MW00812381

DISCARD

A Rabble in Arms

THE WARFARE AND CULTURE SERIES
General Editor: Wayne E. Lee

A Rabble in Arms
Massachusetts Towns and Militiamen during King Philip's War
Kyle F. Zelner

Kyle Zelner's *A Rabble in Arms* serves as a fine inaugural volume in the Warfare and Culture series. In many ways his in-depth examination of the militiamen of seventeenth-century Essex County represents a modern version of the best of the now-old "new" military history that delves deeply into the social and economic background of soldiers and their communities. It is the kind of study that is a necessary foundation for deeper cultural examinations of those soldiers' beliefs and choices in wartime. But Zelner's work is not merely a repetition or reaffirmation of old truths about those militiamen. It is an exciting exploration of a heretofore little understood mechanism: How do certain men get chosen for wartime service while other men remain at home? We have long more or less accurately assumed that this process of selection in the early modern European world was likely to focus on the poor, the rootless, or the socially disconnected. That image has taken a beating for various places and times, and early colonial New England has long been considered a major exception. Their militia was supposed to be a truly representative cross section of the colonial population. In contrast, Zelner finds strong evidence for the more usual biased selection process, and he also reveals something entirely new about that process as conducted by the town committees of militia. It was the town committee, a select group of men, who sat down to hammer out who would go and who would stay. This mechanism of local choice and its idiosyncrasies produced county-wide patterns, but it also produced contingent difference based on personality and local politics. Understanding the myriad contours of creating the committee and of their selection process allows Zelner, in his concluding chapter, to begin to outline exactly what that meant on the battlefield. And that is precisely what the Warfare and Culture series hopes to accomplish.

—Wayne E. Lee, series editor

A Rabble in Arms

Massachusetts Towns and Militiamen during King Philip's War

Kyle F. Zelner

NEW YORK UNIVERSITY PRESS

New York and London

NEW YORK UNIVERSITY PRESS
New York and London
www.nyupress.org

Library of Congress Cataloging-in-Publication Data

Zelner, Kyle F.
A rabble in arms : Massachusetts towns and militiamen
during King Philip's War / Kyle F. Zelner.
p. cm. — (The warfare and culture series)
Includes bibliographical references and index.
ISBN-13: 978-0-8147-9718-1 (cloth : acid-free paper)
ISBN-10: 0-8147-9718-0 (cloth : acid-free paper)
1. King Philip's War, 1675–1676. 2. Massachusetts—Militia—History.
3. Impressment—History. 4. Essex County (Mass.)—History—17th
century. 5. New England—History—Colonial period, ca. 1600–1775.
I. Title.
E83.67.Z455   2009
973.2'4—dc22

New York University Press books are printed on acid-free paper,
and their binding materials are chosen for strength and durability.
We strive to use environmentally responsible suppliers and materials
to the greatest extent possible in publishing our books.

Manufactured in the United States of America
c 10 9 8 7 6 5 4 3 2 1

For Tisha
and
in memory of the militiamen of King Philip's War

The Ruine of a choice Company of young Men, the very Flower of the County of Essex, all called out of the Towns belonging to that County, none of which were ashamed to speak with the Enemy in the Gate.

—Rev. William Hubbard, describing Captain Thomas Lathrop's company, ambushed at the Bloody Brook on September 18, 1675, in his *The History of the Indian Wars in New England,* 1677

Resolved that from the Massachusetts bands/Be pressed on service some Hurculean hands. . . . Our walking castles, men of noted worth.

—Benjamin Thompson, describing the colonial soldiers of King Philip's War in his epic poem *New England's Crisis,* 1676

The object of history is, by nature, man. . . . Behind the features of landscape, behind tools or machinery, behind what appear to be the most formalized written documents, and behind institutions which seem almost entirely detached from their founders, there are men and it is men that history seeks to grasp. . . . The good historian is like the giant in the fairy tale. He knows that whenever he catches the scent of human flesh, there his quarry lies.

—Marc Bloch, *The Historian's Craft,* 1941

Contents

List of Figures, Maps, and Tables

Maps

Tables

Acknowledgments

I am extremely grateful for the support and encouragement of the faculty, staff, and graduate students of the Lyon Gardiner Tyler Department of History at the College of William and Mary, especially James Axtell and Philip Daileader. I must single out James P. Whittenburg, whose patience, understanding, and insight made writing a joyful experience rather than a dreadful task. Thanks also to John Shy of the University of Michigan for his discriminating comments and suggestions. I also want to express my sincere gratitude to Gerald F. Moran at the University of Michigan-Dearborn for his help over the years. Gerry, first my undergraduate mentor and now a trusted friend, is a historian's historian and I thank him for the lessons he taught me and the example he still provides.

My appreciation of librarians grows daily; without their efforts, the work of all scholars would be impossible. Kathy M. Flynn, MaryAnn Campbell, Charity Galbreath, Marla Gearhart, Britta Karlberg, Christine Michelini, and Jean Marie Procious at the James Duncan Phillips Library of the Peabody Essex Museum in Salem, Massachusetts, were extremely generous with their time and expertise. At the Earl Greg Swem Library at William and Mary, John Lawrence, Cynthia Mack, Wendy Webb-Robers, Don Welch, and Hope Yelich were all tremendously helpful. I also want to thank the librarians and staff members at the Massachusetts State Archives (especially Jennifer Fauxsmith), the New England Historic Genealogical Society, the Massachusetts Historical Society (especially Elaine Grublin), the Library of Congress (especially the librarians in the Local History and Genealogy reading room), the Burton Historical Collection of the Detroit Public Library (especially David Poremba), the Harlan Hatcher Graduate Library at the University of Michigan, the Mardigian Library at the University of Michigan-Dearborn, the Purdy/Kresge Library at Wayne State University, the John D. Rockefeller Jr. Library of the Colonial Williamsburg Foundation in Williamsburg, Virginia, the State

Library of Massachusetts in Boston, and Cook Library at the University of Southern Mississippi in Hattiesburg.

Jesse Little Doe Baird of the *Wopanaak* (Wampanoag) Language Reclamation Project and Kate LaPrad and Roger Pickering of Plimoth Plantation were extremely helpful in solving a seventeenth-century mystery that cropped up during my research of the war's aftermath. Special thanks also go to David Barber, who did a masterful job creating the maps for this volume. I received financial support for this project from several sources, including several years of fellowships from the Lyon Gardiner Tyler Department of History at William and Mary. The history department at the University of Southern Mississippi helped fund several of the illustrations herein.

Over the years, numerous scholars have offered observations about my work or asked questions that focused my arguments and forced me to examine evidence in a different way. Whether at a conference or through correspondence, their contributions are many, and I thank them: Fred Anderson, Emerson W. Baker, Jeremy Black, T. H. Breen, Denver Brunsman, Thomas Chambers, Guy Chet, David Corlett, Jonathan Dull, Stephen C. Eames, William M. Fowler Jr., Carolyn Duckworth Fox, John Grenier, Evan Haefeli, Richard H. Kohn, the late Douglas Edward Leach, John A. Lynn, Paul Mapp, Michael McGiffert, John Murrin, Scott Nelson, Jim Piecuch, David Preston, John P. Resch, Carol Sheriff, Linda Smith Rhoads, George F. Sanborn Jr., Melinde Lutz Sanborn, Harold E. Selesky, John Shy, David C. Skaggs, Sandra VanBurkleo, and Daniel Vickers. Several people read all or part of the manuscript and offered invaluable suggestions, including Holly Mayer, Wayne E. Lee, two anonymous readers for New York University Press, and Phyllis Jestice, who did "yeoman's service" editing the final draft of the manuscript. Of course, the errors or omissions that remain are mine alone.

I did not realize how lucky I was when I met my soon-to-be-editor Deborah Gershenowitz of New York University Press at a military history conference. No first-time author (or any author) could hope for a more caring and supportive editor. Debbie, her editorial assistant, Gabrielle Begue, and the rest of the editors and staff at the press made the complicated progression from unrefined manuscript to book as painless as possible and for that I give them my thanks.

I would also like to show appreciation to my colleagues in the history department at the University of Southern Mississippi for creating an encouraging and supportive atmosphere in which to pursue scholarship.

While all in the department have been helpful, I want to particularly thank the members of the junior faculty "lunch group"—Andrew Haley, Sarah Franklin, Amy Milne-Smith, and Brian LaPierre—who were forced to listen to me talk about this project far too often. In particular, Andrew Haley had to endure thrice-daily interruptions of his own work as I asked his opinion on mine. Phyllis Jestice, Shelia Smith, William Scarborough, Bradley Bond, Greg O'Brien, Elizabeth Drummond, and Charles Bolton all offered words of encouragement along the way. In addition, I want to single out my fellow members of the Center for the Study of War and Society at Southern Miss, especially co-directors Andrew Wiest and Michael Neiberg, for their friendship, support, advice, and nearly constant pestering to "get to work on the book," without which I might not have finished.

Without the love and support of my parents, Lee and Sheila Zelner, none of this would have been possible. From giving me an early and lasting love of history to supporting me in every way imaginable, they never doubted that I could accomplish my goals. My thanks and love go to them. This book is dedicated to my wife, Tisha. No one contributed more to the completion of the project. From supporting us financially when I took time off for research to reading every word of the manuscript numerous times, Tisha's encouragement was indispensable. For that, but more importantly for the life that she and I have created together, I offer her my eternal thanks and my everlasting love.

Introduction

On a late August day in 1675, a lone rider arrived in the coastal town of Marblehead, Massachusetts, bearing dispatches for the local committee of militia.[1] The message came from Major General Daniel Denison in nearby Salem, the commander of the Essex County Regiment. King Philip's War had been raging since June and Massachusetts Bay was mobilizing its militia as quickly as possible. The rider found Samuel Ward, lieutenant of the town's militia, and handed over a single sheet of paper. As Ward took the dispatch, he knew that the day he dreaded had finally arrived; in his hand was an impressment notice. The document ordered the militia committee to select five men to serve in a newly formed expeditionary company under the command of Captain Thomas Lathrop of Beverly. Lathrop's company was urgently needed in western Massachusetts to defend the towns of the Connecticut River Valley against attacking Wampanoags, Nipmucks, and other Native Americans. Lieutenant Ward quickly called a meeting of the town's militia committee. Richard Norman (the town militia's ensign), Major William Hathorne from Salem, and Lieutenant Ward quickly assembled, most likely in the town's meetinghouse. The three men had some hard choices to make. Who from the town would they send to war?

The impressment order called for able soldiers to be sent—the colony needed good men to stop the Indian onslaught and strike back at the enemy. But the three men on the committee knew that they would have to answer to their town if the soldiers were lost in battle; they might even have to tell the men's families the grim news of defeat and death if the worst occurred. Probably after much discussion and debate, the men drew up a list of five names. Then they summoned Marblehead's constables, Richard Hanniford and Nicholas Andrews, and gave them the signed impressment warrants. The constables had the unenviable task of finding William Dew, Samuel Hudson, John Merrett, Mark Pittman, and Thomas Rose and informing them that they had been pressed "for the county service." It is hard to imagine the response of the men. Some were probably afraid, although they dared not let it show. Others might have felt an excited anticipation, knowing they were escaping Marblehead and going "off to the wars." Over the next few days, the five readied their seldom-used weapons, put their affairs in order, and said goodbye to friends and families before marching out of town. They most likely met up with the rest of the company in Beverly, Captain Lathrop's home, or possibly in Salem, home to the Essex County Regiment. Now combined with men from almost every town in the county, the five Marblehead soldiers formed up behind their new commander and quickly marched west. Those who came to see them off watched as the company swiftly passed from view.

The town waited anxiously for news of their soldiers' safe return. Then one day, in late September, another rider came galloping into Marblehead. The report that he carried was devastating. Captain Lathrop's company had been ambushed and destroyed south of Deerfield, at a place now called Bloody Brook. Four of the five Marblehead soldiers died on that bright and sunny day. The shocking story was told in full when Thomas Rose, the sole survivor, finally came home. Less than two months later, as horrific reports from the frontier continued to pour into town, yet another messenger rode into Marblehead. Lieutenant Ward probably stared long and hard at the document in his hand before he finally opened it. It was another warrant—this time, thirteen Marblehead men were needed. They would serve on a perilous winter campaign to attempt to crush the Narragansetts in Rhode Island. The town reeled at the news. Would this group of its citizens also be annihilated? Who should the militia committee send?

The question of who *was sent* to fight colonial New England's wars is a deeply complex and important one. Its answer offers crucial insights into New England's society. An examination of the choices that community leaders made when faced with total war offers vital clues to the values, hopes, and fears both of individual towns and the entire society. The culture's principles were in flux as the seventeenth century crept by. But for the majority of people, those values still centered on the Puritan goal that brought them (or their parents) to New England in the first place—the desire to build a godly, well-ordered society. The great hope of the people in the colony (or, at the very least, its leaders) was that the second generation of New Englanders would live up to the standard set by their parents, the "first generation," who made the Great Migration from England in the 1630s. The great fear was that the second generation was flawed, especially

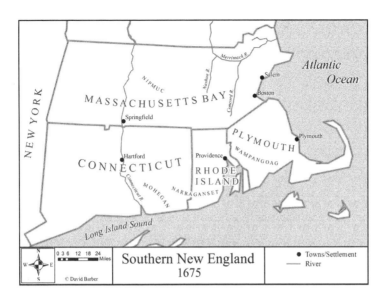

in comparison to their parents. The concern, best articulated by Puritan ministers, was that New England's second generation was failing on two basic levels. First, they were too focused on worldly goods, opening the door to sins such as pride and greed, which in turn manifested themselves in excess in apparel and drink, deceit, quarrelling, and other misbehavior. Worse, according to the ministers, was the decline in the second generation's individual piety, which was ultimately the root of all other decay, itself bringing a lessening of respect for church, government, and family.[2] Proof positive of this deterioration was a series of calamities that had beset the colonies from the 1630s to the 1670s, culminating in King Philip's War in 1675.[3] The war was truly of a size and scale never before seen in New England. Fighting ranged across the region and every single family in the area was affected. By the conflict's end, large portions of the region were devastated and thousands were dead. Amid this catastrophe came a realization: not only did New England have to fight the war to survive in a physical sense, but the society, especially its second generation, had to triumph in order to prove that it had not lost its faith or God's blessing. The seriousness of the situation meant that the militia of New England was now as crucial to the survival of the Bible Commonwealth as the congregational church. While they had not fought a major conflict until 1675, the leaders and people of Massachusetts Bay had established a well-organized military system for just such an emergency. When the hostilities began, they mobilized that system in order to win the war and save their "City on a Hill."

The Massachusetts Bay military system, its conduct during King Philip's War, and most importantly the identity and character of its soldiers are at the heart of this study. Yet, this is not a study of New England's military alone; it is an examination of war *and* society.[4] A society's military must be examined within the context of its culture. The militia of the colony was made up of individuals, and thus its study lies squarely within the realm of social history. The following work draws much of its focus and many of its methods from that field. This work is, in fact, a community study—the community being a group of soldiers, their families, hometowns, and the men who impressed them. Thus, the pages that follow are filled with considerations of marriage rates, the meanings of probate inventories, and how socioeconomic status affected recruitment—the stuff of the social historian's trade. But there are discussions of military policy and the conduct of war as well. Most of the book's military focus is centered on issues of militia institutions, policies, and especially recruitment, although combat, which was ultimately what these men were impressed to do, plays a small role as well. That war and society must be studied together in this way is particularly true of colonial America, where the militia system, in theory based on a citizen-soldiery, united the military with society in unique ways. New Englanders had created their military as they had their churches, towns, and other critical institutions, basing its structure and mechanism on their core values and beliefs. Thus, an examination of how this colonial society fought its wars—and who they selected to fight them—is foremost an examination of the society itself. This particular historical examination is thus driven by three core questions.

First, how did Massachusetts Bay go about choosing which men would actually fight the war? This question requires an in-depth analysis of not only the military institutions of the colony, but also how those institutions actually functioned. How did the militia companies and militia committees operate in the towns? Was it the same in the large towns as it was in the small ones? How were the men recruited—did they volunteer or were they impressed? How did impressment work? Who chose the men? Who made them go? Were substitutions allowed? Did the system work as planned or were adjustments needed mid-war to ensure that the colony could put enough men in the field? All of these questions are crucial to understanding the way that Massachusetts readied itself to fight.

The second core question centers on the soldiers. Massachusetts impressed the vast majority of men who fought for the colony in King Philip's War. Who did the militia committees impress and why were they chosen and not their neighbors? How old were they? What did they do for a living? What were their roles in their communities? Were there any commonalities or was each unique? The answers to these questions and many more follow in a detailed analysis of not only the men themselves, but also their birth families, their communities, and the individual members of each town's committee of militia, the men who made the decisions about each soldier's fate. Only with a total immersion in the society and the culture of each town can we understand how and why society elected these particular men to fight and not their brothers, neighbors, or friends.

The third question is the most essential of all. By examining the militia system of the colony, its impressment system and leaders, and their choice of individual men for soldiers, what can we learn about the society of colonial New England itself? Why, for example, was it so important that the men were selected for impressment in their local communities? Did specific community values drive impressment decisions? Did the military recruitment system change during the war? Finally, was the system of war making in New England transformed after the war and if so, why?

Of course, other historians have studied the militia system of New England. Institutional studies of the militia were once common, as were surveys of the battle exploits of colonial militias and militiamen. Fewer studies exist, however, that place at the center of their analysis an examination of the interaction between war and society. On the issues of recruitment and the identity of soldiers in the early colonial period, very little work has been done and almost all of it by traditional military historians. The works that examine methods of recruitment rely more on impressions from the records and anecdotal evidence than from any systematic survey of muster lists or the men's backgrounds. This is true of the first modern historian to look at the topic, Douglas Edward Leech. Leech wrote extensively on the early history of the New England militia and also authored *Flintlock and Tomahawk* in 1958, still considered by many to be the standard narrative history of King Philip's War. In his work, Leech described the colonial recruitment system as highly disorganized and locally controlled, relying on volunteers to fill the ranks and only turning to conscription when necessary; he never mentioned the all-important committees of militia.[5] In a later work, Leech commented that the recruitment system in New England was "so haphazard as to suggest that the weighty responsibility of sending a man out to risk his life for the community was taken rather lightly."[6] This view came to represent the conventional wisdom on the subject. It is not surprising, given the sheer amount of data and work involved, that most historians would accept Leech's commonsense assessment of the colonial manpower system when their own studies did not deal specifically with recruitment. Thus, the badly flawed notion of an unsystematic and volunteer-based conscription method in the colonial era still exists in numerous studies that touch on King Philip's War or the history of the early militia.[7]

Another major focus of inquiry for war and society scholars is the identity and character of soldiers. Unfortunately for students of colonial America, there has been very little social history work done on the personal histories and nature of the men who actually fought the earliest wars. There have been some preliminary studies, however, and even a few calls for more work to be done. The topic of soldiers, rather than movements of units and armies, was an early interest area of the founders of the more sociological study of war that at first was called the "new military history." John Shy, in his seminal 1963 article "A New Look at the Colonial Militia," turned his attention to the identity of early militiamen. In the article, Shy offered some early impressions about the social identity of early militiamen. He argued that the militiamen who fought most of the colonies' wars in the seventeenth century were representative of their society at large: "Whatever the process of selection[,] military organization and social structure seem[ed] as yet undifferentiated. In the beginning, of course, this is true quite literally: social and military organization were the same thing. When John Smith wrote of 'soldiers,' he meant only those inhabitants who at that moment had guns in their hands and who had been ordered to help Smith look out for danger."[8] But Shy also cautioned that his arguments only scratched the surface of the work to be done on the issue and acknowledged that the "evidence gathered so far is not full nor does it admit of any quantitative conclusions."[9] For years, however, his preliminary view—that the colonial militia (even its fighting companies) was simply a cross section of society—became the conventional wisdom on the issue.[10]

Richard Kohn, yet another "new military historian," urged colleagues to undertake more of the historical legwork on this important topic. In a 1981 article entitled "The Social History of the American Soldier: A Review and Prospectus for Research," Kohn warned that historians needed to cast a suspicious eye on the old assumptions, especially the idea that

American soldiers "comprised a representative cross-section of the American population."[11] In order to find the truth, he laid out a plan:

> First, historians must discover who served, who enlisted in a community and who did not, whom the draft caught and who escaped: their age, ethnic background, wealth, occupation, length of time in the community, and whatever additional information can be gathered or wrung indirectly out of the sources. Except for a few case studies, this basic spadework has never been done, and, until it is, any theories or generalizations about soldiers will not be persuasive. Further, understanding the true identity of the soldiers means grounding them in the communities and times in which they lived. . . . Historians must find all of this out.[12]

Kohn pointed out that without this type of detailed but difficult inquiry, scholars would only know the stereotype of early America's fighting men, not their true character.

Several historians heeded Kohn's call, but they all examined soldiers in eighteenth-century America. Perhaps the best known of these studies is Fred Anderson's *A People's Army: Massachusetts Soldiers and Society in the Seven Years War*, published in 1984.[13] Marking an important milestone in the history of war and society, Anderson scrutinized muster lists to discover the age, residence, birthplace, occupation, and condition of service of the Bay Colony's eighteenth-century warriors, offering a detailed social portrait.[14] Other historians investigated the militiamen and soldiers of the American Revolution, most notably Steven Rosswurm's 1988 *Arms, Country, and Class: The Philadelphia Militia and the "Lower Sort" during the American Revolution* and Charles Neimeyer's 1996 *America Goes to War: A Social History of the Continental Army*.[15] Through the work of these and other fine historians, we now know much more about the identity of the men who fought in America's late eighteenth-century wars and we understand better how their service represented the societal values of their time. No one before now, however, has systematically examined the identity of soldiers in the seventeenth century, the structure that selected them to fight (and left others safe at home), and the way in which those choices reflected early colonial values.

In this book, I first argue that a unique, locally controlled institution—the town committee of militia—impressed the seventeenth-century soldiers of Massachusetts Bay. While much of the Massachusetts militia system was based on the English model, the committees of militia were a completely new invention, directly linked to the insistence of Puritan New Englanders that they control, at the local level, the chief institutions of their lives.[16] Because the committees were housed in each community and both military and civilian elites controlled them, they, and in particular their impressment decisions, offer a rare glimpse into the fundamental values of each individual colonial community. Each man sent to war was selected for a reason and the grounds varied from town to town, as did the rationale for why certain men were allowed to stay safely at home. In other words, a close examination of the type of men that the town's militia leadership thought most expendable is also an excellent indicator of the type of men that the community valued. For example, Ipswich cherished order and authority—it sent young troublemakers off to war and left young men who conformed to community principles at home. Marblehead and Topsfield chose town outsiders or men who lived on the fringes of town society to do their fighting, preserving from harm the sons of their own principal families. A few militia committees, specifically those in Rowley and Andover, pressed large numbers of men from families that were relatively new to the town. This left the sons of the town's original founding families safe. This case suggests that preferential treatment of original families, a pattern in New England's religious and political life, was present in military life as well. Most towns tried to protect themselves and their families by sending those men to war whom they could most afford to lose. In doing so, they also protected the men vital to communal success. By examining each town committee's particular standards of impressment, we see a mirror image of the values of their town, or at the very least those of the town elite.

While impressment choices were distinctive depending on the locality in which they were made, certain common characteristics among pressed men speak to colony-wide values and ideals. Most of the men sent to fight King Philip's War were young and unmarried. It made sense to send soldiers who did not have a family to support, in case the men did not survive the war. Eldest sons, so vital to inheritance and the transmission of family economic stability, were normally spared from town levies. Farmers were generally underrepresented in the draft, despite their predominance in society, which is strong evidence of an acute concern on the part of militia committees over maintaining the colony's food supply during wartime. Almost every town sent men with criminal pasts to fight rather than sending men who had never broken the law. Men who questioned, or even worse, challenged authority were very likely to be sent to the front in an attempt to maintain the hierarchy so vital to New England society, while those men who followed the rules were less likely to be chosen. These wider societal factors highlight the dual role of impressment in New England: some decisions were aimed at actively ridding the towns of troublemakers while at other times the committees selected certain men simply to protect more essential men from the dangers of the war.

Many of these societal values were under considerable discussion in the colony during the war, as ministers and even the colonial government debated the reason why God had brought war on New England. Much of the blame was laid at the feet of the rising second generation. When the General Court or prominent divines such as Increase Mather blamed the war on the actions of drunks and criminals and those who did not respect the clergy, the militia committees obviously listened. Not only did they try to curb such behavior in their towns, but in an attempt to atone they sent those guilty of such actions off to war. This not only rid the community of the sinner but also spared those who followed God's law. At the same time, the committees placed those blamed for sin in a unique position— they could actively repent and atone by fighting for their own and their society's survival.

This study proves, despite a continuing belief to the contrary based on some early preliminary studies of military historians, that the men sent off to war in seventeenth-century New England were *not* a representational cross section of their communities. While the peacetime general militia operated under a universal military obligation (of every man from sixteen to sixty), such was not the case during wartime. The militia committees worked hard to protect their towns, families, and the entire society by choosing the right men to send to war and the right men to keep at home. The active-duty, impressed companies of King Philip's War were thus made up in large part of two types of men. First, the committees pressed men who were actively blamed for bringing about the very war that they had to fight. The second group was made up of men who were simply less vital to society and thus expendable. As the colony soon found out, however, such men, especially the troublemakers, often made poor soldiers.

King Philip's War was a turning point in the history of war in New England. As such, it offers a perfect opportunity to inspect the changing nature of early American warfare. The war was the first and last conflict fought in colonial New England with a mass impressed army, making it a crucial event in the history of the region. A study of the conflict also fosters an awareness of how early colonial military systems worked in general and how militia impressment worked in particular. This knowledge is crucial in recognizing the changes that occurred in recruitment and the waging of war, both in the period of King Philip's War itself and afterward.

The book follows both a thematic and a roughly chronological framework, starting in England in the 1550s and ending with the aftermath of King Philip's War in the 1680s. Chapter 1 offers an institutional history of the New England militia, starting with a short overview of its English precedents. A careful study of the English background to New England's militia tradition is vital to a complete understanding of the colonial militia, much more so than has previously been understood. While it is clear that the militia of Massachusetts Bay was based on the system in England, the question is which English militia served as inspiration. From the 1550s to the 1630s, the English militia was in a state of nearly constant flux as queens Mary and Elizabeth, as well as King Charles I, all instituted military reforms. The Puritans who founded the Bible Commonwealth constructed their military system in a very deliberate fashion, with specific goals in mind. Having been persecuted in large part by Charles I's military machine before they left England, the Puritans of New England hearkened back to the days of the Elizabethan militia for their model military system. This included a fascination with the Elizabethan system of impressment, which utilized locally minded lords lieutenant in each county. The first chapter continues by outlining the establishment of the Massachusetts militia and its history up to the time of King Philip's War. Lastly, I examine the establishment of one of the most important institutions within the new militia system. In 1652, Massachusetts Bay instituted its own locally based system of militia control and impressment: town committees of militia. The history of these militia committees, up to the time of King Philip's War, is summarized in this chapter, demonstrating their significance to the colonial militia.

An overview of the changes made to Massachusetts's militia amid King Philip's War, including the establishment of strict new rules for war and the efforts of the colony to adapt to the complex military situation of the conflict, starts the second chapter. It continues with an examination of the committees of militia and their role in impressment. By the time of King

Philip's War, the militia committees had amassed a tremendous amount of authority to oversee the militia in their towns. The most important of their powers was their sole responsibility to select soldiers in times of war. This chapter briefly traces the history of recruitment in Massachusetts Bay from the colony's founding to 1675 and then focuses on the recruitment role of the militia committees during the war. The fundamentals of impressment are explored, including details on how the system worked and the roles of the different individuals and institutions involved. Not everyone whom the committees chose to go to war was pleased by the choice; the issues of draft resistance and how the colony and the militia committees dealt with it are also examined. While the town militia committees pressed for service the vast majority of the men who fought King Philip's War, a few men did volunteer to serve and a minuscule number of men possibly hired substitutes. Both of these alternatives are also explored in chapter 2.

The third chapter is the first of two detailed examinations into the practice of impressment in the towns of Essex County. Chapter 3 examines four of the county's large or more prosperous towns. Ipswich, the largest town in the county, was economically diverse and socially stratified. It was also a community at war with itself, as the town elite had come to despise certain "undesirables" in their midst and began to harass them. Once the war started, the committee of militia, made up of these same elites, used impressment toward the same ends. In Rowley, a medium-sized town with a textile production background and a nasty religious controversy brewing, local concerns translated into very specific recruitment orders from the committee of militia. Topsfield, the smallest of these towns, was nonetheless a thriving agricultural community. Its recruitment record during the war was one of the most complex; it suggests that some men in the smaller towns were volunteering to fight, especially early in the war, while the committee filled the rest of its quota with town outcasts. Marblehead, the last town examined in chapter 3, exhibited a different pattern. After losing most of its early recruits in the disastrous Bloody Brook ambush, the town committee levied only men with no real connection to the community. It did not want to lose any more stable citizens to the conflict. Examining the impressment choices that the militia committees in these towns made not only offers a detailed look into the workings of the system in each community, but it also proves that in towns with large or growing populations, the militia committees had a vital advantage that small towns did not—an abundance of choice.

Chapter 4 continues the in-depth look at local impressment, but with a crucial difference. It examines three of Essex County's smaller or struggling communities. Andover did not have a sizeable number of troublemakers to impress, unlike the larger towns of Salem and Ipswich. In many ways the model New England town, Andover recruited a number of men from the ranks of its leading families. Those impressed, however, came from a very specific group of allied elite families—and not the elite group in control of the militia committee. The examination of Manchester, the smallest town in the county, offers a unique insight into a community with a nonfunctioning militia structure and how it dealt with recruitment during the war. Manchester's men were, in effect, pressed on orders of the nearby Beverly militia. The linkage of the militias of a small, struggling town with a larger neighboring town is an important facet of the working of the colonial militia and one never before examined. Lastly, the militia committee in Wenham, like the one in Andover, had few obvious choices of men to recruit. The few options offered to the militia committees in these small towns made for a fairly representative impressment pool. Thus in some cases the ideal, often touted in the historic literature, of a cross section of society defending the colony from danger actually occurred in some of these small towns. However, the number of men that such towns sent to fight, even collectively, was extremely small, especially in proportion to all the men impressed in the county. Most men in the county were pressed for a specific reason—not just because they happened to be available at the right time, which was often the only criterion used in the small towns.

An exhaustive study of every man whom Essex County towns impressed for service in an active-duty company is the heart of chapter 5. Looking at all 357 known soldiers as a group proves that the men pressed for service in King Philip's War were not representative of the entire male population of the county. Despite the fact that recruitment in New England was locally controlled and each community had its own criteria for impressment, certain common factors and traits existed. Looking first at factors such as age, birth-order, marriage, and family, a number of patterns are explored. The men were relatively young and overwhelmingly unmarried. Most were not the vital first sons of their birth families. When looking at the man's prewar participation in the religious or governmental lives of their communities, it is noteworthy that the greater part of pressed men played no such role. They were busy at work, but not the type of employment that one would assume. Relatively few of the pressed men worked in agriculture, which is particularly surprising given the county's largely agricultural economy. Militia committees needed to keep food production apace with the needs of a society at war, and they did so by limiting the number of farmers that they impressed. The last section of chapter 5 examines the soldiers in relation to possible damaging societal factors in their past. These incidents, which had come to the attention of the militia committees, made a difference in the minds of the committee members. Criminal acts, little or no connection to the community, low socioeconomic status, and other damaging factors contributed to these men being selected for impressment rather than their more upstanding neighbors. In other words, for the vast majority of men pressed, there was a reason that they marched off to war, be it their occupation, their marital status, or the type of men they were or were perceived to be.

The final chapter offers a narrative of the war that these men fought, with special attention paid not only to the campaigns of the "Essex companies" but also to how the war touched the towns of Essex County. Some may find it strange to include a narrative of the war and its aftermath in what is essentially a study of military recruitment and societal values. While it is true that the book is not specifically about warfare and campaigning, combat was ultimately what these men were being chosen or impressed to do. Chronicling the men's service is thus important, if only to understand what happened to them once they had been selected. It is also important to note these soldiers' active-duty experiences because the militia committees kept a close watch on the war news and sometimes adjusted their impressment decisions based on that knowledge, as Marblehead's committee did after the Bloody Brook ambush. The chapter ends with a look at how the men fared after the war, including a detailed consideration of those killed and wounded, a brief sketch of what happened to the veterans who came home, and what effect the war had on their place in society, especially in regard to their ability to marry. The afterword offers some final thoughts on the influence that these men had in the grand scheme of military manpower in the colonial era and how they, the last troops of a mass impressed army in colonial New England, helped bring about a complete alteration in the future conduct of New England's wars.

A Note on Method

King Philip's War (1675–1676) offers the ideal moment in time to study the character of impressed seventeenth-century New England soldiers and how and why they were chosen for service. This study is built primarily on the techniques of historical prosopography, or collective biography. In order to capture their true identity, I created a social portrait of every man from Essex County, Massachusetts, who served in an active company or garrison during the war. Men were determined to be active-duty soldiers either by their appearance on the official pay lists of the colony (with a unit and commanding officer listed) or if two other credible sources (predominantly town, probate, and court records or reliable town histories) recorded active war service.[1] In all, at least 434 Essex County men received some kind of payment from the colony during the war. Twenty-four of these men were officers or noncommissioned officers, 53 men were paid for some unknown reason, and 357 were soldiers or troopers in active-duty companies or garrisons (see appendix 1). While it is possible that the 53 men who were paid for an unknown service were actually pressed into one of the colony's fighting companies, it is much more likely (given the extensive manpower records on the active fighting units) that these men received compensation for some other service that they performed during the war, such as providing troops with military supplies or building fortifications. Men who simply received payment from the colony, with no confirmation of active-duty service, are not treated in this study.[2] In all, 357 biographies of the active-duty soldiers of Essex County inform the conclusions of this investigation. While a few men who served from the county have undoubtedly been lost from the historical record, I am confident that all but a scant few of the men who actually fought in the war from Essex County are examined in this study.

Once I authenticated the identity of each soldier, genealogical and community records were explored in order to create a social portrait or biography of each man. Because many of these young men still lived with

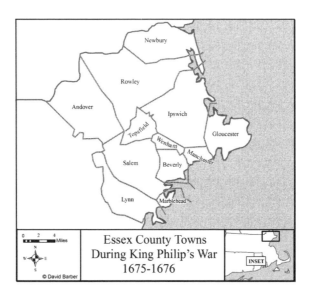

Essex County Towns
During King Philip's War
1675-1676

their parents, their birth families were also examined for clues into the soldiers' status in their community. A large variety of records were consulted in order to create each soldier's profile, including: birth, marriage, death, probate, church, town and colony government, land, military, and court records. In addition, I carefully examined both published and manuscript genealogies to glean important information, as well as town, county, and colony histories.[3] In order to place the men and their families in the proper context, a short social history of each town in Essex County was also constructed. In addition, the members of each town's militia committee were researched and their place in the community (and in relation to each soldier) was examined. While some data has undoubtedly been lost, a considerable amount of information about the men, their families, and their communities inform the conclusions offered here.

I selected Essex County in the Massachusetts Bay Colony as the subject for this study mainly for the diversity of its towns. When the war broke out in 1675, Essex County was home to twelve towns (see map 2).[4] Historians of New England claim that there were either three or five different types of towns in colonial New England.[5] Essex County contained at least one town of every type, from commercial Salem to Lynn, the market center, as well as Andover, the farming hub, and the isolated Wenham. Essex County is thus representative of the entire colony and, in a way, all New England. As one of the first counties organized in the colony, it had a large, stable, and mature population; thus it produced almost a third of the soldiers who fought in the war for Massachusetts Bay.[6] These factors, along with the fact that Essex County has incredibly rich surviving records from the period, made its soldiers the best subjects for this study. Lastly, by studying an entire county, and every active-duty soldier pressed from that county, I do not claim to be choosing a representative sample for examination; instead, I am analyzing an entire population, which has clear statistical advantages.

There are numerous instances throughout this study where I compare information about the soldiers of Essex County to the community at large. One example of this is a comparison of marriage rates among pressed militiamen in Ipswich and the marriage rate in the town in general. I easily established the prewar marriage rate of the soldiers. Determining the rate for all the males in Ipswich was a very different problem. While it would have been fantastic to have detailed community information on every category of analysis included in this inquiry, that is simply not possible given the large population and complexity of Essex County and its twelve communities. The nature of historical prosopography is such that we have much more detailed information about the group under study than we can possibly know about society in general. As this inquiry deals with an entire county, the only way to construct such a control group would have been to conduct a systematic statistical study of every male in Essex County, a task nearly impossible given the immense population of the county and the duplication of names in the various towns. In order to compensate for that historical dilemma and give comparative meaning to the conclusions here, I have used secondary sources when they are available to compare the impressed soldiers to the overall male population of the communities on a number of different subjects, such as economic status, crime rate, religiosity, political participation, and a host of other topics.

In the text, I have used the term Puritan, as well as New Englander, Englishmen, settler, and colonist, to denote the European inhabitants of Massachusetts Bay (and the other colonies) of early New England. While it has fallen out of favor to use the term Puritan in some historical circles (especially in the United Kingdom), I believe that its use here is not only accurate but necessary.[7] As Virginia DeJohn Anderson eloquently asserts in her book *New England's Generation*, the vast majority of those who moved to New England did so for religious motives, and even those who were not Puritans, strictly speaking, realized that they were moving to a

Puritan commonwealth, thus implicitly agreeing to abide by the community's shared culture. Anderson argues, and I agree, that this shared belief system, no matter how it was defined, created a commonality that bound individual colonists into a single culture, and that culture is best labeled as Puritan.[8] When speaking of the men who fought King Philip's War for the colony of Massachusetts Bay, I have used the terms soldiers, militiamen, and pressed men interchangeably for stylistic reasons, although I have made a determined effort to distinguish between the regular militia of the colony and those men pressed into active-duty companies during wartime. When discussing Native Americans, I have attempted to use the correct tribal designation when possible. Otherwise, I use the terms Indian, Native, and Native American interchangeably.

In quotes, I have left the original forms of spelling, punctuation, abbreviation, and capitalization as much as possible, making only slight changes for the sake of comprehensibility. To avoid confusion over dates, I have employed the New Style for all dates. Thus, all dates from January 1 to March 24 are given as the new year, and the double year designation of the original documents (January 1, 1675/76) is dropped in favor of the New Style (January 1, 1676).

1

"For the best
ordering of the militia"
English Military Precedent and the
Early Massachusetts Bay Militia

The 1628 Charter of the Massachusetts Bay Company gave the company and its "chief commanders, governors, and officers" an order to provide "for their special defense and safety, to incounter, expulse, repell, and resist by force of arms" all enemies of the colony.[1] The governor and General Court of Massachusetts Bay took this charge seriously, writing that it was as important to the success of the "City on a Hill" as their preparations for a godly church: "As piety cannot be maintained without church ordinances and officers, nor justice without laws and magistrates, no more can our safety and peace be preserved without military orders and officers."[2] As they established their own military system, New Englanders understandably looked to earlier English military practices for inspiration, both positive and negative.

The English Military Background

England's military tradition of employing subject-soldiers to defend the realm had deep roots in the country's history. The Assize of Arms in 1181 and the Statute of Winchester in 1285 both required all able-bodied men in England to keep arms for use in defense of the kingdom.[3] England resisted the creation of a professional military even in the early modern era. As Europe underwent a military revolution in tactics and organization, brought about by the widespread introduction of gunpowder, however, the Tudor monarchs felt pressure to effect great changes in the English militia system, attempting to keep up with the standing armies of France and Spain. Mary Tudor (1553–1558) initiated a series of significant militia reforms, but she was unable to complete the job during her short reign.[4] The urgent task fell instead to Queen Elizabeth I (1558–1603). While the law prescribed that all men between the ages of sixteen and sixty, with few exceptions, were required to keep arms for militia service, few of the men had any genuine training in the use of those weapons. England's deplorable military condition was even worse when set against the ever-increasing professionalism of most European armies in the sixteenth century. With the hostility of Spain finally urging her to action, Elizabeth set about reforming England's military establishment in the 1570s.

Although it was considered impossible to train every man in the realm adequately, Elizabeth retained the universal service obligation for every male subject in the general militia. In 1572, however, she established "trainbands" throughout the nation, issuing specific orders for their regular mustering and training. The queen and her advisers intended the new units to be made up of the more desirable members of society, including gentlemen, merchants, farmers, and sturdy yeoman—the men of the crucial, rising middle class.[5] Elizabeth ordered the lords lieutenant in every county to acquire (from the general militia) "a convenient number of able men [to] meet to be sorted in bands and to be trained and exercised" in the new ways of war.[6] The government even planned to distribute weapons based on class and ability, with those in the upper classes, "the strongest men and best persons," given the best new weapons while "the least" would be given older, less complicated arms.[7]

The trainbands were defensive troops only, by law and tradition meant to serve only in England, not overseas or even in Scotland. Thus, for offensive forays in Ireland or on the Continent, England had to rely on impressments from the untrained men of the general militia, not the better sort from the trainbands. Numerous contemporary observers commented on the quality of men obtained this way. Writing in 1587, the military critic Barnaby Rich observed, "In England, when service happens, we disburden the prisons of thieves, we rob the taverns and alehouses of tosspots and ruffians, we scour both town and country of rogues and vagabonds."[8] A few times, the government even let men out of jail and shipped them immediately to the front as reinforcements.[9] Thus, while in theory the Elizabethan reforms should have greatly improved the English military, in practice the institution was still largely untrained and ill-prepared, especially when compared to its European counterparts.

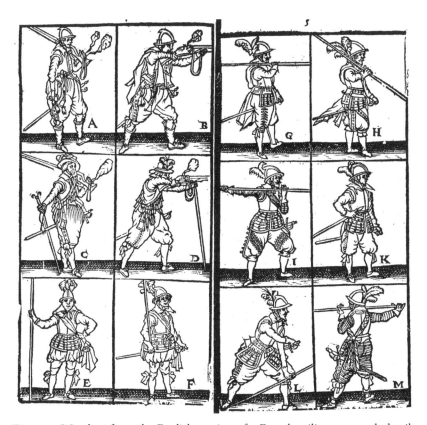

Figure 1. Woodcut from the English version of a French military manual, detailing several stances for the use of the matchlock musket and the pike. As England reformed its military forces, starting in the mid-1500s under Queen Elizabeth, such manuals became important for members of the new trained bands. Woodcut from *The art of Warre* by Sieur Du Praissac. Printed in Cambridge by Roger Daniel, 1642. Courtesy of the Birmingham Central Library, United Kingdom. Image published with permission of ProQuest. Further reproduction is prohibited without permission.

This system, ineffective but inexpensive, continued through the reigns of Elizabeth I and James I (1603–1625). With the coronation of Charles I in 1625, however, the military in England underwent another transformation. Whereas his father, James I, had expressed little interest in the military, the same was not true of Charles, who vowed to set up a "Perfect Militia." Soon after his coronation, Charles dissolved the old, now corrupt trainbands (which had suffered a serious decline in social class). He set up new units with a property requirement for entrance, restoring them to the stable, merchant-based middle class as Elizabeth had originally planned.[10] He also modernized all militia weapons and placed veterans in the trainbands to infuse firsthand military knowledge into the militiamen's training.

Charles levied vast numbers of men for active military service; the number of soldiers impressed by Charles in peacetime was double that levied under Elizabeth in time of war.[11] He also undertook several offensive military incursions and the armies for those expeditions caused considerable trouble back in England. Many soldiers, on their way to coastal towns to disembark for war, razed the English countryside. After the fighting was over, many army units, back in England waiting for their pay and formal discharge, spent their spare time pillaging English towns and villages.[12] The people of England came to see their own army as the enemy, as dangerous to life and property as a foreign foe: "Men under arms had a fearful reputation among English people for casual violence, robbery, and rape and few events were viewed by villagers and townspeople with as much alarm as the arrival in the locality of a contingent of troops, friendly or otherwise."[13] The heavily Puritan East Anglia counties, where most English armies embarked (and returned) for overseas service, were especially distressed by this military abuse, something the East Anglians and their descendants would not soon forget.[14] Worst of all, the system of impressment created feelings of deep distrust in the populace toward their own military. The men at the heart of this trouble were none other than Charles's own lords lieutenant.

English Impressment: The Lord Lieutenant System

King Edward VI (1547–1553) appointed England's first lords lieutenant in 1549.[15] Before 1558, the English militia was organized on the local level, which led to great inefficiencies.[16] With the Arms Act of 1558, Queen Mary reorganized the militia on a county basis, greatly strengthening the role of the lords lieutenant. Appointed by the Crown, the lords lieutenant became responsible for collecting tax money from the gentry and nobles for all military expenses, a fee known as "coat and conduct money." They also had the task of levying, mustering, training, and inspecting men in their counties for active-duty service. By establishing the power of the lieutenancy, the monarchy removed the militia establishment, especially the impressment of men, away from local officials such as sheriffs and justices of the peace.[17] At first, people in the countryside saw this as progress, because the local officials were often corrupt and saw impressment as the perfect opportunity to solicit bribes from common folk who wanted to avoid service.[18] Yet, the lieutenants soon found that they had to maintain a delicate balance between the needs of the Crown and their own counties, a precarious situation that could jeopardize their standing in either community.[19]

The lord lieutenant was always a nobleman, often the most powerful man in his county. Many were also privy councillors with high connections at Court.[20] Assisting the lords lieutenant were deputy lords lieutenant. Each county had two or three deputies culled from the foremost members of the local gentry.[21] In England's larger counties, the deputies had the requisite local knowledge and influence to ensure that the various duties of the lieutenancy were carried out. Even so, each had a large territory to control. Some counties also had muster-masters, professional, experienced soldiers who took charge of training the men and assisted the lords lieutenant in all things military. Rounding out the personnel of the system were local justices of the peace and sheriffs, who still retained a few duties during musters and troop levies. The power of these local officials, however, was on the wane. By the 1630s, local control had completely disappeared from the system.[22] This lack of local control in Charles I's "Perfect Militia" became a major concern of many of the Puritans who left England to start the Massachusetts Bay colony.[23]

Lords lieutenant and their subordinates oversaw the maintenance and training of the trainbands. The lieutenancy's most important military function was to call up men to fight, either from the general militia for foreign military service or men from the trainbands for local defense in case of an invasion. This process of levying soldiers was the most complicated aspect of any lieutenant's duty and required a whole host of actors, from the monarch all the way down to village constables. The process began when the ruler and Privy Council decided how many soldiers to call up and ordered each county to provide a set number of men. The Privy Council informed each county's lord lieutenant of the number of men needed and the time and place of rendezvous. The lords lieutenant in turn informed their deputies; some lieutenants did nothing more than that, while some were very involved in the entire process.[24]

Typically, the deputy lieutenants did the real work of the press, first apportioning the number of soldiers to be levied from each town and village. They also had to collect money to equip and feed the men until they were turned over to the royal officers at the ports and transferred to

Figure 2. As most Englishmen had no experience with muskets, especially mid-dle-class men from the country's cities, military manuals were crucial to trained band members trying to learn the intricacies of the matchlock. These woodcuts show the proper stance and form for presenting and firing such a weapon. Wood-cut details from *The Military Art of Trayning* by Jacob de Gheyn. Printed in London and "solde by R. Daniel" in 1622 or 1623. © British Library Board. All Rights Reserved C.27a21. Image published with permission of ProQuest. Further reproduction is prohibited without permission.

the Crown's expense. The deputies usually had the monumental task of choosing which men to press into service.[25] They would then issue warrants for the local constables to deliver to the pressed men. It was at this point that the dual nature of the lord lieutenant system is most clear. The deputies (or lords themselves in some counties) had to balance their national duty—to provide the Crown with able soldiers—with their local affiliation and concern for their communities. Trying to maintain this delicate equilibrium was difficult and problems sometimes erupted, especially as Charles I began to centralize and nationalize the militia establishment.

The choice of who to press was greatly complicated by law and custom.[26] Decisions on impressment also depended on the specific duty for which the men were required. Custom dictated that the sturdy yeoman of the trainbands stay in England. The trainbands had always been envisioned as containing the better sort of people in the country, especially "well-to-do householders, farmers, franklins, yeomen, or their sons."[27] These men were thus exempt from overseas service; they were needed for a strong home defense and no one wanted to endanger the country by their departure. The "better sort" were also the most likely to be able to afford and learn to use modern weapons, especially firearms. The trainbands, containing as they did property holders, were also considered more reliable if the Crown needed to put down an internal revolt.[28] Some even argued that getting as many "masterless men" (those men most likely serving in the general militia) as possible out of London on overseas service lessened the chance of civil unrest breaking out in the first place.[29]

The preference given to the trained bands, however, caused two problems. First, it triggered a rush of men into the trainbands who wanted to avoid overseas service. In 1601, when the Nine Years War in Ireland was at its height, the Earl of Hertford, lord lieutenant for Wiltshire and Somerset, said that he found "many hired persons, manservants, and . . . inhabitants of the meanest sort such as have ever been held fitter for foreign service" in the ranks of the local trainband.[30] The earl was most upset that these men of the "meanest sort" were no longer eligible for "foreign service" now that they were safely ensconced in the exempted trainbands. His plight highlights the second major problem with the trained band exemption: England's expeditionary armies of the period were largely made up of society's rabble.

When the deputy lieutenants set out to fill their quotas for overseas service, they did so from the general militia and thus from the lower reaches of society. The Crown's unwillingness to lose men of the better sort meant that most soldiers pressed for foreign service came from the mass of the general militia, men from sixteen to sixty who were generally untrained and often lacked weapons. Deputies or constables who went looking for men to press for foreign service turned to the troublemakers in their villages or towns as the first prospects. Almost every locality had a few men that "it could safely spare for the wars; many had men they positively delighted in sending away. The press was sometimes seized upon by the deputies as the perfect solution to the problem of an antisocial or troublesome neighbor."[31]

There are many examples of this type of selective recruitment. The Middlesex County deputy lieutenant selected Samuel Hubbard, a wifebeater and ruffian, for the press in May 1627. When the constable finally found him, Hubbard was in bed with another man's wife, ensuring that few in town were unhappy to see him march off to war.[32] It was not always so easy for the pressing officials. Constable John Plowright had considerable trouble meeting his quota of pressed men for the Bishops' Wars (1638–1639). The impressment warrant had arrived in town open, ensuring that all of the town's troublemakers and tosspots got advance notice of the press and quickly scurried out of town or into hiding.[33] Unable to procure any town vagabonds, Plowright was finally able to press a passing stranger.

In some areas, whole groups of undesirable men were swept into the army. In the 1560s, Newgate Prison was emptied and the prisoners sent to reinforce the garrison at Le Havre.[34] In 1597, the government authorized the impressment of seven hundred vagrants from the neighborhoods of London for an expedition to Picardy.[35] Other men sent were simply unfit for duty, some so diseased or crippled that it was questionable whether they would make it to the embarkation point.[36] Accounts of the poor quality of soldiers pressed by this system are frequent in the military literature of the time. Professional soldiers warned about the use of such "poor specimens" in the armies; sometimes the monarchs agreed, especially when the men were in such bad shape that the Crown's money had to be spent clothing the recruits for service.[37] As time went by, the Privy Council began to see the wisdom of recruiting a slightly better sort into the expeditionary forces; orders went out to the lieutenants to select the men more carefully. The Council even reprimanded some lieutenants for the poor quality of recruits that they sent.[38]

The system was awkward, placing the officials in a bind between local interests and national ones. As foreign military ventures became more common, impressment became an increasingly delicate act. Young single men were preferred for impressment, particularly if they had no ties to the community: "The wandering poor and the sturdy beggar were the ideal candidates, but they were not always enough of these to satisfy the king's conductors."[39] Still, if officials spared the local population and recruited only the worst men, "if they leaned too much towards the needs of their county and neighbors, they risked the severest displeasure of their lieutenant, the council, and even the king."[40] It was then the deputy lieutenant faced a hard choice, forced to press soldiers from among the local population of upstanding young men with wives and children at home. Yet, soldiers had to be sent, even if that meant leaving families at home without support. Thus the lords lieutenant under Elizabeth I and James I were torn between two very demanding masters.

The system changed, and not for the better, during the reign of Charles I (see figure 3). Under his plan for a "Perfect Militia," lords lieutenant were chosen who were more national in their outlook. These increasingly

Figure 3. King Charles I (1600–1649) tried to transform England's military into a "Perfect Militia" as soon as he ascended the throne in 1625. His efforts at military reorganization, especially the reforms of the lord lieutenancy and impressment, caused havoc in England and compelled the founders of Massachusetts Bay to devise a very different system for the militia of New England. Woodcut detail from *The Faithful, yet Imperfect, Character of a Glorious KING, KING CHARLES I*. Written by a Person of Quality. Printed for Richard Royston at the Angel in Ivy-Lane in London, 1660. © British Library Board. All Rights Reserved E.1799.(1.) Image published with permission of ProQuest. Further reproduction is prohibited without permission.

nationalistic lords lieutenant pushed aside local customs by pressing the ablest men for Charles's foreign military adventures, including those traditionally exempt from such service. This caused trouble in the counties and towns, as the loss of good men was often a hardship to the locality. In addition, several trainbands were sent on the ever-growing number of overseas expeditions, upsetting the customary balance in the military system and condemning more middling men to die in the fields of the Continent or Ireland. This angered many, so much so that "after 1625 they [lords lieutenant and their deputies] became the most active, the most visible, and the most despised royal officials in the land."[41] This was the military atmosphere in England when the Puritans fled to Massachusetts Bay in the 1630s. Frightened by the specter of undisciplined and violent English armies let loose on their home countryside and a breakdown in the traditional system of military impressment, the soon-to-be colonists took their negative memories of Charles's "Perfect Militia" with them to New England.[42] They were determined never to live under such military tyranny again.

The Massachusetts Bay Militia, 1630–1675

As early as 1631, just one year after the beginning of the Great Migration, the Massachusetts General Court began to legislate for public safety by requiring all men who traveled outside of Boston to carry a weapon and for each home to be stocked with arms.[43] With the cruelty of Charles I's "Perfect Militia" fresh in their collective memory, however, the Puritan founders of Massachusetts Bay set out to establish a different militia, a militia rooted in the Elizabethan tradition.[44] Although universal military service for all males between the years of sixteen and sixty was retained, the founders dropped the idea of an untrained militia existing alongside select trainbands. In its place, Massachusetts attempted to erect a system exclusively of trainbands, where every male in the militia—not only a select few (as in the case of Elizabethan trainbands)—was vigorously trained and well armed.[45]

In another shift from how the system operated in England, as early as 1636 the men in the Massachusetts militia companies nominated their own officers. Thus they created what T. H. Breen calls a "Covenanted Militia" along the lines of the participatory leadership model of Massachusetts's churches.[46] Later, the men even nominated regimental officers and the military commander of the colony, although the General Court confirmed their appointments. "Voting" for officers was so common that most men believed that they were actually electing their officers outright.[47] The election of officers was born from both the spirit of broad popular participation in the governance of the colony and memories of the untrustworthy and sometimes treacherous English military officers of Charles's "Perfect Militia."[48] A few professional military men in the colony were appalled at the thought of recruits choosing their commanders; however, the practice remained, despite a few difficulties, until 1668.

The town companies in Massachusetts, composed of every male in a town between the ages of sixteen to sixty, were never intended to fight offensively as a whole. While the town company might come together as a unit (in the case of an alarm or attack) to defend the town, the entire company would not be sent away on offensive missions; that would have left the town utterly defenseless. In times of emergency or war, offensive detachments were instead formed by recruiting men from various town companies into a composite company. This process would leave some men in each town for defensive purposes and still allow the colonial government to marshal troops for offensive missions. It was thus a hybrid of the English system, with its two separate forces: untrained militia for offensive missions and trainbands for defense. In Massachusetts, each militia unit was a trainband, so arrangements had to be made to provide offensive troops from those units, unlike in England, where the bands were never supposed to take part in offensive forays. This was the system used, to a very limited degree, to assemble troops for the few military emergencies that the colony faced before 1675.

The government of Massachusetts Bay first compiled its militia law into a single statute in 1643.[49] Five years later, *The Book of General Laws and Liberties* further codified the colony's military laws and continued to do so in its many subsequent editions.[50] The 1672 edition of *The General Laws and Liberties of the Massachusetts Colony*, its subsequent supplements, and militia laws passed by the General Court from 1672 to 1676 offer a complete picture of the state of Massachusetts's militia establishment just prior to King Philip's War.[51] The General Court spent a significant amount of time and effort establishing Massachusetts's militia system and a complete system of safeguards to control it. Having witnessed firsthand the terror of an abusive military back in England, the Court assured strict civilian control over the military at all times by legal statute, funding limits, and direct operational control of militia officers and units.[52]

The 1672 law begins with the organization of the militia, mandating that the military force of each county (called a regiment, such as the "Essex Regiment"), both infantry and cavalry, be under the command of a sergeant major.[53] The sergeants major reported directly to the highest military officer in the colony, the sergeant major general, along with the governor and General Court, or, in time of war, the Council of War. Despite the fact that the General Court appointed and could remove county sergeants majors, a considerable safeguard, the sergeants major of the counties looked suspiciously like English lords lieutenant in their power to organize and command the militia. There were, however, real differences. While the sergeants major for the various counties were required to bring their entire regiment together for a mass military drill every three years, they were prohibited from doing so more frequently—to prevent them from gaining too much power.

There was also a strict prohibition that the county's militia units could not be "drawn out of the said County to any Regimental exercise" by a sergeant major, creating a safeguard against the types of abuses that were common in the English system.[54] Amazingly, the sergeants major were also forbidden to march the regiment or any part of it out of the county during time of war, unless given specific permission from the General Court, council, or the major general; an exception was made if "it be in Pursuit of the Enemy upon a Rout."[55] In addition, sergeants major, unlike their English brethren the lords lieutenant, had very little control over the recruitment of men for active duty. They were given broad powers to oversee the officers under their command, however, including calling them together for meetings.[56] Thus, like so much of the militia system of Massachusetts, the role of the sergeant major, even as late as the 1670s, was a hybrid of English practice and Massachusetts conditions.

The 1672 codification of military law describes at length the all-important town companies. The size of a full-strength foot company was set at a minimum of sixty-four soldiers (not including officers). A full-strength company would be led by a captain, assisted by a lieutenant and an ensign, all to be appointed and commissioned by the General Court. All inferior officers (sergeants and corporals) were "to be chosen and appointed by the Commissioned Officers in that Company."[57] Smaller towns, which could not muster the required sixty-four soldiers for a full company, were to serve under a sergeant or inferior officer.[58] The sergeant major of the county also had the option of combining smaller town units together to make a complete company. Militia officers were to "take care that their Soldiers be well and completely Armed and shall appoint what Arms each soldier should serve with; Provided two thirds of each Company be Musquetiers" while the rest carried pikes (see figure 4).[59] It is telling that the officers were allowed to decide which weapon each man under his command would carry. This mirrors an English practice of assigning weapons based on the class and abilities of individual soldiers.[60]

Town companies were to be inspected and drilled six days a year. The drill was usually held on the town common, where the men practiced marching, skirmishing, ambushing, developing battle formations, and

(1)

✤✤✤✤✤✤✤✤✤✤✤✤✤✤✤✤✤✤✤✤✤✤✤✤✤✤✤✤

THE
Exercife of the English,in the
Militia of the Kingdome of
ENGLAND.

 He Souldiers are divided into two kindes, *Foote* and *Horſe*. The *Foote* againe are of two kinds ; *Pike-men* and *Muſketiers.*

· *Pikemen* are armed with a head-piece, a Curace and Taſes defenſive, & with a Pike of fifteene foot long, and a Rapier offenſive. The Armour is all iron ; the Pike of Aſhen-wood for the Steale, and at the upper

B   end

Figure 4. This military manual, printed in England only a few years after the founding of Massachusetts Bay, clearly highlights the two wings of the seventeenth-century infantry: musketeers and pikemen. While the armor on the pikeman is more extensive than that usually seen in America, many colonists and the Massachusetts Bay Company itself imported military equipment into New England from the earliest days of the colony. Woodcut detail from *The Exercise of the English* by an anonymous author. Published in London in 1642. © British Library Board. All Rights Reserved E.136[23]. Image published with permission of ProQuest. Further reproduction is prohibited without permission.

firing their weapons in concert.[61] The law required all males over sixteen years old to "duly attend all Military Exercise and Service as Training, Watching, Warding, under the penalty of five shillings for every fault."[62] However, there were several categories of men excused from training, including: "Magistrates, Deputies and Officers of Court, Elders and Deacons, the President, Fellows, Students, and Officers of Harvard College and professed School-masters, Physitians and Chyrurgeons allowed by two Magistrates, Treasurer, Surveyor General, Publick Notary, Masters of Ships and other Vessels above twenty tuns, Fishermen constantly imployed at all fishing seasons, constant Herdsmen and such others as for bodily infirmity or other just cause."[63] Also exempt from militia duties were "Negroes and Indians"; the only exception was a brief period from 1652 to 1656, when "all Scotsmen, Negroes, and Indians inhabiting with or servants to the English" were included in militia trainings (although it is unclear whether these groups ever actually trained with their local militia companies).[64] The men who did appear were to be exercised in the military arts of the day. Their officers would also inspect each man's weapon. Those not appearing with the correct arms (based on extensive description in the law) were to be fined ten shillings for every fault. The law made provisions for those too poor to procure arms and ammunition: the colony would provide the musket or pike, and the man, if single, would be employed as an indentured servant in order to pay for the weapon.

An official, known as the clerk of the band, was responsible for inspecting each man's weaponry over the course of the year. The clerk was also empowered to keep the company's muster roll and be on constant watch, during training, for "any defect by absence of Soldiers or other offenses that may fall out in time of Exercise."[65] The law stipulated that after informing the company's officers, the clerk would assess and collect fines for a variety of defects in arms, attendance, or behavior.[66] More serious infractions were to be dealt with by the officers, who had the "power to punish such Soldiers as shall commit any disorder or contempt upon any day or time of Military Exercise or upon Watch or Ward, by Stocks, Bilboes, or any other usual Military punishment, or by fine . . . or may commit such Offender to the Constable, to be carried before some Magistrate, who may binde him over to the next Court of that Shire [county], if the cause so require, or commit him to Prison."[67] In a May 1672 addition to the codification, military punishments were further defined as "Riding the Wooden Horse, or by Bilboes, or lying Neck and Heels or acknowledgement at the Head of the Company."[68] Judging from the amount of

Figure 5. A depiction of the first muster of the East Regiment of the Massachu-setts Bay Militia in Salem, December 1637. The regiments mustered periodically for training; the unit in the foreground is receiving instruction in the use of the matchlock muskets, while in the background men practice with the pike. *The First Muster* by Don Troiani. www.historicalimagebank.com.

time that the issue was discussed and the laws passed, the legislature was quite concerned with misconduct during training.

One of the most pressing problems on training days was the tendency for the men to treat the exercise as a social gathering, drinking and shoot-ing weapons into the air. By 1672, the General Court declared that all sol-diers after training "shall repair to their several Quarters and Lodge their Arms, immediately after the dismission upon Training Days and whoever shall either singly or in companies remain in Arms, and vainly spend their time and Powder by inordinate shooting in the day or night . . . shall be punished by their Superior Officers . . . by sharp Admonition or otherwise with any usual military punishment."[69] The same punishment was pre-scribed for those soldiers who disobeyed any lawful command. Any refusal from a soldier to obey his officer was a serious affair; there is evidence that this independent streak in Massachusetts's militiamen was one reason that the government did away with the election of officers in the 1660s.[70]

In addition to training, the other military duty most men participated in was watch and ward. Ward was the normal policing of the town, usu-ally by the town constable; he could call up armed militiamen, however, if the need arose. Watch, a form of sentry duty, was only performed in time of alert or war and was for the protection of the town from outside enemies.[71] The 1672 law ordered that watches of militiamen be set after sunset every night by the town's military officers and kept by the soldiers until they were dismissed by their officers the next morning. Towns were charged with providing a "sufficient Watch house . . . and a safe and convenient place to keep all such powder and ammunition in toune."[72] Men on watch were forbidden to fire a gun after the watch was set, except in the case of an emergency, or they would suffer a stiff forty-shilling fine.[73] The law also established detailed rules of conduct for the watch when encountering disorderly persons in peacetime (the watch was warned not to risk killing anyone except in self-defense) and prescribed how to raise an alarm when danger approached.

Massachusetts established a cavalry arm for its militia in 1652, and the 1672 militia law contains extensive regulations on their makeup and employment.[74] A troop, the standard unit of cavalry, was considered to be at full strength when it had at least forty men. Troops were assigned three commissioned officers: a captain, lieutenant, and a cornet (instead of an ensign). Troopers were required to "keep always a good Horse and be well fitted with Saddle, Bridle, Holsters, Pistols or Carbines and Swords . . . and having Listed his Horse, shall not change or put him off without License from his Captain" with a penalty of five pounds for each defect.[75] To offset the expense of these requirements, the colony exempted troopers from paying normal county rates (taxes), a sizable incentive to serve as a trooper. Even with this exemption, however, the added expense of owning a horse and all the necessary equipment caused the government to institute a property requirement to join a troop; by 1672, men would only be admitted as troopers if they (or their parents, if they lived at home) paid "in a single Country Rate for one hundred pounds estate and in other respects qualified as the Law provides."[76] A trooper had to attend six training days annually and was, in the case of an alarm, to "fit himself in all respects for service and shall speedily repair to the Guard in the Town" or face a penalty of five pounds.[77] Troops, like infantry regiments, were forbidden to travel out of their county, except in pursuit of the enemy in a rout or with an express order from the sergeant major general of the colony.

The 1672 codification highlighted one more important addition to the militia of the colony, one that had also been established in 1652. This innovation, the town committee of militia, grew into one of the most important institutions within any militia system in colonial America.

The Town Committee of Militia, 1652–1675

All of New England was on alert in 1652 after the Netherlands declared war on England in response to newly passed Navigation Acts. Being so close to the Dutch stronghold of New Amsterdam (later New York), New Englanders kept a close eye on the coastline for an expected seaborne invasion. In addition to normal military preparations, concern over the 1652 Anglo-Dutch War (the first in a series of conflicts) prompted the Massachusetts Bay General Court to establish a new command structure to oversee the militia in Boston; they called the group the committee of militia. The organization was to "consist of the magistrate in the sd towne & the three chief military officers inhabitating the sd towne . . . The sd committee of militia shall have power to appoint military watch, when they shall se cause, for the safty of the towne and country."[78] The 1652 act also stipulated that similar committees be created in Charlestown, Salem, Ipswich, and "all other towns within this jurisdiction where there is one or more magistrates."[79] In towns without a magistrate, the law declared that the town's deputy (or deputies) to the General Court, along with the top military officers in town, would make up the community's militia committee. This was an entirely new development in the militia system; no such group appeared in the English militia.[80]

This unique group developed thanks to a series of crises in the 1640s and 1650s surrounding militia-officer elections in several Massachusetts towns, including Hingham, Newbury, and Ipswich. Disagreements over the form and/or outcome of these militia elections caused severe problems in the towns; the situation was so dire in Hingham and Ipswich that mutinies of the militia nearly broke out.[81] It seems that militia elections often inspired "an excess of democracy" in the Bay Colony.[82] The General Court was extremely troubled by these events and the disorder they caused in society, so much so that it reconsidered the prudence of an elected officer corps, one of the bedrock institutions of self-rule in the colony.[83] The advent of the militia committees in Massachusetts was part of the Court's solution to the problem, dividing control of local militia bands between politically powerful civilians and militia officers.

The new committees of militia in the towns offered another layer of civilian control over the militia, even in times of military crisis or conflict, whereas before the militia officers would have enjoyed full control. The 1652 act gave the committees various powers, most importantly "power of counsell for the best ordering of the militia of their several towns, till the

General Court or councell of the country can be informed."[84] The committees, not militia officers (although the committees included militia
officers), would authorize the mobilization of a town's militia "uppon all
occasions of alarme or any invasion" and would see to it that the town
company readied itself "to oppose any approaching or assayling of them
in any way of hostilitie."[85] The General Court clarified its position on the
power of the committees in May 1654 when it ordered that "it is by this
Court declared, that the committee of militia in the several towns *hath
power to supress all raysinge or gathering of soldiers, but such as shalbe by
authoritie of this gouvment.*"[86] The General Court had come to doubt the
ability of soldier-elected militia officers alone to order their men to stand
down if passions became heated, as they had during several recent militia elections. The memory of an uncontrolled army under corrupt lords
lieutenant back in England still haunted many in Massachusetts Bay. The
committees of militia were the government's attempt to prevent that type
of disorder from recurring in New England. As the elected officer corps
was not up to the task, the government hoped that the militia committees
would be.

In August 1653, the militia committees received a new and very important power. The General Court ordered "that all warrants for impressing
men for warr shall henceforth be directed to the committee of militia in
each town, to execute . . . by the cunstable."[87] The committees were given
the sole power to choose which young men from their community would
be called up for active service; for many of the young men, the decision
of the committee would mean the difference between life and death. This
power had once been in the discretion of the elected militia officers:
now it was to be more broadly based in the joint civilian-military militia
committees.

At the end of the Dutch crisis, in October 1654, the General Court ordered the committees "to release their soldiers under presse."[88] Those men
pulled from the towns' militia companies and called to active duty by the
committees were sent home. While the committees had been established
in response to the Dutch crisis, they did not dissolve with the end of the
emergency in 1654. Instead, they grew into one of the most vital elements
of the militia system in Massachusetts Bay.

The role of the town committees of militia was refined and the committees given heightened powers as time passed. During another Dutch crisis,
in August 1664, the General Court clarified the makeup of the committees, declaring that "the commission officers of horse" or cavalry officers

could sit as members of town militia committees.[89] Earlier laws had stated (probably unintentionally) that only infantry officers could serve as members of the committees. The wartime emergency also inspired the General Court to remind the militia committees for Boston and the other towns of all of their various duties:

> You are hereby required to take into your care & Chardge the soldiery, great artillery & fortification within your towne, and precinct & harbor, & to see that the peace be kept; and in case any shall act upon the shoare or water, in ship, barcque, or boate, contrary to the peace & safety of the toune or country, yow are them to repress by force of armes or otherwise, and doe all things that is requisite in your wisedome for the preservation of the peace of the country, and to comand all to assist yow therein, who are hereby required to yield their obedience to yow; & yow are from time to time to observe all orders yow shall receive from the General Court, councill of the collony, or major generall.[90]

These instructions lay out for the first time in precise detail the government's expectation of the various committees in safeguarding their towns.

In May 1667, the General Court expanded the duties of the militia committees further by instructing them to take charge, together with the town's selectmen, of the fortifications in each town. The men were "to erect or cause to be erected within their tounes, either inclosing the meetinghouses, or in some other convenient place, a fortification . . . in which fortification the women, children, & aged persons may be secured in case of any sudden danger"[91] With their dependants safe from harm in the town's fortification, the town's militiamen would be free to engage the enemy. The committees of militia also organized the labor necessary for this laborious task.

The militia committees had gained considerable power between their inception in 1652 and the codification of their duties in 1672. The militia committee portion of the 1672 act brought all the committees' duties together under one statute for the first time.[92] The committees were to be made up of any magistrate or magistrates living in town, or if there were no magistrates, the town's deputy or deputies to the General Court, together with the three chief military officers (from either foot or horse companies) or a majority of them. In times of emergency, any three of the committee members could act as the entire committee with the power to "order and dispose of the Militia of their Town for their own safety and defense."⁹³ The committees' ability to control the regular militia company in town during a crisis was extended to the local cavalry troop. The 1672 codification continued by confirming the committees' sole power to issue "all Warrants for impressing and raising of soldiers for any expedition . . . who may execute the same by Constable and the said Committee are herby impowered and required to supress all raising of soldiers but such as shall be the Authority of this Government."⁹⁴

A codicil to the 1672 codification, written on May 15, 1672, allowed some coastal towns and their militia committees to take the county rate for the year and put it toward finishing and fixing their fortifications, which were either in bad repair or nonexistent. Most importantly, the General Court ordered "that *each of their Rates be committed into the hands of the Committee of Militia* in each of the aforesaid towns."⁹⁵ This was an entirely new occurrence and added considerably to the power of the committees while taking power away from each town's selectmen, who had controlled such funds in the past.

In December 1673, the colony began mobilizing a force of over five hundred men for a possible expedition if the Dutch fleet that had suddenly appeared in American waters should attempt a landing; the militia committees of each town were entrusted with the job of impressing, listing, and arming the newly created army.⁹⁶ Apparently, this order caused some confusion in the town committees. In January 1674, the General Court issued a clarification that the impressment order was only for the men to be "listed and fitted with firearms & required to be in readiness at all warnings to attend the service of the county," not actually called to duty.⁹⁷

The power of the town committees of militia was expanded one last time before the outbreak of King Philip's War. In 1668, the General Court had asserted its sole right to choose all militia officers, ending the practice of officer elections (in reality, nominations) by members of the local militia companies. It did so because of the continued unrest occasioned by the militia elections. The Court had no idea, however, how difficult the task of identifying suitable men for military commissions in each and every town would prove. As relations with Native Americans deteriorated in the late 1660s and war became ever more likely, the General Court sought help in finding officers, while taking care not to open any discussion of the possibility of renewed elections by the militiamen: "Whereas the allowing & appointing of all commission military officers in this jurisdiction belongs properly and only to this Court by law and *is found both peaceful and satisfactory*, and inasmuch as this Court may not be acquainted with many useful and fit persons for that Service. It is therefore hereby ordered, that henceforth it shall & may be lawful for the committee of militia in the several tounes where there shall be neede to present two or three meet persons in their Tounes for such service & office to this Court for their approbation."[98] Established as a civilian safeguard to the militia system in the 1650s at a time when the General Court was beginning to question the prudence and power of electing officers, the militia committees had come full circle. Ironically, they were no longer needed to safeguard against the disorder and controversies of officer elections; now they were given the sole power to nominate all officers to the legislature. The power of the committees in the local militia system was now second only to the General Court's, giving the community-based committees wide discretion in local militia affairs. Massachusetts had preserved community control of the militia, once embodied in the local election of officers, by instituting instead the town militia committees as a resident command structure that was jointly civilian and military. Militia committees were not only responsible for naming men to serve during war; they played a large part in picking new officers to lead the towns during the coming calamity.[99] The Massachusetts militia, established in the 1630s and in a constant state of change and adjustment up to 1675, was about to face its greatest challenge.

2

The Massachusetts Bay Militia and the Practice of Impressment during King Philip's War

When King Philip's War broke out in the Plymouth Colony on June 20, 1675, the authorities in Plymouth immediately alerted their allies in Massachusetts Bay. The Massachusetts General Court was not in session, but during its first meeting after receiving news of the hostilities, on July 9, 1675, the Court began to prepare for conflict, voting for several war taxes and empowering local constables to amass supplies for an army. The legislators also ordered that cavalry troopers, traditionally exempt from paying regular county rates, pay the new war tax.[1] The language of this first wartime session, however, exposes the Court's cavalier attitude toward the conflict, which had not yet struck Massachusetts. Throughout the proceedings, the Court talked of "the present expedition against the Indians," as if one short battle would settle the conflict; there was no mention of a wider war and little genuine concern.

By the October meeting of the Court, after Indian attacks had laid waste several towns in western Massachusetts and the Massachusetts militia had suffered several setbacks, the cavalier attitude had disappeared and the Court began to prepare its response to the very serious "present warr with the Indians."[2] The legislature quickly enacted several changes to the militia structure to meet the conditions of the war. Court members, following recommendations from commanders in the field, changed the makeup of the forces in the militia: "Wheras it is found by experience that troopers and pikemen are of little use in the present warr with the Indians . . . All troopers shall forwith furnish themselves with carbines . . . and also be lible . . . to serve as foot soldiers during the said warr; provided one fourth part of the troopers in each toune be reserved for the use of the county as such, and all pikemen are hereby required forth with to furnish themselves with fire armes."[3] The necessity of changing one-third of all militiamen from the pike to the musket, in the middle of hostilities, prompted the government to order one thousand muskets from England and to pay for them out of public funds.[4] This late change in armament and the length of time it took to import new muskets from England is almost certainly the reason nearly every town reported that a number of their men lacked muskets when impressed in the coming months. It is probable that those men, required by militia law to own weapons prior to the war, were former pikemen who had yet to acquire their new muskets. Once the muskets arrived, the new weapons from England were distributed to the towns, where local selectmen raised funds to pay for their town's portion of the armament.[5]

In that same October 13, 1675, session, the General Court came to the realization that the crisis was larger than any they had faced before and would require many soldiers and a large army. Never before had Massachusetts Bay fielded such large forces and the men, who were not professional soldiers, needed considerable guidance on how to act in the new army. To deal with this circumstance, the General Court passed the "Lawes and ordinances of Warr . . . for the better regulating their forces, and keeping theire soldjers to theire duty."[6] The regulations were born out of several impulses: the Puritan fear that a loss of godliness had caused the war, the need to establish military discipline for effective army operations, and specific concerns about the conduct of the troops on campaign.

During the war, there were numerous attempts to reform civil society, returning it to the ideals of the colony's founding generation. Many believed that Puritan society had lost its way on the road to a godly "City on a Hill." The first three war ordinances dealt with this loss of the "Puritan Way" and began to rectify it, at least in the army.[7] Soldiers were admonished not to "blaspheme the holy & Blessed Trinity . . . upon payne to have his tongue bored with a hott iron." This, along with regulations against "unlawful oathes, & execrations, & scandalous acts in derogation of Gods honour" and the frequent absence of men from public worship, were meant to begin society's reclamation of its religious heritage through the practices of its soldiery.[8]

The need to inculcate discipline for effectual army operations was the driving force behind the next section of the new regulations. Members of the government believed that the men, who had never been fashioned into a mass army before and had not trained as such, needed a strong statement of what the government expected of them. This required that the men recognize the crucial importance of the chain of command; wartime was not the moment to question the authority of militia officers. The time for militia dispute and protest, a common occurrence in Massachusetts's militia establishment during peacetime, was over. The regulations reminded the men to mind their officers and never to argue with or strike one, on pain of death. Death was also the penalty for men who left the army without permission. Rule 7 told men to be quiet in the ranks, on pain of imprisonment, so that "the officers may be heard and their commands executed."[9] The regulations contained an additional capital prohibition against men who would "resist, draw, [or] lift . . . his weapon against his officer."[10] The men were to take great care to obey the provost marshals and other officers. Any soldier who "utter[ed] any words of sedition or mutiny" was also to be put to death, while those who heard "mutinous speeches and [did] not acquaint their commander with them" were to be "grievously" punished.[11] The fact that most of these infractions were punishable by death is telling—the General Court was taking no chances, knowing the independent spirit of their militiamen.

An equally pressing concern of the Court was the conduct of the army in the field. The experience that they or their fathers had had in England made most Massachusetts settlers wary of any form of powerful army. Long-held memories of uncontrollable Stuart armies raiding the English countryside most likely prompted the General Court to pass these laws of war. Such rules had never been needed before, because Massachusetts had never before put so many soldiers in the field. Even with an all-trained band militia, made up of citizen-soldiers, there was great concern about the behavior of the men on campaign. Rule 12 prohibited drunkenness, the punishment for officers being a loss of their position, while enlisted men would stand for a court-martial. "Rapes, ravishments, unnaturall abuses, and adultery" were to be punished by death, while individual officers decided the penalty to be carried out for fornication or "other dissolute laciviousness . . . according to the quality of the offense."[12] Pillaging, whether theft or robbery, was to be punished with restitution to the victim. Murderers were to be executed. These crimes were a real problem in the memory of many, especially those who remembered rampaging English armies.[13] The legislature did its best to preclude any abuse by soldiers on campaign by instituting a harsh set of statutes and hefty punishments for sin and misconduct.

The last four regulations in the 1675 rules of war focused on particular problems of discipline in the ranks. These regulations were based on actual combat experience; they were the legislature's response to specific

information, reported by active-duty officers, of wrongs being committed in the field by Massachusetts's soldiers. Rule 17 stipulated that all soldiers on watch or at drill be completely armed as the regulations set forth.
Soldiers who "shall negligently loose or sinfully play away their armes at
dice or cards or other wayes" were to stay with the army as pioneers or
scavengers until they could furnish themselves with new arms; losing his
weapon would not win a soldier a quick way home.[14] The colony's ever-
short supply of ammunition and gunpowder was at issue in rule 18, which
made it a capital offense to "spoyle, sell, or carry away any ammunition."[15]
Soldiers were warned not to abuse leave by extending their stay away from
the army, on the loss of their pay. Lastly, the regulations clarified what was
meant by "grievous punishment" ("disgracing, cashiering, the strappadoe,
or riding the wooden horse to fetch blood") and "arbitrary punishment or
punishment at discretion," which precluded any sentence that threatened
life or limb.[16] These twenty rules of war were crucial to regulating the conduct of the Bay Colony's soldiers during the conflict.

When the war broke out, the colony had quickly established a number
of protective garrisons in several towns, especially those communities in
the western Connecticut River Valley and other backcountry areas. Their
proximity to the enemy and the small number of inhabitants in these
settlements made them particularly vulnerable to attack.[17] Ultimately, the
government placed garrisons in over fifteen towns, employing hundreds of
soldiers.[18] There was some question, however, of how these men fit into the
existing command structure: to whom did they report and who should pay
and feed them? In order to clarify this question, in their October meeting
the General Court issued a series of regulations clarifying the command
structure and duties of garrison soldiers. Members of a garrison were
"under the comand and dispose of the chief military officer . . . wither as
scouts, warding, watching, [or] fortifying of garrison places."[19] Thus, area
commanders, not local militia officers, had direct control over the garrison troops in their areas. This gave the theater commanders greater flexibility to move garrison troops to the posts where they were most needed.

The Town Committees of Militia at War

In the same October 1675 meeting of the General Court, the legislators
gave new orders to the militia committees, which were to inspect their
town's stocks of arms and ammunition, to "alter, augment, and dispose"
those supplies, remind the clerks of the bands to inspect the towns'

militiamen's weapons regularly, and order those townsmen who had been exempted from military training to furnish weapons to the town in case they were needed for service.[20] The legislature also addressed those soldiers who had been issued weapons by committees of militia for earlier campaigns, instructing them to return the arms to their rightful owners once such service was over. The committees were required to certify, before any such soldier was paid for his service, that he had returned the borrowed weapon to its rightful owner.[21]

During that first wartime session, the General Court also granted the committees of militia substantial new powers. The committees would assume control over the entire population in times of attack. Militia committees were to:

> setle and dispose the seuerall inhabitants of their respective tounes . . . into one or more garrisons, all persons in the severall tounes, upon penalty of five shillings per day, being herby obligated to labor in and prouide such fortiffication or fortiffications as they [the committee of militia] shall agree upon; and all inhabitants to attend their places in such fortiffication or garrison as they are appointed unto, and in casc of alarm or invasion, to appear at and for the defense of such places . . . no inhabitant or soldier to leaue his station upon any imploy whatsoever but according to [an] order from the chief officer.[22]

Small frontier towns were allowed to evacuate their women and children to the next defensible town, but their husbands were to join their town's garrison.

Militia committees were also ordered to assume the power to "heare, determine, and setle the whole accounts of the several tounes respecting all disbursments of armes, ammunition, horses, furniture, provisions, &c" that were to be sent into the colony's wartime treasurer.[23] This greatly expanded the power of the committees in each community. They were now in charge of every aspect of a town's defense, including its impressment decisions, officer nominations, war accounts, fortifications, garrison assignments, military intelligence gathering, and command of the town in case of attack. As early as October 1675, the wartime powers of the town committees of militia were second only to the power of the General Court itself.

While the records of the General Court from October 1675 on are full of references to militia musters and the operational conduct of the war, the next change in militia law or structure did not come until February

21, 1676. The government, sensing that flexibility in troop movement was paramount, issued new orders. They gave the county sergeants major and other inferior officers permission to take troops out of their county if "engageing, pursuing, or destroying the enemy," as long as it was not expressly "contrary to [a] particular order from a superior officer or authority."[24] The Court thus rescinded one of the most important safeguards against the army, realizing by this time that it was in a fight for the colony's very survival. The legislature overturned another of its orders in February 1676, when it reinstated restrictions against impressing troopers into infantry units.[25] At the beginning of the war, the government believed that troopers were of little use against the Indians, but hard-fought experience taught them otherwise; the scouting abilities and swift response of cavalry troopers were absolutely necessary for success in the conflict. All troopers were needed in the saddle and were no longer to be drafted away into active-duty infantry companies.

The February meeting of the Massachusetts legislature also saw an expansion of the duties of the militia committees in order to improve each town's defenses; too many Indian raids on the towns were breaking through town defenses—by February, the enemy had destroyed many of the towns of western Massachusetts or forced the inhabitants to flee.[26] Fearing that garrison soldiers were not paying close enough attention to their duties, especially in keeping the nighttime watch, the Court instructed the militia committees to ensure that their garrison soldiers adhered to the law. The militia committees were to provide that garrison soldiers in every town take turns "scouting and warding, to prevent the skulking & lirking of the ennemy about the said tounes, & to give timely notice of approaching dainger."[27] The committees were also instructed to ensure that each town watch was kept until the sun rose. Local militia committee members were to see that brush was cut down along the roads and highways to deny hiding places to the enemy; too many men and boys were being killed along the roadways and in pasture lands while trying to move farm goods to town or while grazing livestock. The General Court also ordered the local committees to ensure that young men, even those below militia age, attend militia training musters in order to acquaint themselves with methods of warfare—the government was obviously preparing for a long and bloody struggle.[28]

The new orders for the committees of militia did not stop there. Militia committees had become the main instrument of control in many towns, displacing in some ways the town selectmen. The committees were to make payment to anyone who killed or took prisoner any Indian skulking outside a town: "three pounds per head or prisoners so taken" as long as the committee was provided with the evidence.[29] The General Court ordered the militia committee of Milton in Norfolk County to enforce its directive that people not leave town and order those who had left to return, lest the defense of the town be compromised.[30] In Maine, where civil administration had completely collapsed in the face of massive enemy attacks, the militia committees were given vast powers, usually reserved for town selectmen. They were ordered to make and collect nine separate tax rates and to "audit all acco[unts] . . . of the charges expended in the war."[31] While it seems as if the war was striking at the very heart of Massachusetts's system of government, it was still the locally controlled militia committees, made up of civilian and military leaders, who were controlling the action—meaning that even in this time of crisis, "persistent localism" in the government system remained sound.

By May 1676, the war was having a drastic effect on the ability of many families to survive. As the conflict dragged on, more and more men, including large numbers of young adult sons, the essential farm laborers of New England, and even some married men, were being called up for service. So many young men were being impressed that the ability of many families to farm their land was in doubt. The General Court ordered that soldiers' families in trouble be assisted. Town selectmen (expressly not the members of the militia committees, who were far too busy) were to "impresse men for the management and carrying on of the husbandry of such persons as are called . . . into the service, who have not sufficient help of their oune left at home to manage."[32] The selectmen would oversee the labor of these substitute farmers and pay them from town funds. This gave the town selectmen, who had seen their power dwindle during wartime, an important new assignment.

Militia committees became especially important (and selectmen less so) in towns under threat of direct Indian attack, which by 1676 was true of the entire colony. The town records of the period bring home this fact. Almost all the records kept by the selectmen of each town virtually ignore the war.[33] The records are full of normal town business, local elections, property disputes, or local ordinances passed. They rarely, if ever, even mention the war. In most towns, "scant reference is made upon the records to the transactions of town business [at all] during the first year of the war. . . . Military affairs were the most important and they were managed by the military committee."[34] Other than a possible reference to a war tax, most town documents are silent about how each town handled the calamity swirling around it. The reason was that the selectmen did not handle the war: the committees of militia did.[35] The selectmen, whose power in many towns was considerable before the war, were marginalized during the conflict. While there may have been some overlap of members between the two groups, the new power arrangement caused some distress. The General Court may have sensed this and acted accordingly when it assigned the job of supervising helpers for local soldiers' families to the selectmen, even though this type of wartime duty seems more in keeping with the duties of the militia committees.[36]

In May, the General Court also answered a petition from the committee of militia in Cambridge, which complained that it was having a hard time getting the citizens to labor on the town's fortifications. Work on fortifications was physically demanding and difficult. Many men, already overburdened by their own farm work (possibly lacking a son or two, sent off to the war) and the possible extra obligation of helping a neighboring family with a father off fighting the war, did not have the time or energy to help build fortifications.[37] Yet the work had to be done for the good of the towns. The legislators ordered that the selectmen "joyne with the militia [committee] for the finishing thereof, and for their furtherance heerein doe referr them to the lawes already published."[38] Obviously some militia committees were not getting the assistance they needed from their selectmen, as had been required in a May 1667 law.[39] When the committees asked the legislature to intervene, intervene it did, reminding the town selectmen of their duty and ordering them to assist the militia committees.[40] The loss of political power by town selectmen, along with the detached record of the war in the selectmen's official town histories, demonstrate the truly immense power the militia committees commandeered in the towns during the war.

While the situation was bad throughout the colony, by May 1676 the backcountry of Massachusetts was in a total state of shock and ruin after almost a year of hard fighting. Enemy attacks had destroyed many towns or led to their abandonment. Hundreds of families were scattered to the far corners of the colony, as women and young children were spirited away to the relative safety of the coastal towns, while their husbands, sons, and sweethearts were sent off on military expeditions or assigned to garrisons. The refugee crisis in New England was critical; it was so bad that a number of churches in Dublin, Ireland, dispatched a ship with donated money to assist the war's victims, and money poured in from churches in England as well.[41]

In frontier towns that had not been abandoned, the militia committees were placed in total control. The committees were ordered to divide
all townsmen in certain frontier towns into scouting parties to scour the
nearby landscape, constantly looking for the enemy. The committees selected suitable officers for each party and arranged for them to be paid
from the colony's treasury. Then the General Court took an extraordinary
step. For "the more effectuall carrying out of this worke . . . the soldiers
abroad in service" who lived in the frontier towns were ordered to leave
their units and return home to perform this important local scouting duty.
They would also be "freed from the impresse during their attendence to
the service above said for their own and the countrys defence."[42] The state
of many frontier communities was so fragile that the government stripped
badly needed soldiers from offensive fighting units and sent them back
home to defend their towns. Andover, in Essex County, was one of the
frontier towns singled out in this order, and the town's soldiers soon came
home to protect their own fortified garrison houses. It was almost as if
the Elizabethan system, of trained bands for local defense and a general
militia for offense, was reemerging, fifty years later and three thousand
miles away. The new law also required the chief military officers in every town to send aid to neighboring towns in case of attack, as long as
that aid could be "spayred with safety at home for the security of the distressed."[43] At the same time, the committees of militia were required to
press additional men for war service, a task that was increasingly difficult
as many men refused to serve and those actually impressed failed to show
up for duty.[44] To help combat this shortage of troops, the General Court
authorized and organized the raising of friendly Indians into companies
to fight on the side of Massachusetts Bay.[45]

The lines of colonial settlement were being pushed further and further
eastward. Too many towns were being abandoned and the shrinking frontier was inching ever closer to Boston, which had been in a state of near
shock since February 1676, when enemy attacks came within ten miles
of the town. Something had to be done; the enemy advance had to be
stopped. In order to hold the line, the General Court ordered that "it shall
not be in the liberty of any person whatsoever, who is by law enjoyned to
train, watch, ward, or scout, to leave the town he is an inhabitant of, upon
any pretence whatsoever, without liberty first obtained from the committee of militia . . . upon the penalty of twenty pounds."[46] This order was
vital to the legislature's plan to stop the backcountry from being lost completely to the enemy.[47] If a person had moved away before the new order

or left after—and did not return when the militia committee instructed them to—a twenty-pound fine would be assessed and even taken out of the individual's estate if necessary. It is not known how often this step proved necessary, but it is clear that the militia committees now held every backcountry citizen's future in their hands.

Not only did the committees decide who was sent out to fight, but they now decided who could and could not leave the towns. To make sure that those in garrisons attended to their duties, the Court further ordered that "no person capeable to assist in securing the garrison [house or fort] he belongeth to shall absent himself, by going out of toune, without acquainting of and liberty obtained from the commander of said garrison, upon penalty of five shillings for each offense in that kinde, that so the danger to which the garrisons in the respective tounes are exposed too by frequent absence of such . . . may be prevented."[48] This strengthened an earlier order by the area commander, Major Samuel Appleton, to the same effect.[49] The government was serious about stopping the outflow of its frontier citizens, especially males, which was "enfeebling the remote parts of the country and tending to the damage of the whole."[50] While the situation in the backcountry was grim in the spring of 1676, by midsummer the fortunes of the war were turning. That was due, in large part, to the soldiers of Massachusetts's militia, men who came to serve their society through the colony's complex impressment system.

Massachusetts Bay Impressment at Work, 1630–1675

When Massachusetts Bay established its militia in the 1630s, the Puritan founders created a military force based on a combination of Elizabethan military thought and their own high regard for local control. It took a long time for their system to be fully tested under fire; there was not a major conflict in New England for more than forty years. But while King Philip's War was the first true military emergency that Massachusetts faced, it had called up militiamen for service before, in the Pequot War and a few other minor conflicts from 1640 to the 1660s. Massachusetts's government learned its lessons well during those early incidents and applied that education to impressment during the 1675–1676 conflict.

In 1636, when Massachusetts sent a force of ninety men to take vengeance on the Pequots of Block Island for the murder of dishonest trader John Oldham, every man was a volunteer.[51] Massachusetts Bay decided to join the Connecticut and Plymouth colonies in their war against the

Pequots in 1637. Relatively few Massachusetts soldiers fought, as Connecticut forces won the war's key battle before most Massachusetts forces could be dispatched.[52] In all, fewer than two hundred Massachusetts soldiers actively served in the Pequot War; only around twenty fought in the main battle at Mystic Fort.[53] These men were raised from several Massachusetts towns through a mixture of volunteerism and impressment. The Massachusetts General Court placed a limit on the press, ordering that the towns "may impress such as are not freemen, at their discression."[54]

With the end of the Pequot crisis, the military situation in the colony settled somewhat. Between 1638 and 1655, Massachusetts raised small forces of soldiers, to deal with Indian threats or exact tribute from tribes, only five times.[55] The method of recruitment was far different from the system in England, where impressment from the general militia reigned. Because the number of troops needed for these early emergencies was so small, most of the men who fought in them were volunteers, although a few were pressed.[56] This was generally the case until the 1670s, when the volunteer system began to break down.

Although militia law had made provisions for the town committees of militia to impress soldiers by 1653, the early confrontations (they can hardly be called wars) were so small that impressment was unnecessary. Instead, volunteers were deployed. A good example of the old volunteer system and its faults was the call-up of men for the Second Anglo-Dutch War (1664–1667). The General Court ordered, in May 1664, that "there shallbe *voluntary soldjers* in this jurisdiction for his majestjes service agt the Dutch, not exceeding the nomber of two hundred."[57] The commissions that placed captains Hugh Mason and William Hudson in command gave them specific instructions on how to raise the men: "Yow may or shall, by beate of drume or drumes in each of the tounes . . . proclajme & publish this your power and comission; & leave under your comand & conduct all such persons as shall willingly lyst themselves for that service."[58] To assist in the quest for volunteers, the General Court issued instructions: "To all serjants, corporalls, & drummes in the respectiue companjes within this jurisdiction. Yow . . . are hereby required, in his majesties name, upon the request & desire of Capt Hugh Mason or Capt Willjam Hudson, or either of their officers, to assist them to publish such proclimations within your toune as they shall communicate to yow for the raysing of voluntary soldjers for the service . . . & to returne to them a list of names of such as offer themselues willingly to that seruice; hereof yow . . . are not to faile."[59] There were immediate problems with this effort. The two captains raised only one hundred men, not the two hundred originally called for, despite the fact that the men were promised that they would serve a maximum of six weeks.[60] Captains Mason and Hudson sent two queries about their instructions to the General Court, which offer clues to the problems inherent in the recruitment drive. They asked whether men without weapons should be refused and which men were to be refused because of a prior legal engagement, such as minors or those under an indenture or apprenticeship.[61] It is readily apparent from these questions that the types of men culled from the "beating of the drum" were far less than satisfactory. The low turnout of men also shows that the volunteer system was flawed.

When the next crisis arose, the government changed its approach to recruiting. During preparations for a call-up during the Third Anglo-Dutch War in 1673, the General Court planned to use impressment exclusively; there was no mention of "beating the drum" for volunteers this time around.[62] While the volunteer system had worked to a certain extent during early minor struggles in the 1640s and 1650s, it had become ineffectual by the 1660s, as Massachusetts's experience in 1664 had demonstrated. It is unclear whether the reason was a lessening of civic duty among the second generation of Puritan settlers, a sense that the threat was not as pronounced as it had been in the earlier days of settlement, or the lack of financial incentive to volunteer in an increasingly commercial society. But there was no doubt that the old volunteer system was broken, a fact that the government knew well even in the earliest days of King Philip's War.

The Practice of Impressment in Massachusetts Bay, 1675–1676

Massachusetts's militia committees were instrumental to the conduct of King Philip's War, especially in the impressment of men for combat. The crisis of King Philip's War swelled the number of men pressed for service far in excess of any previous experience in the colony's history. Knowledge of the nature and practice of impressment is essential to understanding the way that the colony fought the war and why it chose the soldiers that it did.

In the early summer of 1675, when news of the troubles with King Philip and his allies in Plymouth and Rhode Island first reached Massachusetts, the General Court believed that the emergency was a small, local affair, like most incidents involving the neighboring tribes in the preceding years. They sent a small force to assist Plymouth colony and believed that the crisis would soon end. By late summer, however, they knew that this war was completely different. The government ordered the entire militia mobilized and directed commanders to prepare all of their units in "a posture of warr."[63] This conflict would not be won with two hundred volunteers; the entire society would need to rally to achieve victory. Despite the severity of the situation, the colony's leaders, who had established the militia system for just such a contingency, were able to keep true to their ideal of locally controlled military impressment. A unique military institution—the committee of militia—safeguarded their ideal, with its mixture of military and civilian officials based in and part of the local community.

Each locally controlled militia committee acted much like an Elizabethan lord lieutenant, deciding who went to war with the interests of the community in mind. The system was a perfect example of "persistent localism," that fierce determination by the citizens of Massachusetts Bay to control all local affairs in the towns and resist any outside intervention.[64] One incident in particular highlights how seriously Massachusetts's citizens regarded local control of their militias. In Beverly, Massachusetts, Thomas Lathrop, the town's militia commander and militia committee leader, was killed in battle in September 1675. The General Court appointed Major William Hathorne, a prominent military and political leader from nearby Salem, to replace Lathrop and fill his post on the Beverly committee. Town leaders immediately protested, writing to the Court, "praying for a substitution of a nomination made by themselves [Beverly's leaders]," stating that "while the gentleman [Hathorne] may be worthy to lead a far more honorable company than ours, yet in regard of his distance of place . . . he is wholly in a manner uncapable to be serviceable unto us, especially in times of war, [and especially for] . . . impressing soldiers."[65] Even though Hathorne, who was well-known in the town, lived just across the river in Salem—only about a mile away—the people of Beverly thought it too far, especially when it came to knowing which soldiers to impress. The General Court agreed with the citizens and instead appointed a Beverly native to the town's militia committee.

The practice of impressment during King Philip's War was very different from the older practice of beating the drum for volunteers. This distinction is lost in most histories of the conflict. In almost every discussion of recruitment, there is a mistaken belief that recruitment during King Philip's War was simply a matter of asking for volunteers.[66] However, even the very first company that Massachusetts mustered for the war was created through impressment. In June 1675, the General Court sent notice to the militia committees of Boston and surrounding towns: "You are hereby required in his Majesty's name to take notice that the Gov. and Council have ordered 100 able soldiers forthwith *impressed* out of the severall townes according to the proportions hereunder written."[67] This is the same language that the Court used during the 1673 crisis, when impressment was chosen as the primary means of recruiting necessary manpower. There is no mention of volunteers and certainly no instructions to the militia to "beat the drum" looking for any. A crisis was at hand and men were needed for service. While there were probably a few volunteers in every company, each recruitment order from the General Court during the war except one refers to impressment as the method for filling the ranks.[68]

The practice of impressment during the war deserves close scrutiny. Entire town militia companies themselves could not be sent; that would have left the towns defenseless. Instead, composite companies, based on the county regiments, were formed. When there was need for a new expeditionary company, the governor and council, or the General Court if it was in session, decided on the total number of men needed to man the company for war service.[69] They named an officer to command the new composite company and gave him the necessary commission. While this was sometimes done when a town called for assistance, it occurred most often when area commanders called for additional troops or in response to a plan of the United Colonies to assemble an intercolonial army.[70] The command majors (or sergeants major, depending on how the order was written) of each county were then told their county's quota of men (see figure 6). An example clarifies the process. In May 1676, the Court wrote: "The whole Court, being mett together, ordered that the major for the county of Essex, Daniel Dennison, Esq, forthwith issue out his orders to the committees of militia in the severall tounes in that regiment for the raysing of their severall proportions of eighty able foote souldjers, well and completely armed, & furnished with ammunition & six days prouission for each souldjer."[71] The major of the county regiment was thus ordered to proportion the target number of soldiers among the towns in his county and inform each town's militia committee of its quota of men for service.

The committees, consisting of the town's top three military officers and any magistrates or deputies living in town, would then convene to

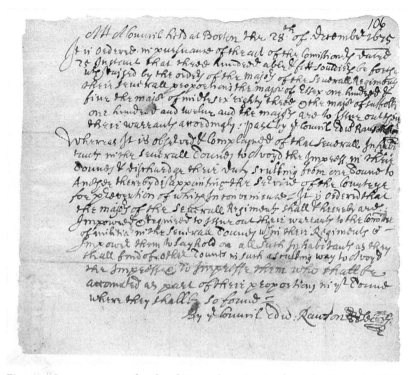

Figure 6. Impressment order dated December 28, 1675 from the Council of Massachusetts Bay to the Sergeant Majors of three Massachusetts counties ordering an additional three hundred "able and fitt soldjers" into the field, just days after the Great Swamp Fight. The men were to be impressed by the town militia committees in Essex, Middlesex, and Suffolk counties. Courtesy of the Massachusetts Archives.

decide which men from town would be sent to fight. The militia committees were servants to two masters during these meetings, much like Elizabethan lords lieutenant before them in England. For the good of the whole society, the militia committees had to impress "able souldjers" from their town, yet at the same time, local interests compelled them to protect their town from serious loss if those soldiers were killed. For frontier towns especially, retaining able soldiers in the community for defense was a priority. Thus, as shall be seen, most committees displayed a preference for pressing single men over married men and men with children.[72] Transients were desired over stable town citizens, while militia committees also sent men with criminal records to the front in large numbers.[73] Once the impressment decisions were made, the militia committees issued warrants to the selected men, via the town constables. Next, the militia committees generally wrote a report to the sergeant major of the county or the General Court itself, listing their choices and detailing the soldiers' preparedness (see figure 7). These reports offer an important glimpse into the types of men sent and their fitness for the coming fight. Many expose problems with the soldiers' equipment; a lack of muskets was especially prevalent in the early days of the war.[74] A message from the Marblehead militia in response to the Narragansett campaign call-up is a case in point:

Marblehead 2 November 75

to the honnored major generall now sitting at Salem,
responding to your honners warrant: we have given your honner this list of the men's names impressed here at marblehead according to your honners warrant for the counties service and for this present Expedition: Also for there clothing wee doe certifie to your honner that they are to the beast of our apprehensions generally well clothed and for armes wee doe certifie to your honner that they are all of them well provided with fier lock musketts powder bags bullets and powder; as for cuttlesses and swords wee doe certifie your honnour that wee can not geett them; if wee could have gott them wee would: nothing else at present and [illegible] your honneres servant to command

richard norman, ensign[75]

The militia committee had done its job. It was now up to the constable to inform the men that they were now soldiers "on the county service."

Besides their normal peacetime duties, wartime constables had a large number of additional tasks to fulfill, many of which were quite difficult.[76] They had to collect war taxes (several times a year), ensure that the watch and ward was kept, and, most importantly, deliver and oversee the militia committee's impressment warrants. Drafted men were then expected to show up at the prearranged place and time. If all went according to plan (which was not a foregone conclusion, especially later in the war) each town's pressed men gathered together on the appointed day, most likely on the town common, and began marching to the rendezvous point for the newly formed company. Along the way, they met with other pressed men from neighboring county towns and soon a sizeable force was on

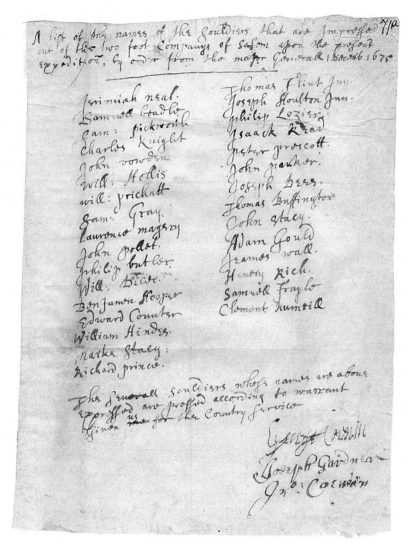

Figure 7. Dated December 1, 1675, this impressment report from the committee of militia of Salem to the General Court was signed by three committee members: George Corwin, Joseph Gardner, and Jonathan Corwin. Most of the thirty-one men listed ended up serving with Captain Gardner at the Great Swamp Fight. Courtesy of the Massachusetts Archives.

Figure 8. Captain George Corwin (1610–1685) was an elite merchant, powerful political figure, and a militia commander in Salem. As the commanding officer of one of Salem's troops, he sat as a member of the Salem committee of militia and was responsible for sending many young men from that town off to war. *Captain George Corwin*. Painting attributed to Thomas Smith, Boston, 1675. Photograph courtesy of Peabody Essex Museum.

the move. In one example, during preparations for the December 1675 expedition against the Narragansett Indians, ninety-four militiamen from seven different Essex County towns marched to Dedham, Massachusetts, to form up under their new captain, Joseph Gardner of Salem. There the new expeditionary company joined with the other Massachusetts companies and marched south to rally with Connecticut and Plymouth forces, forming an army of the United Colonies.

Before they left their towns, the soldiers needed provisioning. Commissioners of the United Colonies instructed town militia committees to supply the soldiers with weapons, food, and all other necessary items. An army travels on its stomach and the armies of New England were no exception; they took bread and biscuits as their main provisions, although supplemented with numerous items such as pickled meat, raisins, and cheese.[77] The men had to provide their own clothing and shoes, which was not a problem for most, except possibly for the cold and wet winter campaigns. The men also needed functioning weapons and ammunition. During the December 1675 expedition, Andover's militia commander, Lieutenant John Osgood, wrote of the hardship that provisioning created for his town (see figure 9): "They [the impressed men] are most of them now well fixed with arms and ammunition and clothing. Edmund Whittington wants a better musquette which we know not well how to supply, except we take from another man which these times seems hard; we air now sendin to Salem for some . . . for shoes and cloth for a coate for one or two."[78] Despite the difficulties and expense of equipping the men for the campaign, Osgood proudly reported that the town's contingent was "now well fixed" for the campaign.[79]

While many men did their duty and mustered for active duty on time, impressment was never an easy task for the constable, especially as the war dragged on and bad news from the front became commonplace. As early as September 1675, the secretary of the General Court, Edward Rawson, wrote to Major John Pynchon, the commander of the western theater, "The slaughter in your parts has much dampened many spirits for the war. Some men escape away from the press, and others hide away after they are impressed."[80] In one incident in Connecticut, the impressment warrants were opened before they arrived in town and their contents were soon well-known. When the constable made the rounds, not a single man on the list was still at home to be pressed.[81]

These problems worsened as the fighting continued. Many came to believe that the militia committees were unfairly targeting certain men for

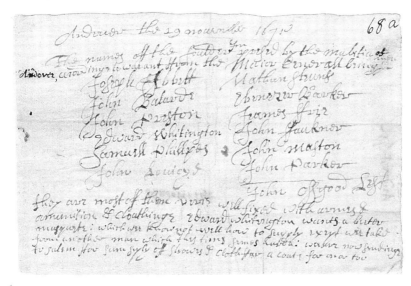

Figure 9. Impressment report written by Lieutenant John Osgood to the General Court on November 19, 1675. Osgood lists the twelve men pressed by the Andover committee of militia and comments on the town's provisioning of the men, remarking on the lack of effective muskets in town. Courtesy of the Massachusetts Archives.

service. Some militia committees, for example, required several of the families in their towns to send multiple sons to fight while other families' sons were spared the press completely. In Andover, Joseph Parker and his brother John both marched off to war, while none of the Osgood, Poor, or Ingalls boys did so.[82] In Beverly, William, John, and Josiah Dodge all served. Samuel, Philip, and John Stainwood of Gloucester served multiple times, while other families in town sent nary a militia-aged son to fight. Such examples are numerous in the impressment records.[83] Certain servants were also pressed into service multiple times. One such incident caused Sudbury's minister, Edmund Browne (writing on behalf of a widowed parishioner whose only servant had been impressed time and again), to question the fairness of the system: "The poore fellow hath nothing to fight for (or land or cattle) as many have both . . . wth choyse of able persons in their familys, of wch not any one hath bin impressed, . . . I heare . . . it may stirr up evill blood or Spirits if impresses continue."[84] Historian Jenny Hale Pulsipher has pointed out that it is not clear whether the poor were in fact unjustly targeted. She argues, however "that there was a significant undercurrent of resentment in the colony, enough to make the Council cautious."[85] The colonial government sent a special warning to the militia committees because "complaint had been made by some against committees of militia in several townes," and the government cautioned committee members to "carry it impartially in the execution of warrants for Impressing soldiers."[86] As shall be seen, it was a warning that went mostly unheeded.

Resentment against the system manifested itself in the increasing number of draft evaders. As the war dragged on, more and more men hid from the press. When the constables could not find the men to be impressed, others had to be pressed in their place.[87] Many an impressment report sent to the General Court listed men who were the militia committees' second or third choice for service—the first choice having evaded the press. The constables and other military leaders, at a loss for how to slow draft resistance, began to threaten parents and other family members with military service if they tried to hide or otherwise protect pressed men. Major Daniel Denison described a Salem incident:

> Only you may please to understand that some of the persons now returned [impressed] hath withdrawn themselves. Although warning hath been left at the places of their abodes and their parents required to be ready to goo in their stead if their sons should fail . . . Other men [have been] warned to make up the number of 28, which is our towne's proportion if any of those now returned should fail. . . . [Three] very lusty young men . . . have by the artifice of their parents, absconded for the present, though their parents hath beene required to bring them forth or be ready themselves to march.[88]

As the letter demonstrates, impressment was not easy, even early in the war. Not only did parents try to protect their sons, sometimes whole towns did as well. Later in the war, as the frontier collapsed, entire towns petitioned to be excused from sending soldiers in order to retain them for town defense. This is exactly what the General Court did in certain circumstances, starting in May 1676.[89]

Some resisted impressment as early as the December 1675 Narragansett campaign, and the problem worsened as the war continued. Groups at every level of society resisted the press, including colony and town leaders, parents, and masters. This opposition points to a battle between power groups in the colony and the realization that the individual could, at times, be more important than the society itself.[90] This resistance to impressment, especially by well-established and powerful individuals and families, was well-known to the colony's military commanders as well as members of local militia committees (see figure 10). Knowing that politically powerful families wanted their sons protected from danger obviously shaped some militia committee decisions. As the war dragged on, numerous young men (those not lucky enough to have some influential connection in towns to help them legally evade the press) gained great skill at avoiding draft calls by "skulking from one Toune to Another."[91] According to the law, such men were liable, if caught, to be pressed to fill the quota of whatever town apprehended them.[92]

As the war proceeded and avoiding the draft became common, the government repeatedly issued measures against draft evasion. By May 1676, the situation had grown so drastic that the General Court passed a stringent new law. "Taking into consideration the great disappointment the country hath suffered by reason of non appearance of souldjers impressed for severall expeditions," the government ordered that every person "neglecting to make his appearance according to order" would be fined a considerable amount: regular militiamen would pay four pounds while troopers were assessed a penalty of six pounds.[93] The duty to enforce the strict new order was given to "the committee of militia in the severall tounes where the offense is committed," and the committees were "impowered and required to call before them all such as shallbe delinquents . . . and on conviction of their neglect, to give warrant to the constable to levy the said fines, which said fines shall be improoved to purchase armes for the tounes use."[94] The committees of militia were thus given the role of judge and jury over those who evaded the impressment orders that the committees themselves issued. The law did, however, establish a mechanism for review and possible reversal of the cases by a higher authority: "It shallbe in the power of the council [the colonial council in Boston] upon the petition of any person agreived, and just reason alleadged and prooved, to make abatement of the said fines as in their wisdom and discretion they shall judg meet."[95] Some historians claim that fines and other punishments were almost never enforced to the fullest extent possible under the law. This nonenforcement was a symptom of the division rampant in the colony at the time; colonial leaders did not enforce the law because they feared that focusing on society's problems would tarnish their image or demonstrate how ill prepared Massachusetts Bay was to fight a war.[96]

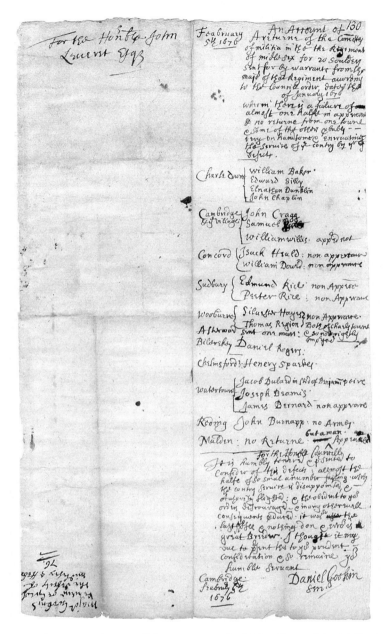

Figure 10. A report written on February 5, 1676 by Major General Daniel Gookin listing twenty-one draft evaders from Middlesex County. Gookin, who reported that almost half of the pressed men had failed to appear and one town had sent no men at all, lamented "the county service is disappointed and Authority slighted." As the war continued, draft evasion became a serious problem for colonial forces. Courtesy of the Massachusetts Archives.

Impressment was not only difficult but also occasionally dangerous for constables. A few constables were attacked (either verbally or physically) while fulfilling their duty. For example, John Elithrop, the constable of Manchester, was verbally and physically abused while trying to press Samuel Leech in 1676. Elithrop testified in court that when he approached Leech, "He answered that he thought he should not go, saying 'You may goe your selfe if you will' and presently Rose up and bending his fist threatened to strike me [Elithrop] and struck my pipe out of my mouth. He [Leech] lifted up his foot and threatened to kick him [Elithrop], called him rogue and said he would turn him out of his house."[97] During another attempt to impress him, Leech "in a scoffing manner . . . said that he would take no notice for it was more than the Selectmen or the Major General or the Governor himself or the King could do and he would . . . publish what fools they were."[98] Leech was severely fined for his actions. While physical violence was not a common occurrence, the constables were under a constant threat of such action while issuing militia committee warrants. Taking such special circumstances into account, the General Court passed an addendum to the May 1676 anti-resistance law, ordering that if the nonappearance was accompanied by "refactorines, reflections, or contempt upon authority," the culprit would be put to death or punished with "some other grievous punishment."[99] The colony felt the need to protect its constables and the impressment system in general. As a society in a fight for its very life, the colony was not about to suffer abuse from its own citizens.

Some men had traditionally been exempt from the militia before the war and were not generally regarded as eligible for service during it. Magistrates, ministers, elders and deacons, students and professors at Harvard, and shipmasters and full-time fishermen, along with several others, were not enrolled in the militia. Indians and blacks had also been stricken from the militia rolls, although the colony increasingly used friendly Indians as scouts and in volunteer companies as the war went on. The law stated that no man could be impressed "that is necessarily and sufficiently exempted, by any natural or personal impediment, as by want of years, greatness of years, defect of minde, failing of sences, or impotency of limbs."[100] Before the war, quite a few men had been granted an exemption by the quarterly courts, either from militia service itself or training musters. In pre-1675 Essex County, for example, over a hundred men were exempted from militia training. Most had to pay an annual fee for their absence "to the support of the company."[101] Some were old; some lived a long way from the training field. These men were generally regarded as exempt from the active-duty press for the war as well; most of them were too old for service anyway. Yet, they were not without value.

The colony turned to the exempt men in the early days of the war to furnish sorely needed weapons. All men "of estate within their tounes as are, by the county courts or committees of militja exempted from ordinary trainings" were required to "prouide three fire armes," which ensured that they "shall be freed from being sent abroad to the warrs, except in extreme & utmost necessity."[102] Such exemptions were dangerous, however, because the public perceived them as a way that the wealthy could avoid service. To combat this, the General Court cautioned committees of militia to take care to limit the number of such exemptions granted.[103]

Hiring a substitute to avoid service during the war also caused great resentment in the colony. There is no mention of this practice in any Massachusetts Bay militia statute enacted before 1675.[104] While there is little question that substitution was practiced during the war, the question is *how often* it took place. Jenny Hale Pulsipher claims that most substitutes, hired by men of means from among men of lower rank, came from towns with unequal wealth distributions, especially the commercial centers of Boston and Salem.[105] Both towns had large numbers of wealthy merchants and larger numbers of men who needed cash. The best-known instance of substitution during the war comes from an often-cited court case from Suffolk County. In May 1676, Eleazer Phillips sued John Smith. Smith had promised to take Phillips's place after he was impressed for an expedition to Black Point in Maine: "After the reciept of which [money and arms from Phillips, however,] he [Smith] never went forth, but absented himselfe from the said Service whereby the said Phillips is greatly damnified for wont of his mony armes & ammunition & is also liable to bee impressed again."[106] This one example of a substitution gone awry has been used time and again, in numerous histories, as the primary evidence for what many historians claim was the widespread use of substitutes during the war.

Very few other records of substitution exist. John Laighton of Rowley, when he was called before the Court for nonappearance, claimed that he hired a substitute in November 1675. No direct evidence, however—even the name of the supposed substitute—was offered that he had indeed done so.[107] Zachary Curtis of Topsfield served as a substitute in 1675. The evidence for this comes from a report sent from Topsfield's militia to Major General Daniel Denison: "Zacviah Curtis he is praised [pressed] and was

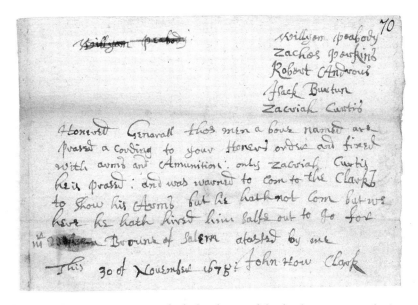

Figure 11. Impressment report which details one of the few known cases of substitution during the war. John How, the clerk of the militia of Topsfield wrote "Honored General" Daniel Dennison on November 30, 1675 that "Zacviah Curtis he is praised[pressed] . . . but he hath not Com but we here[hear] he hath hired Himself to go for Mr. Browne of Salem." Despite this example, the vast majority of men who served in the conflict were impressed. Courtesy of the Massachusetts Archives.

warned to come to the Clerks to Show his arms but he hath not Com but we here [hear] he hath hired Himself to go for Mr. Browne of Salem" (see figure 11).[108] Very few other examples of substitution exist, and *all* are from Boston.[109] While substitution was apparently available as an option, if it was common it is strange that it does not appear more often in the court records, especially in Essex County. Other than the two cases related above, there is no mention of militia substitution in the Essex County Quarterly Court records, a troubling fact when one considers that the county was brimming with young men, like the transient fishermen of Marblehead, who would have been prime candidates to hire themselves out as substitutes. If the practice had occurred with any frequency in Essex County, there should be several court cases, like the Suffolk case, on the books. It appears that the practice was extremely rare in Essex County and anywhere outside the urban center of Boston during King Philip's War.[110]

If substitution was rare during the war, so too was volunteering for service. After the failed experiment in 1664 with "beating the drum" for troops, the government was not about to rely on that system to fill the ranks in 1675. Few muster records report men volunteering for service during the war, with some notable exceptions. There is evidence of at least one troop of volunteer cavalry being raised during the war.[111] More memorably, Captain Samuel Mosley raised at least two all-volunteer companies in Boston. The first was made up of "apprentices or servants and probably many boys not yet enrolled in the militia and therefore not subject to impressment . . . [including as well] a sprinkling of Frenchmen and . . . ten or twelve privateers."[112] Mosley and his men were notorious. Many of his men felt that their volunteer status gave them the right to choose which (and whose) orders to obey. This created a real problem of command; the legislature dealt with it by statute, decreeing "that all such persons so listing themselves [as volunteers] shall be subject to all such martial lawes as are or maybe provided for the well ordering of the forces of this jurisdiction."[113] Although it posed certain difficulties, Mosley's first company was very successful in battle and the colony highly desired such service.

When Mosley went to raise his second unit of volunteers in May 1676, after having earned a reputation as an able battlefield commander and his volunteers as effective, if ruthless, soldiers, he entered into negotiation with the General Court about the nature of his command. Mosley demanded that he be allowed to accept up to sixty friendly Indian volunteers, that his company could be as large as he deemed fit, that his men would have the same privileges as impressed soldiers (such as having wounded men cared for at the colony's expense), and that his men never be assigned to a garrison. Most importantly, he wanted total control over his command "that he not be ordered under the command of any comander in chiefe . . . unless uppon a suddaine exigent." He also demanded freedom of movement and that he and his company "not be bound up in . . . marches or executions to particular places, but to leave it to their best discretions for destroying the ennemy."[114] Despite the extraordinary power that Mosley demanded, which basically placed him outside the military command structure, the General Court ruled that "he ought to haue all due encouragement in this affaire."[115] The Court even ordered the militia committees to assist in the raising of money to pay and provision his volunteers.

While some men volunteered to fight with Mosley, most men tried to avoid service at every opportunity. The question is why. Massachusetts Bay volunteers for the special companies, as well as some Plymouth volunteers, were given incentives to fight. Most importantly, Mosley and his men were to divide among themselves any "benefit that may accrew by captives or plunder."[116] At the same time, they received the same pay as impressed men, without the worry that they could end up assigned to a garrison for long stretches of time. In Plymouth, the colony encouraged soldiers to join these special units by pledging that lands captured in the war would be held as security for their militia pay.[117] Many historians credit this type of volunteer unit, especially the ones that Plymouth Colony fielded under Captain Benjamin Church, with winning the war.[118] Felix Zarlengo even argues that Massachusetts only avoided defeat "with the assistance of volunteer bands of bounty hunters who were largely outside the militia structure."[119] This is an oversimplification of the situation; without the regular militia to provide manpower for protective garrisons and regular expeditionary forces to fight major battles, the special volunteer units would not have been able to function in their role as "seek and destroy" raiders. There is little doubt that these units of volunteers, while effective fighters, were outside the norm of service during King Philip's War. The vast majority of men who fought during the war did so in regular expeditionary companies, drawn from the mainstream militia by impressment.

While the number of special, all-volunteer units was small, there were, in every town, some men who came forward to serve in normal companies of their own free will. The volunteers for regular-duty companies were simply different. They volunteered for any number of reasons. The threat of conscription itself probably induced some men to volunteer, particularly if by doing so they could serve under an officer whom they knew and trusted.[120] Some volunteered from a sense of civic duty, while others had the desire to escape their town or family. There is some evidence that a large proportion of the men who volunteered for service were second (or lower) sons of their families.[121] They had to wait a long time for any financial support from their fathers, if they got much at all; for these men, volunteering might have offered some advantages. There was actually little incentive to volunteer, however, especially if there was a chance to avoid the press altogether. While in the past some regular volunteers had been given a bonus of some sort, it was not common during King Philip's War. For example, during the Pequot War, Connecticut gave land grants for military service. Thirty-six Connecticut Pequot War veterans eventually received over three thousand acres of land for their service.[122] Yet, Massachusetts never gave land to any enlisted man for service, something most men probably realized.[123]

The government offered no reward to Massachusetts Bay volunteers in regular units except the standard pay, which was quite low because the colony always tried to keep the cost of war to a minimum.[124] Despite this, some men undoubtedly volunteered for the pay, but the number was probably very small. On average, enlisted men made eight pence a day, which amounted to two or three pounds for a term of around six to nine months.[125] While two to three pounds was not much money, it was not insignificant and was undoubtedly useful to many soldiers. The pay was not enough, however, to set them up as independent adults, free from the economic control of their birth families. It certainly was not enough to buy or establish a farm.[126] Volunteering for military service in the seventeenth century was not the same as doing so in the eighteenth. Fred Anderson argues that Massachusetts soldiers of the French and Indian War in the 1750s and 1760s were induced to volunteer for provincial service by "relatively large sums of cash," which made "military service . . . a reasonably lucrative proposition, providing cash income to hasten his [the soldier's] attainment of independence . . . and perhaps an accelerated entry into real manhood."[127] This was not the case during King Philip's War. While the number of men who volunteered was never high, that number shrank as the war went on and the news from the front lines got worse.

There is no doubt that the town committees of militia impressed the vast majority of men who fought for Massachusetts Bay during King Philip's War. Some historians have commented on the arbitrary nature of the militia committee system that sent these men to war. Douglas Edward Leech, in *Flintlock and Tomahawk*, mused that "possibly the town authorities have a grudge against some ne'er-do-well or a certain family that has proved uncooperative in civic affairs. Such a person usually finds himself at the top of the list."[128] While Leech was correct in his assessment of the final result of many impressment drives, his characterization of the process was flawed. Leech argued that the system was highly decentralized and unregulated, writing that how the soldiers were selected was of "no concern of the central government at Boston" and that the men were probably chosen by an ad hoc meeting of selectmen, which decided who to send based on the criteria of "who can best be spared by their families."[129] Leech went on to characterize the recruitment system as disorganized and almost random, although "flexible." The committee of militia system, which Leech failed to mention, was actually very organized, as it was established by the "central government at Boston."[130] George H. Martin offered a more enlightened critique of the committee system:

This seems a large power to put into the hands of a few men, to select from all the eligibles in town the persons to be sent on military expeditions. What principles of selection they acted on, we do not know. The phrase "all things considered" [in the 1689 Militia Committee Act] left much to the fallibility of human judgment, and we can imagine that the selection seemed as mysterious as the choice of the women grinding at the mill, of whom it was predicted "one shall be taken and the other left." That there should be much masculine anger and much feminine bitterness and many personal and family feuds resulting from this system of impressment was inevitable.[131]

Martin's concerns echo those of the people of Massachusetts over two hundred years earlier, who, as the war raged on, had begun to question the methods of the militia committees. The examination in the following chapters of the towns of Essex County and the soldiers chosen to fight by their militia committees attempts to shed some much overdue light on these "mysterious" choices in order to determine just what the militia committees' "principles of selection" really were.

3

Many Men, Many Choices
Impressment in Essex County's Thriving Towns

Impressment for active military service was a local matter in colonial New England. The militia committees, which made the fateful decision of who went to war, resided in each community and were made up of local elites who personally knew most of the men they sent off to fight. That was the reason that the General Court established the committees of militia in the first place—to institutionalize the "persistent localism" so cherished in Puritan New England within the military command structure, especially the arm that made impressment decisions. To truly understand how Massachusetts Bay chose its soldiers and why, it is important to dig deeply into the localities. The towns of Essex County offer the perfect opportunity to examine seventeenth-century military impressment. Essex County, just north of Boston, was the heart of colonial Massachusetts Bay. By 1675, it held every type of New England town, from major seaports like Salem; to small, failing communities like Wenham; to thriving commercial centers like Ipswich; to quintessential farm towns like Andover. The details of recruitment in these communities are key to understanding who the soldiers of seventeenth-century New England were and why they, and not their neighbors, were chosen for military service.

Essex County contained a number of important commercial and trading towns that dominated the region and played an important part in the Massachusetts economy. The most important of these was undoubtedly Salem, which by 1670 was the colony's second largest port and a major shipping center in the growing Atlantic world.[1] Commercial centers like Salem were densely populated and had greater degrees of both wealth and poverty than other towns. Yet, as vital as Salem was to Essex County, so too were the county's other commercial and market towns. Newbury and Lynn were significant communities in their own right, as chief regional trading towns and agricultural and population centers.[2] Ipswich, Rowley, Topsfield, and Marblehead, the towns examined here, were also important, both in the county and the colony as a whole. Ipswich, the most populous town in Essex County, was a major center for agriculture and trade. Rowley had become an important commercial center for the production of textiles. Topsfield, while smaller than the other towns examined, had all the characteristics of a town on the rise. Marblehead was extremely important in the profitable transatlantic fishing trade. The large or growing populations of these thriving towns offered the men who sat on their militia committees options, a real choice of men to send to war. In addition, as the home of a large proportion of Essex County's citizens, these and similar towns supplied the overwhelming majority of the soldiers impressed from the county during the war. The largest percentage of those men came from the affluent town of Ipswich.

Ipswich: Essex County's Largest Town

Situated almost in the middle of Essex County's Atlantic coastline, Ipswich's land extended inland more than ten miles and was bisected by the Ipswich River (see map 2). Founded in the early spring of 1633 under the energetic leadership of John Winthrop Jr., son of the famous governor, Ipswich quickly rose to prominence. The town established mill and meetinghouse alike that first year, while laying out streets and assigning house lots. Nathaniel Ward, the town's influential first minister, arrived in the early years, as did Thomas Dudley, a former governor of the colony. While both Dudley and Winthrop eventually moved on, a number of prominent men in the county and the colony, including the Rev. William Hubbard and Samuel Appleton, continued to reside in Ipswich. As the settlement grew, with a large influx of settlers from East Anglia, it developed a decidedly mixed economy, much like that of England. The town displayed an understanding and appreciation of the "important role of merchants, tradesmen, artisans, and manufactures."[3] In addition, the town was home to a large number of prosperous yeomen. Ipswich was becoming a powerful town; only four years after its founding, it ranked second only to Boston in wealth and population in the colony, a distinction it retained throughout the seventeenth century.[4]

By the early 1660s, the townspeople had amassed substantial capital, although there was a great disparity of wealth between Ipswich's large landholders and merchants and those inhabitants just trying to feed their families. The leaders of Ipswich's local government, chosen from among the leading citizens, stayed in office for long stretches, many (especially selectmen) serving almost yearly in the same office.[5] These circumstances allowed the top 10 percent of the town's original families to control almost half of the town's wealth.[6] This, in combination with an East Anglian consciousness that "divided men into specific political gradations, leaders, freeman, commoners, and inhabitants," severely stratified the town.[7] In turn, the privileged families developed an intense dislike of anyone who tried to upset the town's economic, political, or social balance.

Ipswich's leaders went to "great lengths to close ranks against undesirables."[8] The town closed itself to new inhabitants in 1659 by declaring that anyone who did not already have a house built in town was forever excluded from the privileges of commonage; they would get no land in Ipswich.[9] This made any future in the town especially bleak for younger sons, who could not expect to inherit their family's main homestead.[10] Sale of land to newcomers by established residents was considered alarming and happened infrequently.[11] Soon after the town closure, the leadership brought court cases to remove a number of men who had refused to leave when warned out of town, including a number of former servants who had lived in Ipswich and tried to return after an absence.[12] Town leaders also cracked down on inhabitants whom they deemed "undesirable" with a variety of harsh actions and fines. By the 1670s, even "strangers of 'honesty and ability' had to be vouched for by their hosts, post security, and obtain a license to remain in town."[13] Ipswich even attempted to create a place for "undesirables" to go—it sponsored a new town on the frontier at Quabaug (later Brookfield).[14]

The attempt to purge Ipswich of undesirable residents, along with a constant campaign to cleanse the town of sin (especially sins instigated by the lower orders), led to a rise in court cases in the 1670s and an inevitable backlash. Many lower and middling citizens of the town were angry and resentful of the leading families, "while some in the upper echelons openly expressed disdain for those in the lower echelons."[15] The town became even more stratified when, in an attempt to enlarge the meetinghouse, a crisis over the seating in the building caused an open split between ranks. In this stratified and contentious atmosphere, the calamity of King Philip's War unfolded.

The civilian-military leaders of Ipswich's committee of militia were solidly part of the town's upper echelon. The committee consisted of the town's militia captain, Daniel Dennison, who was also the colony's major general; Lieutenant Samuel Appleton, who was also a deputy to the General Court; his brother John Appleton, captain of the town's cavalry troop; and Mr. George Gittings, the other deputy. It is possible that up to three other men—John Whipple, cornet of the troop; and Thomas French and Thomas Howlett, the ensigns of the infantry company—served on the committee at various times.[16] Major General Dennison probably had little time to devote to the Ipswich militia committee, since he was in charge of the entire colony's war effort. Dennison held simultaneous positions as captain of the regular Ipswich militia company and major general (or commander in chief) of all Massachusetts Bay forces.[17] When Samuel Appleton left to command a company in August 1675, his place on the militia committee was probably filled by one of the town's ensigns or Cornet Whipple. Every regular member of the committee was among the town's powerful political leadership.[18]

The town leaders, who blamed "undesirables" for any discord in Ipswich, continued their practice in the early days of the war. In her exhaustive study of the town, historian Allison Vannah argues that "Ipswich needed someone to blame for the cataclysm of war, a war that symbolized righteousness against evil and called into question the right living of the godly."[19] When they looked around for a culprit, the town's godly leaders "saw in their midst newcomers and poorer folk who breached communal rules and who dared to cross social boundaries by wearing the clothing of their betters."[20] This was the type of sin that many believed caused the conflict with the Indians in the first place. This prompted a heightened number of presentments to the law courts at the beginning of the war, as the town's leaders tried to correct the problem. After looking at the choices made by the militia committee, it becomes clear that the Ipswich committee made the impressment of undesirable elements a crucial step in the town elite's continued effort to rid itself of troublemakers and undesirables.

Men from Ipswich served in almost every phase of the war. The town sent at least eighty-eight men to fight as enlisted soldiers in active companies.[21] More than 20 percent of the male population of Ipswich was impressed during the war. The main impressment drives for Ipswich came in August 1675, when Captain Appleton formed his company for service in the Connecticut River Valley; in November 1675, when Appleton returned to Ipswich needing more men for the Narragansett campaign; and throughout the later months of the war when troopers and garrison soldiers were recruited in substantial numbers. A large number of Ipswich men (twenty-seven; 31 percent of those serving) served in at least two different military units, most often an infantry company and then a garrison. This was in large part due to soldiers serving with Appleton being transferred from his command to various garrisons in the Connecticut River Valley. Thus, Ipswich men were present at almost every major campaign and battle of the war.

In recruiting eighty-eight men, the Ipswich militia committee had the greatest burden of any Essex committee during the war, raising almost a third of all the county's troops for wartime service. Salem, the next largest town, was the only community close to Ipswich in its contribution to the war effort, with seventy recruits. Unlike smaller and more static towns, Ipswich's size and the mobility of some of its population must have made recruitment a monumental task. The town's large population of around 440 militia-age males also offered the militia committee a distinct advantage over smaller towns.[22] Even with the county's largest impressment quota, the Ipswich committee had options—it could pick and choose its soldiers based on a wide number of variables, something that small towns could not do. With a high degree of choice, the type of men impressed by the committee is a mirror of how the town's military leadership perceived its citizens and their value to the town.

When looking at the men chosen for impressment, certain characteristics stand out. Unlike many other towns, the Ipswich militia committee sent a large percentage of eldest sons off to war. Often protected as the main guarantors of a family's future success, it is surprising how many of the town's first sons were levied.[23] Out of men whose birth order is known, 51 percent were first sons of their families, a much higher number than in most towns. In addition, twenty-three of the eighty-eight men sent were married, more than 25 percent. This number is very high indeed, higher than any other Essex town. Why did the town send so many valuable first sons and married men to war? Clearly, birth order and marriage were not the most important factors in impressment in the town; the committee had other issues in mind when making their choices.

Occupation was a slightly more important consideration for the committee in determining who would serve. Of the eighty-eight men whom the town sent off to fight, the occupations of fifty are known.[24] It should be noted that because a number of men had two or more listed vocations, the number of listed occupations (fifty-seven) is higher than the number of men in this analysis. The mixed economy of Ipswich is evident in its soldiers: fifteen men (26 percent) were engaged in agriculture as their primary occupation, twenty-one (37 percent) were employed in trades (including a few merchants or innkeepers), fourteen (25 percent) were servants, while seven (12 percent) were either fishermen or mariners.[25] While this distribution may look reasonable at first glance, there were in fact far more farmers than tradesmen, servants, and fishermen in Ipswich in 1675, especially among men of the age likely to be sent off to war.[26] The militia committee clearly preferred to send far more nonfarmers to war than farmers, despite the preponderance of yeomen in town. This could simply be because Ipswich, with a large native population and countless refugees streaming into town, had to protect its ability to feed the populace. It seems likely that a desire to preserve the town's food supply was an important consideration. It is also a fact, however, that large landholders were powerful enough to protect their rent-paying, farming tenants from the press. As proof of this, not a single tenant farmer in the town was impressed for the war. Their absence "suggests that they were protected from service by their landlords, who undoubtedly secured their own [economic] interests in the face of war."[27] It is likely that these influential, elite landowners also protected their farm-working sons from military service, accounting for the small proportional number of farmers impressed from a large agricultural center like Ipswich.

The impressment of a relatively large number of fishermen (for land-locked Ipswich) suggests that the committee believed that these men, often transient members of the community, could easily be removed from town without ill effect. Fishermen also had the reputation in colonial Massachusetts of being a rough and unruly group—one that would not be missed by a town trying to ensure good order.[28] While the data on the soldiers' occupations suggests a certain bias toward impressing nonfarmers, this bias was in no way the only one at work in the town.

Unquestionably, the long-standing discord between Ipswich community leaders and those whom they considered undesirable played out in the impressment of soldiers for King Philip's War. Of the eighty-eight men pressed out of the town, seventy-two (82 percent) had at least one negative factor against them in the minds of the committee of militia. These negative factors took many different forms. The first and most important was the socioeconomic status of the men. In Ipswich, which was socially stratified to an extreme degree, one's place in society (or more likely for many of these young men, their families' place) played a large part in determining whether the young men went off to war. Out of the eighty-eight men pressed into active companies from Ipswich, sixty men (68 percent) were on the lowest rungs of the town's socioeconomic ladder. These Ipswich men were either from the "lower-middle" or "lower" families in town or were "underlings," beholden to someone else, most likely a master, for their economic situation.[29] Historians of wealth in Essex County maintain that only around 25 percent of the population was in the lowest economic stratum.[30] For a supposedly representative group of male citizens to contain 68 percent from the lowest layer of society, instead of the expected 25 percent, proves that socioeconomic status was a vital, determining factor in military recruitment.

The militia committee, made up of members of the town's elite, was representative of that very element in town that had come to plainly disparage and disapprove of the lower sort by 1675.[31] Few of these "undesirable" men were commoners (those due to receive land allotments from the town in the future), making it unlikely that they would ever become upstanding members of the town's economy. There is little doubt that the elite saw impressment as a way to clear the town of some of the sons of the "lower orders," especially when otherwise the sons of the elite would have to serve. For years the town elite had ordered undesirables out of town and even taken many to court to force them to leave; the war was the perfect opportunity to be rid of many of them at least temporarily.

The second most important negative factor that caused some men to be impressed was crime. Twenty-three of the men sent to war from Ipswich had criminal records (26 percent of the men pressed from the town).[32] This is a much higher rate of lawbreakers than in the general society. In all of Essex County in any given year, on average only eighty-five criminal cases were brought to court, spread throughout the county's twelve towns.[33] Even taking Ipswich's large population into consideration, one would expect only around twenty criminal cases a year to occur in the town.[34] The town's upstanding citizens did not tolerate crime, no matter how small the infraction, particularly after they became convinced that the war was God's punishment for society's sins, especially the sins of the lower sort.[35] Even the colony's General Court attributed the start of the war to crime and sin, including in its pronouncement a list of the most common depravities that had angered God.[36] Sins were commonly prosecuted as crimes in the county courts. While criminals had always been undesirable in Ipswich, once the war started, the need to rid the town of these men was even greater.[37] The militia committee was glad to oblige.

The eventually impressed men had been found guilty of a number of different crimes, some more serious than others. Some men had angered the wrong people. One prime example of this is Samuel Hunt, who had a series of run-ins and court cases during 1674 and 1675 with Samuel Appleton, the town's militia lieutenant and a prominent member of the militia committee. Hunt accused Appleton of "detaining a horse" that in effect Hunt's son had taken without permission. The court found against Hunt and fined him for a pernicious lie against Lieutenant Appleton.[38] Hunt had been in trouble before in the town: his daughter had caused a stir in the meetinghouse throughout the 1660s by disturbing the services and his son had also been brought to court for the same, "laughing and talking and spitting and striking boys with sticks and throwing things into the gallery."[39] Samuel Hunt's wife, Betty, was so often in trouble with the town's leadership that they thought her worse than her husband and did their best to evade her, even crossing the street to do so.[40] It is no wonder Hunt found himself marching off to war.

Other men who had offended the Ipswich leadership landed on the constable's impressment warrant. Seth Story had cut and carried away valuable marsh grass from the town commons.[41] Thomas Knowlton had been admonished for being disorderly during public worship and breaking the meetinghouse's windows in 1674.[42] Richard Prior, one of the married men drafted by the committee, had been prosecuted for fornication in 1666; in the 1670s, he was again in trouble and jailed for living apart from his wife for over four years. He later escaped jail, only to be returned to prison until he promised to stay with her.[43] Edward Neland had been arraigned as far back as 1659 for excessive drinking and was still indulging to excess into the 1670s.[44] Drink was also the problem of John Browne; in 1675, he was fined for drinking, idleness, and stealing cider.[45] John Chub was almost as much a problem for the town's leaders as Samuel Hunt. Chub was constantly in trouble with the law, especially for trying to act above his station by "excess in apparel, beyond that of a man of his degree."[46] This common New England offense was particularly serious in Ipswich, where the elite took an exceedingly dim view of the lower classes acting above their station. The town's elite vigorously enforced all sumptuary laws and often made an example of offenders.[47]

Freegrace Norton, the town's miller, had been hauled into court in 1674 to answer questions about the accuracy of his scales, a problem that the Court declared "a great misdemeanor being in the public trust, either through falsehood or extreme negligence."[48] Norton's crime or negligence affected everyone in town, but above all the major landowners who had their grain ground at the mill. Norton was heavily fined for his attempt to cheat the town. But, perhaps more seriously, he found himself serving under Captain Appleton once the war started. Thomas Dennis and his wife were similar thorns in the town elites' sides; they had affronted the marshal, "done the selectmen wrong," stolen from Major General Denison, and been presented for "oppression in . . . trade."[49]

It was not only members of the lower middle class who gave the town fathers fits. Many of the servants in town who had been in trouble with the law also found themselves drafted into the colony's forces. In 1673, Nathaniel Emerson and Richard Pasmore were admonished for drinking stolen wine; in addition, Pasmore was found guilty of "carrying himself irrevently and Unchristianly upon the Sabbath day . . . wispering during service to smaller boys and setting a bad example."[50] In the same year, John Thomas was fined and imprisoned for "attempting the chastity of Elizabeth Bassit and running away from his master"; he was also made to add a year and a half on to his service to repay his master for time lost and the fine.[51] In 1664, then-servant George Stimson broke into the house of the prominent Daniel Epps and stole several items, threatening Epps's children with death if they told who had done the deed. Stimson and his accomplices were fined triple damages, whipped, had time added to their terms of service, and spent time in jail.[52] Stimson's partners had all left town by 1675. Yet, the crime was so frightening, being aimed at one of the town's elite, that even after ten years, it is possible that the memory of it spurred Stimson's impressment. The sheer number of pressed men from Ipswich with criminal pasts—along with the relative seriousness of their crimes or the fact that the crimes were aimed at the elite—is a clear indication that the militia committee was using impressment as a powerful tool to rid the town of troublemakers.

Men who had serious debt problems, along with a number of men with no known connection to Ipswich, made up an equal number of soldiers on the town's muster rolls. While normal operating debt was common in colonial New England, men who had been singled out and taken to court for their excessive debts were different, which got them noticed by the town's elite. Four men in Ipswich had this type of serious debt; interestingly, all four also had criminal records.[53] Four other men impressed by Ipswich had no known connection to the town.[54] Whether they were impressed while in town on business or if they were men who had left their hometowns in hopes of avoiding the press, these four men had no records of ever living or doing business in Ipswich. As such, the militia committee had little to lose by pressing them. With a number of war refugees in town already, the last thing the town needed was to house and feed possible draft dodgers.[55]

Two men in town had negative marks against them for making trouble with the town itself. One was the now-familiar Samuel Hunt, who sued the selectmen on several occasions.[56] The other was Joseph Jewett, whose family sued the town over the closure of the town commonage.[57] These actions did not endear the men to the town elite. Several men in Ipswich picked for service had multiple infractions. Nineteen men in town (22 percent of the eighty-eight pressed) had a number of different strikes against them.[58] John Knowlton, a lower-middle class man, had both crime and debt problems, while John Thomas, a servant, had also been in trouble with the law.[59] These men represented perhaps the easiest decisions that the militia committee made when filling their draft quotas.

In the end, of the eight-eight men sent to fight from Ipswich, sixty (68 percent) were from families in the lowest socioeconomic groups town, while twenty-three (26 percent) had criminal records. Four men (5 percent) had serious debt problems, while four had no known connection to the town. Two men had actually attacked the town's leaders in court. Nineteen of these men (22 percent) had multiple infractions. Looking at these numbers, there is no doubt that the Ipswich committee of militia used the war and impressment to continue their long campaign to rid the town of undesirables. While they surely did not wish for all the men they sent off to die, impressment would get them out of town for a while, and possibly for good, especially if the soldiers found better homes during their wartime travels. And if they did not come back from the fighting, Ipswich would be little worse, perhaps a little better, than before they left. Ridding the town of these miscreants was also an important step in fighting the sin and disorder that many believed had caused the war in the first place.

What of those men without a negative factor who left Ipswich to fight? Sixteen men from town had no known strike against them, yet they fought alongside those who did. All these men were socially either members of the local elite or the upper middle class. Why they were chosen or even if they were impressed is unclear. While the vast majority of those who fought in the war did so after being impressed, there were some men in every town who volunteered for service. There are two factors in Ipswich that suggest that a number of these sixteen men did just that. First, eleven out of the sixteen (69 percent) served in the early days of the war under their own militia lieutenant, Samuel Appleton.[60] It is not hard to imagine a number of men of the same social circle coming forward in the early days of the war to join their lieutenant in an adventure. The horror of the front lines was not yet widely known when these men volunteered.

Another possible factor in each man's decision to volunteer was his place within those elite or upper-middling families. Six of the men to join Appleton (55 percent) were not their families' first sons. They had less to lose and longer to wait for their inheritance.[61] This was especially true in Ipswich, where many second and younger sons were not guaranteed sustainable commonage, because the town had stopped its land distributions. Also, many of the Ipswich men from the upper ranks served in garrisons near the end of the war, when the colony's heavy impressment load and increased draft evasion caused a severe shortage of troops, necessitating even the better sort to be sent, albeit to a somewhat safer posting. While it is impossible to know if these men of the town's better families volunteered or were reluctantly impressed by their militia committee, it is certain that they constituted a small proportion, only 19 percent, of the town's soldiers. The rest, a clear majority, went to war in the name of a town that no longer wanted them around.

Rowley: Essex County's Thriving Textile Town

The town of Rowley is situated between Ipswich and Newbury in the heart of Essex County. The Rev. Ezekiel Rogers and his flock arrived in Massachusetts near the end of the Great Migration in October 1638.[62] Rogers and around sixty families settled Rowley after land negotiations were concluded in early spring 1639.[63] Rogers's political skill had assured the town a large land grant from the General Court. The original grant to the town included some land along the Atlantic shore and a small corridor between Newbury and Ipswich to link Rowley to the ocean. The town center lay in the corridor about two miles inland, along a small stream.

The townspeople quickly went about the task of laying out the town by assigning house lots. The town layout included three major streets where most of the earliest settlers lived. By the 1660s, around eighty families lived in the community.[64] These families were linked by a number of bonds, especially their Puritanism, their Yorkshire roots, and their common skills in the textile trade.[65]

Ezekiel Rogers wielded considerable political influence during the town's early years and was also an authoritative presence as the spiritual leader for the town's earliest settlers. More than two-thirds of the early inhabitants enjoyed the privileges and responsibilities of full church membership.[66] Even those in town who were not church members attended meeting and were highly influenced by the "Puritan Way" in Rowley. Yet, all was not peaceful and quiet in town. In some Massachusetts towns, religious controversy broke out and threatened the stability of the communities. Several religious arguments occurred in Essex County, one at Newbury from 1669 to 1672 and another in Salem from 1672 to 1676.[67] The same fate befell Rowley, where the conflict was so severe that it divided the town into two camps just before King Philip's War.[68]

Rowley's church supported two ministers from its founding, one as pastor and the other as teaching minister. Ezekiel Rogers, the town's founder, was the church's pastor, and Samuel Philips came to town as the teacher in 1651. When Rogers died in 1661, the town brought in Samuel Shepard to fill the post. His premature death in 1668 opened a void in the church, which was finally filled in 1673 when Samuel's older brother, Jeremiah Shepard, was called by the town for a yearlong trial. In February 1674, the church members voted to extend the pastor's trial for another year and Shepard stayed on, but trouble was already brewing. A small minority had spoken out against the new preacher at the vote (Shepard's qualifications and the cost of keeping two ministers concerned some) and dissension grew as time went on. The town's population soon divided into pro-Shepard and anti-Shepard camps. Things got worse in late 1674 as the Rev. Samuel Philips, Rowley's teaching minister, entered the fray against Shepard. This controversy consumed Rowley and alienated the townsfolk through November 1675, when a council of five elders from surrounding towns convened to settle the matter. The elders commended Rev. Philips, the teacher, for his actions on behalf of the "church's peace," while the congregation was both "praised and chastised" for their part in the affair.[69] Rev. Shepard was dismissed from the church at the end of his one-year term and encouraged to move on. Still smarting from his dismissal, Shepard stayed in town three more years, his presence in Rowley a constant reminder of the town's division.

If strong faith was the first compelling bond between the inhabitants of Rowley, the second was their northern English background. This was quite different from the majority of settlers in Massachusetts Bay, most of whom came from East Anglia. The town's Yorkshire roots caused great differences in many aspects of its settlement and life, including governance, town layout, and occupational patterns. The wealth distribution of Rowley was skewed compared with most Massachusetts towns, with a

high concentration of wealth in the upper tenth of the population, remi-
niscent of the manorial economy of Yorkshire.[70] The land allotments that
the town made were also less equal than those of other Massachusetts
towns, as the top 10 percent of inhabitants were given 44.5 percent of the
town's land by 1642.[71] Later allotments of pastureland, calculated in "gates,"
confirm that this trend of inequality continued into the 1670s.[72] Even the
street placement of the house lot given by the town conferred social and
economic status.[73] Rowley, like the manor towns of Yorkshire, was economically stratified—to a much greater degree than most medium-sized
Massachusetts towns.

Paradoxically, Rowley was exceedingly democratic in its politics. Their
Yorkshire background gave Rowley's inhabitants specific ideas about who
should govern and how. Rowley men imported a political system where
almost every male citizen assumed one or more town government posts.[74]
Even men at the low end of Rowley's economic scale frequently served as
officeholders.[75] This widespread office holding meant that "not only were
local inhabitants constantly involved in executing duties as officers, but
they also took an active part in formulating local regulations."[76] The town
collectively made all major decisions in frequent meetings, leaving the
selectmen simply to carry out the town's wishes. This was very different
from the majority of Massachusetts towns, settled by East Anglians, where
selectmen quickly took over not only the executive role in town government, but also the formulation of policy.[77] In Rowley, the town leaders were
simply caretakers who followed the town meeting's instructions rather
than making policy in their own right. While this wide base of political
participation and leadership seems at odds with the stratified economy of
Rowley, the discrepancy was consistent with the Yorkshire background of
a majority of the settlers, where the same paradoxical situation existed.[78]

The last important bond between the families of Rowley was their
common skill in textile manufacturing, a trait shared by many from the
Yorkshire region. While most towns in Massachusetts Bay were pursuing limited grain crop or subsistence agriculture in their earliest days of
settlement, such was not the case in Rowley. From the very beginning,
the town's economy was based on raising sheep and producing cloth. The
reliance on textiles rather than planting is seen in the relatively small size
of planting land that the town gave compared to larger common pastureland allotments.[79] In addition, investment or speculation in farming land
was very low, unlike most Essex County towns, where farming was the
main focus. Well into the 1670s, Rowley continued to focus on textile

production, as seen in the description of traveler Samuel Maverick: "The Inhabitants are most Yorkshiremen very laborious people and drive a pretty trade, making Cloth and Ruggs of Cotton Woll, and also Sheepe wooll with which in a few years the county will abound not only to supply themselves but also to send abroad. This Towne aboundeth with . . . a great number of sheep."[80] Most Rowley homes contained a spinning wheel and a fair number had their own looms.[81] While it is certain that all the inhabitants also practiced traditional farming to sustain themselves, there is little question that Rowley was a growing textile center by the time of King Philip's War.

Rowley's militia company was established when the town was settled in 1639. In 1673, the General Court confirmed the militia officers of the Rowley foot company as Mr. Samuel Brocklebank, captain; Philip Nelson, lieutenant; and John Johnson, ensign.[82] The appointment of a captain in 1673, for the first time since the company's inception, signified that Rowley's militia company was finally at full strength, with at least sixty-four men. It is possible that the three officers also made up the town's committee of militia, although, according to law, a magistrate or the town's deputy to the General Court should have sat on the committee. Rowley, however, had no resident magistrate.[83] Rowley's deputies to the General Court for the first year of the war, 1675, were Richard Swan and Maximilian Jewett.[84] In 1676, only Maximilian Jewett represented Rowley on the Court.[85] It is probable that Jewett sat on the militia committee for the town instead of Ensign Johnson, especially since Jewett was more powerful in town affairs. Because no records exist from the committee, the membership remains uncertain.

In August 1675, Rowley's committee of militia summoned nine men to join Captain Lathrop's company for the campaign in the Connecticut River Valley. Seven of the soldiers were killed, a frightfully large percentage (78 percent): two in a skirmish at Hatfield, and five during an ambush at the infamous Bloody Brook.[86] The community was utterly stunned by the loss of so many of its sons. The town was still reeling when the General Court called for more recruits, this time to serve in Major Appleton's company. The members of the militia committee—Brocklebank, Nelson, and Jewett (and/or Johnson)—must have had a very difficult time calling up more men to fight so soon after the tragic loss. Nonetheless, they impressed ten more men from Rowley to fight under Appleton in December. Almost as soon as the men had marched off to the Narragansett country, Captain Brocklebank was given command of his own composite company, which was needed to relieve the army after the deadly Narragansett campaign. While most of Brocklebank's men came from other Essex County towns and Boston, four men from Rowley found themselves marching off with their old militia commander in January 1676.[87] The last two Rowley men who served with a recognized unit during the war were Samuel Cooper and Thomas Lambert, who were troopers in Captain Whipple's troop from February 1676 until summer.[88]

Most of the men in the fighting units were unmarried at the time of their service. Of the twenty-three enlisted men, only two of them (9 percent) had wives.[89] After the horrendous losses at Bloody Brook, Rowley's committee of militia made sure that it sent only single men into harm's way. None of the ten soldiers sent to fight with Appleton or Brocklebank's men, except the captain himself, was married. The militia committee obviously made a priority of recruiting unmarried and childless men for active duty, especially after they realized how deadly the conflict had become. For the committee, keeping families intact was a top priority, as they were the bedrock of New England society.

Because most of the men sent to fight were not married and thus still living with their birth families, an examination of those families offers clues into the militia committee's impressment decisions. The economic and social position of the soldier's birth family was crucial to his eventual standing. For this study, each family was placed in one of four categories: elite, leading, middling, or subordinate. This categorization of socioeconomic status is based on information on the men themselves and their birth families. Every family's economic records and political power were taken into account in assessing the soldiers' place in the socioeconomic hierarchy of the town.[90] "Elite families" had considerable wealth (over eight hundred pounds in taxable property) or immense political power (such as a family member serving on the Court of Assistants or as a longtime deputy to the General Court or both). These families were leaders on the colonial level, not just in their towns. "Leading families" were upper to upper middling in wealth (three hundred to eight hundred pounds) and held occasional colonial office and frequent town leadership positions, most often as selectmen. "Middling families," the vast majority in the county, were of average wealth (one hundred to three hundred pounds) and held occasional town offices, sometimes as selectmen, but usually lower offices such as constable or fence viewer. "Subordinate families" were worth less than one hundred pounds (many were actually in debt) and rarely, if ever, held any government office.

A number of different sources exist that make it possible to determine the relative place of families in Rowley around the time of King Philip's War. One of the most important of these sources is the probate record of each family's patriarch, which gives a relatively clear picture of each family's overall economic status.[91] Also useful is the record of the original land grants (house lots). When the town was originally laid out, each family's socioeconomic position was taken into consideration, with the elite's house lots being placed along the common, close to the meeting-house and the center of town, while others of lesser stature were assigned house lots on the town's outskirts or backstreets.[92] Thus, the size of lots and their location, even years later, help establish the hierarchy of social and economic standing in Rowley at the time of the war.[93] A tax list from 1662 also exists, which, although it dates to a decade before the war, offers a clear picture of the relative economic situation in town for all the families who had settled in Rowley to that point (see appendix 2).[94] Because there was relatively little movement into and out of Rowley, the list contains almost all the families in this study.[95]

The third and last source of information is a listing of "gates" or rights to common land in 1678, just three years after the conclusion of the war.[96] The town assigned families a number of "gates," which limited the number of animals that a family could place on common pastureland (the gates were not physical gates, just the town's label for the amount of access a family had to common pastureland). While in agricultural towns the amount of farming land assigned was important, in a textile center such as Rowley, it was the pastureland that was crucial. Rowley assigned gates based on the economic and social status of its citizens; thus, wealthier families received more gates while poorer families received fewer or none.[97] The number of gates held by each family is a good clue to the social and economic position of the town's families shortly after the war. A comparison of the gate numbers to the 1662 tax list demonstrates the remarkable stability of the town's socioeconomic status over time.

Just which Rowley families were required to send their sons to fight? In economic and social terms, the militia committee of Rowley sent a very representative group of its sons to fight King Philip's War. There were young men from all parts of town and all types of families. The majority of soldiers impressed, twenty-one out of the twenty-five active soldiers (84 percent), came from middling families, by far the largest category of families in town. Only two soldiers (8 percent) came from a leading family, while another two men (or 8 percent) came from subordinate families. It

TABLE 1
Town Rankings of Rowley Soldiers Based on
Tax Rates, House Lot Size and Location, and Gates, 1643–1678

Tax Rank	Cat.	Company	Soldier's Name	Father's Name	House Lot & Street	Town Status	Gates 1678
3	L	Lathrop	Pearson, Joseph	John	1½	Latecomer	7
8 (tie)	M	Brocklebank	Hobson, John	William	Unknown	Latecomer	
10	M	A=Lathrop[1] J=Appleton	Stickney, Andrew Stickney, John	William	1½ Wethersfield	Original	6
12	L	Unknown	Lambert, Thomas	Francis, Thomas Barker[2]	2 Holme	Original	
17 (tie)	L	Brocklebank	Brocklebank, Samuel	Jane (Mother)	2 Bradford	Original	
17 (tie)	M	Lathrop	Palmer, John	John	1½ Bradford	Original	7
23	M	Lathrop	Bayly, Thomas	James	1½ back street	Latecomer	
24	M	Appleton	Palmer, Thomas	Thomas	1½ Bradford	Latecomer	
26	M	Whipple	Cooper, Samuel	Peter	1½ Bradford	Original	
29	M	Appleton, Brocklebank	Jackson, John	William	1½ Bradford	Original	
32	M	Appleton, Brocklebank	Boynton, Joshua	William	1½ Bradford	Original	
34	M	Whipple	Lever, Thomas	Thomas	1½ Bradford	Original	6
39	M	Appleton	Jackson, Caleb	Nicholas	1½ Holme	Latecomer	5
45	M	Lathrop	Kilborn, Jacob	George	1½ Bradford	Original	5
48	M	Lathrop	Harriman, John	Leonard	1½ Bradford (bought)	Latecomer	5½
49 (tie)	M	Lathrop	Scales, Matthew	William	1½ Wethersfield	Original	3
51 (tie)	M	Lathrop	Holmes, Richard	Richard	1 back street	Latecomer	5
51 (tie)	M	Quartermaster	Wicomb, Daniel	Richard	1½ Bradford	Original	2 (Son)[3]
58	M	Manning	Smith, Samuel	Hugh	1½ Bradford	Original	
62	M	Brocklebank	Wood, John	Thomas	Bradford (bought)	Latecomer	4

TABLE 1 (*continued*)

Tax Rank	Cat.	Company	Soldier's Name	Father's Name	House Lot & Street	Town Status	Gates 1678
64	M	Appleton	Brown, William	Charles	Unknown	Latecomer	3
65	M	Lathrop	Sawyer, Ezekiel	Edward	1½ back street	Latecomer	
71	M	Appleton	Leyton, John	Richard	1½ Holme	Latecomer	2
76	M	Appleton	Burkby, Joseph	Thomas	1½ Unknown	Latecomer	3
Not on Tax List							
	S	Appleton	Gowen, Symon	Unknown	Unknown	New	
	L	Unknown	Jewett, Jeremiah	Joseph	2 Bradford	Original	
	S	Appleton	Tyler, Samuel	Moses	Unknown	New	

Tax Rank is the rank of the family based on the 1662 Rowley tax rate.[4] Cat. is the family's economic/social category: L=leading family, M=middling family, and S=subordinate family. Company is the military unit that the soldier served with.[5] When two companies are listed, either multiple sons served in different companies (Jackson and Stickney) or one son served in two different companies (Joshua Boynton). Soldier's Name sometimes contains two names when two different sons of the same family served. Father's Name gives the family patriarch's name. House Lot & Street records the original grant size of the family's house lot in acres and then gives the location in town by the street name if known.[6] Town Status is a measure of when the family arrived in Rowley, either as one of the original settling families, as latecomers arriving generally between the late 1640s and 1670, and those new to town who arrived from 1670 to 1675.[7] Gates 1678 refers to the amount of common land available to each family for pasturing their animals; the original number of gates was based on the family's social and economic status in town and about equal to the size of the original house lot given (usually 1½ gates). The number changed over time through additional grants or purchase.[8]

1. Andrew served with Lathrop; John served with Appleton.

2. Francis Lambert, Thomas's father, died in 1647, and Thomas was adopted and raised by his uncle, Thomas Barker. George B. Blodgette and Amos Everett Jewett, *Early Settlers of Rowley, Massachusetts; a Genealogical Record of the Families Who Settled in Rowley before 1700, with Several Generations of Their Descendants* (Rowley, Mass.: Amos Everett Jewett, 1933), 220–221.

3. Gates are Daniel Wicomb's, not his father's, and may be less than his family had as a whole, taking division into account.

4. Matthew Adams Stickney, "Ancient Tax List of Rowley," *New England Historical Genealogical Register* 15 (1861): 253–254.

5. George Madison Bodge, *Soldiers in King Philip's War*, reprint of 1906 3rd ed. (Baltimore: Genealogical Publishing, 1967).

6. Thomas Gage, *The History of Rowley Anciently Including Bradford, Boxford, and Georgetown from the Year 1639 to the Present Time* (Boston: F. Andrews, 1840), 123–134.

7. Patricia O'Malley, "Rowley, Massachusetts, 1639-1730: Dissent, Division, and Delimination in a Colonial Town" (Ph.D. diss., Boston College, 1975), 243–252.

8. O'Malley, "Rowley," 243–252.

is clear that Rowley's militia committee, despite the town's stratification of wealth, did not base its recruitment decisions on economic or social status.[98] This seems strange, given the high level of wealth stratification in the town, yet it mirrors the paradox of widespread political power in Rowley.[99] What the data shows is that representatives of all types of families were sent, from Joseph Pearson, son of John Pearson, the owner of the town's fulling mill and third in town wealth in 1662, to Joseph Burkby, whose father's tax ranking was seventy-sixth out of eighty-five on the 1662 list.[100]

While Rowley's militia committee—unlike Ipswich's committee in large part—did not make its impressment decisions based on socioeconomic status, they did take a number of factors into consideration. While the overall equality of Rowley's recruitment is inescapable, it is worth noting that a sizeable number of the original leading families in town did not send any sons to fight.[101] None of the young men of the original town families—those that received original house lot grants of more than two acres—was pressed for war.[102] This fact is brought home even more clearly when the town's recruitments are plotted on a map of the town. Rowley's town layout was based along three main streets and centered on the meetinghouse and training field. Families were assigned house lots positioned and sized according to their contribution to the settlement of the town and their socioeconomic status. Those families with the largest land grants were assigned lots on Wethersfield Street or the nearby highway to Newbury. The families living on Bradford Street had property at around a half to two-thirds the median wealth, while those just at the middle of the wealth scale in town lived along the length of Holme Street or nearby.[103] The town elite were thus originally concentrated on the choice land between the meetinghouse and the training field. Only one active soldier, John Hobkinson, son of William, lived in this prestigious section of town.[104] Most of the families of pressed men were situated along Bradford or Holme streets, while a number were on a back alley that did not even have a name. Thus, Rowley's recruitment pattern was fairly equally divided in terms of socioeconomic status, yet it appears that very few of the town's founding or original leading families saw their sons impressed by the militia committee. The question is why.

On examination of the soldiers from Rowley, it is clear that the militia committee preferred to impress sons from families not original to the town—in other words, non–town founders.[105] Forty-four of the sixty original families remained in town by 1675.[106] Of those, only ten families (23 percent) had sons impressed during King Philip's War.[107] Sixteen families came to Rowley later, between 1645 and 1669. Seven of those (44 percent) had sons impressed for war service.[108] In addition, two soldiers were impressed from the small number of families that arrived in town between 1670 and 1675. As the large majority of families in town, the original families should have contributed a majority of the soldiers to the companies, but this was not the case. It is obvious that the militia committee preferred to send sons of late-coming families, sparing the original families to a large degree. It seems that the strong common bond of a homeland in Yorkshire between the original settlers was still an important factor when the militia committee, composed entirely of original townsmen and Yorkshire natives, picked its recruits.

As notable as the findings on family are, there was another important factor that the committee took into consideration while making its conscription decisions. The religious controversy that swirled in Rowley over the appointment of Rev. Shepard to the permanent position of town minister in the 1670s deeply affected all aspects of town life and also played an important part in the militia committee's decisions during King Philip's War. The conflict divided the people of Rowley into two camps: the majority, who were against Shepard's appointment; and a vocal minority, who supported the minister. By examining the petitions and court documentation surrounding the case, each family's stance on the controversy was determined for thirteen of the twenty-three enlisted men (57 percent).[109] Ten soldiers were from families that do not appear on any documents concerning the controversy; some were non–church members without a say in the matter, while others surely had an opinion that was not recorded. The town records also reveal the various positions of the committee of militia on the matter. Samuel Brocklebank and Philip Nelson, the two highest-ranking members of the committee, were in the minority pro-Shepard faction. The third member of the committee, whether it was Ensign John Johnson or Deputy Maximillian Jewett, was in the majority anti-Shepard camp.

Looking at the available information on the pressed men, it appears likely that Brocklebank and Nelson were using their seats on the militia committee to take some measure of revenge on the families that had thwarted them in the Shepard controversy. The two men were among Shepard's staunchest supporters.[110] By the fall of 1675, it became clear that their bid to install Shepard would fail. Their reputation as town leaders was seriously damaged and their need to lash out at their political foes was undeniably strong. Rowley's unique situation of widespread political participation and weak town leaders exacerbated the situation.[111] Brocklebank and Nelson had less power than most town leaders in Massachusetts to penalize their detractors, yet colony law and the power of the General Court assured their control of the militia committee. At the very time that they wanted to reassert their power in town, which would have been difficult in the everyday governance of Rowley, they were put in a position to impress men for the war.

Of the thirteen enlisted men with known connections to a faction in the church dispute, only two (15 percent) were from families that supported Rev. Shepard's bid to become the town minister.[112] Eleven men (85 percent) who had publicly come out against the minister or were members of families that had done so marched off to war.[113] While it is true that a majority in town were against Rev. Shepard, the majority was not nearly 85 percent.[114] In addition, it is likely that a majority of the ten enlisted men whose attitudes about the controversy are unknown were in the anti-Shepard camp. Their inclusion would make the percentage of anti-Shepard men impressed even higher.[115] Brocklebank and Nelson, perhaps over the objection of the third member of the committee (Jewett or Johnson, both of whom were in the anti-Shepard faction), were very likely exacting revenge on their political enemies by impressing their sons for war. While such retribution would have been hard to manage in the regular course of Rowley's Yorkshire-inspired, egalitarian town governance, it was facilitated by the colony's militia law in the form of the immense power wielded by militia committees. Similar religious disagreements occurred in Newbury and Salem before the war, making it quite possible that a comparable winnowing of religious opponents occurred in those towns. Regardless of whether it did, there is little doubt that Rowley was a divided town and that many of the men on the "winning" side of the religious conflict found themselves marching off to face a different enemy later that year, courtesy of two of the controversy's "losers."

Topsfield: A Middling Town on the Rise

The town of Topsfield, located in the middle of Essex County, was founded on land that was originally part of Salem and Ipswich.[116] As early as 1639, the General Court allowed settlers from Salem and Ipswich to set up a village in the area, on the northern side of the Ipswich River. On October 18, 1648, the General Court named the settlement Topsfield, after a small parish in Essex, England. Exactly two years later, the village was incorporated as a town in accordance with the request of two powerful inhabitants, Zacheus Gould and William Howard.[117] The vast meadowland around the town made it a perfect spot for mixed agriculture and animal husbandry. While small compared to its immediate neighbors Salem and Ipswich, Topsfield showed signs of steady growth and by the late 1660s had a population of thirty-five to forty families.[118] Topsfield was more prosperous than its small neighbors, Manchester and Wenham, which both grew slowly and had only around twenty-five families each at the time of King Philip's War. Just a few years after the war, in 1681, Topsfield had grown to include well over 105 men on the taxable list, representing seventy or eighty families.[119] Unfortunately for historians, the early town meeting records of Topsfield were lost in a fire at the clerk's house in 1658. The earliest surviving continuous record comes from the town book started in 1675. That volume, however, does contain some of the town's surviving early records.[120]

The existing town records, combined with county and colony records, offer a surprisingly complete accounting of the militia in Topsfield from 1666.[121] In June 1666, the General Court confirmed and approved that "the inhabitants of Topsfield and the villages adjoining thereunto, having by order of Major Danyell Denison, met together in a military way and choose officers of a foot company of train soldiers."[122] This order confirms that Topsfield and its neighboring village, known as Rowley Village, were following an order by Major General Denison to pool their men into a single militia unit. This provision had been incorporated in the law so that smaller towns and villages could combine their forces into a functional unit when the towns could not field their own full-strength company of at least sixty-four men.[123] The order also confirmed the officers chosen by this combined company: "John Reddington as sergeant-in-chief to command the company, Joseph Bigsby, sr. sergeant, Abraham Reddington, sr., clerk and Edmund Towne, John Cummings, and William Smith, corporals."[124] The highest officer listed is a sergeant, meaning that the company, even including men from the outlying village, was still below full strength. In 1667, less than a year later, the General Court confirmed John Gould as ensign (and new commander) of the company, followed a year later by Francis Peabody's appointment above Gould as the new company commander with the rank of lieutenant.[125] Little did Lieutenant Peabody know that he was about to enter into a long and drawn-out controversy over the nature of his militia company.

In the early 1670s, the General Court had to resolve a militia controversy between Rowley Village and Topsfield. Rowley Village was a small hamlet outside the original town center of Rowley that developed near the Topsfield town line in the 1660s. Rowley Village was closely connected to Topsfield; in fact, the inhabitants attended religious meetings and militia training there.[126] In 1671, a number of village inhabitants, led by Abraham Reddington, a former clerk of the band (the militia), petitioned the General Court for permission to sever the ties between Rowley Village and Topsfield. Others asked the Court to allow them to stay connected with Topsfield, claiming great hardship if they were forced to travel several miles into Rowley to conduct civic functions.[127] The matter apparently remained unresolved, so Reddington took matters into his own hands. The result was that in June 1671, charges were brought in the Essex County Quarterly Court against Sergeant Joseph Bigsby and Abraham Reddington of Rowley Village for refusing to attend training in Topsfield, and they were fined. The "rest of the company which did exempt itself from training" was to be fined by the clerk of the band in Topsfield "as his duty entailed."[128]

In November 1671, the controversy continued when the town of Topsfield petitioned the Quarterly Court, stating that the actions of the villagers (not paying their church rate yet still attending services) were hurting Topsfield. In addition, the fact that the villagers were staying away from militia training was seen as damaging to the town's military. The Topsfield selectmen complained that the situation meant that "military discipline and exercise can not be well attended and promoted by reason of the paucity of our trained soldiers listed in Topsfield very few; too few to make our exercise to have any thing of soldier-like luster and beauty in it."[129] Topsfield asked the Court to enjoin the villages to return to the fold, at least temporarily. By March 1672, the Quarterly Court rendered its verdict and "ordered that at the next training day at Topsfield, the soldiers of the Village shall attend there and declare whether for the future they will train there or not."[130] The Quarterly Court's opinion, however, was not the last one heard on the subject.

In May 1672, the matter finally seemed settled when the Essex Quarterly Court, directed by order of the superior General Court in Boston, reversed its own call for a vote on the matter and issued the following clarification: "[The Quarterly] Court being informed that the General Court has allowed the uniting of Rowley Village with Topsfield in one military Company, appointing their officers as their own desire, they revolke their former order of March last, and declare that the said Villagers ought to continue in the military company with Topsfield and to attend all military service and exercise under the established officers of that company until they be released or otherwise disposed of by the General Court's order."[131] Yet, in October 1674, the General Court issued another ruling, its final word on the long-standing case. They allowed the men of Rowley Village to serve either at Topsfield or Rowley, "as shall best suite with their inclinations and occasions."[132] Most villagers complied and a few found themselves fighting for Topsfield during King Philip's War.[133] Some of the families of Rowley Village also sent sons to fight for Rowley in 1675 and 1676.[134] Despite this compromise, the exact status of Rowley Village was in limbo for some time, as both Topsfield and Rowley held power over the villagers' lives. This state of affairs continued until Rowley Village was incorporated as the town of Boxford in 1685 and allowed its own militia company.[135]

Topsfield's committee of militia in the years before and during King Philip's War consisted of the top three militia officers in town, as Topsfield did not have a resident magistrate and did not send a representative to the General Court during the period.[136] Thus, the committee was made up of Lieutenant Francis Peabody, Ensign John Gould, and John Reddington, the town's most senior sergeant.[137] When the war broke out in the summer of 1675, Topsfield's position in the middle of the county offered it a relative sense of security. Yet, the war did come to town. Topsfield's first son was sent to fight in August 1675, when Thomas Hobbs served in Captain Thomas Lathrop's ill-fated company.[138]

In November 1675, the call went out to the towns to ready recruits for a major offensive against the Narragansett Indians.[139] Topsfield sent a total of five men, the largest group of men impressed from the town during King Philip's War. On November 30, 1675, John How, the clerk of the Topsfield militia, made a report to the major general reporting the men assigned to fill Topsfield's quota: "Willyom Peabody, Zachos Perkins, Robert Andros, Jack Burton, Zacviah Curtis . . . are phrased according to your Henered order and fixed with arms and Ammunition: only Zacviah Curtis he is praised [pressed] and was warned to come to the Clerks to Show his arms but he hath not Com but we here he hath hired Himself to go for Mr. Browne of Salem."[140] The absent substitute Zachariah Curtis could not serve for Topsfield in the campaign; the town's militia committee sent his older brother Zacheus to serve in his stead.[141]

John Wild (or Wildes) of Topsfield served with two different companies during the war, starting in the fall of 1675 under Captain Poole in the garrison at Quabaog.[142] Wild went on to serve under Captain Turner when Poole's company was transferred to Turner in the spring of 1676.[143] At the time of the transfer, John Wild had attained the rank of corporal. For his extensive service, he was paid over sixteen pounds.[144] It is not known if he was impressed for service under Poole or if he volunteered. It seems probable, however, based on his elevation to corporal and his very lengthy term of service that Wild either enjoyed or excelled at soldiering.

Records also report that the colony reimbursed three men from Topsfield for unknown military "service."[145] It is not known whether James Stanley and Isaac and Joseph Estey served in an active unit or simply offered other assistance to the war effort. Possibly they were compensated for service in one of the town's own garrison companies, perhaps as leaders of a garrison house company established by the town's watch plan. All together, if the substitute Zachariah Curtis is included, eleven men from Topsfield received payment for war service, only seven of whom, it is assumed, were impressed by Topsfield's militia committee.[146]

Like soldiers from Rowley, the mostly unmarried men levied for service still had close ties to their birth families; most probably still lived at home. A close look at the socioeconomic situation in Topsfield offers some important clues about the families. In addition to the normal probate data on each family and lists of the various government posts that the heads of families held, a listing of the land allotments made in 1668 and a tax list from the same year survives to help establish the town's socioeconomic and political hierarchy (see appendix 3).[147] Looking at the seven men whom the committee impressed into active companies, three came from leading families (43 percent), two came from the middling group (29 percent), and two (29 percent) have insufficient records to make a categorization. Not a single man impressed came from a subordinate family, although the two men without sufficient records, Thomas Hobbs and Isaac Burton, may well have fallen into that category. As in Rowley, it seems as if socioeconomic status was not a crucial factor for the Topsfield committee of militia. In fact, the committee in Topsfield sent some of its own elite sons to fight. William Peabody, the son of Francis Peabody (the town's lieutenant and highest-ranking committee member) fought in Captain Gardner's command. John Gould, the town company's ensign and a militia committee member, sent a number of sons of allied families off to war, including John Wild and William Peabody, who were both related to Gould by marriage. The Curtis brothers, whose family had long been associated economically with the Goulds, also served.[148] The third committee member, John Reddington, was related by marriage to both William

Perkins and John Wild Jr., yet he helped send them off to war.[149] It is difficult to understand why.

It is possible but unlikely that the committee members pressed their own sons in order to prove a point about shared sacrifice and civic duty. It is much more likely that a number of these young men from leading families went off to fight of their own accord. In Essex County, Topsfield held the distinction of being the town with the highest age of marriage for males.[150] The young men in the town were tied to the family farm for many years beyond their physical and mental maturation, working for their fathers and postponing their own independence longer than their contemporaries in other Essex County towns.[151] While the sons of the leading families had every hope of eventual financial independence at their father's death, a few evidently needed some form of temporary independence from their families. The freedom of being on campaign doubtless appealed to these young men, making it the most likely reason why William Peabody and Zacheus Perkins volunteered to serve.

The fathers of both men were prominent. In addition to serving as the town's militia lieutenant, William Peabody's father, Francis, was a town leader in many other ways. The elder Peabody had been a selectman and town clerk, besides owning the local grist mill, which made him a key figure in the town's agricultural economy.[152] Zacheus Perkins's father, Thomas, was a major landowner, a former selectman, and highly active in the Topsfield church, where he became a deacon in 1677.[153] Perkins was twenty-eight years old, while Peabody was already twenty-nine, and neither was an oldest son. Both young men were unmarried and living at home when the war started, where they probably would have remained for quite some time. It seems likely that the two men just wanted to get out into the wider world for a time, and what better way to do that then volunteer to go to war? One can almost hear them trying to convince their fathers to let them leave the farm to go, arguing that it was their turn to serve their community. With their assured, eventual financial independence, it was likely not money that prompted them to serve. Soldiering in seventeenth-century New England, with its relatively short tours of duty, did not offer much of a financial incentive. The pay, however, was not insignificant for all the men.

John Wild Jr. was also the son of a prominent Topsfield family. His father, John, was an important landowner with the seventh-highest tax ranking in the town in 1668, a former town constable, and a common member of the Jury of Trials.[154] The town obviously trusted him to look out for its interest, because he served eleven times as a town surveyor, laying out the town's borders.[155] John Jr. was the first son of his family. Already thirty-two years old in 1675, his father had already granted him the use, but not the title, of some land before the war.[156] It was not enough, however, to become independent and marry. Much like his neighbors William Peabody and Zacheus Perkins, John Wild Jr. probably volunteered to gain a taste of independence from his father's control. He served with Captain Poole and stayed in the army when Poole's command was transferred to Captain Turner in 1676. It is almost certain that he volunteered to remain in service when the company was transferred to Captain Turner; otherwise his length of service would surely have allowed him release from duty. By the time that he mustered out in spring 1676, Wild had accumulated almost sixteen pounds in pay for his lengthy service.[157] Perhaps even more important than the pay, Wild's political status grew when he was promoted to corporal during the war. War service was very good to Wild; he increased his chance to gain early social and economic independence by serving. He had been so successful in the military that in 1677, after King Philip's War was officially over, he volunteered to serve again, this time in Maine with Captain Benjamin Sweet. His second campaign was not as lucky: Wild was killed at Black Point in June 1677.

Although Wild, Perkins, and Peabody almost certainly volunteered for service, the militia committee impressed most of their fellows. What motivated these decisions? It is clear that the committee did not simply choose men from the lower socioeconomic strata in town; most of the men came from leading or middling families.[158] One exception to this might be Isaac Burton.[159] Little is known of the background of the twenty-seven-year-old Burton. He lived with the William Nickols family, who treated him as their "adopted son."[160] While Nickols was the eleventh person in rank on the 1668 tax list, the adopted Burton's socioeconomic status is less certain; he was too young to appear on the 1668 rate list himself.[161] Perhaps even more important than his questionable status in the town's hierarchy is the question of where Isaac Burton lived.

William Nickols and his family, including Burton, belonged to a small group of settlers on the fringes of Topsfield society. These settlers, who lived on the far edge of the town, considered themselves citizens of Salem and disliked their enforced connection to Topsfield.[162] After the war, Isaac Burton, who received a portion of William Nickols's farm as his "adopted" son, continued to live in this outlying area.[163] William Hobbs, the father of soldier Thomas Hobbs, also lived in this community of outsiders.[164] While the Hobbs and Nickols/Burton families joined the Topsfield church, there is no doubt that citizens of Topsfield regarded them and the other families in their fringe settlement as outsiders—and not just outsiders, but annoying ones who sparked conflict and cost the town great expense for constant court cases over which town, Salem or Topsfield, controlled the area. In addition to the men who lived in the outlying areas of Salem, the Curtis brothers and Robert Andrews came from the outlying sections of Topsfield associated with Rowley, known as Rowley Village. The early 1670s militia controversy over the village made it a problematic region for the town of Topsfield.[165] Thus, five out of the eight men in known combat units (63 percent) lived on the periphery of the town and not in Topsfield proper. Their status as outsiders in all probability had a direct bearing on the militia committee's impressment decisions once war came.[166]

The militia committee in Topsfield, like its counterpart in Ipswich, took criminal behavior into consideration in its recruitment decisions. A number of Topsfield's impressed men had been in trouble with the law in the years preceding the war. The low crime rate in the colony and the small number of men from each town arraigned each year of a crime made the accused stand out in the sight of their more upstanding townsmen, especially those in power.[167] Topsfield's first soldier, the outsider Thomas Hobbs of Lathrop's command, had been fined in September 1668 for excessive drinking, and he also had debt problems, including not paying the town rate for the minister's house in the late 1660s and early 1670s.[168] In April 1672, Robert Andrews (along with his brother Thomas and others) was fined for breach of the peace and swearing.[169] While not a serious crime, it might have made all the difference to a militia committee trying to decide whom to send off to war in November 1675, especially because crime was relatively rare in colonial Topsfield.

Of the five men recruited for Gardner's company, two (40 percent) had criminal records. In reality, three men had criminal records, Robert Andrews and both the Curtis brothers, Zachariah and Zacheus. Despite the fact he did not serve when called by Topsfield on account of his employment as a substitute, the committee most likely impressed Zachariah Curtis because he and his family were known troublemakers in town. In June 1672, Zacheus Curtis Sr., his sons Zacheus Jr. and Zachariah, along with Abraham Reddington Jr. and John Everitt, were "complained of for smoking tobacco in the meetinghouse at Topsfield in the time when most people were met on a Lord's Day to the great offense of the assembly."[170]

Massachusetts had banned smoking around crops and buildings; the fact that the offense took place in the meetinghouse on a Sunday made the matter very serious indeed.[171] All five men were presented in court and admonished for their behavior.[172] It was quite a scandal in tiny Topsfield. John Everitt, a crippled man, sincerely apologized to the Court for his actions.[173] Abraham Reddington Jr., another of the convicted troublemakers, was not impressed; it is possible that his relative on the militia committee, John Reddington, saved him from that fate. Both the Curtis brothers, however, found themselves called for service. It seems probable that the committee, having called the disorderly younger Zachariah for service, turned to his troublemaking older brother Zacheus when Zachariah was not available.

Zacheus's difficulties had not begun with the meetinghouse incident; he had a long and troublesome criminal record. He would in all probability have been the committee's *first* choice for service had he not been married. Zacheus Jr. started getting in trouble early in life. In May 1663, at seventeen years of age, he was presented for publishing a false intention of marriage of a couple in town, against their will and without their knowledge.[174] He was sentenced to stand in the church door and wear a sign on his hat reading, "For setting up a false purpose of marriage."[175] In March 1664, he was in more serious trouble. He was sentenced to be whipped and pay a fine for abusing Mary Hadley. Her statement reads:

> When I was goone by Thomas bucrs hous where Zacheus Curtious was and he followed me and overtook me and he had a rood and he whipt me with that and then he let me goe and puled another rod and he ouer tock [overtook] me agayne and whipt me with the 2 rod with my feet under his arms and my head on the ground and then he let me goe and gathered two rods and ouertwoke me and made me pull of my cloths and whipt me with both them rods the thurd time and then he let me gooe agayne and got another rod and wypt me with that rod . . . and then he bid me goe and dress my selfe but . . . he would a had me to a gone in to a swomp and I would not: and when I tould him that I would tell my aunt he sed he would whip me fower times as much.[176]

A secondary note explains that Curtis was being presented for whipping and abusing several children.[177] This physical abuse (and possible attempted rape) was shocking to the tiny town. It was not, however, Curtis's last bout of trouble.

TABLE 2
Impressment Factors in Topsfield, 1675–1676

Soldier	Company	Factors in Impressment
Thomas Hobbs	Lathrop	Town Outsider Criminal Record (September 1668)
Robert Andrews	Gardner	Town Outsider Criminal Record (April 1672)
Isaac Burton	Gardner	Town Outsider Questionable Economic Status ("Adopted")
Zacheus Curtis Jr.	Gardner	Town Outsider Serious Criminal Record (1663, 1664, 1672)
William Peabody	Gardner	Probable Volunteer
Zacheus Perkins	Gardner	Probable Volunteer
John Wild Jr.	Poole, Turner	Volunteer
Zachariah Curtis	Unknown- Substitute	Town Outsider Criminal Record (1672)

In 1672, there was the smoking in the meetinghouse incident and in 1675, Zacheus Curtis was sought as a witness in the fire that destroyed the Saugus ironworks.[178] While he was not directly implicated, he was friendly with some of the men who were. When the militia committee tried and failed to fill its quota with his younger brother Zachariah in November 1675, his absence was easy to rectify by impressing his more troublesome older brother, despite the fact Zacheus was married at the time. He was, in fact, the only married man that Topsfield sent to fight during the entire war. Clearly, the militia committee felt that if it had to send men off to war, better to send some of the community's troublemakers.

On the surface, Topsfield's recruitment picture seems murky (see table 2). The large percentage of sons from leading families seems an anomaly, especially when compared to recruitment in other thriving towns like Rowley and Ipswich, where the elite sons were mostly protected.[179] Yet, this unique situation is perhaps explained by the high age of marriage in town and the relative smallness of the community. When the incongruity of the leading sons is explained, recruitment in Topsfield takes on a whole new look. Like those in neighboring larger towns, Topsfield's militia committee exercised its prerogative and chose outsiders or criminals. One could easily see this list originating from Ipswich, with its high intolerance for undesirables being translated into recruitment warrants. Choice also made a difference to the committee in neighboring Marblehead, which used its own local preferences in recruitment to come to a similar overall result.

Marblehead: Essex County's Fishing Settlement

The area of Marblehead was settled as early as 1629. Situated on a peninsula jutting out from the Massachusetts shore, Marblehead's history is closely intertwined with that of Salem, the much larger and more powerful town to the east. The area of Marblehead was small, "not much bigger than a large farm," and its rocky coastline and hillsides afforded little in the way of good farming land.[180] The harbor, however, was deep and well protected. At first, Marblehead was simply a district within the town boundaries of Salem. As early as 1631, the area's economic potential was foreshadowed by the establishment of a fishery station; fishing and shipping dominated the economy of Marblehead throughout the colonial period. From its earliest days, merchants from Boston and Salem, backed by London fish importers, outfitted fishing voyages from the little town. In May 1635, the Massachusetts General Court ordered that there should be a plantation at Marblehead and that it should have a measure of independence from Salem: "The inhabitants now there shall have liberty to plant and imp've such ground as they stand in neede of . . . The inhabitants of Salem shall part with such ground . . . being payed for their labor and costs."[181] The very next year, a ship of 120 tons, the third ship built in the entire colony, was launched at Marblehead, the first of many vessels constructed there.

In January 1637, Salem's selectmen, who oversaw Marblehead, ordered that "for the better furthering of the fishing trading" no one in Marblehead could be granted more land than that given by the town to fishermen; the town's future was to be tied strictly to fishing, not agriculture.[182] More fishermen could be accommodated in town if the lots were kept small. The large number of fishermen in town were ethnically diverse, predominantly male, and very mobile. The nature of the fishing trade meant the town endured an endless cycle of in- and out-migration. Marblehead's unstable population made it unique in Puritan New England.[183] Crime was also a constant problem.

Two distinct social groups coexisted in Marblehead during the period: the men who managed the fishery and the fishermen who did the work.[184] The town was socially and economically stratified to an extreme degree. While the fishermen greatly outnumbered their employers, they had much less power.[185] Both groups continued to grow through the seventeenth century as the town blossomed. In 1648, Marblehead received full political independence from Salem and the General Court incorporated it the following year. Shortly thereafter, the townsmen chose selectmen to oversee the town's business. Despite this, Marblehead remained tightly linked to its former parent because of Salem's merchants' powerful position in Marblehead's economy.

There were few viable institutions in the town, which also made it different from its neighbors. The church, usually the first institution established in any New England town, was not founded in Marblehead until 1684, more than fifty years after the town's founding. Historian Christine Leigh Heyrman wondered "whether Marblehead held more village atheists than any other New England town?" and concluded, "If the majority of inhabitants were not actually hostile to religion, they were indifferent to Congregationalist orthodoxy."[186] The majority of the population gave little respect to town government either. Most inhabitants had little to do with local government and when they did, it was usually in opposition to it. The turnover of selectmen in Marblehead was almost constant, suggesting a distinct lack of public support. The town's population even took their own selectmen to court three times during the 1660s over local tax disputes.[187] With such scant regard for local government and religious institutions, it is unlikely that the militia establishment in town would fare any better.

Marblehead's militia band was a part of Salem's militia until the separation of the two towns in 1648, but Marblehead's militia troubles began even before that date. The town's difficulty in establishing a militia company was one of the factors that convinced the General Court to leave Marblehead linked to Salem for so long.[188] In 1644, the General Court ordered Marblehead to fortify the harbor, an order that was ignored.[189] At the same time, the Court ruled that "in consideration of the great default and neglect of the inhabitants of Marblehead in not exercising themselves in Martiall discipline—It is ordered that the inhabitants of Marblehead shall make choyce of some one who shall exercise the rest, that they may not be to seeke when special occasions call for their assistance."[190] Because the first town officers were not confirmed until the 1660s, it is unlikely that these orders were carried out either. The community simply did not have a militia structure in its earliest days.[191] Not a single Marblehead resident is listed in the town records with a military title until 1672, well after its militia company was finally established by direct order of the General Court.[192]

In 1666, during the Second Anglo-Dutch War, the General Court once again instructed the people of Marblehead to fortify their harbor. In addition, the Court, for a second time, ordered that a militia company be organized to ensure that the inhabitants were drilled and disciplined in military tactics.[193] This order would not have been necessary had the town followed the 1644 order. Next, the General Court took an extraordinary step, placing Major William Hathorne, a powerful merchant and political figure from Salem, in command of the new militia company. Hathorne, a magistrate of the Court of Assistants, was widely disliked in Marblehead as a powerful outsider and politically conservative figure who did not suit the town's rough political landscape.[194] The town, however, evidently took heed of the legislature's orders this time; the fort was completed in 1667 and later that year, the town elected Samuel Ward as the first lieutenant of its own militia company.[195]

The status of Major Hathorne in the Marblehead militia after Ward's election and confirmation as lieutenant is unknown, but Hathorne's continued presence in some official capacity is evident from the Essex County Quarterly Court records.[196] Hathorne probably retained his special position in Marblehead's militia as an overseer, to ensure the town's obedience to the law.[197] Only one other record of the Marblehead militia exists, a list from November 2, 1675, of soldiers impressed for active duty. It was signed by "Richard Norman, Ensign."[198] Norman had appeared in the town records as early as 1672 as "Ensign Norman," but no other evidence of his appointment survives. This is not surprising, as after 1668 the General Court appointed officers and did not always publish notices of the commissions.[199] It is likely, therefore, that Major Hathorne, Lieutenant Ward, and Ensign Norman made up the town's committee of militia. No other officers for the town are listed in the records and Marblehead had no magistrates (other than Hathorne) or even a deputy to the General Court.[200] There is little reason to believe, and no evidence to suggest, that the command structure of the town changed between 1667 and the start of King Philip's War in 1675.

The two Marblehead men on the town's militia committee were prominent members of the town's elite. While the so-called elite in Marblehead were not generally up to the standards of other Massachusetts Bay towns and thus did not enjoy the normal influence and power of their position, Richard Norman and Samuel Ward seem to have been the exceptions.[201] Neither had ever been in trouble with the law, unlike most of Marblehead's elite.[202] Although neither of them were among the town's original settlers, this was not nearly as important in Marblehead as elsewhere because of its high level of migration.[203] Ensign Norman had been a resident since 1648 and by 1658 was a selectman.[204] His name is almost constantly listed in the town records. Samuel Ward arrived in Marblehead later; the first record of him in town is in 1660 when he was made a "Packer and Gager."[205] He climbed the social ladder quickly. By 1662, he was a selectman (for the first of several terms) and was chosen town constable as well.[206] He continued his rise in the town hierarchy in 1666, when the General Court appointed him the town's first militia sergeant. The next year Ward became the company's lieutenant. It is quite clear that despite the dismal record of most of Marblehead's local leaders, the General Court had picked two of the town's ablest men to lead the militia and serve on the militia committee (along with Major Hathorne).

Twenty Marblehead men served with a known active-duty company or companies during the war. Unfortunately, little is known about most of these men. The muster rolls show that the Marblehead militia committee twice sent groups of men to fight. The first five recruits fought under the command of Captain Lathrop starting in August 1675.[207] Marblehead's largest contribution to the war effort, though, came with the call-up for the Narragansett campaign in November 1675; twelve men from town fought under Captain Joseph Gardner.[208] Three others served on active duty during the conflict: Enoch Lawrence in Paige's troop early in the war and Rowland Ravensbee and Thomas Stamford under Captain Brocklebank in the early months of 1676.[209]

Of the five men recruited into Captain Lathrop's command from Marblehead in the early days of the war, three had solid connections to the town. John Merrett was the son of Nicholas Merrett, one of the original settlers and a prominent figure in town politics.[210] Nicholas had been a selectman numerous times and held various other offices. His son John, thirty-two years old and married at the time of the war, had already been the town constable and a deputy marshal of Salem.[211] In 1674, John was listed as a householder and allowed one cow on the town common, suggesting that he already had an independent household.[212] Mark Pittman had roots in Marblehead reaching back to 1648, when he appeared on the list of town householders with commonage for two cows (by 1674, he had three).[213] Pittman was born around 1625 and was about fifty at the time of the war.[214] He was married to Mary Shapligh and they had at least one child.[215] Thomas Rose appears for the first time in the town records on the 1674 commons listing where his space for two cows is acknowledged.[216] In postwar court records, he is named as a shoreman or mariner, a step above a fisherman and one with a more definite link to the town.[217] While it seems that he was just starting out in Marblehead, he appeared to be doing well, based on his middling position on the householder list.

It is curious that these men were called to serve. Not only did they have connections to the town, but two of them, Merrett and Pittman, were quite well placed in the town's society. Merrett was the son of a powerful man in town, as powerful as any political figure could be in Marblehead's antiestablishment climate. John was himself on the road to power in the town, serving as a constable. Pittman was not much involved in town government, but he was a stable, longtime resident. Pittman and Merrett were also old for soldiers—Merrett was thirty-two and Pittman was fifty, one of the three oldest soldiers recruited in all of Essex County.[218] Both were married and Pittman had children. It is hard to understand why these men were chosen for service. Perhaps their sense of civic duty was strong and they volunteered to go; this could especially be the case with John Merrett, who possibly saw military service as a way to solidify his rise to political prominence and escape his father's shadow. The fact that both served early in the war, before they realized how dangerous the war would become, also points to the possibility that these men volunteered.

It is easier to understand the militia committee's other choices. Thomas Rose had just moved to town; his possible loss was not of much concern to the committee. The last two soldiers listed as serving with Lathrop had little or no recorded connection to the town other than their names on the pay lists. Samuel Hudson does not appear on any listing of townspeople from Marblehead before the war. The one incident that places him there is a court record from June 1670. It is perhaps this incident, where Hudson was sentenced to be whipped or fined "for not assisting the constable, discouraging others, and using provolking speeches," that brought him to the attention of the committee.[219] While it may seem unlikely that a crime five years before would carry much weight with the committee in crime-ridden Marblehead, the details of the incident offer a clue as to why it might.[220] Not only had Hudson's behavior been extreme in its disregard for proper authority in the person of Constable

William Beale, but two of Beale's close friends were Major Hathorne and Ensign Norman. These militia committee members witnessed the crime and testified to Hudson's guilt.

The last Lathrop soldier, William Dew, had a very tenuous connection to Marblehead. Dew was born in 1653 and raised in Salem and Beverly by Edward Bishop, who in 1662 was given custody of Dew "after a manner of apprentice" for seven years.[221] Bishop apparently released Dew around 1670, freeing him to make his own way in life. He had "worked" as a soldier before; his probate record lists pay "for ye County servise under Captain Page of Boston" as an asset.[222] The only other asset in the record was a stock of "merchantable fish"; Dew was probably a drifter who had spent some time in Marblehead as a fisherman. It is likely that this is how he was known to the militia committee. It is also possible, especially because he had already served in the military, that he volunteered for service when he heard that Lathrop needed men.

While the recruitment pattern for the first five men is somewhat obscure, the same cannot be said of the men who were impressed later in 1675. Of the twelve men from town listed as impressed for service with Captain Gardner, only two (17 percent) have any meaningful connection to the town in the surviving records: Henry Codner and Thomas Russell. Codner and Russell were familiar last names in Marblehead on prewar householder records, although Henry and Thomas themselves do not appear.[223] Codner was a servant to Jeremiah Gatchell, a member of one of the town's original families.[224] A few court records also place Codner and Russell in Marblehead in the 1670s.[225] There is little question that the two were living in or very near Marblehead in 1675.

The other ten men (83 percent of the total) pressed for the Narragansett campaign are a different story. Not a single man has a known connection to the town before the war—they simply do not exist in any town, county, or colony records before appearing on the impressment lists. There is no doubt that when it came to pressing men for the dangerous Narragansett campaign, the Marblehead militia committee decided to scour the streets for transients rather than send their own permanent citizens. The town was bursting with a transitory population of maritime laborers from all over the Atlantic world, most notably England and Newfoundland. Even the Marblehead elites, who were dependent on the labor of these men, complained of "the concourse of many strangers" in town.[226] These men often "worked for a season or two, took up a page in a merchant's book, and then vanished without making any further imprint on the colony."[227]

They were relatively poor, socially unstable, and, according to many Puritan leaders, not very bright. William Hubbard, writing in 1677, described the men as "a dull and heavy-moulded sort of People, that had not either [the] Skill or Courage to kill any thing but Fish."[228] These were the men whom the militia committee did not mind losing and whom they sent to fight the war, much as Elizabethan lords lieutenant had done in England's past.

One question that emerges is why the majority of men pressed for the earlier campaign under Lathrop had town connections while the later soldiers did not. There are a number of possible reasons for this. First, Marblehead suffered a tragedy with its first group of soldiers; four out of the five men sent (80 percent) were killed in action.[229] Hathorne, Ward, and Norman on the militia committee presumably did not want to lose any more of the town's permanent citizens. The possibility that they might, however, was strong; the General Court had warned the towns of the dangerous nature of the upcoming Narragansett campaign in its December impressment order.[230] Who better to send than the transient fishermen who prowled the streets of Marblehead every day? There is some evidence from the postwar period that this is exactly who these men were—Leonard Belinger and David Shapligh are listed as fishermen after the war.[231] The men were strong and fit, and their loss would be of little burden to the town. William Dew, the former apprentice with few ties to Marblehead who had been killed at Bloody Brook, created no burden for the town—his probate inventory was taken, his debts settled, and that was that.[232] From the militia committee's standpoint, transient fishermen were the perfect soldiers, although professional military men might have disagreed.[233]

It is bewildering, given the large number of eligible transient fishermen in town, that the militia committee did not press only such men for service in Captain Gardner's company. Yet, the fact that two men with town connections were singled out for impressment is not altogether surprising. Henry Codner and Thomas Russell had both been in trouble with the law. That in itself was not special in Marblehead, but both cases had special circumstances. In 1669, Henry Codner was sentenced to be whipped or fined for abusing William Beale and his wife with "reproachful speeches."[234] William Beale was the same friend of Ensign Norman and Major Hathorne who was the victim of the incident with Samuel Hudson. The Beale family had several enemies in town; it appears that they also had strong allies on the militia committee. In addition, Codner had been accused of burglary (the charges were later dropped), had lost a case for debt in 1670 and was known to owe the estate of Mr. Croad of Newfoundland, a well-known fishing merchant, a staggering thirty-three pounds.[235] It seems that this was enough to land Codner, a servant, debtor, and troublemaker, in Gardner's company that November.

Thomas Russell had also experienced trouble with the law and with debt. In 1673, he was twice sued for debt and lost both times, prompting the constable to attach some of his property.[236] He had made no friends among the town's elite when he signed a petition in 1674 protesting the actions of the town selectmen, a petition directly opposed to the views of Samuel Ward and Richard Norman of the militia committee.[237] With such a record, it is no surprise that when the Marblehead militia committee needed to press men for a dangerous expedition, Thomas Russell found himself in the ranks.

Further proof that the committee of militia preferred to press men not connected to town is the fact that the other three men who served, Rowland Ravensbee and Thomas Stamford in Brocklebank's command, along with Enoch Lawrence in Paige's troop, were non-householders with no known connection to Marblehead in the prewar records. It is extremely unusual that Lawrence, a trooper, is missing from the records. Troopers were usually culled from the county's better families, yet no records of Lawrence exist other than his enlistment record.

After losing four of their own citizens to enemy action in their very first impressment group, the militia committee was not in any hurry to send more of the town's permanent inhabitants to war. They instead chose transients from among the huge population of temporary maritime laborers in town or, in a few cases, troublemakers. Ironically, none of the men pressed into service after the first group was listed as being killed or wounded in battle.[238] It did not really matter very much to the town in any case; most of its sons stayed home, thanks to the local committee of militia.

A detailed study of the militia decisions made in these towns is instrumental to understanding the nature of impressment during the war. Each town, through its locally controlled militia committee, made impressment choices based on the town's needs, or at least the town elite's needs or priorities. With their large or growing populations, the militia committees in these communities had choices and they used that power of choice to great effect. Ipswich's committee continued its campaign against undesirables. Rowley's leaders protected original families from the press while exacting revenge on some of its political enemies. Topsfield filled its ranks with a mix of men; volunteers seem to have come forward for service, but the militia committee chose the remainder from among town outsiders and men with criminal pasts. Topsfield's levy, once the high percentage of serving leading sons is explained, mirrors those of the other communities. Its insistence that town outsiders and men with criminal records make up the ranks of active-duty men from the town could easily be the story of Ipswich. Marblehead sent transient fishermen to war after losing some of its better citizens in an early war ambush. The question that arises is whether the same choices and similar trends occurred in the small, isolated, and weak communities of the county, those towns that had relatively few men and most likely fewer choices.

4

Few Men, Few Options
Impressment in Essex County's Small Towns

Local control of the militia was a hallmark of seventeenth-century Massachusetts Bay. As has been demonstrated, the power of locally controlled committees of militia to levy soldiers was nearly absolute in most of Essex County's large or thriving towns. Militia committees used their impressment power not only to raise the troops necessary to fulfill their military manpower quotas, but did so in a way that affirmed the community's (or at least its elite members') values. Ipswich's committee continued a long-running battle with town undesirables, while the committee in Rowley dealt with the aftereffects of a religious controversy. Marblehead's military leaders avoided sending any more citizens with a stake in their community to war after their first foray into impressment ended in the death of so many fine citizens. But all these towns, from large, prospering Ipswich to small but growing Topsfield, had options. They had the necessary population base to make choices about who should serve, using locally decided criteria. But that was not the case in all of Essex County's towns, especially the smaller or less successful communities. Even amid flourishing Essex County, some towns were isolated, small, or even shrinking and in trouble in the days before King Philip's War. The militia committees in those towns, like small and secluded Andover or tiny, shrinking Wenham, had far fewer options when it came to impressment. Still, the colony needed soldiers and the committees had to press them. Yet, in the small communities, the militia committees found their choices severely limited by the very nature of the towns they served.

Andover: The Quintessential New England Town Offers Few Choices

The town of Andover is as good an example of the stereotypical "New England town" as any.[1] Situated on the Merrimack and Shawshin rivers, the town sits northeast of Salem and was, in the seventeenth century, on the outer edge of English settlement in Essex County. While its location—a long day's walk or a half day's ride from Salem—made it relatively isolated in the early days of settlement, its potential for growth was ensured by its position on the Merrimack River. With such great potential and plenty of land, Andover became a desirable location for settlement soon after the colony was established. Settlers started to arrive in the early 1640s and the town was incorporated on May 6, 1646.

Designed with a cellular or nucleated layout, common fields and pastures surrounded the homes and meetinghouse in the town center. All the original families were proprietors, a status that entitled them to future land divisions.[2] Because they needed clear title to land, citizens in the small farming towns "married somewhat later than their counterparts elsewhere in New England; needing farm workers, they had larger families than typical; and . . . they lived longer lives than most New Englanders."[3] As time passed and the economy grew, the yeomen of Andover (and other small farming communities) moved beyond mere subsistence farming, but even then they were connected to local, not regional or colony-wide, markets. The result was a relatively equal distribution of wealth and low levels of social strife, especially when compared to larger, more commercial towns like Ipswich or Marblehead.[4] By 1660, the English traveler John Josselyn noted that Andover was a small but prosperous community with much land under cultivation.[5] So it remained through the seventeenth century.

As ordered by the governor and the General Court, Andover established a militia to protect itself soon after its formation. The town had close ties to the military hierarchy of Massachusetts Bay and Essex County; both the first major general of the colony, Thomas Dudley, and the sergeant major of the Essex County regiment, Daniel Dennison, had relatives in Andover.[6] The Essex County Quarterly Court approved John Osgood as the town's sergeant and commander in June 1658.[7] The company renominated Osgood as commanding officer in 1666, this time as a lieutenant (in recognition of the increased size of Andover's militia company).[8] They also elected subordinate officers; Thomas Chandler was named ensign and Henry Ingalls became the company's sergeant.[9] As the three highest-ranking members of the military in the town, they also constituted Andover's committee of militia, since the town had no resident magistrate or deputy.[10] These three officers—Osgood, Chandler, and Ingalls—remained in power throughout King Philip's War.

Sixteen men from Andover served the colony during the war.[11] The first call for men came in November 1675 and the committee of militia set to work impressing the allotted number of soldiers to serve under Captain Joseph Gardner. All the men pressed were single at the time of the war and none had children. Most likely, these young men still lived in their fathers' houses and worked their fathers' fields. It was not unusual for sons of New England's second generation to marry relatively late; the average age at marriage for second-generation males in Andover was 26.7 years.[12] Sons needed their father's permission and, more importantly, access to family land before they could marry. Because both farm labor and available land were scarce, fathers kept close control of their sons by limiting their access to land, and thus their ability to marry and support a family.[13] Fathers and sons were interdependent—sons needing access to land and fathers needing their sons' labor in the tight labor market. Fathers and sons regularly came to an important yet informal understanding when the son turned twenty-one and reached social and political, but not yet full economic, independence.[14] The two agreed on which portion of the father's estate the son would eventually receive. He would then start working that section independently, while still assisting his father on the home farm. While most of the militiamen's occupations are not listed in the surviving records, it is certain that almost all the men worked in agriculture, most probably for their fathers. Only two of the pressed men had listed occupations. Edward Whittington was named as a weaver, even though he owned neither a loom nor a mill (he probably made his living as both a farm laborer and an itinerant weaver).[15] In addition to helping his father on the family farm, Ebenezer Baker sometimes worked as a carpenter.[16]

If they were not yet the heads of their own families, to what kind of families did the Andover soldiers belong to as offspring of first-generation settlers? Probate records for the men and their fathers, tax lists, family histories, and town land records make it possible to determine the relative standing of each family in town. By 1675, there were between forty and fifty families, some with several branches, living in Andover.[17] The economic and social data allows a categorization of the families of Andover into one of four categories: elite, leading, middling, or subordinate. Of the eleven men impressed for Gardner's company in 1675, two were members of leading town families (18 percent), seven came from middling families (64 percent), and two were from subordinate families (18 percent). There was a wide range of families in the middling category, from upper middling to almost subordinate. No enlisted man from Andover came from an elite family.

When examining the Andover committee of militia's choices for service in the dangerous winter offensive of 1675, a number of characteristics about the soldiers' families become evident. They constituted a cross section of the community; the committee did not simply pick sons of the poorer families in town. While no members of the contingent were from elite families, in reality only one family in the entire town qualified as elite: John Osgood, the town's militia commander, and he was needed at home. However, it is noteworthy that none of his sons, two of whom were of militia age, fought in the war.[18] While this could be mere coincidence, it appears unlikely in view of the town's overall family rankings.

Many of the most powerful families in town, such as the Osgoods, the Poors, and the Ingalls, did not have any of their sons impressed—despite having numerous militia-age sons. The top five families in the small town included three families directly represented on the committee of militia (see table 3). Significantly, not one of the sons of these families, the Osgoods, Chandlers, or Ingalls, was sent to war. Two of the militia committee families, the Osgoods and the Ingalls, were closely linked by marriage. The Poor family was also linked to the Osgood and Ingalls families by marriage.[19] Although not directly represented on the committee, the Poors also avoided sending a son to war. Thus, these three leading families, all linked by social, economic, and marital ties, and all with militia-age sons, sent none of those sons off to fight.[20] The other allied family of the Osgood group, the Marstons, did have a son who served. The importance of allied families has been noted by historians such as Laura Thatcher Ulrich, who points out that "marriage was never just a private contract between a husband and wife, it was an alliance of families and a *linchpin* in the social structure."[21] Lieutenant John Osgood was not merely the principal figure in a cluster of families in town allied by marriage—he was the undisputed leader of the town and the leading presence on the militia committee. It is obvious that he, and the members of the militia committee connected to him, protected from the press their own sons, as well as the sons of their allied families.

Of the wealthiest five families in town, only one had a son impressed: Ebenezer Baker. Baker and his family were not linked to the Osgood/Ingalls/Poor group. The Bakers were instead associated with the Stevens family, forming a competing family cluster in town. Both of these families had sons impressed for service.[22] While it seems unlikely that the Baker/Stevens sons were "targeted" for impressment, they certainly did not have the political

TABLE 3
Top Families in Andover and Their Sons during King Philip's War, 1675–1676

Town Rank	Family Name	Town Position	Son(s)	Served	Notes
1	Osgood	North	Y	N	Member-Committee of Militia Osgood Group
2	Poor	North	Y	N	Osgood Group
3	Ingalls	North	Y	N	Member-Committee of Militia Osgood Group
4	Barker	North	Y	Y	Barker/Stevens Group
5	Chandler	South	Y	N	Member-Committee of Militia Southern Family Group
6	Marston	North	Y	Y	Osgood Group
7	Abbot	South	Y	Y	Southern Family Group
8	Phelps/ Philips	South	Y	Y	Southern Family Group
9	Ballard	South	Y	Y	Southern Family Group
10	Stevens	North	Y	Y	Barker/Stevens Group

Table shading represents those who had sons of militia age who did not serve during the war. There are a total of around forty-six family names present in Andover by 1679. Town Rank is the family's rank based on the 1679 minister's tax list of all families in town.[1] Family Name is based on the patriarch. (The eighth family—Philips/Phelps—almost certainly included the soldier Samuel Philips.) Town Position indicated which pole of town, north or south the family lived in. Son(s) is an indication that the family had a son of militia age during the war years (1675–1676). Served is an indicator of a son of that family serving in the war. Notes indicates positions of power held in Andover (members of the committee of militia) and membership in allied family groups.

1. Elinor Abbot, "Transformations: The Reconstruction of Social Hierarchy in Early Colonial Andover, Massachusetts" (Ph.D. diss., Brandeis University, 1989), 242–248.

clout to avoid the press; that was a privilege of the families in the Osgood faction alone. When looking beyond the top five families in town, a curious pattern emerges. As we have already seen, economic position had little to do with impressment in Andover. While several of the leading families avoided sending their sons to war, this was due to family alliances, not economics. The case for this is strengthened when one considers that of the top ten families named on the tax lists, six *did* send sons to fight (see table 4).

Andover's families were divided not only by social and marriage alliances, but by geography as well. Andover had been divided down the middle from its inception. The split, between the northern, prosperous end of town and the southern, subordinate end of town, was based on the different groups or "companies" that settled the town.[23] This division

TABLE 4

Ranking of Andover Soldiers Serving with Captain Gardner
by Town Socioeconomic Rank and Land Status, 1675

Family Name	Cat.	Father or Son	N/S Rank	1679 Tax Rank	House Lot Size	Total Acres	Overall Land Rank
Baker	L	F	N-4	4th	10	310	5th*
Marston	M	F	N-5	6th	n/a	n/a	n/a
Abbot	M	F	S-2	7th	4	84	11th*
Philips	M	F	S-3	8th/32nd[1]	n/a	n/a	n/a
Ballard	M	F	S-6	9th	5	105	10th*
Stevens	L	F	N-32	10th/53rd[2]	12	252	4th
Frye	M	F	S-9	14th	8	168	6th*
Lovejoy	M	F	S-33	50th	7	200	7th*
Parker	M	F	N-33	70th	n/a	n/a	n/a
Preston	S	S	S-40	74th	n/a	n/a	n/a
Whittington	S	S	S-41	75th	n/a	n/a	n/a

Cat. is the family status as classified in this study, L=leading, M=middling, S=subordinate.
Father or Son indicates whether the tax record is the families' (father's, mother's, or brother's)
or son's (the militiaman). N/S Rank is the rank order of the family (or the son in the case of no
father) in their town section, north or south, based on the 1679 minister's rate. 1679 Tax Rank is
the rank order of the father (or other family members if the father is not available) in the town
overall by the minister's rate; the rank includes all the families of Andover, not just those who
sent sons to fight. The father's tax rate is used, where available (see column Father or Son) to
determine the family's rank. In cases where the father was not known or not listed in the tax list,
the son's tax rate (or other family member's) is used.[3] House Lot Size is the size of the house lot
allotted by the town by 1662. Total Acres is the minimum amount of land that the family had,
based on the house lot size and the formula developed in Andover (twenty acres of upland allotted for each house lot acre). It does not measure extra or extraordinary land allocations to
certain families. Overall Land Rank is inclusive town rank based on house lot (acreage) size and
the formula employed by Andover for future land allocations. It does not take into account extra
land allocations to certain families, which is why the rankings may not coincide with the actual
acreage numbers. This ranking includes all the families of Andover, not just soldier's families.
An asterisk denotes a tie for town rank based on the formula acreage.

    1. Town rank of eighth is based on his older brother Edward, the nominal "leader" of the
family; Samuel's rank alone is thirty-second.
    2. Town rank of tenth is based on his mother's (Widow Stevens) ranking; Nathan's rank alone
is fifty-third in town. If the two were combined, the family ranking would be close to fifth or
sixth in town.
    3. This data and the rankings established from it must be viewed with great suspicion be-
cause of the real possibility that the son's tax rate was based on the divided property of the
father at the time of the father's death, which would significantly underrepresent the wealth of
the family as a whole. In these cases, it may be best to rely on the land data, if available, to give
a truer picture of the family's wealth and status.

is visible even on the town's tax lists. The prominent Osgood group and
the Barker/Stevens families inhabited the northern section of town. In the
southern end of town, another group of important families had formed,
much like the northern Osgood group. These families, despite being in
the town's top ten in terms of economic status, came from the less affluent side of town and held less political power. Most soon found their sons
heading off to the wilderness to fight the Narragansett Indians.

The southern group included the Chandler, Abbot, Ballard, and Phelps families.[24] A series of marital, economic, and social bonds linked this group, including both leading and upper-middling households. Except for the Chandlers, whose patriarch, Thomas, sat on the militia committee, each family in this group had a son impressed to fight. As only one member of three (and not the leading member) of the militia committee, Thomas Chandler obviously did not have enough power to protect his neighbors' sons from the press, as Lieutenant Osgood had done for his circle. Chandler was able to keep his own sons out of harm's way, but he was not able to extend the safety net to others in his group, and Joseph Abbot, Samuel Philips, and John Ballard all marched off to war.

Family connections played a large part in recruitment in Andover. The Osgood group (the Osgood, Ingalls, Poor, and Marston families) had only one son go off to war, probably as a volunteer, because it seems unlikely that the committee would have impressed him. The other prominent family groups, the northern Barker/Stevens group and the southern group (with the exception of the Chandlers, who were directly represented on the militia committee), all sent sons to fight, despite being economically among the top ten families in town. The families at the very top of the militia power structure in Andover, especially those in the Osgood group, protected their own and allied sons from service.

Yet, the militia committee was not simply sending sons of the poorest and least powerful families away to fight, as was the case in many larger towns, such as Ipswich. A careful study of the Quarterly Court records turns up few other factors that could have influenced impressment decisions. No member of the Andover contingent had a criminal record. This makes them quite different from many of their fellow soldiers from Essex County. The low crime rate in town prevented the militia committee from filling its militia quotas by simply turning out the jail. Court records mention a few of the pressed men as owing debts, yet none were serious or litigated debtors. The question remains: why did Andover's militia committee impress so many young men from its leading and middling families to fight in what would surely be a harsh and dangerous campaign?

There are several possible answers. From the record of the levies, it appears likely that the leading families of Andover saw military service as an important civic duty—one that sons of the town elite should carry out (as long as it was not the decision makers' *own* sons). In a sense, the pressing of a number of well-to-do Andover sons resembles the Elizabethan idea of a trainband made up of the best middling sort. This New England trainband would march off to fight, however, unlike the original incarnations back in England, where only unruly and low-class men from the untrained general militia fought in Elizabeth's overseas expeditions.

In addition to this sense of duty, there is a good chance that at least some of the young men of Andover volunteered to go; the lure of glory on the battlefield has been a strong motivator throughout history. The attraction was doubtless strong for young men in a farming town such as Andover, where fathers controlled their sons' labor, limiting their ability to start families of their own by manipulating access to farming land.[25] While the prominence of impressment over volunteerism is well established for the war, there is little doubt that a certain number of men did volunteer for war service. This possibility, which could account for the relatively large percentage of leading and upper-middling sons going to war, is strengthened by an examination of exactly which sons went to fight. The birth order is known for nine of Andover's eleven soldiers (82 percent). While six of the leading families in town had sons serve, either as volunteers or levied, none of those families sacrificed their oldest son to the war effort (see table 5).[26] The militia committee seems to have avoided sending men from the ranks of the town's first sons. Only two of the nine soldiers sent to Gardner's command with known birth orders were first sons; both of those men, John Lovejoy and John Parker, were from families far down on the town's socioeconomic scale. They were also younger (Lovejoy was the youngest at twenty, Parker was twenty-two) than the other soldiers (whose average age was twenty-four). They might have been the only sons of militia age available for impressment from those particular families. Thus, while Andover was sending members of its best families to war, for the most part it was not sending the all-important first sons of the leading families, on whom great expectations had been placed.

The birth-order data strengthens the case for volunteerism. It is logical that sons not first in line to inherit or receive pre-probate title to some of their father's land (a necessary step in starting their own families) would seek some escape, albeit a temporary one, from their father's control. While New England did not practice primogeniture, second and third sons did know that they would be far behind their oldest brother in gaining control of any family land and would be tied to their fathers for much longer. Some may well have sought to get away for a short time because of that fact. Later sons also knew that while they would get some land from their fathers, it would not be the choicest plot.[27] Historians have shown that first sons in seventeenth-century Massachusetts married earlier and received

TABLE 5
Birth-order Status for Andover Soldiers in Gardner's Company, 1675

Name	Birth Order	Age at War	Family Status	Town Rank
Ebenezer Baker	3rd Son	24	L	4th
John Marston	Unknown	Unknown	L	6th
Joseph Abbot	3rd Son	23	M	7th
Samuel Philips	Younger Brother	21	M	8th/32nd[1]
John Ballard	3rd Son	22	M	9th
Nathan Stevens	2nd Son	31	L	10th
James Frye	2nd Son	26	M	14th
John Lovejoy	1st Son	20	M	50th
John Parker	1st Son	22	M	70th
John Preston	5th Son	Unknown	S	74th
Edward Whittington	Unknown	Unknown	S	75th

Birth Order is based on probate or other records. Family Status is based on the classification in this study, L=leading, M=middling, S=subordinate. Town Rank is the rank order of the family in the town overall by minister's rate of 1679.

1. Town rank of eighth is based on his brother Edward; his rank alone is thirty-second.

more financial support than their younger brothers, who were then held at home longer than first sons in order to work the family farm.[28] This supports the idea that some younger sons who marched off to fight probably volunteered to go, in order to escape their controlling families for a time. The soldiers' ages, all over twenty-one (except John Lovejoy) gave them the necessary political freedom to volunteer without their fathers' permission.[29] It cannot be argued, however, that these possible volunteers expected military service to gain them the means necessary to escape their father's control for long. Military pay was not sufficient for permanent escape. However, the glory accrued and the ability to flee their fathers' control, even if for a short time, may have been enough incentive to garner a few volunteers for the Andover contingent of Gardner's company.

Nevertheless, the most plausible explanation for the large number of men from leading and middling families pressed into service is simply that Andover was a peaceful and homogeneous town in 1675. Few men had criminal records or substantial debt problems. Almost every family in town fit the leading or middling category. Unlike Marblehead with its population of transient mariners or Ipswich with its large number of subordinate families, Andover was simply less stratified. There were not great numbers of unattached farm laborers roaming around the agricultural sections of Essex County in the seventeenth century waiting to be impressed.[30] The reason that more militiamen were not taken from the lower elements of Andover society was simply that few men in town belonged to that category.

About the time that the men of Gardner's company were returning home in early 1676, three Andover men found themselves serving with Captain Samuel Brocklebank of Rowley. One of them, Nathan Stevens, had been with Gardner on the Narragansett campaign; it is probable that he volunteered to stay with the army. While he had already received a portion of his father's estate (he was eighteen when his father died in 1662), there is no marriage record for him until 1692.[31] Even though he was thirty-one years old at the time of the war, it is likely that he was still living at home and caring for his mother and younger siblings in 1675.[32] It is possible that Nathan enjoyed the life of a soldier over that of mother's helper. The other two soldiers recruited for Brocklebank's Company were Zechariah Ayers and Joseph Parker.[33]

Zechariah Ayers was a newcomer to Andover. He was born in Haverhill on October 24, 1650, to farmer John Ayers and his wife, Mary.[34] Undoubtedly, Zechariah arrived in Andover too late to profit from the town's land divisions. He settled in the less prominent southern sector of town and by 1679 had a taxable worth at thirty-eighth place in the southern section and sixty-fourth out of eighty-six in town overall.[35] He married only after the war, in 1678.[36] While his tax rank qualifies him for the middling category, it places him in the decidedly lower spectrum of that scale.

Joseph Parker belonged to the prominent Parker family and was a kinsman of the Gardner militiaman John Parker. The Parkers were the only Andover family that contributed more than one man to the war, but John and Joseph came from different branches of the family. Militiaman Joseph Parker's father, Joseph, was an original settler; the elder Joseph was a tanner, married to a Mary Parker. The Parkers were important citizens in the northern part of town, owning a tannery, the town's gristmill, and considerable land.[37] According to land records, the Parker family received the fifth-largest division of land from the town, with a house lot of ten acres and corresponding farming land of at least two hundred acres.[38] They were "citizens of much consideration."[39] Joseph the elder died in 1678 "at a great age and infirm" and his estate was valued at over 546 pounds.[40] His first son, Joseph, inherited the largest portion of that, including the gristmill.[41] Accordingly, Joseph was ranked at fifteenth place in the north end of town and twenty-second in town overall, even after the division of his father's property between four sons and three daughters.[42] After the war, Joseph married Elizabeth Bridges in October 1680 and was beginning a family when he took ill.[43] In his own will of 1684, as a carpenter and innkeeper, Joseph's place in society comes into even clearer detail. By 1684, his estate was worth 402 pounds, the mill alone valued at 100 pounds.[44] While there is little doubt that the Parkers were important members of Andover society, their lack of political power in town placed them in the middle of the town's status system, not among the leading families.

None of these three men—Joseph Parker, Zechariah Ayers, and Nathan Stevens—had been in trouble with the law, nor did any of them have a problem with debt. Yet all three served in the war. None of the men was protected by an alliance to the Osgood group, which controlled the militia committee, even Joseph Parker. Once again, the Andover militia committee placed in harm's way townsmen in good standing but continued to protect its own. The three men were all back in Andover after about five weeks of service. They were the last men from the town to perform militia service during the war, however, as the war came too close to Andover for comfort.[45]

On February 10, 1676, enemy warriors attacked the frontier town of Lancaster, an attack that became famous because of the abduction of Mary Rowlandson.[46] Fear spread throughout the countryside, and Andover's location on the frontier looked even more dangerous than in the past. Reports of Indian movement along the Merrimack River sent Andover into a panic. The town had just been ordered to send ten men to Woburn for its defense, which worried Lieutenant Osgood so much that he wrote to the Council in Boston on February 16 requesting reconsideration. His letter conveys some of the sense of urgency in the community: "If it may stand with you honors wisdom & favour to release our men that are to goe forth, as wee being an outside town & in greate danger in our apprehension as any and may stand in as great need as any other town of help, this makes us bould to request this favour att your hands."[47] His request was granted. Andover sent no more of its militiamen out of town for the duration of the war.[48]

Two other Andover men appear on the pay lists of Massachusetts Bay during the war. Their service is unknown; their names do not appear on any muster lists. It is highly unlikely that either actually served as soldiers during the war. Both men were much older than the others paid by the colony and were established town leaders. The first is Stephen Johnson, thirty-five years old and married.[49] Johnson was a town leader, having been a constable in 1672 and a selectman for the last year of the war in 1676.[50] He was listed as a carpenter and in 1671 the town granted him was granted a license to operate the first saw mill in Andover, where he cut lumber and made thousands of wood shingles every year.[51] The payment that Johnson received from the colony is most likely a reimbursement for lumber used to build the town's fortifications during the war.

The last of the men compensated by the colony for service from Andover was John Osgood, the town's leading citizen and lieutenant of its
militia company. He was the only man in Andover to enjoy elite status
in 1675. Osgood's central role in Andover is evident. He was the son of
the elder John Osgood, one of Andover's founders. Born in England in
1630, John Jr. traveled to America with his father and mother, Sarah, in
1638, where they first settled in Ipswich and Newbury before finally ending up in Andover in 1645.[52] Andover's first town meeting was held in the
Osgood home. The elder John Osgood was one of the first ten members
of the Andover church and the town's first representative to the General
Court. He died in 1651, halfway through his first term as a deputy. John
Osgood Jr., as the eldest son, inherited his father's house and lands, while
his brothers and sisters received money as their inheritance, a decision
that kept intact the Osgoods' lands and power base.[53]

John Osgood quickly replaced his father in the town's hierarchy. John
settled in the more prosperous northern section of town and eventually
controlled over 610 acres, second only to the absentee Simon Bradstreet,
who lived in Boston and would become the colony's governor in 1679.[54]
Osgood married Mary Clements in 1653 and they had three children.[55] He
was at the top of Andover's political and economic structure, as can be
seen by his place as the first individual on the town's tax lists.[56] Although
Osgood reported his occupation as a tanner, he was also by far the largest
farmer and landowner in Andover. From 1659 on, he also ran an ordinary
(tavern) in town.[57] In 1672, he had a spot of trouble with the law and the
Essex County Quarterly Court fined him for "giving some Indians cider at
his house."[58] This incident did little to damage his position in Andover.

John Osgood had a long history of public service to his town. In 1658,
Osgood took the freeman's oath and started his career as a town leader.[59]
By 1659, not only was he serving on the grand jury, but also was, as we
have seen, the sergeant and commander of the town's militia.[60] He was
named lieutenant in 1666 and served as a town selectman from 1670 to
1673 and again in 1676.[61] In 1674, the quarterly court made him one of
three commissioners to hear and judge minor cases in Andover, in effect
making him a small claims judge.[62] Osgood's status as the leader of Andover cannot be questioned.

Osgood never left the town during the war; he earned his compensation while dealing with the crisis at home. Perhaps the pay was for his
work on the committee of militia, although the other two members of
the committee, Thomas Chandler and Henry Ingalls, did not receive any

money for their service.[63] Osgood's pay may have been a reimbursement for supplies that he procured for Andover's soldiers before they marched off to fight.[64] As commander of a town on Essex County's frontier, Osgood was forced to deal with a number of emergencies that crept up during the war, the most important being to ensure the town's defenses and hold the frontier to shield interior towns from Indian attack. It is possible that he was paid for war service while commanding the town, although no other men on regular town militia duty (sentry, garrison, drill, etc.) were compensated. Because the details of his compensation are missing, we will never know exactly what he was paid for, but it is well-known how important his service was to Andover.

The last few months of the war were nervous but quiet in Andover. Andover's impressment record during the war is dominated by family status and family connections of political and military power. It is quite clear that the town's militia committee, made up of Osgood, Chandler, and Ingalls, protected their own militia-age sons from the press. It also seems clear that Lieutenant Osgood protected at least some sons of allied families, especially the Poor family, who were linked to the Osgoods by marriage. Ensign Chandler does not seem to have had the same clout on the committee. Most of the sons of his group of allied families went off to war, although Chandler was able to protect his own sons from the press. Among those soldiers from leading families, it is remarkable that no first sons served; the committee seems to have protected them as well. Some of the men might have been impressed to fulfill their civic duty while some may have volunteered to go for the same reason or because they were lured by the glory of battle.

In the final analysis, though, the most plausible reason for the social and economic makeup of Andover's pressed militiamen is simply the town's homogeneous nature. Andover was in many ways the model seventeenth-century New England town, harmonious and without enormous economic stratification or numerous social divisions. The reason that Andover did not send mostly "rabble" to fight the war, as so many other towns did, was that it did not have a "rabble" to send.

Manchester: A Town with No Choice

Manchester was the smallest town in Essex County at the time of King Philip's War. Located on the seacoast, it is sandwiched among Ipswich, Gloucester, Wenham, and Beverly. Unlike its neighboring towns,

Manchester's rugged shoreline of cliffs and boulders offers no safe harbor for ships. The area was first settled in the late 1630s.[65] In 1640, a total of around seventeen families "jointly and humbly" petitioned the General Court in Boston to grant them permission to establish a village.[66] The General Court never formally incorporated the town during the seventeenth century and Manchester remained small. Town records reveal fewer than twenty family names at any one time.[67] While fifty-two different individuals are named in the town records (representing forty-six distinct family names) up to 1676, many appear to have been transient.[68] The town leadership positions circulated among the same eight to ten men from about 1660 to 1680.[69]

The traces of Manchester's militia are very faint. There is not a single reference to a militia unit of any kind in the town records.[70] In the militia reorganization of Massachusetts undertaken in 1680, just after King Philip's War, Manchester was missing from the 2nd (North) Essex Regiment, indicating that the town had no militia organization.[71] Nor are there any definite clues to any militia officers in town. Manchester, as a small and insignificant town, had no organized militia unit or militia committee at the time of the war. Yet, five men from Manchester fought in the conflict. John Allen, John Bennett, and Joshua Carter served with Captain Lathrop during his ill-fated campaign in the fall of 1675.[72] Samuel Pickworth was a corporal under Captain Gardner during the Narragansett campaign of 1675.[73] And finally, John Knight was recruited in November of 1675.[74] The long and confusing process by which Knight finally ended up in the militia ranks offers important clues into militia selection in Manchester during the war.

The sole surviving evidence for what happened comes from the record of a series of cases that appeared before the Essex County Quarterly Court in March 1676. They tell a strange tale of militia recruitment gone awry the previous fall. The court convicted Manchester's Samuel Leech for "abusive speeches, affronting and not obeying authority, when impressed for the county's service" and ordered him to be whipped or to pay a hefty five-pound fine.[75] The account behind this conviction is complex. On November 3, 1675, the lieutenant of Beverly's town militia, William Dixsy, had sent a warrant to John Elithrop, the constable of Manchester. The warrant ordered Elithrop to impress one soldier for service and bring him to Beverly to join that town's company on an appointed day. Apparently Manchester's militia and militiamen were under the control of the Beverly militia. After Beverly received a summons for men from the General

Court, it allotted a portion of its quota to Manchester. When comparing the recruitment patterns for both towns, the case for this becomes stronger; not a single soldier from Manchester served in a company that did not also include men from Beverly's militia. The quotas for Beverly became Manchester's quotas and men from the two towns served side by side.

The relationship between the two towns and their militias, however, was more convoluted and troubled. Rarely in the history of the Massachusetts militia had so many different warrants been issued to impress one man. The first of four warrants was dated September 18, 1675. It reads: "To the constable of Manchester you ar required in his maiestys name to impress one able man of yor towne for the servis of the Contry complete in armes & to be at an owers warning by order of ye Comander Leftenant William Dixsy [of Beverly's militia] & John Knite [Knight] I will not except of."[76] This warrant was too late to be the instrument that impressed the men for Lathrop's command from Manchester and was too early for the impressment of Samuel Pickworth for the Narragansett campaign. It appears likely that no one was ever impressed based on this warrant, which prompted the militia committee of Beverly to issue a second warrant on October 10, 1675. This warrant to Elithrop was more precise in its requirements and included a threat to Manchester's constable: "Faill not upon ye peril by order of the melette [militia] of Beverly."[77] The court records convey that Constable Elithrop tried to impress Samuel Leech of Manchester. According to Elithrop's later testimony, Leech fiercely refused to go, even attacking the constable.[78] Despite his violent refusal to serve, Leech eventually reported to the muster at Beverly; the twisted tale, however, does not end there.

Manchester's quota of Beverly's militia, which was supposed to have been filled by the impressment of Samuel Leech, was still incomplete in January 1676. In early January, two additional militia warrants were sent to Constable Elithrop in Manchester. The warrant of January 11, 1676, stated: "To the constabell of manchister you ar Requiered in his magesteys name to bring up your imprsed man by to morrow ten of the clock to beveley: . . . with eight days provsion by order of the millisha [militia] Left William Dickse."[79] The second warrant, issued the very next day, was even more precise, naming the soldier to be impressed (John Knight) and adjusting the time of his muster, armed and equipped, to eight in the morning on January 14, 1676, at Beverly.[80] William Dixsy, the militia commander of Beverly, was leaving nothing to chance, giving constable

Elithrop very explicit instructions and making him deliver John Knight in person to the muster. What is strange about all of this is that Samuel Leech was supposed to be Manchester's contribution to the Beverly militia back in October. Yet this was not the case; Leech had been released from service by the "militia of Beverly," after Elithrop had impressed him in the fall of 1675.[81] He never served. How Leech convinced Dixsy to release him without fulfilling his service is unknown. What makes it even stranger is the fact that Dixsy allowed Leech to leave and later accepted for service John Knight of Manchester, despite the fact that the very first warrant, in September 1675, had said that Knight was not acceptable.[82] In the end, John Knight served under Captain Poole in the garrison forces of western Massachusetts.[83]

While is seems that William Dixsy of the Beverly militia was controlling the militia situation in Manchester, this state of affairs did not sit well with the town's selectmen. They entered the fray by swearing out a warrant, to be served by poor constable Elithrop, to compel Samuel Leech to care for John Knight's wife, who was now at home without a husband. They also severely criticized the methods of the Beverly militia. The Manchester selectmen, Thomas Bishop, John West, and Samuel Freed, laid out their concerns in a petition to magistrate and Major General Daniel Denison:

> Respecting a woman and her child that is left in a very poore Condition her husband being prest for the service of the country whereas another was prest that was in every Respect more fitt as we conceive namely Samuel Leech who was sett fre by the malitia of bevarly which was contrary to order as we conceive we do intreat your worship that you would be pleased to direct us what to doe in such a case the inhabitants of our village doe manifest as there inability so there unwillingness to contribute to her present nessessity and the Reason they aledg is that Samuell leech was prest before and did not goe and therefore was a delinquent. . . . We conceive that the malitia of beverlay had no power to give any warrant to pres another man therefore we hope that your worship will Judge that either the malitia of beverlay or Samuel leech should maintain this woman in her husbands absence.[84]

The selectmen were bolstered when Major General Denison answered their petition, commenting that "if there were any irregularitie in sending away that soldier [John Knight] and releasing Leech . . . the selectman must take care that his family does not suffer in his absence."[85] Dennison went even further, giving the selectmen the power and authority to force Leech to care for Knight's family and suffer a stiff penalty if he refused.[86]

When Constable Elithrop tried to serve this latest warrant, an order to assist Goodwife Knight, the uncooperative Leech once again failed to follow the selectmen's orders. Leech shrugged off the warrant and questioned the entire impressment system, insulting all of its participants—from the constable up to the king—along the way. Elithrop testified that "Leach [*sic*] did nothing for Goodwife Knits [Knight] though she was in a suffering condition for want of wood and other necessaries."[87] Leech's disrespect for authority and his physical attack on Constable Elithrop prompted the entire series of court cases and caused the Quarterly Court to issue a strong ruling against Leech. He was convicted and ordered to be whipped or pay a fine of five pounds.[88] The case, and others like it, was so upsetting to the government that in May 1676, the General Court passed a new law, stating that men who failed to appear when impressed would be fined and "if their neglects or refusal shall be accompanied with refractions, reflection, or contempt upon authority, such persons shall be punished by death or some other grevious punishment."[89] In addition to Leech's fine, the Court ordered that he pay Constable Elithrop's expenses related to the matter. While a unusual step, it was the least the Court could do for such a faithful and often-abused public servant. Mary Knight and her family got little relief, however, and the Essex Quarterly Court ordered, as late as June 1676, that both the militia committee in Beverly and the selectmen of Manchester "forthwith take care that they may be relieved and not suffer" because the family was still "in great need."[90]

The episode offers several important insights into the militia in Manchester, including details of the relationship between the militia in a small town and a larger, neighboring town, as well as a glimpse into how a town too small to have its own militia went about selecting men for service. There is simply no way to know, for the records are silent, the peacetime relationship between the Beverly and Manchester militias. It is likely that the men from Manchester trained with the Beverly militia prior to the war. Until 1668, Beverly was a part of Salem and not a distinct entity of its own, so it is possible that the men from both Manchester and Beverly joined the Salem militiamen for training in the early days of settlement. The link between the Manchester and Beverly militias was clear by the time of King Philip's War, as seen in the Leech court case. If the same relationship existed before the war, as seems likely, the absence of militia officers in Manchester and the total absence of militia records (to say nothing of any mention of the militia in the Manchester town records) is much easier to understand.

Another question that the incident hints at, but does not answer completely, is who was choosing the men of Manchester to serve when called. Normally, the town's committee of militia would determine which men to impress. Manchester did not have a single militia officer (or noncommissioned officer), however, let alone a militia committee. From the records in the Samuel Leech case, it seems that the constable of Manchester himself simply made the choice once the warrant arrived from Beverly's militia commander. The case for this is strong; each of the four impressment warrants was addressed to Manchester's constable, John Elithrope.[91] In addition, in the first warrant, of September 1675, Lieutenant Dixsy of Beverly names a man, John Knight, who will *not* be acceptable as an impressed soldier. This implies that the choice was up to Manchester's constable, with some guidance from Beverly's militia establishment. Early in the war, Captain Thomas Lathrop commanded Beverly's militia; he recruited five men from Beverly and three from Manchester for his own campaign in August 1675.[92] While no warrants from this impressment survive, if it followed the same pattern as occurred later in the war, Constable Elithrop of Manchester probably chose the three men from the town who served with Lathrop.

Compared to the men in several other towns, very little is known about most of the Manchester soldiers. Two of the three men who served with Captain Lathrop, John Allen and Joshua Carter, are absent from the records except for their names on the original muster lists.[93] It is probable that John Allen was the son of William Allen of Manchester, one of the first eight settlers in the area in the late 1630s.[94] William had come from Salem, was a member of the Salem church, and served in various posts in the town.[95] His 1678 will and probate inventory makes no mention of a son named John; but since John Allen had in fact died in the war years before, there is no reason that it would. The probate inventory totals 180 pounds and is consistent with the belongings of a middling farmer of the period.[96] Of Joshua Carter there are no records whatsoever.

A little more is known about the family of the third man sent to fight under Lathrop, John Bennett. His father was Henry Bennett, who was born in England in 1629 and had come to Massachusetts in 1650.[97] He settled in Ipswich and married Lydia Perkins there in late 1650; they had five sons between 1651 and 1667, of whom John was the second.[98] His farm of two hundred acres was in the extreme southeastern section of Ipswich, very close to the town boundary of Manchester.[99] He also held considerable land on a number of islands off the coast. He died sometime after 1679.[100] John, Henry and Lydia's second son, was born in 1655, which would make him twenty years old at the time of the war.[101] It is likely that he worked on his father's farm; Henry Bennett kept direct control of all his land until 1682, when he gave his eldest son, Jacob, fifteen acres.[102] It is unlikely that as a twenty-year-old second son John would have been granted any land or had any independence from his family at the time that the war broke out in 1675.

John Bennett had run into some legal trouble in July 1675. Magistrate Major William Hathorne of Salem fined Bennett for "affronting" the constable while he was gathering the minister's rate.[103] Disrespect toward authority was taken seriously in Massachusetts Bay and probably had a great impact on the man responsible for choosing soldiers from Manchester, himself a constable, John Elithrop. The record is silent as to whether John Bennett's altercation had been with Elithrop or a different constable (perhaps in Salem or Beverly), but the fact remains that less than a month after Bennett had committed this crime, a constable sent him off to war. He and the other two young men from Manchester paid the ultimate price, for all three were killed in the horrific carnage at Bloody Brook in September, 1675.

Only one man from Manchester was involved in the next major campaign of the war; Samuel Pickworth fought in the Narragansett campaign under Captain Joseph Gardner. While it may seem strange that the town only contributed one man to the campaign, from the records of the Leech/ Knight impressment, it is known that Manchester was asked to submit only a single man for service. Manchester's small size and subordinate militia relationship to Beverly makes this impressment of a single soldier reasonable. Samuel Pickworth's background is problematic. First, Pickworth had strong ties to both Salem and Manchester, making it difficult to determine where he was recruited.[104] Documentation that his wife and children were living in Manchester during and after the war suggests that Samuel too resided there.[105] It is most likely that he lived in Manchester for years (there are numerous instances of the Pickworth family in Manchester's town records) and simply had strong ties to Salem.[106]

Pickworth served as a corporal in Gardner's company from December 1675 to February 1676.[107] There is very little evidence in the primary or secondary literature about the recruitment or appointment of noncommissioned officers during wartime. While there are several instances of the quarterly courts appointing or confirming sergeants, there are very few records relating to the assignment of corporals.[108] It is simply not known how these men were treated in regard to recruitment. Most were probably noncommissioned officers in their town militias before the war; some served with the same rank (and some with reduced rank) in composite companies created to fight the war. This is not the case, however, with Pickworth—there is no record of him serving in such a capacity before the war.[109] How he was selected we simply do not know. Noncommissioned officers could have found themselves serving in assembled active-duty companies in several ways: some volunteered, officers asked others to serve, some were appointed, and a few might have been impressed.

Samuel Pickworth's precise birth date is not known but was probably close to 1640, making him around thirty-five at the time of the war.[110] His father, John, was a longtime resident of Manchester, appearing in the town records as early as 1637.[111] The elder Pickworth was active in town affairs, serving as commissioner of the minister's rate, timber overseer, and selectman.[112] John Pickworth lived and farmed in Manchester with his wife and their four children.[113] Pickworth died in 1663. His will and probate inventory detailed the holdings of a middling farmer: a dwelling sitting on twenty-five acres of land, a few additional parcels around town, a share of the town's sawmill, and a normal assortment of household goods for a total estate of 168 pounds.[114] Samuel, as the second son, was co-executor of the will and received two small parcels of land and his father's share of the sawmill.[115] In addition, he was to act on his mother's behalf, overseeing her part of the estate (the eldest son, John Jr., was apparently too busy running the main family farm).[116] At the time of his father's death, Samuel was not yet married, but, as he had been given a small parcel of land by the town in 1661, it is not known whether he still lived at home.[117] Samuel served on a special jury of inquest in Salem in 1666, showing his tendency to range widely around Essex County in his affairs.[118]

Samuel married Sara Marston on September 3, 1667, in Salem.[119] The next summer they had their first daughter, Sara, then a son, Samuel Jr., in 1673, and another daughter, Hanna, in May 1675.[120] Samuel Sr. was a member of the First Church in Salem and had his son Samuel, Jr., baptized there in 1672.[121] When he marched to war in December 1675, his family anxiously awaited his return, but they waited in vain. Samuel was killed on December 16, 1675, with two others while leading a scouting party before the Fort Fight.[122] An inventory of his estate offers a detailed view of Samuel's economic status. The inventory includes a house and land worth fifty-five pounds, household goods, swine, lumber, carpenter's tools, and "several years time in a youth."[123] From this account of his possessions, it becomes clear that while he owned a small farm, Pickworth's primary occupation was as a carpenter. His total worth was only eighty-three pounds once his debts had been paid.

His inventory places Pickworth in the subordinate category in socioeconomic status and offers a clear example of the economic hardship that second sons of lower-middling families faced once the first-generation patriarch died. The eldest brother got the majority of the family's land and the family house, which forced Samuel to pursue another income source in town. Pickworth's situation offers both clues and questions about his status as a noncommissioned officer. It is possible that Manchester impressed him as a regular soldier because of his secondary status in town and later promoted him to corporal, even without holding a rank in the peacetime militia.[124] Being ten to fifteen years older than the majority of the militiamen and having experience overseeing an apprentice may have given him the credentials to become a corporal under Gardner. The fact that Pickworth joined Gardner's company amid the impressment controversy between Beverly and Manchester, however, is probably a clue that he was not impressed. The impressment system between Beverly and Manchester had broken down and was not fixed again until January 1676, by which time Pickworth had already served.[125] It is possible that he volunteered for service, needing additional income, and was eventually promoted for the above reasons. It is also possible that in his business and social connections to Salem, Pickworth knew Captain Joseph Gardner, who may have asked him to join the campaign as a corporal.

The last soldier to be chosen for militia duty was John Knight, who served with Captain Poole after the long and drawn-out impressment saga in town was resolved. Constable Elithrop, working under the direction of Lieutenant Dixsy of Beverly, selected him for service. There are no records of John Knight before the war in any of the standard sources. He simply materialized in 1675 during the impressment controversy. No record exists of a Knight family in Manchester before 1675.[126] His name is first mentioned in the first warrant sent to Constable Elithrop from Beverly in September 1675, in which Lieutenant Dixsy calls for a man with the following caveat: "John Knight I will not except of."[127] What had Knight done to make himself unacceptable? There is no record of wrongdoing in the county or colony court records.[128] Perhaps Knight was a drifter who had made a bad impression in Beverly when passing through and was not wanted back. Perhaps he had been sent to Beverly in the earlier press (for Lathrop's command?) in August and was deemed, for some reason, unsuitable. Perhaps Lieutenant Dixsy did not think that he would appear for muster if pressed and Beverly would have to send one of its own sons in the Manchester man's place. In January 1676, Dixsy finally accepted Knight as Manchester's recruit, after the Leech impressment affair was finally concluded; in fact, Knight was named specifically as acceptable in the final warrant.[129] In the postwar period, John Knight seems to have become just another middling farmer in Manchester; it is a mystery why he evoked such a strong response during the war.

As a group, the impressed men of Manchester were unremarkable. Little is known about them, as is the case with the town in general. It is not even certain whether Samuel Pickworth was impressed or if he joined Captain Gardner's company some other way. It seems likely that John Bennett's offense of confronting a constable in July 1675, perhaps even the man who eventually impressed him, led to his service. The reasons that the other men were chosen, however, are much harder to understand. There is so little information available that further analysis is simply not possible. Yet, the lack of data on the soldiers does not mean that Manchester's story is not important.

The impressment system of Manchester was unique, made so by the lack of a committee of militia in town. The small community relied on a combination of outside advice from the Beverly militia commander, Lieutenant Dixsy (who issued the warrants), and the decisions of one man in Manchester, Constable Elithrop, to make its impressment decisions. As has been demonstrated, however, this system did not work smoothly. The two men involved, Lieutenant Dixsy and Constable Elithrop, clashed repeatedly over impressment, and the selectmen of Manchester even entered the fray to support their constable. The Leech/Knight impressment controversy shows a system in disorder. The General Court had established town committees of militia to exert local control over impressment, giving those who best knew the men of any town the power to pick who would serve as soldiers. Because the town did not have a committee, local control of impressment was not assured in Manchester. This void in the local militia system led to a system of chaotic and unreliable recruitment, conflict within the town, and, most importantly, a quarrel between Manchester and its neighbor.

Wenham: A Small Population Leads to Fewer Choices

Wenham, like many towns in Essex County, began with the settlement of Salem in 1628.[130] Located between Salem and Ipswich along the road linking the two towns, the area was known for its beautiful lake and plush meadows. Wenham became an outlying township of Salem in 1637. To further increase its own settlement and population, Salem offered house lots around the lake to about twenty families to establish a town center for the settlement in 1639.[131] The founding of Wenham was made official by the General Court in 1643. The settlers, now with four thousand acres of land to manage, began the process of building a community. The town gathered its church in 1642 and had a meetinghouse well underway by the time that it called John Fiske as its pastor in 1644. The church, like the town, was very small, having only nineteen members in 1645.[132] Despite its early promise, Wenham stagnated for the next ten years. Fiske, who had hoped to develop an important settlement in Wenham, became frustrated with the lack of growth, so in 1655 he and several families moved to the settlement of Chelmsford, leaving a gaping hole in the small and struggling community of Wenham.

The town suffered a forceful blow with the removal of the minister and seven families. Only the intervention of Charles Gott, a prominent Salem inhabitant who had recently moved to Wenham, saved the church. As a selectman, Gott convinced the Rev. Antipas Newman to become the town's minister, a post that he retained until 1672. Despite the infusion of new blood, Wenham remained small and continued to struggle, having only two hundred inhabitants as late as 1662.

Few surviving records discuss the town's early militia. While it is known that the town, as required by law, had a training field and the men trained occasionally, no list of town officers exists.[133] The first mention of the militia is a reference in the town records to a Sergeant White in November 1670, apparently the town's militia sergeant.[134] The next time that the town's militia is mentioned is in the official records of the Essex County Quarterly Court. In May 1674, Charles Gott, the clerk of the militia band in Wenham, swore out a case against Walter Fairfield for abuse. The Court issued a warrant that Fairfield's property be detained until he paid a five-shilling fine for not appearing at Wenham's last militia training. The Court fined Henry Haget "for like Defect" and suggested that the money be given to the town's militia "for the use of the Companye."[135] According to the testimony of Charles Gott and the town's new militia commander, Sergeant Thomas Fiske Sr., Walter Fairfield and Henry Haget had failed to appear for militia training on the scheduled day. When Gott went to Fairfield's house to collect the normal militia fine, Fairfield replied that he would not pay.[136] Gott returned to Fairfield's house a week later and once again read the warrant. Saying that he "cared nothing for Captain Tom [Sergeant Thomas Fiske, apparently known as captain even though his rank was officially sergeant], with many filthy speeches," Fairfield again refused to pay.[137] When Gott attempted to seize two pewter vessels in place of payment, Fairfield wrested them away.

The next day, Gott and Thomas Fiske Jr., the sergeant's son, returned to Fairfield's house and tried to seize some corn in lieu of the fine. This time, Fairfield first threatened them and then assaulted Gott, who related that Fairfield "shooved me with violans [violence] several times & tooke A greate Club in his hand and vowed if I came theare he woulde knock me down."[138] Further struggle ensued. Fairfield testified that he had offered Gott several boards in place of the fine, but Gott would not consider them.[139] Most of the witnesses told a version consistent with Gott's account. Fairfield, apparently a hotheaded man, had numerous other court cases pending at the same time, all of which he lost. He later appears to have moved to Ipswich.[140] In the end, the Court ordered Fairfield to pay a five-shilling fine to the company and twenty shillings to the county.

The incident offers a rare glimpse into the workings of a small-town militia. Walter Fairfield asserted that he thought Gott was joking the first time he demanded the fine, a misunderstanding born out of the fact that Gott was new to his post. Sergeant Fiske had appointed Gott to the office of clerk of the band only after the company's choice, by vote, had refused to serve in the highly disliked position.[141] This case highlights why the General Court instituted fines against men who refused to serve as militia clerk.[142] In addition, the case indicates that Fairfield and Haget, the other men fined for nonappearance, were confused by the company's procedure regarding rainy training days. The company had agreed that if the weather were bad on the morning of training, the training day would automatically be postponed, in order to save the men from traveling all the way to the training field. This was a simple yet important agreement, because the men could not fire their weapons if the firearms were wet.[143] Yet, this also caused confusion; several men testified that they thought training would be postponed on the training day in question because of threatening weather.[144]

The Fairfield case also demonstrates the high level of frustration and bad feeling within the small town's militia company. Sergeant Fiske seems to have been out of favor, at least with some of his men. Fairfield's derisive comments about "Captain Tom" harbor sarcasm and disdain.[145] The fact that five men testified against Fiske and Gott in court sends a signal that not all was well in the Wenham militia.[146] In less than a year, King Philip's War would break out and the small town's troubled militia would be tested for its first time in more than thirty-five years of existence.

The lack of official militia records for Wenham makes identifying its entire militia committee difficult. Sergeant Thomas Fiske, as the only officer in town (and a noncommissioned officer at that), was undoubtedly a member. Fiske's colleagues, however, are harder to identify. The law stated that any magistrate living in town, or, in the absence of a magistrate, a deputy to the General Court, should join with the highest-ranking militia officers in town to constitute a three-man militia committee.[147] No magistrate lived in Wenham at the time of the war, however, and the town did not send a deputy to the General Court in Boston between 1674 and 1677.[148] Thus, it is not known if Wenham even had a committee of militia or if Sergeant Fiske simply chose the men to serve. Fiske's name alone appears on the report dated November 30, 1675, to the General Court about the recruits for the Narragansett campaign.[149] It is also possible, although unlikely, that the town's selectmen helped make the decision. Perhaps Charles Gott, the clerk of the militia for Wenham, was on the committee. The records are simply too meager to know for certain.

Wenham sent a total of nine soldiers to fight during King Philip's War.[150] This was the second smallest number of soldiers impressed from any town in Essex County, which fit with the town's minute population. Two men, Thomas Kimball and his cousin Caleb Kimball, served with Captain Lathrop during his disastrous mission.[151] The town impressed seven men for service in the Narragansett campaign. Mark Batchelder, Richard Hutton, Samuel Moulton, Philip Welch, and Thomas Kimball (the Lathrop veteran) served under Captain Gardner.[152] Thomas Abbe and Thomas Killom received credit for service under Major Appleton. Later in the war, Henry Kimball (brother to Caleb and cousin to Thomas) served with Captain Benjamin Sweet's company from February to June 1676, while Thomas Kimball, already a veteran of two campaigns, went out again with Captain Brocklebank from January through March 1676.[153]

It is possible that these last two men were volunteers, because it was uncommon, although not unheard of, for the General Court to issue any town a quota for just one man. The likelihood of volunteerism is even stronger in the case of Thomas Kimball, who served in three different companies; it seems unlikely that Wenham's militia committee would impress one man multiple times when other young men in town had not served. One explanation for his service in multiple companies is that Kimball felt soldiering suited him. It is also possible, however, that the committee selected him multiple times because it had little choice. With such a small population from which to draw, the committee of militia in Wenham was likely hard-pressed to find suitable young men to draft into service, especially as the war dragged on and more men evaded the press. This also may explain why so many members of the extended Kimball family were sent.

Of all the men who served in the war from Wenham, only one was married, the drifter Philip Welch.[154] None of the full-time inhabitants of Wenham was married. The militia committee ostensibly placed a high premium on the fact that the militiamen it chose had no dependents for whom the town would be forced to care if their breadwinner was killed.[155] The town was also keeping its existing families intact. This was especially crucial in small and struggling Wenham, which did not have a large population to begin with. The militia committee worked hard to protect heads of households in town, at the expense of its young, single men.

Wenham's committee of militia did take advantage of one troubled man to spare the rest of the town's families the heartache of losing a valued community member. The committee impressed Philip Welch even though it appears that he was not a resident of the town.[156] It is possible that Welch was impressed while in town on business or that he and his family were in town for a short time, his wife having once lived in Wenham. Impressing men while they were in town on business was fairly common during the war, although it did not always sit well with colonial authorities.[157]

Most local records about Welch come from Topsfield and Ipswich, towns where he had strong roots. Philip Welch was well-known in the county from the time of his arrival. He and another boy from Ireland had been brought to Massachusetts Bay in May 1654.[158] Welch, eleven years old, and William Dalton, nine years old, "were stolen in Ireland by some English soldiers in ye night out of theyr beds & brought to Mr. Dills ship, where there were diverse others of their country men, weeping and crying because they were stolen from their friends."[159] They were transported to Boston and their indenture (nine years for Welch, eleven for Dalton) was sold to Mr. Samuel Symonds, a prominent citizen of Ipswich.

In 1661, Symonds brought a suit against Dalton for refusing to work, and the young men petitioned the General Court to end their contract. In defense, they argued: "We were brought out of our country contrary to our own wills & minds and sold here . . . notwithstanding we have indeaured to do him [Symonds] ye best service wee Could these seven Complete years. . . . Now 7 years being so much as ye practice in old England . . . & wee being both above 21 years in age, we hope this honored Court and Jury will seriously consider our Condition."[160] The General Court sided with Symonds and the two men served him until 1663, as per the original indenture agreement.

No further mention of Welch appears until after he was free of Symonds in 1663 or 1665.[161] He married Hannah Haggett of Wenham in February 1667.[162] In November 1668 and November 1670, the couple appears in the court records concerning a land sale in Topsfield.[163] It would appear that the couple and their five children, born between 1668 and 1675, were living in Topsfield at the time of the war. But it was the Wenham militia committee that impressed Philip Welch for the Narragansett campaign.[164] To make matters even more confusing, a Philip Welch (possibly the same man) also appears on several lists as coming from Lynn or Beverly.[165] The probable explanation is that Welch and his family were drifters, moving from town to town. There is little doubt that as a poor, unskilled indentured servant with a large family, Welch was in the subordinate category. His status and the assumption that the family moved from place to place is strengthened by a 1676 court case.

Almost as soon as Welch got back from his war service in early 1676, he moved his family from Topsfield to Marblehead. The selectmen of Marblehead petitioned the Essex County Quarterly Court: "Whereas the laws of this common wealth ordereth that every towne shall provide for its own poore: Philip welch of Topsfield being reputed A very poore man & of late com with his family into our towne of Marble Head without Leave obtained from either towne or Selectmen, also, being according To our towne order warned either to depart or give bond for ye townes securitie hee refusing to doe either, wee doubte not but this honnoured court will give releeffe against this unjust intrusion."[166] The Court permitted Marblehead to disallow Welch and his family as inhabitants worthy of town support. Welch was still in Marblehead in 1677, but by 1679 he had moved back to Topsfield.[167] There is little doubt that he and his family were seen as a nuisance and a potential drain on town coffers wherever they went. It is not surprising that Wenham's militia committee jumped at the chance to send Welch to war in place of one of its own. Not only would no family in town be harmed if he didn't come back, but if that happened, Topsfield, not the citizens of Wenham, would have to care for Welch's widow and children.

Wenham, being so small, did not have many choices of its own young men to send to war. A 1659 tax list of the town, the closest to the war years available, shows only twenty-seven men in town, living in around twenty-three households (see table 6).[168] While the list was compiled over fifteen years before the war, it offers important clues into the community's social and economic hierarchy. There were probably even fewer families in town by 1675, as Wenham experienced high levels of out-migration. The 1675 colony assessment for Wenham was considerably less, in proportion, to its assessment twenty years before, and the town faced such financial hardship because of the "feeble and drooping condition of the place" that the colony discharged Wenham from paying the Harvard University subscription (tax) in early 1675.[169] Despite the downturn in Wenham's fortunes, the 1659 list does lay out the social and economic hierarchy of the town, which, when compared with probate records, shows little variation between 1659 and 1675.[170]

Looking closely at the tax list and other socioeconomic data, it becomes apparent that Wenham's militia committee impressed sons from families all along the town's economic scale; it probably didn't have a choice if it wanted to primarily impress unmarried men. Thomas Kimball, the three-time soldier, was the son of one of the town's most important citizens. His cousins, Henry and Caleb Kimball, came from one of the town's lower-middling families. Yet all three went to war for Wenham. The committee displayed a slight preference to enlist the sons of families on the lower end of the socioeconomic scale. This preference is apparent when examining the 1659 tax list. Only three of the men impressed (37 percent) came from families that paid above the average tax assessment (£1–18–0), while five men (63 percent) came from families that paid below the average.[171] While there seems to be a minor inclination to send sons of middling to lower-status families, the real interest of the committee seems always to send unmarried men.

In addition to the tax data, the categorization system used in this study also highlights the fact that the town impressed sons all along the socio-economic scale. Wenham's small size meant that a large number of the fathers of militiamen had served in town governance; however, only a few had the mixture of political power and economic clout to be called leading

TABLE 6

Wenham Tax List with Soldiers' Families Highlighted, 1659

Rank	Name	£-s-d	Note	Soldier's Name
1	Richard Kimball	3-15-0		Thomas
2	John Fisk	3-0-0		
2	Mr. Gott	3-0-0	in corn	
2	James Moulton Sr.	3-0-0		Samuel
5	John Dodge	2-15-0	third in corn	
5	Thomas Fisk	2-15-0		
7	Richard Coy	2-15-0		
7	Phineas Fisk	2-10-0		
9	John Gooland	2-0-0		
9	Richard Hutton	2-0-0		Richard Jr.
9	Austin Kilham	2-0-0	in corn	
		Average Value £1-18-0		
12	John Abby	1-15-0	in corn	Thomas
12	Mark Batchelder	1-15-0		Mark
12	Richard Goldsmith	1-15-0		
12	William Gore	1-15-0		
12	Henry Haggett	1-15-0		
12	John Kilham	1-15-0		
12	John Powling	1-15-0	in corn	
19	Alexander Moxey	1-12-0		
20	Daniel Kilham	1-10-0		Thomas
21	John Batchelder	1-0-0		
21	Robert Gowen	1-0-0		
21	Henry Kimball	1-0-0	half in corn	Caleb, Henry
21	James Moulton Jr.	1-0-0		
21	Abner Ordway	1 0-0		
21	Edward Waldron	1-0-0		
21	Thomas White	1-0-0		

Source: Myron O. Allen, *History of Wenham Civil and Ecclesiastical from Its Settlement in 1639 to 1860*, reprint of 1860 ed. (Ann Arbor: Edwards Brothers, 1975), 33.

TABLE 7
Soldiers' Families and Town Rank in Wenham, 1659–1675

Tax Rank in 1659	Category	Family Name	Soldier(s)'s Name	Father's Name
1	L	Kimball	Thomas	Richard
2 (tie)	M	Moulton	Samuel	James Sr.
9 (tie)	M	Hutton	Richard Jr.	Richard Sr.

Town Average–£1-18-0

12 (tie)	M	Abbe	Thomas	John
12 (tie) *his rank[1]	L	Batchelder	Mark	Joseph
20	M	Killom	Thomas	Daniel
21 (tie)	M	Kimball	Henry Jr. Caleb	Henry Sr.
Not on List	S	Welch	Philip	Unknown

Tax Rank in 1659[2] is the family's rank; Category reports the findings of the categorization system used in this work, L=leading family, M=middling family, and S=subordinate family.

1. Mark Batchelder's father, Joseph, died in 1647. Mark's ranking is his own, not his family's as a whole. Before the split of family assets at the father's death, the Batchelder family would have been at the top of the town hierarchy. See Sidney Perley, "Batchelder Genealogy," *Essex Antiquarian 7*, no. 3 (1903), 105–109; Frederick Clifton Pierce, *Batchelder, Batcheller Genealogy: Descendants of Rev. Stephen Bachiler of England . . . Who Settled the Town of New Hampton, N.H. And Joseph, Henry, Joshua, and John Batcheller, of Essex Co., Mass* (Chicago: W. B. Conkey, 1898).

2. Myron O. Allen, *History of Wenham Civil and Ecclesiastical from Its Settlement in 1639 to 1860*, reprint of 1860 ed. (Ann Arbor: Edwards Brothers, 1975), 33. Philip Welch was not on the 1659 tax list, as he was not an inhabitant.

citizens. Two of the men who served came from Wenham's leading families, about the correct proportion in regard to the town's economic hierarchy. In addition to being in the number-one position on the town's tax list in 1659, Richard Kimball (militiaman Thomas's father) was very active in town government, holding numerous town offices, including being a town selectman eleven times between 1657 and 1674.[172] Richard Kimball was even a member of the highly prestigious Artillery Company in Boston, as was Sergeant Thomas Fiske.[173] Militiaman Mark Batchelder, despite his relatively middle position on the tax list, was the son of a founder of the town, who had also been Wenham's first deputy to the General Court in Boston.[174] Mark had served on the jury of trials, as town constable, and as selectman at least three times between 1668 and 1673.[175] The Batchelders were also active members of the Wenham church, the only family of a soldier to leave a record in the church of any consequence.[176] The rest of the Wenham families, middling all, had fathers who served the town, but none had power on the scale of Kimball and Batchelder.

Much like the town's overall social and economic order, two of the soldiers (25 percent) came from leading families, while six (75 percent) came from middling families (see table 7). While Philip Welch did not appear on the list, it is apparent from all the evidence that he was from the subordinate category. Despite the declining position of the town, no native Wenham families seem to have belonged to the subordinate category in the 1670s. Socioeconomic status played at best a slight role in Wenham's impressment decisions; the committee was far more concerned with pressing men without families of their own than they were with drafting only the sons of the town's lower-middling sort.

None of the native Wenham men pressed into military service had a criminal record. In the ten years before the war, only one serious crime of a physical nature occurred in Wenham.[177] The perpetrator of that act, and the only man with a criminal record drafted, was the drifter Philip Welch. In November 1668, Welch (this time listed as an inhabitant of Ipswich) was fined for breach of the peace in Wenham, "striking John Abbe, Jr. with his fist, blows upon his face with much violence."[178] There is little question why Wenham's committee impressed Welch.

While Wenham experienced a few crimes in the ten years before the war, none of them were of a serious nature.[179] Two incidents involving the fathers of three soldiers, however, might have made an impression on the militia committee. In November 1668, Thomas Fiske, the town's sergeant and militia committee member, sued James Moluton (the father of soldier Samuel Moulton) for an undisclosed reason.[180] The Quarterly Court threw the case out and Moulton was allowed costs by Fiske as the case was "not prosecuted." Also in 1668, Richard Hutton and Daniel Killom (the fathers of militiamen Richard Jr. and Thomas) were accused of disturbing the assembly during the Lord's Day.[181] Hutton and Killom spoke out of turn at a church meeting after service and would not be quiet, eventually threatening the constable. One of the main witnesses against them was Thomas Fiske. It is possible that Fiske impressed the sons of these men in order to take long-delayed revenge for personal wrongdoing against him or disturbances in his town. This possibility, while not known for certain, is chilling. In small, isolated Wenham, being the sons of men whom Fiske or the committee perceived as troublemakers might just have been enough to be sent off to war.

When faced with quotas for soldiers from the General Court, Wenham's committee scrutinized the available men in town very carefully. The easiest choice for the committee must have been drifter and troublemaker Philip Welch. After that, it became more difficult. There were no serious native troublemakers in town to ship off. It is possible that the committee practiced corruption by blood and sent the sons of some citizens perceived as difficult. The committee did send three native citizens at the lower end of the town's economic scale to war, but it also sent at least one son of a leading family. In the end, Wenham's committee chose men from all parts of the socioeconomic spectrum who were unmarried younger sons, those men who could most easily be sacrificed if the war went badly.

The militia committees of the small, shrinking, or isolated towns of Essex County had few options of men to send to war—or in the case of Manchester, no choice at all. Yet, even though limited, impressment remained local in almost all cases—officials in the communities chose soldiers for expeditions, not the General Court or the governor or the Court of Assistants in Boston. Andover sent a mixture of men, many well-respected, leading and middling sons who resembled the Elizabethan trained bands of old; the colonists, however, were meant to fight. Manchester was so small that it did not have a say in who went; the militia committee of its neighboring town, Beverly, decided the fate of Manchester's militiamen. And stagnating and contracting Wenham was able to protect its married citizens but only by shipping off single men from the breadth of the town's socioeconomic scale. The details of how the committees chose who would serve (or not) offers an important glimpse into the workings of interdependent militia systems in small communities. This examination of the smaller towns with few recruitment choices, and even fewer choices of "undesirable" men (who were simply were not present in measurable numbers in the smallest of towns), offers important clues as to the nature of recruitment in certain parts of the society. While impressment in the large or prosperous towns was not at all representative of the community as a whole, the impressment pools of the small towns were much more representative of their societies. In many ways, this is because the populace in these small communities was so homogenous compared to the more diverse larger towns. They did not have large numbers of young men with problems in the community like the larger towns did. Thus, for the very small towns of Essex County, military service was a burden shared relatively equally across society. As important as this finding is, however, it does *not* mean that an equal burden of military service across society was the norm. In reality, the minuscule number of men that these small towns contributed to Essex County's war effort meant that for the county as a whole, the incidence of truly representational impressment was negligible. That point becomes abundantly clear when taking a detailed look at impressment for the entirety of Essex County.

5

The Pressed Men of Essex County

The Social Identity of the Soldiers of King Philip's War

Many documents from the period of King Philip's War and countless sources after—town histories, genealogies, community records, and other sources—claim to record the men who served in King Philip's War. Yet, scores of the men so listed were never on the front lines; some received payment for services or provisions they supplied, while others were compensated for some now unknown reason. These men were not soldiers. Even leaving these noncombatants aside, from July 1675 to September 1676, well over a thousand men from Massachusetts Bay were soldiers. They served in active-duty militia companies, fighting in the most important and deadly conflict of colonial New England's history. Of those men, 357 came from Essex County and served in infantry companies, cavalry troops, or garrisons.[1] As we have seen, a uniquely New England military command structure, the committee of militia, had selected them from the pool of available men in their town. The committees were as important to the smooth operation of a town's militia as selectmen were to town governments. This was especially true during wartime, when the militia committees took over most functions of town governance. The most important power of the militia committees was the right to choose which citizens of their towns would be sent to war. This was a matter for local communities, not the governor or the General Court in Boston or even the county's own major general. For individuals, their families, and their towns, the town committees of militia held in their hands the power of life and death.

Each town militia committee had different criteria for choosing soldiers, and the soldiers from each town could differ considerably from their fellows from other towns. As has been seen, Andover sent a specific subset of its leading sons to fight, while Rowley and Topsfield chose town outsiders, Ipswich "undesirables," and Marblehead strangers. Yet, despite the "persistent localism" of Massachusetts Bay's impressment system and the diversity of the men whom it picked, certain common characteristics did exist among the soldiery. Most active-duty soldiers of King Philip's War were in their mid-twenties when the war began, unmarried, and childless. These facts are not surprising. A fourth common characteristic is surprising, however, given the conventional wisdom in the history of colonial war and society. The soldiers of seventeenth-century New England were not a straightforward cross section of their communities. They were not simply "those inhabitants who at that moment had guns in their hands."[2] Instead, the men were *chosen*, and chosen for particular reasons.

Age, Marriage, and Family as Factors in Impressment

While the New England militia is perhaps best known for its inclusion of every male in the colony between the ages of sixteen to sixty, actual wartime service was understandably quite different. For instance, the men sent out during wartime did not represent this age range. Out of the 357 active-duty men from Essex County, the ages of 191 (54 percent) are known (see appendix 4).[3] Of the men whose age is available, on average the committees chose men in their mid-twenties to fight the war (see table 8). The mean age was 26.6 years. More than 70 percent of the army was made up of men under thirty years old and 93 percent were under forty. The vast majority of the men who fought as enlisted men, 76 percent, were either in their twenties or thirties when enlisted. The next largest age group was men between sixteen and nineteen years old. Clearly, the active-duty forces of the county did not constitute a cross section of men from sixteen to sixty (the age range for men in the general militia). This is just one piece of evidence that proves that universal military obligation to serve in the militia was not the same thing as service in an active-duty, pressed expeditionary company. Understandably, the average ages of noncommissioned officers and officers were quite different. The twelve officers commissioned out of Essex County to lead wartime companies were forty-six years old on average, with an age range from thirty to sixty-five years old. Noncommissioned officers were younger, but on average still older than enlisted men; the average age of the twelve known sergeants and corporals was thirty, with an age range of nineteen to fifty-two years old.

    There are many reasons why most soldiers were levied when in their twenties. As seen in the descriptions of recruiting in the individual towns,

TABLE 8
Overview of Soldiers' Ages

Age Group	Men	Percentage of Soldiers	Cumulative Percentage
16–19	32	17%	17%
20–29	102	53%	70%
30–39	44	23%	93%
40–49	9	5%	98%
50–52	4	2%	100%
Overall	191	100%	

men in their early to mid-twenties were fully grown but not yet wholly self-sufficient. At around the age of twenty-one, men were considered semiautonomous adults both politically and legally. Even this measure of age, however, is not concrete. Historian John Demos claims that "twenty-one would in any case represent only a minimum."[4] Other historians argue that it was between the ages of twenty-two and twenty-six that men acquired greater political and legal control over their lives.[5] Even if the young men were of legal age, they were not yet independent, especially socially or economically. Most lacked the one thing that they needed to reach true independence, marry, and start their own families: clear title to farmland. Usually their fathers held that land and continued to need the labor of their sons for the economic good of the whole family.[6] Often, fathers did not allow sons to independently obtain land and livestock until they reached their late twenties or early thirties.[7] The ten or more years of labor that a son offered between his sixteenth birthday and the day he married in his late twenties were crucial to the well-being of the family: "The families that had sons to work their fields . . . were the wealthiest households" in colonial New England.[8]

As was demonstrated in the specific case of Andover, this situation left most men in their mid-twenties in limbo. Physically and legally they were grown men, but they were often forced to remain on the family farm in the role of son (and laborer) even though they were ready to become husbands and fathers in their own right. It is no wonder that a small number of these semi-dependent sons volunteered for military service, if just to get away for awhile. It is even less surprising that the local militia committees impressed them—they were the obvious choice. Their years certified that they were legally of age for service and most had the physical ability necessary for soldiering. More importantly, few of these young men were the head of a household yet. If they were lost in the war, it would be a

TABLE 9
Soldiers' Ages by Town

Town	Average Age	Men	16–19	20–29	30–39	40–49	50–52
Andover	23.8	9		8	1		
Beverly	28.7	12	3	4	4		1
Gloucester	21.7	9	3	6			
Ipswich	26.9	46	6	25	12	3	
Lynn	27.8	23	6	7	8	2	
Manchester	20.0	1		1			
Marblehead	32.5	4		2	1		1
Newbury	22.4	29	2	25	1	1	
Rowley	26.1	15	5	7	2		1
Salem	31.9	30	5	10	13	1	1
Topsfield	31.0	7		4	2	1	
Wenham	24.2	6	2	3		1	
Overall	26.6	191	32	102	44	9	4

blow to their birth families; their deaths, however, would not leave a wife and children behind to be cared for by the community.

When the age of soldiers is examined town by town, other noteworthy considerations come to light. Most of the towns had age ranges that are close to the county averages, with a few exceptions (see table 9). Marblehead appears to have recruited relatively older soldiers than the rest of the county, but that is a function of the small sample size; Marblehead levied a large percentage of men who were most likely transient fishermen without a clear link to the town and few records, including age data. The town of Salem, however, does appear to have recruited slightly older men on average than the rest of the communities.

It is the only town in the entire county to recruit more men in their thirties than in their twenties, although the difference is small. This result could simply be a statistical anomaly, but it is worth noting that Salem had been the first town founded in Essex County and as such was slightly further along in the transition between the first and second generations than the county's other towns. Forced to levy large numbers of men for the war in 1675, Salem may have had to dip into an older age group because its second-generation sons were simply older than the same group in the younger towns of the county.

It is also worthwhile to examine the issue of age in relationship to the unit in which the men served (see table 10). This data reveals the point in the war when they were recruited, which might have had an effect on who was impressed. Essex County supplied men for a large number of units during the war, but four combat companies in particular received a large

TABLE 10
Soldiers' Ages by Company or Unit

Unit	Dates of Service	Men	16–19	20–29	30–39	40–49	50–52
Appleton	Aug. 1675–Jan. 1676	60	5(8%)	39(65%)	9(13%)	3(5%)	1(2%)
Lathrop	Aug. 1675–Sept. 1675	40	7(18%)	23(58%)	7(18%)		3(6%)
Gardner	Nov. 1675–Feb. 1676	46	7(15%)	24(52%)	19(30%)	1(2%)	
Brockle-bank	Jan. 1676–Apr. 1676	18	3(17%)	10(56%)	4(22%)	1(6%)	
Multiple Billets	War 1675–1676	23	2 (9%)	17(74%)	4(17%)		
Troopers	War 1675–1676	18		7(44%)	6(38%)	2(13%)	1(6%)

percentage of Essex men. Captain Samuel Appleton (later Major Appleton) commanded troops from the early days of the war in Massachusetts until January of 1676. His men took part in the defense of the western frontier, the attack on the Narragansetts at the Great Swamp Fight, and the Hungry March. Captain Thomas Lathrop was also active early in the war, until he and most of his men fell at Bloody Brook in September 1675. Captain Joseph Gardner's unit was raised specifically for the Great Swamp Fight, while Captain Samuel Brocklebank's command was raised to relieve the army after the Hungry March. In addition, a number of men served in multiple billets or as troopers during the war.

There does not appear to be any age pattern to the recruitment of men in the infantry companies, other than a very small increase of thirty-year olds in Captain Gardner's company. Gardner's company was raised, in large part, from men in his hometown of Salem, the only town to recruit a larger number of thirty-year-olds. It is important to note that among the cavalry troops, the age distribution was distorted. There is a much higher average age among the troopers, 32.4, than the enlisted men in general (26.6). This is to be expected. With stiff property and income requirements written into colony law for troopers, it is no surprise that the men would be older. Actually, it is surprising that the men were not older still. It appears likely that some peacetime troopers in their thirties and forties allowed or required their sons to take their place when the cavalry was called up for active service during the conflict, in order to spare the older men arduous war service. Unlike the infantry companies, whole sections of established troops seem to have been called up for service together during the conflict. Because the cavalry units were often organized at the county level and not by towns, this did not pose a problem for home defense. In addition, because there were relatively few troopers, compared to scores of men who could be called on as infantry, assembling composite companies of cavalry from the whole would have been quite difficult.

It is apparent that some militia committees took birth order into consideration when making their impressment decisions. The order that males were born in a family had large implications for New England society. Colonial New England was a healthy place, especially when compared to England or the Chesapeake colonies.[9] Large families were the norm. In his study of families in colonial Andover, Philip Greven discovered that on average, first-generation families had 8.3 children, with 7.2 children surviving until the age of twenty-one.[10] Of first-generation families, one quarter had one to six children, while a startling 75 percent had seven to thirteen children.[11] This meant that each family had a considerable number of children to care for and set up as independent adults. For sons, this usually meant providing land, and land was usually formally transferred through inheritance.

Both law and family custom ruled inheritance. New Englanders of the colonial period did not practice a strict form of primogeniture—the leaving of the entire family estate to the eldest son in order to maintain the overall economic status of the family. Nor did the colonists follow ultimogeniture (the practice of leaving everything to the youngest son), nor strict partible inheritance, which split the family's assets equally when the father died. Instead, most families practiced a modified form of primogeniture. The biggest portion of the estate, a "double portion," went to the eldest son, usually including the family's main house, barns, and prime fields. Younger sons received outlying parcels of land and livestock to establish them economically. Very often, the widowed mother and the eldest son would receive the double portion together and the first son was expected to care for her until her death. In a few cases, the double portion (and care of the mother) fell to the youngest son in the family, a modified form of ultimogeniture. This inheritance system kept the family's main estate intact, under the control of the eldest son; with luck it maintained at least one branch of the family on the same economic level that the family had worked so hard to obtain.[12] This made first sons crucial to the survival of their family's social and economic status, making it less likely that

TABLE 11
Soldiers' Birth Order by Town

Town	Men Known	First Sons	Other Sons	Men Unknown
Andover	10	3 (30%)	7 (70%)	4
Beverly	10	4 (40%)	6 (60%)	12
Gloucester	6	3 (50%)	3 (50%)	9
Ipswich	46	22 (48%)	24 (52%)	41
Lynn	15	8 (53%)	7 (47%)	29
Manchester	1		1 (100%)	1
Marblehead	0			21
Newbury	22	4 (18%)	18 (81%)	17
Rowley	10	4 (40%)	6 (60%)	6
Salem	16	8 (50%)	8 (50%)	60
Topsfield	2	2 (100%)		7
Wenham	3	1 (33%)	2 (66%)	6
Overall	141	59 (41%)	82 (59%)	216

they would be chosen by militia committees for impressment, as the committees uniformly gave priority to social concerns over military ones.

Of the 357 active-duty soldiers of Essex County, birth-order data is available for 141 (39 percent).[13] Of those known, 82 men (59 percent) were not the first sons in their families, while 59 men (41 percent) were. While there is little question that a clear majority of the men impressed were not the vital first sons of their families, in all likelihood the percentage of non–first sons is considerably higher. Clerks almost always reported the birth-order status of first sons, while status as a subsequent son was much less likely to be noted. For instance, in probate records, the identity of the first son is consistently clear in wills and any documents granting executor status, while it was much rarer to label younger sons. Taking this underreporting into consideration, it is almost certain that a substantial majority of the men pressed for service during King Philip's War were not first sons; the committees of militia protected these men from the press.

The protection that the committees offered first sons is also clear in the town-by-town breakdown of the data (see table 11). Even with incomplete data, it is plain that six out of the eleven towns with birth-order data sent fewer first sons to war than subsequent males, with only two of the towns sending an equal number of first and successive sons to battle. Only Lynn sent more first sons to war, and only by one man.[14] Given the underreporting of later sons in the records, however, the percentages in the towns are likely higher than displayed here. Clearly, birth order was a factor in local impressment.

As mentioned, one of the main reasons that militia committees chose men in their mid-twenties for service was the unlikelihood of their being head of a household. The information on the men's marriage status supports this claim. The men chosen to fight as enlisted soldiers from Essex County were predominately unmarried. Of the 357 men, only 77 (22 percent) had wives.[15] Of the married men, 23 (30 percent) had wed relatively recently (between 1670 and the start of the war in 1675). The militia committees tried their hardest to protect married men from the press, and of those whom they did levy, a sizeable percentage were relative newlyweds.

Historians of colonial New England point out that marriage and the family were crucial to the success of the entire society. Once a couple was married, they were considered a family, even before any children arrived. And a marriage and the family was, according to social historian John Demos, "absolutely [the] central institution throughout the whole history" of the colonial period.[16] At the heart of all families stood a marriage. Puritan marriages were in many ways partnerships; they were not, however, equal partnerships. Husbands were the undeniable masters of their households. Yet, as historian Laurel Thatcher Ulrich argues, "the Christian ideal required more. . . . The subjection of wife to husband was never to be confused with the subjection of child to parent or of servant to master."[17] Puritan marriage was a godly partnership.[18] Women had a right to be consulted on important family matters and on any question involving a child, and wives had equal authority to the husband.[19] A wife could, if her husband was away for an extended period, even act as a "deputy husband."[20] Despite this, women who took marriage vows were "solemnly" dependent on their husbands.[21] Husbands were the heart of their marriages and the militia committees of Massachusetts were very reluctant to press them away for dangerous wartime service.

In the role of master of the house, husbands had an exclusive obligation; they had to provide for their wife and family. Gender historian Lisa Wilson contends, "A man felt a unique obligation to support his family. This was society's expectation as well; providing was a husband's legal responsibility, his sacred duty, and his unique burden. He provided what was 'needful' according to his resources."[22] The responsibility of a husband did not even end with death. A husband was responsible to provide for his children and wife even after his demise—the only time that he escaped his duty was when his children came of age and his wife died or remarried.[23] With such a large economic burden placed on husbands and the fact that the community would have to step in to support the family if

TABLE 12
Soldiers' Marriage Status by Town

Town	Number of Married Men Pressed	Percent of Total Men Married	Number of All Pressed Men	Percent of Total Men in Service for County	Difference Percent Married and Percent in Service
Andover	0	n/a	14	4%	-4%
Beverly	5	6%	20	6%	0
Gloucester	1	1%	16	4%	-3%
Ipswich	23	30%	88	25%	+5%
Lynn	13	17%	42	12%	+5%
Manchester	1	1%	5	1%	0
Marblehead	2	3%	20	6%	-3%
Newbury	1	1%	41	11%	-10%
Rowley	5	6%	25	7%	-1%
Salem	24	31%	70	20%	+11%
Topsfield	1	1%	7	2%	-1%
Wenham	1	1%	9	3%	-2%
Overall	77	22%	357	100%	n/a

he failed in his duty, it is understandable why militia committees did their utmost to avoid placing married men into active-duty war units.

Some towns enlisted more married men than others (see table 12). This was undeniably the case in the large towns of Salem (31 percent) and Ipswich (30 percent), and to a lesser degree the medium-sized but thriving Lynn (17 percent). These towns, especially Salem and Ipswich, were large commercial and market centers. Salem and Ipswich were also less economically dominated by agriculture than the small towns in the county, perhaps making the impressment of married men easier. This view is supported by the fact that the towns that impressed the fewest married men (Andover, Gloucester, Newbury, Rowley, Topsfield, and Wenham) were smaller and had economic fortunes more closely linked to farming. The detailed investigation of Ipswich proved that the committee had things other than marital status on its collective mind when it undertook recruiting. It is quite possible this was the case in Salem and Lynn as well.

A few of the towns deserve special consideration. Andover, the most agricultural town in the study, did not send a single married man to war; it was the only town with such a record. Heads of households were evidently too important in the small farming community to endanger in war.

A similar attitude might have influenced Newbury's militia committee, which sent the smallest percentage of married men to fight in comparison to its total soldier population. The fishing village of Marblehead also sent a very small percentage of married men to fight. Marblehead was a special case; after its horrific loss of townsmen in Lathrop's command, the town selected almost all of its soldiers from among its large population of transient fishermen, men with no permanent connection to the town (and who certainly were not married).

An analysis of married men among the different Essex companies, thus recruited at different phases of the war, shows an important pattern (see table 13). As the war went on and the need for men grew, the militia committees were forced to levy more married men as a percentage of combat forces. For example, married men made up only 11 percent of Appleton's company recruited in the fall of 1675, yet they constituted 22 percent of Brocklebank's force, recruited in January 1676. In the first two major companies raised in the county in August 1675 (Appleton's and Lathrop's commands), married men made up only 11 percent of the total manpower in each unit. As early as December, when Gardner's company formed, the committees had to levy more married men (21 percent). Given the great reluctance of the committees of militia to press married men, this relatively early rise in their percentage is proof of the difficulties that the colony was having recruiting soldiers. It was in September 1675, after news of the massacre at Bloody Brook became known, that Secretary Edward Rawson of the General Court wrote to Major John Pynchon (the commander of the western theater) complaining of the large numbers of men that made to "escape away from the press . . . [while] others [that were already pressed] hide away."[24] The colony's leadership warned that they would have to fill their quotas no matter what—it appears that they followed through on their threat by pressing more married men. As the war dragged on and casualties grew, the colony's military leadership was less able to protect them from active service.

It is worth noting, however, that only 12 percent of garrison troops were married; apparently the militia committees wanted to protect husbands from long-term duties that would increase the strain on families at home. Cavalry troopers, whose members came from the more affluent segment of colonial society (and were usually older), included a larger percentage of married men (45 percent). This was not, however, as much of a hardship; most troopers did not stay away from home as long as infantrymen, because they were often engaged in local scouting. A relatively

TABLE 13
Soldiers' Marriage Status by Company or Unit

Company or Unit	Dates of Service	Number of Married Men/Total Men	Percent of Force Married
Appleton	Aug. 1675–Jan. 1676	11/96	11%
Lathrop	Aug. 1675–Sept. 1675	11/68	16%
Gardner	Nov. 1675–Feb. 1676	23/108	21%
Brocklebank	Jan. 1676–Apr. 1676	7/31	22%
Garrisons	War, 1675–1676	5/39	12%
Troopers	War, 1675–1676	15/33	45%

large proportion of the men pressed who had been wed five years or more were part of this group.

If the committees of militia impressed relatively few husbands, they drafted even fewer fathers. Of the 357 enlisted soldiers from Essex County, only 48 (13 percent) were fathers at the time that they were impressed. Even more than men who just had wives, fathers had a special responsibility to provide for their families. Beyond their role as providers—a role that they would have had even if they had no children—fathers had a set of special responsibilities. In colonial New England, fathers were plagued with a great anxiety about their offspring's physical and spiritual well-being. Fathers "allayed their anxieties with scrupulous attention to the upbringing of their offspring. A careful monitoring of a child's growth, education, and religious training marked their love."[25] Fathers had close contact with their children because of the large amount of time that they spent at home.[26] Using the example of God as the ultimate parent, Puritan fathers raised their children with both authority and love. They took an active role in the education of their children, especially once a child moved beyond infancy: "At this point, a father began to parent in a way that distinguished him from his wife. Of course, women trained their daughters for their adult roles and fathers focused on their sons, but their parenting techniques also diverged. Men concentrated their energies on teaching their children the secular and religious truths that would direct them toward adulthood . . . They provided their children with the tools for a productive adulthood and for eternal life."[27] Fathers began instruction on the rules for proper behavior and moved on to more formal education and spiritual instruction. The militia committees respected this

TABLE 14
Soldiers' Family Status by Town

Town	Number of Fathers	Percent of Total Fathers	Number of Men in Service	Percent of Total Men in Service for County	Difference in Percent Fathers and Percent in Service
Andover	0	n/a	14	4%	-4%
Beverly	4	8%	20	6%	+2%
Gloucester	0	n/a	16	4%	-4%
Ipswich	14	29%	88	25%	+4%
Lynn	10	21%	42	12%	+9%
Manchester	1	2%	5	1%	+1%
Marblehead	1	2%	20	6%	-4%
Newbury	1	2%	41	11%	-9%
Rowley	3	6%	25	7%	-1%
Salem	12	25%	70	20%	+5%
Topsfield	1	2%	7	2%	0
Wenham	1	2%	9	3%	-1%

unique role and, worrying about the children who might have to grow up without fathers, strictly limited the number that they impressed.

In addition to formal education for all of the children, fathers had a duty to teach their sons the ways of the working world. This was vital, not only to the eventual survival of the son, but to the well-being of the whole family, which would come to rely on the young man's labor. When a boy was old enough to accompany his father to the fields, he was given small farming tasks as a type of vocational education.[28] These tasks also socialized the boy and "began the process of integrating him into the male world outside the house. A nine- or ten-year old boy who was trusted by his father to carry messages to his neighboring farmers or to drive the family's wagon into town would have been brought more and more into contact with adult men and the male world outside his home."[29] As boys became young men, they were given more and harder jobs to do.[30] Without a father to teach the sons, a family was in real trouble, as was, in effect, the larger society given the central place of the family in New England culture. Knowing this, the great reluctance on the part of the militia committees to recruit fathers is easily understood.

Looking at the small number of men pressed who did have children in relation to their towns offers support for this argument (see table 14). Two Essex County towns, Andover (which had not pressed any married men) and Gloucester, sent no fathers to the front lines at all. A number of towns—Wenham, Topsfield, Manchester, Newbury, and Marblehead— all smaller communities, sent only a single father to fight. Each of these towns was agricultural (except Marblehead) and the thought of losing many fathers to the war was simply too horrible for the militia commit- tees to contemplate. Only the relatively large towns of Beverly, Ipswich, Lynn, and Salem sent more than their share of fathers to serve. A few of these towns had thriving markets and a sizeable number of trades- men, perhaps making the recruitment of fathers more tenable. Much like their attitude toward sending husbands to fight, the smaller, more settled towns fiercely protected their fathers and household patriarchs, while the larger towns sent more of them off to war.[31] Overall, the protection of hus- bands and fathers demonstrates the pivotal role that these men played in their families. Husbands and fathers were "prince and teacher, pastor and judge" in their homes.[32] Militia committees, anxious to preserve the stabil- ity and economic well-being of Bay Colony families during the calamity of King Philip's War, went to great lengths to protect husbands and fathers from the press, and to limit their length of service if they were called. In a related concern for family stability, many militia committees tried to limit the number of eldest sons that they impressed. Age, birth order, and marital and family status all played an important part in the recruitment decisions of Massachusetts Bay's committees of militia when it came time to press men for active service. Other factors, however, mattered as well.

Religious, Civic, and Occupational Factors in Impressment

A young man's place in economic or religious or civic society could influ- ence his chances of going to war, depending on the community in ques- tion. This can best be seen in a through examination of the men in their respective communities. Massachusetts Bay was founded in 1629 by a group of English Puritans who planned to build a godly community with- out interference from the crown. In the famous words of John Winthrop, the first governor of the colony and the leader of the Great Migration, they would build a "City on a Hill" in order to "to improve our lives to doe more service to the Lord."[33] While a few historians have claimed that the Great Migration and founding of New England was mainly motivated by economic factors, most agree that it was primarily a religious move- ment.[34] Virginia Anderson, a historian of the founding of New England, argues that even if not all the people who moved to Massachusetts Bay were Puritans, "prospective emigrants could hardly have been unaware of the peculiar religious character of New England society. Accounts of the region's commitments to Puritanism were simply too numerous to be overlooked . . . People willing to move to Massachusetts then, tacitly, agreed to become members of the Puritan commonwealth, even if they did not quite agree on what that meant. . . . This shared commitment to Puritan principles, however vaguely defined, became the common thread that switched individual emigrants together into a larger social and cultural fabric."[35] By the time of King Philip's War, the Bible Commonwealth was well and truly established.[36]

All was not well, however, in the Bay Colony's churches in the 1670s. Church members were key to the strength and vitality of Puritan congregations. New Englanders had instituted a "purity test" to ensure that only true Puritan "saints," those with a clear connection to the universal church (as established by God's predestination), were admitted.[37] Thus, before they allowed full membership in a church, people had to offer evidence of their "election" or saving grace to their congregation in the form of a "testimony" or statement.[38] Church membership was vital in New England society; not only did it confer religious status (being one of God's elect) but it conferred social, political, and legal status as well. Men could not take the freeman's oath unless they were members of an established Puritan church; legally, without freeman status men were not allowed to vote in civil, church, or even military elections.[39] This was not much of a problem in the early days of the colony, when a very high percentage (upward of 75 to 80 percent) of adults were full church members.[40] By the late 1660s, however, the ranks of church members were dwindling. Many first-generation settlers were passing away and the young adults of the second generation were not feeling the saving grace of God and advancing to full church membership in the numbers or with the rapidity that their parents expected.[41] Some ministers claimed that this decline in religiosity was one of the most important reasons that God allowed the Indians to strike at his chosen people and their new Bible Commonwealth in 1675.

Social historian Gerald Moran's definitive study of church membership patterns shows that the percentage of full church members dropped from a high of 78 percent in 1643 to around 47 percent in 1678, just three years after King Philip's War.[42] In addition, more women than men were joining the church. It would be understandable then that the number of men who were full church members recruited into active-duty companies would be well short of the high percentages seen in the first generation of Massachusetts settlers. Yet, the number is startling low. Of the 357 enlisted men in the study, only 50 (14 percent) were listed as full church members before the war, either by a direct reference to their admission to a church (18 men) or their prewar freeman status (32 men), which was directly dependent on church membership. The records of the various Essex County churches vary in their completeness (especially for the seventeenth century), which could account for this low percentage. Freeman status was quite well recorded, however, as was the holding of any political office, which (as it was dependant on freeman status) is another measure of church membership.[43] Yet, even with the realization that the records on church membership are somewhat incomplete, there is a very large discrepancy between the 16 percent figure of Essex active-duty soldiers who were church members and the 47 percent rate of their presence in society at large.

It seems likely that some militia committees took church membership into account when choosing soldiers. It makes sense that if a militia committee, which was made up entirely of church members (militia officers and magistrates or deputies had to be freemen), was given a choice between two men, one a church member and one not, the nonmember would probably march off to war. This possibility is heightened by the fact that many saw the decline in religion and church membership as either a reason for or a sign of decline in the colony. In his 1676 "An Ernest Exhortation to the Inhabitants of New England," Increase Mather lamented that New England had fallen away from the godly path and that the war was their punishment (see figure 12): "God is never wont to forsake his People except they do first forsake him . . . Inasmuch then as God hath seemed to cast us out, and put us to shame, and hath refused to go forth with our *Armies*, he doth by his Providence testifie . . . that we hath forsaken him."[44] Mather went on to lay the blame squarely at the feet of the second generation:

Surely the times are perillious, and that which brings such times is, the *taking up a form of godliness without the power of it*; and is it not so with us, the *first Generation* which was in this Land, had much of the power of Godliness, but the present *Generation* hath the form, and as to the *body of the Generation*, but little of the power of *Religion*. Alas in our Churches, we have a form of Discipline, but little of the power of it . . . in which respect we have no cause to wonder that sad tydings hath come to us.[45]

Who better to send off to fight than the men of the second generation who had "little of the power of *Religion*"?

Figure 12. Increase Mather (1639–1723), one of the most powerful religious leaders in Massachusetts Bay, was the author of "An Earnest Exhortation to the Inhabitants of New England." Mather argued that the sins of New Englanders were largely responsible for the outbreak of King Philip's War and demanded a renewed effort toward godliness on the part of the colonists. His call for a spiritual renewal and the punishment of sin greatly influenced the impressment decisions of the colony's militia committees. *Increase Mather.* Oil on canvas by John van der Spriett, 1688. Courtesy of the Massachusetts Historical Society.

While it seems likely that church membership played a part in impressment, there is also a level of happenstance with this motive. Almost all members of the second generation were late in gaining church membership compared to their parents. Young and unmarried men were the least likely prospects for early church membership by the 1670s, at the same time that they were in many ways the perfect soldiers in the minds of the militia committees.[46] These two facts make it likely that the lack of full church membership was not a major determining factor in most impressment decisions. However, militia committee members, when given the choice of men with otherwise similar profiles, would most likely press a non–church member to go to war if it meant that a Puritan saint could stay home.

Political office was linked to church membership through freeman status. Service to the community was a very important part of good citizenship in colonial New England. With their deep commitment to local control of their daily lives and governance, the "persistent localism" that was so important to military affairs was, if possible, even stronger in town governance.[47] To ensure that power stayed local, public service "volunteerism quickly became the hallmark of Massachusetts society."[48] Whether it was widespread among the population (as in Rowley) or narrowly defined and controlled by town elites (as in Ipswich), civic service was crucial to a man's status in his town. For this study, political offices were classified into three categories: selectmen, lower town officials, and freemen. In total, 32 men out of the 357 impressed (9 percent) served in a political office or were freemen eligible to do so.[49] Only 22 men (6 percent) had actively held a local government post.

Selectmen were the highest officials in local government.[50] While there might be more powerful officials living in a town, such as a magistrate (also known as an assistant, because they sat on the Court of Assistants) or the town's deputy (representative) to the colony's General Court, they had no power in the daily running of the community (unless they happened to hold multiple offices, which was not uncommon).[51] Of the men impressed from Essex County, eight were or had been selectmen. Depending on the town, selectmen could either wield considerable power by formulating the town's policies or simply act as caretakers of the town's wishes as they were expressed in town meetings. The duties of selectmen included supervising town boundaries, overseeing education, controlling servants, maintaining public works (streets, meetinghouse, and common lands) by pressing citizens to labor on them every year, regulating timber cutting, overseeing town meetings, and overseeing the distribution of town lands.[52] As the legal representatives of the town, they also conducted any lawsuits necessary and often determined the number of families allowed to settle in the town and which should be granted that privilege.[53] Selectmen were quite powerful men, depending on the community, and the fact that so few were impressed is no surprise.[54]

To assist the selectmen, towns appointed one or more constables. If the selectmen were the heart and mind of town government, constables were the arms. They had a wide variety of duties, including, as has been seen, carrying out impressment orders in time of war. Their peacetime duties were almost as important. They were so important to the functioning of the towns that their duties were the first ever enumerated by the General Court.[55] They collected taxes (rates), kept the peace and arrested criminals (sometimes with the assistance of a town marshal), "warned out" interlopers, oversaw the town ward, called citizens to meeting, appointed special juries to investigate unexpected deaths, and handled myriad other important town functions. There were other, lesser town office holders as well, including tithingmen (to oversee behavior during church services), fence viewers, poundkeepers, surveyors of highways, sealers of leather, hogreeves, town herdsmen, wharfmasters, town clerks, and several others, depending on the town.[56] Of the 357 men impressed from the county, only 14 held or had held one or more of these inferior offices. Much like church membership, it is doubtful that serving in a political office was the main (or only) reason that a man might be passed over for military service, but it is possible that such service in the past would have given the man the benefit of the doubt with the militia committee, had other factors been equal.

While the colony of Massachusetts Bay was primarily founded as a religious settlement, the founders did not eschew profit making. The "Puritan Way," however, demanded they not make too much of a profit or care too deeply about it. Most New Englanders strove for "competency" in their economic lives. Those who possessed a competency had, according to Virginia Anderson, "a sufficiency, although not an abundance, of this world's goods."[57] This allowed for a certain level of self-determination. In New England, this took on a special, spiritual meaning. Puritans in Massachusetts Bay strove for enough economic wealth "to support their families, to follow the bidding of their consciences, and to contribute to the maintenance of their new communities. A modest prosperity would reinforce spiritual integrity."[58] Thus economic activity was spiritual activity.

Economic opportunity in Essex County was centered, from the time of settlement to a period well after 1675, on two main types of production. With the exception of Salem, which as early as the seventeenth century was enmeshed in the world of Atlantic trade, the towns of the county were focused primarily on farming and fishing.[59] While a large proportion (two to one) of the men who left England during the Great Migration had been artisans or tradesmen, when they reached New England they became

TABLE 15
Soldiers' Occupations by Category

Occupation Category	Number and Percentage of Men with Known Occupations[1]
Agriculture	64 (41%)
Crafts/Trades	52 (33%)
Maritime Trades	25 (16%)
Mercantile	11 (7%)
Servant	22 (14%)

1. Percentages are based on number of men with a known occupation.

farmers.[60] They practiced subsistence farming, growing the food that their family needed to live, and a bit more that they could sell in the marketplace in order to buy those things that they could not make themselves. Some continued to practice their trades, in addition to working their farms, to make extra money as long as the trade did not require a large capital investment in tools or supplies. Most men, however, abandoned their trades, finding "little time for anything other than clearing, improving, and working the land."[61] By the time that the second generation came along, the vast majority of men in most Essex County towns were farmers.

Thus, one would expect the vast majority of men impressed into the army during King Philip's War to have been farmers. But the record does not support that argument. The occupation (or occupations) of 157 men out of the total 357 soldiers can be established (44 percent).[62] Because several of the men had two or more listed occupations, a total of 174 distinct occupation listings were actually recorded (see appendix 5).[63] Out of the 157 men with identified occupations, only 64 were listed as working in agriculture, either as a husbandman, yeoman, farmer, farm laborer, or shepherd (see table 15). This accounts for a mere 41 percent of the men with known occupations. Some even had a nonagricultural job in addition to their farming duties.[64] This is a truly startling finding. All evidence suggests that a sizeable majority of men in colonial New England were primarily engaged in agriculture, yet less than half of all the levied men (with known occupations) were so engaged. As most were not farmers, the remainder of the pressed men must have had another occupation.

An unexpected 52 men (33 percent) were listed as some sort of artisan, craftsman, or tradesman.[65] A small number of these men were also listed with more than one occupation, often agricultural in nature. The next largest group of men was those working in the maritime trades as fishermen, mariners or sailors, and shoremen.[66] Twenty-five men (16 percent) performed these duties for a living. The next largest group of men was servants—22 men (14 percent) worked for someone else. The last group was made up of men who worked in some type of mercantile capacity, either as merchants, inn- or ordinary-keepers, or as trappers or traders. Just 11 men (7 percent) were in this category. While the diversity of occupations fits, in a way, Essex County's changing economy, it is still a distortion of the overall makeup of the county. The vast majority of men in the county were involved in farming. The fact that a simple majority of the men pressed for service in the county were not farmers is critical.

There are several reasons why militia committee members might not have sent farmers to the front. First, because most farms in New England, including those in Essex County, practiced subsistence agriculture, each farmer that the committee sent away to fight was one less man home feeding his family.[67] While wives and children might have been able to do the work of the patriarch and keep the family farm productive, if at all possible the militia committees did not want to take a chance that they could not. As proof of this concern, there are several recorded instances of pressed farmers informing military authorities that military service would endanger their ability to raise food for their family. Ipswich farmers Nathaniel Adams and Thomas Newman became anxious when they were ordered to transfer to garrison duty after their initial impressment period, as garrison duty could be long and laborious. The two men petitioned the General Court for release in order to get home in time to plant that year's crops.[68] Farmers were the lifeblood of the economy. More importantly, they were the key figures in Massachusetts's ability to feed itself. It was much safer for militia committees to press tradesmen, fishermen, or servants to go to war than to imperil farmers.

There was great concern over the colony's ability to produce enough food during the conflict. Massachusetts Bay lost a great deal of its farm production capacity early in the war. The farms in the Connecticut River Valley were some of the most productive in the colony, as can be seen by the fact that they produced corn for commercial export. When the enemy attacked towns like Deerfield and Northampton and they were either abandoned or destroyed in the fall of 1675, much of the colony's surplus food production went with them. Not only was the grain in storage and in the fields lost, but so too was much of the abundant livestock, a favorite target of the Indians.[69] One episode that illustrates the importance of food stocks in the valley is the Bloody Brook incident in September 1675. Captain Thomas Lathrop and his men were ordered to the already-abandoned Deerfield to convoy wagons full of the town's stockpiled corn back to Hadley for storage. The corn was badly needed to feed the growing number of people in the area, both refugees trying to flee the fighting and soldiers pouring into the region to fight. While escorting the valuable grain, a large force of Indians surprised and slaughtered Lathrop and his men.[70]

As the war dragged on, refugees streamed east from the valley towns (and later south from Maine), increasing the need for food, as did the growing number of men under arms. The last thing that militia committees wanted to do was take men away from their fields during a food crisis. More evidence that the colony was greatly concerned about plummeting food production appears in a series of laws passed in the colonial assembly. In October 1675, the General Court passed a law that prohibited food exports except for fish, "considering the great danger of a famine, or at least a scarsity of bread & other prouissons, by reason of the war."[71] The Court even appointed special representatives to inspect ships leaving the harbor and imposed stiff fines for smuggling. Connecticut enacted a similar ban and even enforced it against its ally Massachusetts Bay by refusing to ship corn to Massachusetts for a time, provoking a dispute that the Commissioners of the United Colonies ultimately had to settle.[72]

In November 1675, the Court ordered that "forasmuch as the preservation of the grajne, both Indian [corn] and English [wheat or oats], in this colony is of great necessity . . . It is ordered by this Court, that there be effectuall care forthwth taken by the seuerall militias and selectmen of the tounes for sercuing the sajd grajne . . . so that the ennemy may not be at pleasure to destroy it, or furnish themselues with it."[73] In addition to the general ban on exporting grain and the order to protect it, by the next spring the colony was very concerned about the effect that impressing farmers was having on food supplies. In May 1676, the Court approved a law that called on the selectmen of every town in Massachusetts "to impresse men for the management and carrying on of the husbandry of such persons as are calld . . . for service, who have not sufficjent help of their oune left at home to mannage the same."[74] Every militia committee member certainly felt the widespread worry over food. They probably did their best to limit the effect that impressment had on food production by drafting men unattached to agricultural occupations, like tradesmen and servants. Even fishermen would have been preferable to farmers, because by the 1670s most fish caught by the fleets of the Bay Colony were exported to the West Indies, not consumed locally.[75] The reluctance of militia committees to levy farmers, in light of the food situation during the war, is perhaps the best explanation of the relatively small numbers of such men pressed.

There are other possible reasons for the disparity. It is likely that many of the men whose occupations are not known (200 men, or 56 percent, of 357) were farmers. A large number of those men, however, were probably employed in the fishing trade as well, as the number of fishermen and mariners impressed (25, or 16 percent) also seems low. In Marblehead, for example, only six of the twenty men who served were listed as fishermen, yet it is likely that a sizeable majority (if not all) of the men impressed from the town were just that. The same is possible for the towns of Salem and Gloucester, which both had large fishing populations. Maybe both tradesmen and servants were more likely to have their occupation named because their occupations were not the norm, but that argument is countered in part by the fact that farmers show up in the numerous land records for the county, making them quite conspicuous in the historic record as well. Another factor to consider is that many of the twenty-two servants listed possibly worked in agriculture as farm laborers, although some of the servant listings were of men who were obviously apprentices to tradesmen. If the servants were added to the agriculture numbers, the percentages would shift. Despite these possibilities, the case for militia committees keeping farmers on the farm is strong.

When looking at the occupations of impressed men in relation to their towns, a number of significant factors come to light (see table 16). While agriculture was still the dominant type of production in every Essex County town in 1675 (with the possible exception of Salem), even the smaller towns did have some economic diversity. For quite a few towns, especially Gloucester, Lynn, Newbury, Rowley, Topsfield, and Wenham, however, the economic domination of agriculture is apparent in the recruitment record; the men whom they sent were predominantly farmers. On the other hand, Andover—the quintessential farming village—only sent one farmer off to war (of the men with known occupations). Despite the fact that Andover was not a market town and was somewhat isolated from the rest of the county, it sent four tradesmen and two merchants to fight. Apparently Lieutenant Osgood and the rest of the militia committee were extremely concerned with feeding their town.

The towns with the most diversified economies, Ipswich and Salem, also sent very low percentages of farmers to fight in the war. While both Ipswich and Salem were commercially diversified, had thriving markets, and a vibrant community of artisans and craftsmen, each also had a sizeable

TABLE 16
Soldiers' Occupations by Towns

Town	Known	Agriculture	Craftsmen	Maritime	Merchants	Servants
Andover	7	1(14%)	4(57%)	0	2(29%)	0
Beverly	10	4(40%)	1(10%)	4(40%	0	1(10%)
Gloucester	10	6(60%)	3(30%)	0	0	1(10%)
Ipswich	57	15(26%)	15(26%)	7(12%)	6(11%)	14(25%)
Lynn	15	7(47%)	5(33%)	2(13%)	0	1(7%)
Manchester	1	1(100%)	0	0	0	0
Marblehead	6	0	0	6(100%)	0	0
Newbury	12	7(58%)	3(25%)	0	0	2(17%)
Rowley	9	6(67%)	2(22%)	0	0	1(11%)
Salem	42	13(31%)	18(43%)	6(14%)	3(7%)	2(5%)
Topsfield	3	2(66%)	1(33%)	0	0	0
Wenham	2	2(100%)	0	0	0	0
Overall	174	64(37%)	52(30%)	25(14%)	11(6%)	22(13%)

hinterland for food production. In fact, Salem was the only town in the county that had enough arable land in production by the 1670s to export a substantial amount of grain before the war.[76] Both towns had large numbers of farmers in residence. Why were they not sent to fight? The answer could well be an even greater than normal concern for the community food supply. Salem and Ipswich, as large and thriving towns, both saw a great influx of refugees during the war. Quabaug, the town that Ipswich elites founded as a place to dispatch undesirable citizens before the war, was destroyed in the fighting. Refugees from the frontier community streamed into Ipswich with nothing but the clothes on their backs and hungry children to feed.[77] Salem was also inundated with families fleeing the destruction of the war. Because of its coastal location, numerous families escaping the fighting in Maine, as well as people from the Massachusetts backcountry, found their way to the town. Salem's leaders took such pity on many of these families that they allowed them to remain in town, assuring them the right to settle there for the duration of the war and possibly permanently.[78] With so many new mouths to feed and large populations of their own, the militia committees of Ipswich and Salem could ill afford to send away farmers. Yet, as was seen in the portrait of the town in chapter 3, something else was at work in the machinations of the Ipswich militia committee when it came to impressment. Perhaps the same was going on throughout the county.

Negative Societal Factors and Impressment

Massachusetts Bay's committees of militia attempted to limit the disruption that impressment caused to individual families when selecting men to fight in King Philip's War, in case the men failed to return. They kept the numbers of husbands and fathers levied low and pressed large numbers of men in their mid-twenties, because those men did not yet support families of their own. Men who had served in government or were church members were quite possibly kept to a minimum as well. Farmers—valued for their vital role producing food for a society in crisis—bore a lighter impressment burden than their tradesmen or mariner counterparts, particularly in relation to their number in the society. Thus, while the military law of the colony implied a universal military obligation for males between sixteen and sixty years of age, that obligation was anything but universal when war came to New England in 1675. Militia committees tried to protect families the best way that they knew how: by impressing those whom they could best afford to lose.

At the same time that they were protecting families, the committees of militia tried to limit hardship to the soldiers' towns. Much like Elizabethan lords lieutenant decades earlier and an ocean away, militia committees served two masters. The military good of the colony required pressing the best men as soldiers, while the towns worried about losing their best citizens. Town leaders preferred that less worthy men be sent to the wars. The towns would need their best citizens to survive the war if the colony had any hope of rebuilding the "City on a Hill." The militia committees asked the question, Who better to send into harm's way than those "undesirable" elements responsible for the war in the first place? Increase Mather himself claimed that in Puritan society "so many evils [were] visible and manifest" that "the Lord hath poured on thee the fury of his Anger and the Strength of Bettel [Battle], and he hath set thee on fire."[79] In order to protect society, either by keeping the worthy at home or forcing those with sin into the fire of "Bettel," the militia committees of Essex County pressed misfits as often as possible. In 1675 and 1676, Essex County's committees of militia were asked to send men to war time and time again. In all, they sent 357 men into battle in active-duty companies or as members of a garrison. Of those men, the town militia committees chose 261 (73 percent) with some black mark on their record (see table 17). As had happened in England in the days before the implementation of the "Perfect Militia" of Charles I, the locally controlled military recruitment

TABLE 17
Soldiers' Negative Impressment Factors by Town

Town	Men	Total with Negative Factor	Low Socioecon. Status	Crime	No Town Link	Town Issue	Debt	Multiple Factors
Andover	14	11 79%	5 36%	0	5 36%	5 36%	0	4 29%
Beverly	20	12 60%	4 20%	4 20%	3 15%	1 5%	1 5%	1 5%
Gloucester	16	10 62%	8 50%	1 6%	6 38%	0	0	4 25%
Ipswich	88	72 81%	60 68%	23 26%	4 5%	2 3%	4 5%	19 22%
Lynn	42	25 60%	14 33%	6 14%	0	7 17%	2 5%	4 10%
Manchester	5	5 100%	2 40%	1 20%	3 60%	1 20%	0	1 20%
Marblehead	20	17 85%	0	3 18%	14 82%	0	1 6%	1 6%
Newbury	41	27 66%	14 34%	4 10%	0	9 22%	0	0
Rowley	25	19 76%	3 12%	5 20%	13 52%	11 44%	0	12 48%
Salem	70	50 71%	34 49%	15 21%	6 9%	7 10%	2 3%	12 17%
Topsfield	7	5 71%	1 14%	3 43%	4 80%	0	0	5 71%
Wenham	9	8 89%	4 44%	1 11%	4 44%	3 33%	0	2 22%
Overall	357	261 73%	149 42%	67 19%	60 17%	49 14%	10 3%	64 18%

system of Massachusetts Bay chose to send the "rabble" of the county to war in order to keep most of the "flower" of the towns at home. Every single town's militia committee selected a majority of men who had some negative societal factor, either past or present. The number and proportion of such men differed town by town, as befit a system of local impressment. Even the town with the lowest percentage of such "undesirables" in its impressment pool, however, levied a clear majority of such men. Tiny Manchester, with a very small recruitment base and a dysfunctional militia system, picked *only* troublemaking men to fight; all five men sent had negative marks against them. Another small town, Wenham, had a very large percentage of soldiers with black marks on their records (89 percent) for the same reason. Marblehead's committee sent a large proportion of men with no connections to the community in an attempt to protect their own citizens from harm. Ipswich, the largest town in the county and one that had a history of trying to rid itself of troublemakers, also sent a large proportion of "undesirables" (81 percent).

In a system of local recruitment, each community (or the elite in the community) selects the factors that matter the most to it when levying soldiers. In the 1670s, this localism in military affairs meant that the type of men coming to the army from each town were different, if only slightly. Despite this individual approach to impressment, certain factors were common across the recruitment spectrum, especially negative factors. This study classifies negative societal factors into several broad categories, including low socioeconomic status, criminality, a slight or no connection to the home community, some type of noncriminal problem (often a political disagreement or being on the losing side in a town controversy), and, lastly, serious debt. The vast majority of Essex County men who fought in an active-duty company had one or more of these damaging factors associated with their name when they were impressed.

For the soldiers of Essex County, low socioeconomic status was the most common negative factor of the men sent to war. Forty-two percent of the levied men came from the lowest rungs of their community's socioeconomic ladder. Given that the best study of wealth in Essex County places only 25 percent of the population in that category, it is evident that in some towns socioeconomic status was a factor in impressment.[80] For this study, each pressed man was classified by economic status based on their, or their birth family's (if the men still lived at home), economic position in their hometown. Both economic records and political power were taken into account to reach these conclusions. As seen in chapter 3, the top of the classification scheme included elite families (who had considerable wealth or immense political power) and leading families (upper middling in wealth and with limited colony-wide and/or stronger local political power). Middling families (of average revenue and little political power) made up the vast majority of the families in the colony, according to economic historian Manfred Jonas, who found that in seventeenth-century Essex County, most families achieved "a comfortable level of prosperity [competency] . . . the average estate having a value of £409 with a median of slightly over £162."[81] Lastly, at the bottom of their communities' economic strata were subordinate families, those of indebtedness or limited income, with no political voice. The men from these families were often newcomers to their communities or drifters who moved from town to town. In Puritan New

England, with its broad and inclusive economic "middle way," members of subordinate families were truly outsiders in most towns.[82]

While being poor was not a sin and certainly not an automatic ticket to the front lines, some committees of militia considered it a valid reason to levy a young man. This seems particularly true in the large communities of Ipswich and Salem. Perhaps the militia committees in those wealthy commercial towns (whose elites had disproportional wealth compared to the rest of the citizenry) believed, along with Increase Mather, that the sins of the second generation lay somewhat at the feet of the poor. In his jeremiads, Mather often railed against the poor, in particular those who demanded high wages—"*Day-laborers* and *Mechanicks* are so unreasonable in their demands"—and those poor who were guilty of the sin of pride, especially in matters of apparel; as he said, "None [are] more guilty than the poorest sort of people."[83] It is also quite possible that the elite men of the militia committees in these large communities relied on socioeconomic status because the town's large populations precluded them from knowing the more mundane details of each citizen's life, such as occupation or family status. This is one likely reason that most soldiers from the lower strata of the socioeconomic pyramid came from the two large trading towns.

As seen in many of the town case studies in chapters 3 and 4, for most of the smaller Massachusetts towns socioeconomic status was not a deciding factor for the militia committees. This speaks directly to the power of local impressment. The large percentage of the economic "lower sort" recruited in the county overall was a direct result of the fact that Ipswich and Salem, whose committees did rely on that negative measure, recruited such large contingents of men (88 and 70 men, respectively), in effect skewing the data for the county as a whole. Of the men that Ipswich recruited, 60 were of low socioeconomic status, while Salem recruited 34. Together, these two towns were responsible for 122 out of the 149 men (82 percent) with low economic status pressed in the county. Most towns levied only modest numbers of subordinate men. For example, in Beverly only 20 percent of all the men recruited were from the "lower sort" while in Topsfield it was 14 percent and in Rowley only 12 percent. While the most common negative factor recorded for the county's soldiers was low socioeconomic status, the war was not just a poor man's fight. There were many other factors at work.

Criminality was an important consideration in most towns. In all, 19 percent of the county's soldiers had been punished for committing a criminal act, from assault and trespass to making "reproachful speeches." While this many not seem like a large percentage, it is unexpectedly high given the crime climate of Massachusetts Bay: "The first settlements were tight social networks that discouraged crime and most forms of deviant behavior. . . . Crimes were few in the early settlements, and those that did occur seldom possessed a threat to public safety."[84] The very nature of life in Puritan New England kept crime rates down; it was common and expected for townspeople to watch carefully and inform on each other. This informal but efficient policing kept crime rates very low during the reign of the first generation of settlers. Yet, as in so many things, the second generation in New England was not able to maintain the high standards that their parents had. By the 1670s, "neighbors were growing reluctant to meddle in the affairs of others unless the peace or safety of the community was directly threatened by antisocial behavior."[85] Thus, law and morality enforcement became increasingly a function of the government.[86] By the 1670s, the Quarterly Courts were hearing many more cases than in the early days of the settlement.

At the same time, the incidence of crime was rising in New England. More people neglected church meetings, and "respect for civil authority also declined and fights and brawls became more common."[87] Increase Mather lamented the rise of several crimes, in his pamphlet "An Earnest Exhortation," as one of the reasons that God was punishing New England by sending the "heathen" Indians against his chosen people. Mather specifically targeted excessive drinking:

> The Plenty [that God had given them] . . . hath been abused unto great Sensuality, and many Professors and Church-members have been shamefully guilty in that respect. How common hath it been with them to haunt Taverns, and squander away precious hours, nay dayes in publick houses . . . our Fathers were Patterns of Sobriety, they would not drink a cup of wine nor strong drink, more than should suffice nature . . . men of later times [the second generation] could transact no business, nor hardly ingage in any discourses, but it must be over a pint of wine or a pot of beer, yea so as that Drunkenness in the sight of man is become a common sin.[88]

Public drunkenness was also becoming a more common crime. But though criminal activity was on the rise, it "hardly amounted to a crime wave."[89]

Even by the 1670s, criminals made up an extremely low proportion of the population. The Essex County Quarterly Court ruled on only 257 cases from 1671 to 1674.[90] An account from 1675 on the population of New England claimed that there were 500 households in Salem, 50 in Marblehead, 50 at Cape Ann (Gloucester), 400 at Ipswich, and 300 at Newbury.[91] Without even accounting for most of the medium and small towns of the county (Andover, Beverly, Lynn, Manchester, Rowley, Topsfield, or Wenham), the figure of 1,300 households places the population of Essex County's large towns alone between 7,000 and 10,000 inhabitants.[92] The fact that over a four-year period, in a county of that size, only 257 criminal cases were prosecuted proves that crime was a rare occurrence indeed. Even if the lowest possible estimate of the county's population is employed (7,000), only 4 percent of the population committed a crime in the four years prior to the war. Yet, 19 percent of men impressed had a criminal record, proving that criminality was a major factor in the impressment decisions of most of the militia committees.

Some of the crimes committed by the pressed men were serious, although none rose to the capital level. In Massachusetts Bay, the Court of Assistants adjudicated such crimes. No Essex soldier committed a crime in that category; crimes of that nature were exceedingly rare in the colony.[93] However, some Essex men did have quite serious, noncapital crimes on their records and it most likely brought them to the attention of their local militia committee. John Chub of Ipswich was sentenced to be fined or whipped in 1669 for killing another man's horse, and he was brought in to court again in March 1673 for abusing and striking his servant on the Lord's Day.[94] Chub's crimes did not stop there. In May 1674, he was fined for "suspicion of chaining up the gate on the highway," and in April 1675, just a few months before he went to war, Chub was hauled into court for "excess in apparel beyond that of a man of his degree."[95] This last crime was serious in colonial Massachusetts and especially so in Ipswich. It was seen as a direct challenge to the hierarchy of the society and was often cited as a major sin. In fact, it was one of many sins responsible for the war, according to the General Court and Increase Mather.[96]

Another sin associated with God's punishing war was the disturbance of worship services. "There is too great a neglect of discipline in the churches" warned the General Court, while Mather stated it even more forcefully: "The body of the present Generation is guilty of *Sacremental perjury* in the sight of God."[97] Not only were children guilty of disturbing worship (and their parents guilty of not controlling the children), but some adults committed this crime as well. John Knowlton of Ipswich was presented in May 1674 for "being disorderly at meeting in time of public worship . . . [he and his friends] sometimes laughing, spitting in one anothers faces, pricking at each others legs, justing boys off their seats, heaving things up into the gallery among the girls who sit there, and breaking the glass windows."[98] "Sacremental perjury" indeed, and something that probably hastened his way into an infantry company just a year later. Richard Pasmore, a soldier pressed in Ipswich, was admonished in September 1673 for "carrying himself irrevently and unchristianly upon Sabbath day by talking, laughing, and whispering during service to smaller boys and setting a bad example."[99] These men exhibited blatant disrespect for the church, its ministers, and its elders—another sin, according to Mather, partly responsible for God's sending the Indians to punish New England.[100]

Disrespect for authority, religious or civil, was a serious crime in colonial New England. In November 1671, Ezekiel Sawyer, a soldier impressed into Lathrop's company, was fined for several misdemeanors committed while he and his friend, Thomas Spofford, were on the night watch in Rowley.[101] They ran a rope across Rowley's main street, causing a rider the next morning to be thrown from his horse. They also ran a cart into the river and placed another cart outside a family's door to trap them inside their home. The teenagers confessed and offered an apology to the Quarterly Court. While this series of pranks sounds harmless, the fact that they endangered the rider's life and exhibited profound disrespect to the importance of the town watch made the crimes severe in the eyes of the local magistrates. The court wrote: "[You were] to watch for the good & safety of the Town to prevent disorder, whereas [you] carried it as if some enemy had broken into town to block the way & lay stumbling blocks & doe mischief."[102]

The court sentenced the young men to be whipped or pay a fine and to go before the church to ask forgiveness. Thomas Spofford appeared before the church in Rowley the next Sunday, acknowledged his wrongdoing, and begged the members' pardon. But when Ezekiel Sawyer rose, he gave a very different speech. Sawyer, "instead of acknowledging his disorderly carriage did charge the church with partiality in letting pass greater matters without calling for repentance from them."[103] Sawyer's speech shocked the congregation and he was ordered to "consider his sin and the offense he had given the church by his speech and carriage at this time."[104] Two weeks later, Sawyer appeared and "his proud and contemptuous spirit was subdued and he made open confession and contrition for his evil carriages."[105] But the damage had been done. There can be little doubt that his actions, particularly his defiance of authority, earned him a reputation as a troublemaker, a label well-known to the militia committee members. It is not hard to see why Sawyer was picked to serve in the first company called up in Rowley during the war, while his truly repentant partner in crime was not. This event happened years before the war, but in the low-crime atmosphere of the county such incidents were likely remembered a long while. When the militia committees were forced to choose between two men for a spot in an expeditionary company in 1675, one who followed the rules and one who defied them, their choice was undoubtedly made easier by such memories.

Many elites, like Increase Mather, were also concerned with the wave of excessive drunkenness in the colony.[106] The General Court itself claimed that "the shamefull and scandalous sin of excessive drinking, tippling, and company keeping in taverns & ordinarys" was one of the reasons that God had decided to rain death and destruction on Massachusetts Bay (see figure 13).[107] Thus it was no wonder that William Bath was recruited out of Beverly for Gardner's command in 1675. He was found guilty of "being much disguised with drink" in March 1670, June 1670, June 1673, September 1673, November 1673 (when he "reeled from one side of the street to the other and could not speak one plain word"), and again in June 1674.[108] Many such men liked their drink and found themselves marching off to war as a result.

Not only was drunkenness a sin in itself, but it led to other sins. The General Court admonished those who undertook the "loose and sinfull custome of going or riding from toune to toune, and that often times men and weomen together . . . to be merely to drinke and revell in ordinarys and taverns, which is in itself scandoluous, and . . . a notable means to debauch our youth and hazard the chastity."[109] Sexual crimes were the most commonly prosecuted acts in Massachusetts Bay in general and in Essex County in particular.[110] In November 1673, Christian Marshman accused John Stainwood of Gloucester in court of fornicating with her and fathering her child, a charge that he denied. Apparently the court did not believe him, as it sent him to jail to wait for the next court to convene (a rare occurrence), unless he could post bail of fifty pounds, an extremely large sum.[111] The case dragged on through the summer of 1674 and allowed everyone in Gloucester to judge Chub's actions, apparently including the local militia committee.[112]

Figure 13. The General Court of Massachusetts Bay published this broadside on September 17, 1675 lamenting the sinfulness of the people of New England. Sin had provoked God to cause "the Heathen in this wilderness to be as thorns in our sides." To rectify the situation, New England needed to repent, cleanse, and undertake a "thorough Reformation." The colony's militia committees obviously took this message to heart when they pressed criminals, drunkards, and other sinners as soldiers. "At a Council held at Boston, September the seventeenth 1675" Broadside, Massachusetts General Court. Cambridge, Mass: Printed by Samuel Green, 1675. Courtesy of the Massachusetts Historical Society.

Ridding the town of "undesirables" was common before the war in some communities, especially Ipswich. It appears that most town militia committees took the opportunity to participate in a similar housecleaning when impressment quotas were issued in 1675. This made sense—send the men with criminal pasts into battle rather than any of the town's more upstanding citizens. The towns with the largest number and percentages of pressed men who had criminal pasts were the large to medium-sized towns of Beverly (20 percent of all men levied), Ipswich (26 percent), Rowley (20 percent), and Salem (21 percent). These towns used their abundant choice of men for impressment to good advantage, ridding their communities of troublemakers. Topsfield (43 percent) and Manchester (20 percent) also appear to have levied a large percentage of men with criminal records. Both of these towns were relatively small, however, as was their recruitment number, and those percentages are possibly skewed. Despite the differences in number and percentage, every town in the county save one (Andover), even those that had little choice in the men they sent (like Manchester), sent men with criminal records off to war.

"Impressment was an unenviable task" contends historian Victor Stater, "it meant breaking up homes, sending young men to their deaths, and often leaving fatherless households" to become dependent on the home community.[113] One of the many ways that militia committees tried to limit this damage to their locality was to press men from outside their community. Men visiting a town for just a few days sometimes found themselves pressed. Even more desirable to the militia committees were the men in town trying to avoid the press in their home communities; by order of the General Court, these men could be and routinely were pressed to fill the quota in the town where they were found.[114] This was not an uncommon occurrence in the history of impressment; it occurred in Elizabethan England when deputy lieutenants pressed "passing stranger[s]."[115] It also happened over one hundred years later, during the American Revolution, when local men chose drifters from other communities as substitutes for the draft.[116] During King Philip's War, several towns in Essex County pressed men to fill their quotas who were either new to town, visiting, hiding out, or passing through. Men with only a slight, or more often no, connection to the town that levied them made up 17 percent of the men that the county sent to the army.

The best example of this phenomenon occurred in Marblehead. As has been seen, after a disastrous loss of men in the first detachment dispatched from the town, the militia committee sent strangers out the next time that they had to fill impressment quotas from the General Court. In Marblehead, 82 percent of the men pressed had no known connection to the town: no prewar birth, marriage, church, town, tax, militia, court, business, or probate records exist that place them in the community that sent them to war. Other Essex towns with high numbers of men with no connection to the community were Andover (36 percent), Gloucester (38 percent), Manchester (60 percent), Rowley (52 percent), Topsfield (80 percent), and Wenham (44 percent). Significantly, neither Ipswich (5 percent) nor Salem (9 percent), towns that based their recruitment largely on socioeconomic status and crime, had high numbers of non-connected men among their recruits. The committees in these towns actively knew which men they wanted to get rid of for the good of the town. The smaller towns were looking for people to levy who simply had little connection to or stake in their community. In a number of towns, such as Rowley and Andover, the militia committees also made a sustained effort to protect sons of the town's original families from war service, sending instead sons of families that had moved to town after the initial founding period, a recruitment strategy that proves the continuation of a strong bond between the original core families of the settlements.

While the evidence is compelling that many towns recruited those with few or no long-term connections to the community, measuring this factor is not without difficulty. In many cases, town connection is difficult to document because it is based on negative evidence—the lack of documentation. The records in early New England, however, are amazingly complete in many ways, especially those of Essex County. The fact that major towns with large populations, such as Ipswich and Salem, have record collections that include many marginal men is a good indication that if a man was in a town for any length of time, he would be in the town's records. This is also true, perhaps even more so, in the communities with small populations, where newcomers were highly visible and their presence recorded.

Men who had had some type of noncriminal trouble in their town made up 14 percent of the total men impressed. Town dynamics in New England were complicated. As has been seen in the studies of the individual towns, it was not uncommon for a once harmonious "City on a Hill" to be divided over an issue, whether it was religious, political, or military. It was also quite common for men (and sometimes women) to cause trouble with the local elite or even the town government. The

General Court saw such division as a serious problem, one that had hastened the coming of the war. They saw that "a wofull breach [is] . . . to
be found amongst us, in contempt of authority, civil, ecclesiasticall, and
domesticall . . . a sin highly provoaking to the Lord."[117] In some cases,
such men were pressed because they had been on the losing side of a
town religious controversy. Such a division occurred not only in Rowley,
but also in Salem.[118] Other men (or their family members) made enemies
of important town elites, some of whom served on militia committees.
In Lynn, William Bassett, John Davis, and Joseph Collins testified in
court against town leader and militia committee member John Hathorne,
claiming in 1672 that Hathorne was selling liquor to Indians at his ordinary.[119] Hathorne was fined and lost his ordinary license—and three
years later, despite the fact that all three hostile witnesses were married
and Bassett and Collins were well placed in town, they found themselves
in a fighting company. Moses Chadwell swore "rashly" at Major William
Hathorne during a trial proceeding and was fined; he was impressed a
year later.[120] This type of dispute often ended with men who had made
trouble for town elites marching off to war.

Some men were in trouble with a number of important officials in their
town. In March 1670, John Dodge, son of a town founder and frequent
selectman, himself a well-placed man in the upper reaches of Beverly's
society, got caught in a legal struggle with the town's selectmen. They
sued Dodge for trespass, specifically for cutting down trees on town land.
Not only was Dodge acquitted of the charges, but he countersued, which
could not have sat well with the selectmen.[121] The tussle, however, was not
over; in June 1674, the Beverly selectmen again prosecuted Dodge for cutting lumber on town lands. While the verdict in this case is unknown,
the fact that Dodge challenged the authority of the selectmen once again
was hardly welcome.[122] Those who sued their towns often ended up in the
infantry, sometimes years later, as did those who affronted the constable.
It was common for constables to be verbally abused when collecting rates
or carrying out their other duties, so much so that few men wanted to
serve in the capacity.[123] In July 1675, John Bennett was fined for affronting the constable collecting the minister's rate. Less than two months later
Bennett went off to fight in Captain Gardner's company; ironically he was
most likely issued his impressment warrant by the very constable whom
he had confronted.[124] The power of the militia committee, like the power
of the selectmen or the church elders, could make life difficult for those
who did not conform.

The last negative societal factor that may have influenced impressment decisions is debt. Debt was a normal part of everyday life in colonial New England. In the agrarian culture that was colonial Massachusetts Bay, specie was scarce and credit relationships were the normal means of business.[125] In the household economy of New England, every family owed something to someone and most were owed. Usually, this normal operating debt was never even noticed in the towns.[126] Family members, friends, and neighbors trusted one another and most debt was paid before death as a man tried to "clear" his obligations. It was also common to see normal operating debt compensated in the wills and probate inventories of Essex County.[127] Almost every soldier in the county had this unexceptional debt, which was in no way a stigma on their record.

There were times, however, that debt reached a level beyond the friendly, everyday variety carried by nearly everyone. At times, "creditors [often merchants] demanded repayment, debtors refused (or were unable) to pay, and creditors sued to recover the money owed them."[128] This type of debt and the resulting court case was likely to catch the attention of town authorities. As elite men, militia committee members were often creditors, and when someone refused to pay a substantial debt, it must have raised some concern. While the number of men in the county who had such exceptional debt was very small and the number impressed was smaller still, 3 percent of the men impressed did have debt problems large and public enough to make them possible targets of their militia committee. This issue, because of the low number of men involved and the nature of debt in New England, is the weakest of the possible negative motives for impressment.

In addition to these specific damaging factors, several men had a multiplicity of negative factors on their records and they often ended up levied for service. Of the pressed men, 18 percent had multiple strikes against them. These men, often of low economic status, had also got in trouble with the law or had little or no connection to the town that recruited them. Others had criminal records and additionally had angered a local elite or the town as a whole. A sizeable percentage of the married men (35 percent) and fathers (39 percent) pressed for service had multiple negatives, perhaps explaining their inclusion in the ranks despite an obvious reluctance on the part of the militia committees to press family men. In an atmosphere in which every troublemaker or undesirable sent to the war meant that one of the town's fathers or farmers or upstanding young men could stay home, the troublemakers went to war. Pressing men with multiple strikes on their records must have been relatively easy for the militia committee, and several towns indeed pressed individuals with multiple strikes against them in large numbers. The two largest towns, Ipswich and Salem, pressed many men with several negative factors. So too did a few smaller towns, including close-knit Rowley (48 percent) and Topsfield, where over 71 percent of their soldiers had multiple negatives. In addition, Andover, Gloucester, and Manchester all had sizeable percentages of men with several black marks on their records.

An analysis of the negative factors of soldiers in relation to their unit (and thus at what stage of the war they were pressed) shows a similar pattern for all the major Essex County commands (see table 18). Of the eight companies formed with a measurable Essex County contingent, all but one was established with a majority of "undesirables" or troublemakers as recruits.[129] In the four major Essex County companies—commanded by Lathrop, Appleton, Gardner, and Brocklebank—the lowest percentage of "undesirable men" in any unit was 61 percent. The infantry company with the highest number of such men was Captain Appleton's company, which was recruited predominantly from Ipswich, a town with a high percentage of troubled recruits and a long history of ridding the town of such men by any means possible. Gardner's company, with many men from Salem, had a similarly high percentage. An even larger percentage of the men who served in at least two separate units (75 percent) had negative factors, which was possibly the reason that they were impressed by a committee numerous times (or perhaps having such bad reputations and prospects at home, they volunteered for service). The differences between the major companies, however, point to at most a slight impact on recruitment based on the stage of the war or the mission of the unit.[130] These facts do put to rest the famous boast of contemporary historian William Hubbard that Captain Lathrop's men were "the very Flower of the County of Essex."[131] Lathrop's men, like their fellow seventeenth-century New England soldiers, were often town "undesirables" whose loss would not damage the town. They were not the sons of the county's best families.

The locally controlled impressment system of Massachusetts Bay meant that each town made recruitment decisions based on unique, native concerns. Ipswich continued a decades-long campaign against lower-income

TABLE 18

Soldiers' Negative Impressment Factors by Company or Unit

Unit	Dates of Service	Number of Men from Essex Co.	Number with Negative Factor	Percentage with Negative Factor
Paige's Troop	July 1675–Aug. 1675	9	7	78%
Lathrop's Company	Aug. 1675–Sept. 1675	68	45	66%
Appleton's Company	Aug. 1675–Jan. 1676	96	75	78%
Gardner's Company	Nov. 1675–Feb. 1676	108	81	75%
Poole's Company	Nov. 1675–Apr. 1675	20	10	50%
Brocklebank's Company	Jan. 1676–Apr. 1676	31	19	61%
Manning's Company	Jan. 1676–Aug. 1676	9	3	33%
Whipple's Troop	Mar. 1676–Sept. 1676	16	11	68%
Garrisons	War, 1675–1676	39	27	69%
Troopers	War, 1675–1676	33	23	69%
Multiple Units	War, 1675–1676	51	38	75%

men and other "undesirables." Almost all the towns in the county sent fellows with criminal pasts off to war rather than press upstanding citizens. Crime was especially important to the committees of Beverly, Ipswich, and Salem, all large, thriving towns (see table 19). While a majority (eight of the twelve) Essex towns seemed to make low economic status one of the most important factors in impressment decisions, this can be misleading, especially in small, struggling towns (like Wenham or Manchester), where many men suffered from low economic status. It is much more likely that other factors, most often crime or a problem in town, caused the men to be called to service. The committees of militia in Andover, Manchester, Marblehead, Rowley, and Topsfield chose men primarily for their lack of connection to the town. These committees were safeguarding their town's stability by sending men who were irrelevant to the town's survival. The second most important negative factor for five towns was either crime or

TABLE 19
Rank of Soldiers' Negative Impressment Factors by Town

Town	First Negative	Second Negative	Third Negative
Andover	Socioecon. Status* Town Problems* Town Connection*	None	None
Beverly	Socioecon. Status* Crime*	Town Connection	None
Gloucester	Socioecon. Status	Town Connection	Crime
Ipswich	Socioecon. Status	Crime	Town Connection* Debt*
Lynn	Socioecon. Status	Town Problems	Crime
Manchester	Town Connection	Socioecon. Status	Crime* Town Problems*
Marblehead	Town Connection	Crime	Debt
Newbury	Socioecon. Status	Town Problems	Crime
Rowley	Town Connection	Town Problems	Crime
Salem	Socioecon. Status	Crime	Town Problems
Topsfield	Town Connection	Crime	Socioecon. Status
Wenham	Socioecon. Status* Town Conn.*	Town Problems	Crime
Overall	Socioecon. Status	Crime	Town Connection

Note: An asterisk indicates a tie between numbers of factors.

a man's negative record in town, with the men most often being singled out for their stance in a town or church dispute. A man's problematic history with town leaders was a considerable factor in almost every one of the smaller, closely knit communities, such as Andover, Lynn, Manchester, Newbury, Rowley, and Wenham.

These facts are crucial to understanding the genuinely local nature of impressment administered by the committee of militia system. Most committees, when forced to ship their citizens off to war, looked to send the men whose absence (or even permanent loss) would not harm the town or its families. Each town's committee, much like locally based lords lieutenant under Elizabeth I and James I in England, decided what was best for their community and impressed men accordingly. When they instituted their militia system, and especially when they created the committees of militia in the 1650s, Massachusetts Bay's leaders strove to preserve local control of impressment. The colonists wanted to avoid impressment by officials with no grounding in the community like the nationalistic lords lieutenant under Charles I's "Perfect Militia." The system that the Puritan leaders established in New England fulfilled their wishes during King Philip's War. However, the committees decided to make their primary duty the protection of local community interests, not the procurement of upstanding men who would make able soldiers. Thus, the majority of men sent to fight King Philip's War were not the "flower" of their towns, but rather the "rabble."

6

The Effects of Impressment
War and Peace in Essex County

King Philip's War raged in southern New England from June 1675 to September 1676.[1] While men from Essex County fought in many different units and capacities during the war, soldiers from the county made up a sizeable portion of eight active-duty units, six infantry and two cavalry. The history of these "Essex companies" is essential to forming an understanding of the nature of the war for the men from Essex. It also offers a glimpse into the minds of the town committees of militia, whose members frequently heard reports about the conditions of the war from their soldiers. The committees almost certainly took stock of that intelligence when recruiting subsequent groups of men. The following narrative of the war focuses on the involvement of the Essex County–based units; it is in no way an exhaustive history of the conflict.

King Philip's War began in Plymouth Colony in June 1675. After John Sassamon, an Indian confidant of the authorities at Plymouth, was killed (for informing on the Wampanoag leader Metacom, or King Philip) and his alleged Wampanoag murderers executed, the simmering tension between Indians and English colonists spiraled out of control.[2] Fighting broke out when a group of Wampanoags attacked the town of Swansea in Plymouth Colony on June 24 (see map 3). Massachusetts Bay came to its ally's aid almost immediately. The first Massachusetts troops left Boston on June 26, and the support was significant. A regular infantry company was raised from the ranks of Boston's militia under Captain Daniel Henchman and was joined by a company of volunteers, mostly from Boston, under Captain Samuel Mosley. In addition, a cavalry troop under Captain Thomas Prentice was raised from Suffolk, Middlesex, and Essex counties and traveled south.[3] On June 29, the Massachusetts force commander Major Thomas Savage arrived on the scene in Plymouth with the reinforcements, which now included another infantry company and the

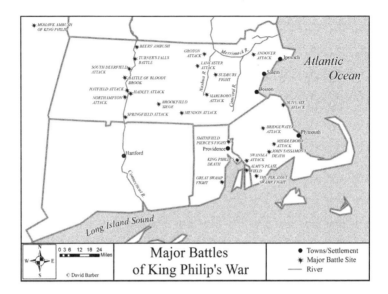

Major Battles
of King Philip's War

cavalry troop of Captain Nicholas Paige. Paige's command, with thirty-six officers and men, included at least seven men from Essex County.[4]

Nicholas Paige, who originally came from Plymouth, England, lived in Boston by 1665 and was very active in the militia before the war.[5] When Paige was appointed captain of the wartime troop sent south with Major Savage, John Whipple of Ipswich went as the unit's lieutenant and Thomas Noyce of Newbury as the cornet, indicating the heavy Essex County character of the troop. Paige and his cavalrymen were deeply involved in the early days of the war. As part of Major Savage's command, the troop moved into enemy territory on the morning of June 30, traveling toward Swansea. They discovered the remains of the Wampanoags' first attacks: several burned English homes and a number of upright poles, on which had been placed the severed heads and hands of numerous colonists. After halting to bury the remains, the men pressed forward but only found a number of hastily abandoned native villages, the enemy having escaped by canoe into Mount Hope Bay. Once they finished searching the rest of the Pokanoket peninsula, the English troops returned to Swansea. The majority of the army lingered there while the militia leaders decided on their next move. Paige's troop of Essex County men was assigned to patrol the area. On one patrol, the troop engaged a number of Wampanoags, including a minor chief, and killed a number of the enemy, taking revenge for the dead colonists whom they had buried a few days before.

In early July, Paige and his men moved west with the rest of the army into Narragansett territory on a diplomatic mission intended as a show of force to keep that tribe neutral. Upon completing their goal, on July 19 Major Savage's command (including Paige's unit) joined with Plymouth forces in an attack on the Wampanoags (including King Philip himself) who lay hidden in a great cedar swamp near Swansea. Attacking into the swamp, the Massachusetts and Plymouth forces, especially the troopers and their horses, had a difficult time maneuvering in the treacherous landscape, which was covered with extensive underbrush. Everywhere they turned, they received fire from a rapidly retreating enemy. Chaos ensued as units of the colonial army advanced and became separated. Confused, they began to fire at anything that moved in the brush, endangering one another. The English lost seven or eight men in the fight and only managed to "capture" some abandoned wigwams and one elderly Indian man, who told them that Philip had escaped early in the fight. As night approached, the commanders decided to withdraw; it had been a very frustrating day.

The colonists applied the hard-learned lessons of the day to their tactics, deciding to abandon the offensive strategy of engaging the enemy on his home territory. Believing that they had Philip and his soldiers localized, the officers decided to build and garrison a few small forts on the Mount Hope peninsula and establish a small mobile force to harass the enemy and cut off his food. The officers surmised that it would only be a matter of time before the Wampanoags surrendered. This wishful thinking fit their understanding of conflict with Indians up to that point. Colonial forces throughout the mid–seventeenth century had been able to compel Indians to capitulate without a fight—why should this instance be any different?[6] Accordingly, colonial leaders sent four of the five Massachusetts units back home, including Captain Paige and his heavily Essex County–manned troop. They returned to the Boston area in August. Paige's service was over for the duration, although some of his men, especially his subordinate officers, would fight again. The plan to trap Philip was a major blunder. He soon escaped and the war expanded in size and scope as more native groups joined the uprising. Soon, war raged across southern New England.

In August, the Nipmucks, allies of Philip's Wampanoags, attacked and laid siege to Brookfield in central Massachusetts, the first direct attack on the Bay Colony. While no Essex County companies were actively engaged at Brookfield, two were raised and sent to the upper Connecticut River

Valley to counter the growing Indian threat there. Captain Samuel Appleton, militia captain and deputy to the General Court for Ipswich, was placed in command of an infantry company in late August 1675. The large company, over one hundred strong, was made up of men from Ipswich and the surrounding towns of Essex County, with some additional soldiers from Boston.[7] In early September, Appleton's command, along with Captain Mosley and his volunteer company of "apprentices or servants . . . boys not yet enrolled in the militia . . . a sprinkling of Frenchmen . . . and ten or twelve [former] privateers [with] several dogs," marched to Hadley on the Connecticut River, north of Springfield.[8] Appleton and Mosley remained in the Hadley area on patrol, keeping in contact with the commander of the region, Major John Pynchon, the prominent leader of Springfield.[9] There was great concern that Indians hiding nearby intended to attack one of the valley towns. Other companies soon joined the English forces, including another Essex County company under the command of Thomas Lathrop.

Captain Lathrop, from Beverly, had extensive experience in the military, serving as lieutenant of the Salem militia as early as 1644 and a captain of the semiprofessional Ancient and Honorable Artillery Company of Massachusetts in 1645.[10] He even had combat experience: he was a veteran of the Pequot War and an expedition to the French colony in Acadia in 1654 and 1655.[11] Lathrop and his new command were raised for the Brookfield siege, but they arrived too late. The company joined up with a unit under Captain Richard Beers and together they moved north to Hadley to link up with the growing army. The mounting concern over enemy attacks forced the abandonment of the frontier town of Northfield. A Council of War decided that the army should strengthen the various garrisons in order to defend the rest of the western towns. On August 24, learning that a local group of formerly peaceful Quabaugs had crept off armed into the night, captains Lathrop and Beers led their companies in hot pursuit. They caught up with the Indians at Hopewell Swamp and battle ensued. Nine English soldiers, including some of Lathrop's men, were killed during the sharply fought skirmish. Lathrop and Beers withdrew, leaving the Quabaugs to continue on their way.

Fighting continued into September, marked by numerous small Indian raids on the towns of the Connecticut River Valley. On September 4, Indians ambushed Captain Beers's company, killing more than half of his thirty-six men, including the unfortunate captain. The extreme frontier towns were indefensible and the military command decided to abandon

Deerfield on September 17. Captain Lathrop and his Essex men were sent north to help with the evacuation of the inhabitants and stores of badly needed grain. As they made their way toward Northampton, the inexperienced warriors of Lathrop's Essex Company felt that they had little to fear. There was no sign of Indians nearby and the officers believed that the enemy would not attack such a large force. On the return trip, as Lathrop's company escorted the wagon train evacuating Deerfield's stores of food, they did not bother with flankers or a vanguard. Increase Mather later reported that many of the men had even stacked their weapons in the carts and started to pick wild grapes growing by the trail.[12] They were taken completely by surprise when the Nipmucks and other Indians attacked in a small clearing; hundreds of Indian fighters charged the bewildered and outnumbered militiamen. Muddy Brook forever became Bloody Brook as Lathrop and most of his command were killed. Hearing the frantic calls of Lathrop's bugler, who had escaped the carnage, the nearby Captain Mosley and his company hurried to the scene. Although too late to stop the slaughter, Mosley's men rushed the remaining enemy to drive them off and stop their grisly trophy hunting. As Mosley's company and a few survivors from the ambush struggled back to Deerfield that evening, Indians in the distance taunted them, joyously holding aloft clothing from the bodies of Lathrop's men.

The next day, Mosley and his men went back to bury sixty-four English dead, including Captain Lathrop. The Rev. William Hubbard tells what happened next in his contemporary history:

> As Captain Mosley came upon the Indians in the morning, he found them stripping the Slain, amongst whom was one Robert Dutch of Ipswich, having been sorely wounded by a Bullet that razed to his Skull and then mauled by the Indian Hatchets, was left for dead by the Savages, and stript by them of all but his Skin; yet when Captain Mosley came near, he almost miraculously, as one raised from the Dead, came toward the English, to their no small Amazement; by who being received and cloathed, he was carried off to the next Garrison, and is living and in perfect Health at this Day.[13]

Hubbard famously called September 18, 1675, "that most fatal day, the saddest day that ever befel New England . . . the Ruine of a choice Company of young men, the very Flower of Essex, all called out of the towns of that County, none of which were ashamed to speak with the Enemy in the

Gate."[14] It was a disastrous day for the people of Essex County, one that they and their militia committees would not soon forget.

The morale of the army was at a low point after the ambushes of Beers's and Lathrop's companies. The mood was no better in the east, where authorities started having difficulty filling militia quotas; many men began to evade the warrant-bearing constables. The enemy continued to raid along the Connecticut River, even burning houses on the outskirts of Springfield itself, the largest and strongest English town in the region. On October 4, Major John Pynchon, encamped with his forces at Springfield, received intelligence that a major attack was planned for Hadley. Pynchon took his small army, including Appleton and his Essex men, and marched to the town's defense. During the night, an Indian friendly to the English arrived with word that Springfield was the real target. When Pynchon and Appleton got back to Springfield the next day, they found it ablaze and the enemy gone. The attacking Agawams had burned some thirty homes and twenty-five barns, along with Major Pynchon's mills. Some fifty homes on the west side of town and the outlying areas were unharmed. The majority of the citizens were safe in fortified garrison houses; remarkably, only three people were killed in the attack.[15] Over forty families were now destitute and homeless, however, having lost everything. The entire region was in danger of being destroyed. Major Pynchon wrote the Commissioners of the United Colonies, advocating that the army abandon the practice of actively hunting the enemy and move to a defensive posture of strong garrisons for the remaining towns—a request that was denied. His town in ruins, Pynchon relinquished his command of the western theater, "being more and more unfit and almost Confounded in my understanding," as he himself wrote.[16] The governor and council of the Bay Colony appointed Samuel Appleton of Ipswich a major and made him the new commander in chief for the western theater.

Appleton was now in command not only of his own company of Essex men, but also a combined force of around five hundred men from Massachusetts and Connecticut. When Appleton inherited the Connecticut troops, he also inherited a troubled command. There was general disagreement over how to proceed; the Connecticut leaders did not agree with Massachusetts's strategy, especially Appleton's interpretation of it. Despite the almost-daily squabbles over strategy and command, with frequent letters sent back and forth between Appleton and the governments in Boston and Hartford, the army remained on alert.[17] They were again concentrated in the Hadley-Hatfield region, with Appleton and his Essex

Company stationed at Hadley. Numerous patrols and forays were undertaken but without success; the army strove to protect the towns while waiting for an opportunity to strike the enemy. On October 19, believing that they had drawn the colonial army out of the town on a ruse, the Indians attacked Hatfield in large numbers. To their surprise, Appleton's company and others still defended the town. Appleton's army forced the Indians to fall back with heavy causalities. Early the next morning, the Indians were seen retreating from the area. The English regained some of their lost confidence, having driven the enemy from the field.[18] The Hatfield fight was the last major action in the Connecticut River Valley that year, but it was not the last fight of the year for Major Appleton and his Essex men.

In mid-November, Appleton was told by the high command that a major new offensive was in the works for southern New England and he would need to ready most of his army to move out. Appleton held a Council of War to decide on how best to continue the defense the Connecticut Valley. He left a number of small detachments to garrison the river towns, released the Connecticut troops under his command, and marched the bulk of his army back to Boston. If his men were expecting to be released from duty, however, they were sorely disappointed. Appleton was placed in command of the next phase of the colonial war plan. The Commissioners of the United Colonies had decided to launch a preemptive strike on the Narragansett tribe. The tribe was officially neutral, but colonial authorities believed that the Narragansetts were aiding Philip's warriors and might be ready to join the war on his side.[19] While the commissioners did not relish sending an army into the worsening winter weather, they decided that the time was right for an attack on the main Narragansett town in the Great Swamp, in Rhode Island. In some ways, a winter campaign was ideal for colonial forces. In summer, swamps proved hard to traverse, and heavy underbrush gave the enemy too many places to hide. In the winter, the swamp would be frozen over and easily crossed, while the lack of undergrowth made ambush much less likely.

The army for this strike was the largest colonial force ever assembled in North America, one thousand strong. Command fell to the aging general Josiah Winslow, governor of Plymouth Colony and a veteran of the early colonial wars. Each colony was expected to muster an assigned quota of men; Massachusetts Bay, as the largest of the three colonies involved, raised six infantry companies and a troop of cavalry, around 540 men in all.[20] Two of those companies consisted largely of men from Essex County: Major Appleton's company (Appleton was, in addition, the commander the entire Massachusetts detachment of the army) and a new company mustered out of almost every town in Essex County, commanded by Salem's Joseph Gardner.[21]

Gardner, the son of one of Salem's most prominent families, had extensive militia experience. He had been a lieutenant in Salem until the town's company was divided and he became captain of one of the two infantry companies. As such, he was an important member of the Salem militia committee and was well acquainted with the soldiers in town.[22] Orders to impress men for the Narragansett campaign came from the Commissioners of the United Colonies, stating that because the winter campaign would be extremely arduous, as well as dangerous, the militia committees should press only men of "strength corrage and activity."[23] Appleton's 136 men (of whom 61 were "new men" and 75 "old soldiers" from the valley campaign) and Gardner's 102 soldiers mustered on the Dedham common with the other Massachusetts companies on December 9, 1675.[24] Major General Daniel Dennison read a proclamation to the men from the Massachusetts Council, "that if they played the man, took the Fort, and Drove the Enemy out of the Narragansett Country, which was their great Seat, that they should have a gratuity in land besides their wages."[25] While this was not an enlistment bounty, being proclaimed after the men were already impressed, it was an incentive for the men to fight well.[26]

The Massachusetts and Plymouth troops marched and sailed for two days to arrive at Wickford, Rhode Island, from which they would invade the Narragansett territory. On December 13, the army moved closer to the enemy, setting up an advance base at Smith's Garrison (now Warwick, Rhode Island) and patrolling the vicinity. Patrols captured a number of Indians, including "Indian Peter," who agreed to guide the English. On December 15, the army entered negotiations with an Indian named "Stone-layer John" who had lived among the English for a number of years and learned the stonemason's trade. While the negotiations (thought by some to be an Indian ruse) continued, a number of enemy fighters crept into the outskirts of the colonial camp. They began sniping at soldiers as soon as "Stone-layer John" left, killing several soldiers from Captain Gardner's company. Later, several more militiamen were killed in an ambush as they set out to escort Major Appleton's company, encamped some distance away, back to the main base. On December 18, 1675, Winslow left a small force to occupy Smith's Garrison and marched the bulk of the army south to meet up with the Connecticut forces. Using intelligence offered by their Indian captives, the colonial army moved toward the Great Swamp.

As they encamped in an open field on the edge of the swamp, a blinding snowstorm began, rendering the night miserable. But the weather would not have been the only reason that the men slept fitfully: the attack was planned for the next day.

Early the next afternoon, the army reached the main Narragansett town. A stone fortress was being built around the Indian town in the middle of the swamp. As luck would have it, the troops reached the wall at one of the few unfinished areas of the palisade. The Massachusetts forces were in the lead (with Captain Mosley and his volunteers in the van) followed by the men from Plymouth and Connecticut. The first companies from Massachusetts rushed the opening. Almost immediately, captains Isaac Johnson and Nathaniel Davenport were shot and killed. The first companies swarmed into the breach without a plan or effective leadership, and they were soon forced back out as the Indians reorganized their defense. By this time, the rest of the army had reached the fort and launched a second assault; the Narragansetts fell back into the town before the superior numbers of the English. The fighting inside the fort walls moved from wigwam to wigwam as the colonial soldiers, led by the Massachusetts companies, worked their way through the fortified town.

Captain Gardner and his Essex militiamen were in the thick of this fight, having been one of the first companies through the wall during the second assault. Captain Benjamin Church, a personal aid to General Winslow (and later one of the most effective commanders in the war), related the story of Gardner's company firsthand:

They [Church and a small force of thirty Plymouth men] entered the swamp and passed over the log that was the passage into the fort, where they saw many men and several valiant Captains lie slain. Mr. Church spying Captain Gardner of Salem, amidst the wigwams in the east end of the fort, made towards him; but on a sudden, while they were looking each other in the face, Captain Gardner settled down. Mr. Church stepped to him, and seeing the blood run down his cheek lifted up his cap, and calling him by name, he looked up in his face but spake not a word; being mortally shot through the head. And observing his wound, Mr. Church found the ball entered his head on the side that the English entered the swamp. Upon which, having ordered some care to be taken of the Captain, he dispatched information to the General, that the best and forwardest of his army, that hazarded their lives to enter the fort upon the muzzells of the enemy's guns, were shot in their backs by them that lay behind.[27]

Figure 14. John Leverett (1616–1679), a veteran of the English Civil War, was the Governor of Massachusetts Bay from 1673 to 1678, during King Philip's War. His impressive buff coat of leather was a type of armor and its like was worn by a few officers during the war. Legend has it that Captain Nathaniel Davenport of Boston, an infantry commander at the Great Swamp Fight, was killed by the enemy early in the battle as his "good Buff Suit" made the enemy think he was the commanding general. *John Leverett.* Unknown artist, attributed to Sir Peter Lely, c. 1655. Photograph courtesy of Peabody Essex Museum.

The fighting continued and the English eventually gained control of the town's grounds, although hundreds of Indians were still in their wigwams.

The hour was growing late and there were still many Narragansetts hiding in the fort, so General Winslow ordered the fort burned to drive out those who remained. Captain Church argued that this was unwise, because the spent and injured colonial army could shelter in the wigwams during the fast approaching night. His objections were overridden. No one knows how many Narragansetts (mostly women, children, and the elderly) died in the fires, but surely the total was in the hundreds.[28] As the weather threatened to turn even worse, General Winslow worried that the enemy fighters who had escaped in the early phases of the battle would return with other warriors in the area and counterattack. He ordered his army to collect its wounded and move out, leaving most of the English dead behind. The army had lost around twenty dead in the attack and over two hundred men were wounded, some severely.[29] The troops retreated toward Smith's Garrison through the night, most finally arriving at 2:00 a.m. the next morning. At least twenty of the wounded died en route. The next few days at the base saw more of the wounded succumb; by a month after the fight, the death toll had risen to between seventy and eighty men. The treatment of the wounded was hampered by the poor conditions at tiny Smith's Garrison. The men were slow to recover, especially as many had suffered exposure and frostbite during the nighttime retreat through the snow. The week after the fight, sailors from Rhode Island finally moved the wounded to Newport by ship. The attacking force paid a particularly heavy price in officers: seven of fourteen company commanders, including Captain Gardner, had been killed. Gardner's company, in addition to its commander's death, lost seven enlisted men killed and ten wounded in total during the campaign.[30] Major Appleton's losses were four men killed and eighteen wounded.[31] The army was in such a bad state that it was declared temporarily unfit for duty. Virtually all military operations ceased while the colonies recovered from their great "victory."

With the death of Captain Gardner, his lieutenant, William Hathorne, son of the prominent magistrate of Salem of the same name, assumed command of the company. Hathorne led the men through the remainder of the battle and the retreat. Major Appleton and his men remained with the army as it prepared a further offensive. The lack of an organized fighting force in the aftermath of the Narragansett campaign was of great concern to colonial authorities and they quickly went about recruiting

new forces. As early as Christmas Day, less than a week after the Great
Swamp Fight, the Commissioners of the United Colonies called for a new
army of one thousand men to take the field; there was a great desire to
strike the Narragansetts before they could recover from their defeat at the
Great Swamp. Reports that King Philip was with the main body of Narragansetts made them an even more important target. Raising new troops
was increasingly difficult, however, as men began to evade the press in
great numbers.[32] One of the first companies formed for this mission was
pressed out of the towns of Essex County and was led by Captain Samuel
Brocklebank of Rowley.

Brocklebank, as captain of Rowley's militia, had led the town's militia committee in recruiting men for the Narragansett campaign before
he was chosen to lead a company after the Fort Fight.[33] The company of
fifty-seven pressed men from Essex County and Boston arrived (along
with two other companies) in Winslow's camp at Smith's Garrison around
January 10, 1676. The march to join the army had been harrowing; many
men suffered frostbite and eleven froze to death during the journey.[34]
Brocklebank's men, the first reinforcements that the army received after
its traumatic offensive, were a welcome sight. Soon other Massachusetts
troops arrived, including a company under Nicholas Manning from Salem.[35] Manning had fought in the first campaigns of the war with Captain
Prentice's troop and was commissioned a captain to take a relief company
to the Narragansett army in early January. He and his thirty-seven men
(who included some men from Essex County) joined the army in time
for their renewed offensive. By late January, the army was somewhat recovered from the Great Swamp Fight and bolstered by the arrival of fresh
troops; it seemed ready to renew the offensive.

General Winslow departed his camp on January 28, beginning a campaign that became known as the "Hungry March." While the general
thought the troops fit to resume operations, it is apparent that many of
his men did not agree. A small number of men from Plymouth even de-
serted on January 29. When questioned later, they "displayed a bitterness
which undoubtedly was shared by many other soldiers who had not gone
so far as to leave their units. In all likelihood, the trouble centered around
such matters as a strong distaste for further winter campaigning, shortage of food, and perhaps the fact that the army had not obtained good
quarters."[36] There is little question that morale in the army had reached a
low ebb. One clergyman who talked with the deserters remarked, "Pride
and rebellion against authority . . . doth soe rage in our Armye that the

Authority of officers will not procure a silent March."³⁷ The army set off in pursuit of the enemy, chasing the main body of Narragansetts for over sixty miles through the snow. While the army fought a few small skirmishes, they captured or killed few of the enemy and Winslow was never able to bring about the decisive battle he desired. During the march, the colonial army quickly ran out of rations and was even forced to kill and consume some of their horses. Finally, realizing that in its present condition the army could not catch the enemy, Winslow dismissed the Connecticut men and marched the Massachusetts and Plymouth forces to Boston. They arrived on February 5, 1676.

Once in Boston, Major Appleton retired from military service and he and his company finally returned to their homes. Appleton and many of his men had been in the thick of the fight for six months, from the defense of the Connecticut River Valley to the Fort Fight to the Hungry March. They deserved a rest. Captain Hathorne took Gardner's men back to Essex County as well. Captain Brocklebank's company was also allowed to return home, but they were called up again less than a week later and sent to Marlboro in central Massachusetts to garrison the town and protect the backcountry. Marlboro had become a military command center on the frontier—a supply hub and transit area for troops and commanders.³⁸ The people of the town felt secure with troops in town but frightened when the soldiers left on campaign. Consequently, the General Court established a military garrison to protect the town and its vital function as a military outpost. Captain Brocklebank and his unit served as the Marlboro garrison until April 1676, when they were ordered to undertake another expedition. Captain Manning and his Essex company also continued the fight until August 1676 (as demonstrated by their pay records), although the details of that service are unrecorded.³⁹ It is quite probable that they, too, were engaged in garrison duty, as the bulk of active campaigning was shifting to special volunteer companies by mid-1676.

Another company with Essex ties, that of Captain Jonathan Poole, also spent considerable time in garrison duty at Marlboro and other Connecticut River towns.⁴⁰ Poole had been an officer under Major Appleton during the valley campaign of 1675. When Appleton was promoted to command the western theater, he raised Poole to the rank of captain.⁴¹ When Appleton left the valley to direct the Massachusetts army at the Fort Fight, Poole took command of all garrison forces there. He remained as commander and president of the local Council of War until April 1676. Many Essex County men who first served with Appleton later became garrison soldiers

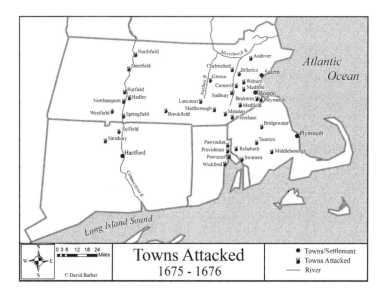

Towns Attacked
1675 - 1676

under Poole. The captain remained on active duty from the fall of 1675 to March 1676. That month he requested to be relieved of his command; a friend wrote the General Court that Poole needed leave "to repair to his very much suffering family at least for a little while."[42] Poole's request was granted and his forces turned over to Captain William Turner on April 7, 1676. It appears clear, however, that some of the Essex militiamen who served with Poole stayed on garrison duty for the remainder of the war.

As the Essex men under Poole, Brocklebank, and Manning stayed alert on garrison duty, the war took an ominous turn in the early months of 1676. On February 10, an Indian force attacked the town of Lancaster, an event chronicled in the legendary captivity narrative of Mary Rowland-son.[43] With the attack on Lancaster and no offensive colonial army in the field, many Massachusetts towns exhibited increasing alarm about Indian attacks. People kept close to their town's garrison houses and local officials begged the colony for more defensive troops. The situation became even worse later that month when the enemy attacked and burned the towns of Medfield and Weymouth, the latter on the Atlantic coast—no longer was this solely a "frontier" war.

In Essex County, Andover was the town most exposed to Indian attack because of its position on the periphery of the county. People in town were alarmed and the local political and military leaders were quick to act. That February, reports of enemy movement along the nearby Merrimack

River sent the town into a panic and Lieutenant John Osgood wrote to the Council in Boston. Andover had just been ordered to send ten men to Woburn for its defense and Osgood was troubled. On February 16, he requested, "If it may stand with you[r] honors wisdom & favour to release our men that are to goe forth, as wee being an outside town & in greate danger in our apprehension as any and may stand in as great need as any other town of help, this makes us bould to request this favour att your hands."⁴⁴ His request was granted. In fact, Andover sent no more men for the duration of the war.⁴⁵ In addition, the town began to prepare for a direct assault. More garrison houses were built. A committee from the Council in Boston reported back in March that "we met at Andover, where we found twelve substantial Garrisons well fitted which wee hope through God's blessing may bee sufficient to secure them from any sudden surprisal of the enemy."⁴⁶ On March 18, two Indian scouts had been sighted looking over the town and Lieutenant Osgood sent an urgent request to Ipswich for aid. Major Daniel Denison, the county's militia commander, led sixty men to the town, but the natives had slipped away.

On February 23, the General Court sanctioned an official Day of Humiliation to encourage the citizens of the Bay Colony to pray and humble themselves before God; that same day they issued new laws instructing towns to tighten their defenses. Novel defensive ideas were considered; the legislature proposed building a twelve-mile-long wall from the Charles River to the Concord River as a barrier against Indian attacks. The Court proposed "that a line or fence of stockades or stones (as the matter best suiteth) be made about eight feet high . . . by which means the whole tract will be environed for the security and safety under God of the people, their houses goods & catell from the rage and fury of the heathen enemy."⁴⁷ Many towns, which would have had to furnish the supplies and labor for this "Great Wall of Massachusetts," argued that the plan was impracticable and that they had enough to do building garrisons houses of their own. The selectmen and people of Newbury wrote to the Court, "We conceive it not feasible nor answering the end propounded."⁴⁸ In the end, the plan was abandoned.

In response to another order by the Massachusetts Council, a committee of Essex County leaders—John Appleton (brother to Major Appleton), John Putnam, and Thomas Chandler—toured the county to inspect the defenses of the various towns. Their March 1676 report showed most of the towns well fortified or on their way to being so. They reported that most towns had "garrisons [houses] well fitted" and had organized and assigned their citizens to gather in specific garrison houses.[49] In addition to isolated Andover's twelve garrison houses, Rowley Village and Topsfield had four, while Lynn, Rowley, and Newbury had sufficient garrisons for all of their citizens. Ipswich and Salem not only had garrison houses in place, but they were building larger fortifications; Salem was actually building "a fortification around ye towne."[50] Yet, the defensive situation was not good in all the towns. Marblehead's inhabitants deemed garrisons "needless," and in Wenham the inhabitants did not appear to discuss their defensive preparations when the committee appointed a meeting time and place.[51]

In early March, the Commissioners of the United Colonies organized a new army of Connecticut soldiers and around three hundred Massachusetts men under Major Thomas Savage (see figure 15). This force, which was to be stationed at Marlboro, incorporated Captain Samuel Brocklebank's Essex command. Also included was the last Essex County unit raised during the war. Recruited in March 1676, thirty-one Essex men served as a cavalry troop under the command of Captain John Whipple. Whipple, from a prominent Ipswich family, had been appointed cornet of the Ipswich troop before the war began.[52] He served as lieutenant in Captain Paige's troop at the beginning of the war and received his captaincy in March 1676 to join the army under Major Savage. Dissent among the officers and men marred the expedition before the army even left. The debate centered on the question of employing Indian scouts; unbridled hatred of all Indians, friendly or not, increased as the war persisted.[53] The army operated in the Connecticut Valley for the next few weeks but was soon recalled to protect the increasingly threatened settlements further east.

While the force was stationed around Springfield, Captain Whipple's troop pursued a small number of native fighters who had killed several men and women from the town. The enemy also took a number of women and children captive; Whipple's troopers had been dispatched to rescue them. As Whipple and his men approached the enemy force, the Indians killed the two child captives and struck the women on their heads with hatchets, leaving them for dead before fleeing. Whipple and his men recovered the bodies and one woman who survived the ordeal. They then returned to camp, letting the Indians go without a chase. Historian George Bodge credits a popular rhyme of the period to this incident, although it inexplicably misnames Whipple as Nixon: "Seven Indians and one without a gun, / Caused Capt. Nixon [Whipple] and forty men to run."[54] There is little question that the captain was widely known for this failure; in April 1676, the Massachusetts Council wrote to Whipple's immediate

Figure 15. Major Thomas Savage (c. 1608–1682) of Boston was a prominent military leader during King Philip's War. He played a crucial role in the early campaigns of the war on the Mount Hope peninsula. Later, in the spring of 1676, Savage was in command of the army in the Connecticut River Valley which incorporated two Essex County units: Captain Samuel Brocklebank's infantry company and Captain John Whipple's troop. It fell to Major Savage to issue the "Rebuke of God upon Capt Whipple [for his] . . . great shame" in not pursuing the enemy. *Major Thomas Savage.* Attributed to Thomas Smith, 1679. Photograph © 2009 Museum of Fine Arts, Boston.

commander, Major Savage, to raise the question of the "Rebuke of God upon Capt Whipple . . . it is a great shame and humbling to us."[55]

On March 18, scouts in northern Essex County reported Indians massing near Andover and Haverhill. Major General Dennison dispatched troops to the area, but they did not find the enemy. The situation on the western frontier had grown so perilous that the colony decided to abandon several towns there, including Groton, Lancaster, Wrentham, and Mendon. On March 28, enemy raiders attacked the town of Marlboro while the inhabitants were in church. With the majority of its former defenders out on campaign with Major Savage, including Brocklebank's company, the few soldiers in town could defend only their garrison houses against the enemy. Hearing of the attack, Captain Brocklebank and his Essex men rushed back to the town, only to find it in ruin. Brocklebank wrote to the Massachusetts Council on March 28, 1676, "This may let you understand that the assault the enemy made upon the town of Marlboro upon sabbath day did much dammage as the inhabitants say, to the burning of 16 dwelling houses besides about 13 barnes."[56] While a small force from the town followed the enemy and killed some as they slept that night, the citizens had had enough. The civilians were evacuated, leaving the town as a military outpost only. It seems as if Captain Brocklebank and his men had had enough as well. He requested to be released, citing the fact that he and his men had been in service since early January without pay and noting their frustration at not defeating the enemy: "[We] doe little where [we] are."[57] The request was denied, as the colony needed every man. A few short weeks later, the crisis hit close to home for the Essex men: in April, the enemy struck Essex County itself.

On the morning of April 8, an enemy war party was spotted crossing the river near Andover and alarms rang as the citizens rushed to the safety of their garrison houses. While most townspeople quickly secured themselves from harm, Joseph and Timothy Abbot were caught out in the fields working their father's land. Twenty-four-year-old Joseph had served in Gardner's command during the Narragansett campaign and had returned home unscathed from that ordeal. Now Joseph's luck was out: he was killed, although according to tradition he took at least one of his attackers with him.[58] Timothy, aged thirteen, was whisked away as a captive; an Indian woman later returned him, apparently taking pity on the boy's mother.[59] Ironically, not only was Joseph the only Andover soldier slain in the war, but his father George Abbott's house was a town garrison and its shelter saved many Andover citizens that day. In addition to the death on the Abbott property, the Indians also attacked the house of Edmond Falkner and killed and maimed a large number of his farm animals.[60]

Lieutenant Osgood, in his April 1676 report to the Council in Boston, wrote of the town's fear and utter sadness at these events:

We have had some forces to help us but the enemy cannot be found when we go after them; and we find that we are not able to go to work about Improving our lands but are liable to bee cut off nor are we able to raise [illegible] men at our charge to defend ourselves. We fear greatly that we shall not be able to live in the town to Improve our lands to raise a subsistence without some force be kept above us upon the river of Merrimack and to Concord river, which being speedily and well defended with a competent quantity of soldiers all the Towns within might be in sum reasonable safety to follow their Employs to raise corn and persu their cattle . . . for now we are so distressed to think that our men are libel to be shot whenever we stir from our houses and our children taken by the cruel enemy, it do so distress us that we know not what to do; if some defense be not made by the forces above us we must remove off if we can tell where, before we have lost all lives and cattle and horses to the enemy; we are completely able to fend ourselves in our garrison houses if we have warning to rest in, but otherwise out of our house we are in continual danger . . . Praying God to directe & counsel you we rest.[61]

Osgood was rightly concerned about the future of his town; Andover was in a bad way. Corn was in such short supply that those who had enough to sell insisted on hard currency rather than credit for payment, an impossible situation for many hungry families.[62] Many were ready to quit the town and the General Court cancelled the town's county rate for the year.[63] Local leaders took further steps to defend the community and more garrison houses were erected. Most important was a contingent of forty soldiers, sent to assist the local militia in protecting Andover. From then on, farming parties toiled in the fields under the watchful eyes of armed military patrols.

By mid-April, the General Court decided that they had to stop the slow erosion of the frontier—a stand had to be made. The place chosen was the town of Sudbury, now the westernmost backcountry town with a civilian population. That Sudbury was only seventeen miles from Boston highlights how desperate the situation had become. On April 19, large numbers of hostile natives, possibly including King Philip, gathered in the vicinity of Mount Wachuset, intent on attacking Sudbury the next day. Around five hundred warriors invested the town on the evening of the twentieth and attacked the next morning. The inhabitants were housed in strong garrisons and the Indians had to content themselves with burning several uninhabited homes. Help came from nearby Watertown and the men were able to push the attackers out of the center of town to the western bank of the Sudbury River.

As that fight was taking place, captains Samuel Wadsworth and Brocklebank, hurrying from their base at Marlboro with their companies (totaling fifty or sixty men), saw a party of retreating natives and pursued them. Suddenly, several hundred warriors confronted the two companies; they had fallen into a trap. Almost surrounded, Wadsworth, Brocklebank, and their men fought their way to nearby Green Hill. There they struggled for their lives throughout the afternoon. Forces from Sudbury tried to break through to the now-surrounded units to no avail. As the afternoon wore on, the enemy set fire to the brush on the hillside, blinding and choking the colonial defenders. In a moment of panic, a few of the militiamen began running down the hill to escape. This caused others, who could barely see, to follow, thinking that a retreat had been ordered. As the defenses splintered, the Indians sensed a rout and fell on the men, hacking them to pieces. Both Wadsworth and Brocklebank were killed, along with at least forty of their men. Only a few escaped the carnage, finding their way off the hill in the smoke. Following the slaughter, the enemy withdrew from the town. The next day, a force of men from Sudbury, along with a contingent of Christian Indian allies, crossed over to bury the dead. At about the same time, the garrison soldiers at Marlboro "watched silently as the victorious natives shouted seventy-four times to indicate the number of English they believed were lying dead in Sudbury."[64] The few remaining soldiers of Brocklebank's command were sent home to Essex County.

In May, Massachusetts began preparations for a new offensive. Tactics were changing as the colony employed more Indians as scouts. Much of the offensive capability of the colony was turned over to hybrid volunteer companies like that of Captain Samuel Mosley. Plymouth and Connecticut had both organized this new type of unit earlier in the war; the most famous of these companies was the Plymouth force of mixed colonial volunteers and friendly Indians under the command of Benjamin Church.[65] These companies received more latitude to pursue the enemy without formal battle plans. The men in these volunteer companies were motivated to enlist and fight by a new, more liberal policy that allowed them to collect pay from the colony, keep any plunder, and profit from the prisoners they took.[66] Indian captives, mostly women and children, were sold as slaves in the West Indies and brought high profits for the officers and men who seized them.[67] While there were a few men from Essex County in these new units, none of the companies was based in the county. The only Essex County unit in active service in the closing months of the war was Captain Whipple's troop, which remained on patrol until discharged in September 1676.[68] The war was coming to an end, however, in the summer of 1676. Most Indians were defeated or surrendered because of hunger, thanks to the colonial tactic of destroying food crops. At the end of July, King Philip's wife and son were captured and sold into slavery. On August 12, Captain Benjamin Church and his hybrid company of Plymouth men and friendly Indians cornered and killed Philip himself not far from his home at Mount Hope, the place where the war had begun. Church and his men, along with others, continued to round up Indian leaders; by October the war in southern New England was over and the colonies started the long road to recovery.[69] The militia veterans had much to recover from as well. Impressed into service by their towns' committees of militia, the men of the Essex County companies had done their duty and many had paid the ultimate price.

The Aftermath of War for Essex County's Fighting Men

King Philip's War was the deadliest war in American history in terms of the proportion of people killed to those in the population.[70] In a report of the Council of Trade in October 1676, Edward Randolph reported to London that 600 Englishmen had died.[71] Another observer, Nathaniel Saltonstall, believed that around 800 English had perished.[72] An estimated death toll of 800 and an estimated population for New England of 52,000 English colonists equates to 1,538 deaths per 100,000 people, which makes King Philip's War far more deadly per capita than the American Revolution (180 deaths per 100,000), the Civil War (857), or World War II (206).[73] The war took an even greater toll on the Native Americans of southern New England. According to one learned estimate, the war claimed 7,900 Indian victims, with over 1,250 deaths in battle alone.[74] And these were just the war losses in southern New England; fighting continued and increased in ferocity in the district of Maine after the conflict ended in the south.

Fifty-two of the 357 men sent to fight from Essex County were killed in action, 15 percent of the total.[75] This is considerably higher than the total estimates for the war of an 8 to 10 percent battle death rate among the colonists.[76] Considering that three of the Essex County companies were engaged in some of the deadliest battles of the war—the Bloody Brook ambush, the Great Swamp Fight, and the Sudbury Fight—the high percentage of battle dead is understandable. In addition to the deaths, twenty-three men (6 percent) were listed as wounded. This accounting of wounded, however, is too low. Unlike the reliable records of battle deaths, the records of men wounded in battle are quite unreliable—there is no doubt that a much larger number of men from the county were wounded, because the number of wounded in battle almost always exceeds the number of dead. It is likely that the twenty-three Essex men listed as wounded in battle were those whose wounds were so severe that it had a long-term effect on their ability to support themselves after they returned home. Men like William Peabody of Topsfield, who lost an arm in Gardner's attack on the Narragansett Fort, or John Bullock of Salem, who was crippled during Lathrop's campaign in western Massachusetts, fit this pattern.[77]

Of the Essex County men killed, the vast majority (forty-one soldiers, or 79 percent) died at the Bloody Brook ambush in September 1675. The frightful loss of men in Lathrop's command inspired much sorrow throughout the colonies, but nowhere was the grief felt more over "that most fatal Day, the Saddest that ever befell New-England" than in Essex County.[78] Of those forty-one men killed with Lathrop, six were married.[79] Only seven married men from the county were killed during the entire war. The high number of married men killed in action early in the war was another incentive for the militia committees to avoid pressing more married men as the war dragged on. The campaign to defeat the Narragansett Indians in December 1675 was also deadly for Essex County forces. At least nine men (17 percent of those killed) died while under the command of Major Appleton or Captain Gardner on that campaign, with most falling in the assault on the enemy fortress in the Great Swamp. At least two other men from the county were killed during the war. Samuel Pickworth of Salem survived Gardner's command in 1675 but died in 1676, possibly during the Hungry March.[80] Jacob Burton of Salem was killed at the infamous Falls Fight of May 19, 1676, under the command of Captain William Turner.[81]

Every town in the county save one lost at least one man killed in battle, although Andover too had its own "battle" death (see table 20). The cities with the most men killed in action were Salem (thirteen dead), Ipswich (seven dead), and Rowley (seven dead). The large number of dead from Salem is explained by the large percentage of men recruited for Captain

TABLE 20
Soldiers Killed and Wounded in Action by Town

Town	Total Men	Killed in Action	Percent of Town's Force Killed	Wounded in Action	Percent of Town's Force Wounded
Andover	14			3	21%
Beverly	20	4	20%		
Gloucester	16	2	13%		
Ipswich	88	7	8%	5	6%
Lynn	42	5	12%	1	2%
Manchester	5	2	40%		
Marblehead	20	4	20%		
Newbury	41	4	10%	8	20%
Rowley	25	7	28%	1	4%
Salem	70	13	19%	3	4%
Topsfield	7	2	29%	1	14%
Wenham	9	2	22%	1	11%
Overall	357	52	15%	23	6%

Lathrop's company from that community. Lathrop, the ill-fated com-mander ambushed at the Bloody Brook, was a native of Beverly, a com-munity next to and closely tied to Salem. All four of the dead from Bev-erly, Lathrop's hometown, were also killed under the command of their own militia leader. Salem was also a prime recruiting ground for the com-pany of Salem native Captain Gardner, while Ipswich saw large numbers of troops recruited for its hometown militia commander, Major Appleton. With the second-largest number of battle deaths occurring at the Fort Fight, it is no wonder that Ipswich and Salem took heavy casualties, be-cause both Gardner and Appleton were heavily engaged in that campaign.

Some of the smallest towns took the largest proportion of casualties. While this may simply be a reflection of the small number of men that they sent and proportionally larger numbers of men killed, it does bring home the fact that King Philip's War was particularly deadly. When 40 percent of the men sent to war by Manchester failed to return, or when Rowley and Topsfield lost large percentages of their war contingents (28 and 29 percent, respectively), it must have been devastating to the small communities. As was seen when Marblehead lost four out of the first five men it sent to war, the tragedy radically changed subsequent recruiting criteria. Even when the men made it home, they were not always safe.

Thus, although Andover suffered no battle deaths among the men it sent to war, Joseph Abbott, the former Gardner soldier, died in the April 1676 attack on Andover. Joseph Abbot's experience was replayed many times during the war and not only speaks to the deadly nature of the war, but also to the fine line between the deaths of combatants and noncombatants in colonial warfare.[82] The effect of such losses on communities in colonial America is a history waiting to be written.

An examination of the probate inventories of the men who fell in action offers an insight not only into the type of men killed but also an additional opportunity to look at the social makeup of those who served. Daniel Rolfe of Newbury was killed at the Fort Fight. Before he was posted to Appleton's command, Rolfe was credited with service under Captain Lathrop. It is not known whether he was one of the lucky few who escaped the ambush at Bloody Brook or if he was transferred to Appleton's unit before the attack on Lathrop's command. Rolfe did take part in the assault on the great Narragansett fortress on December 19, 1675. As Daniel was not married, his brother Ezra Rolfe handled his estate.[83] When Rolfe's goods, due wages, and debt were inventoried, they included:

> One cloke, 2Li. [pounds] 12s [shillings]; one Koote [coat] made of Sarch, 1Li. 10s.; one Cloth Koote, 18s.; a payre of drawers, 6s.; a doublet & britches, 1li.; one old Cloth Clooke, 1li.; a payer drares [drawers] and waskot [weskit or vest], 1s.; 2 payer old Bridges [britches], 1s.; thre hats, 6s. 6d. [pence]; one shirt and drawers, 8s.; 2 bands, a Neck Clooth, and one payer of sellfes, 12s.; one belt and ponts, 4s.; small Tools, 12s. 3d; Coopers tools, 3li. 7s; one axe, 2s. 6d.; one gone stik bore, 1s. 6d.; Debts due by a bill of Schoer Wilson, 3lis, 9s., 5d.; Jo. Clark for a gun, 8s.; my father Rolffe, 13li. 6s.8d.; Jas. Smith, 8s.; Jos. Lee, 5s.; Mr Lord, Clerk 10s.; Jon Kindrik, 3s.; total 18li. 10s. 1d. More by 2 goons and 4 barrels of goons, 3li. 1s.; Goodman Wood of Rowley, 2li.10s.; James Myrick of Newbury, 1li. 10s.; 3000 of Barrel Staves and heading, 4li. 10s.; a bill of Joseph Wilson of Andovier, 3li. 10s.; debts due from the estate, 4li. 4s. 6d.; total clear estate, 42li. 8s. 4d.[84]

From this probate inventory, it is clear that Daniel Rolfe was a fairly typical recruit of the age. He was not married (his estate going to a brother) and did not own any land. He obviously was trained as a cooper ("3000 of Barrel Staves and heading"). However, Rolfe most likely also worked as a farm laborer for a number of men, including his father. The fact that

Rolfe's father owed his son over thirteen pounds is good evidence of his farm-laborer status, as that amount of back wages seems much too high for just coopering services (few men other than merchants would need that many barrels). Rolfe moved about a bit—he was owed money by men in Newbury, Rowley, and Andover. He needed to purchase a musket before he went to war, going into debt to do so ([owed] "Jo. Clark for a gun, 8s"). Daniel Rolfe was, from his probate inventory, a young man just getting started in life. He died owning only the clothes on his back, a few tools, and the fruits of his labor. He was a perfect impressment choice for the militia committee—he left behind no dependants and his loss did not break up a family or even put much food production at risk.

This pattern is seen time and again in the probate records. William Dew of Marblehead died with twelve pounds to his name, most of that in "Marchandable fish."[85] Ipswich's Samuel ·Crumpton, who was married, died with a net worth of eight pounds.[86] George Ropes of Salem died in debt and his brother William was ordered to pay the creditors eleven shillings on the pound.[87]

Few of the young men made wills before going off for service, either because they did not believe that they would need them or because they simply had nothing of substance to bequeath. Those who did have wills or those for whom the court chose administrators and beneficiaries left their estates to their brothers, sisters, fathers, mothers, or sister's children; servants even left their small estates to their masters. The listed items in the inventories include clothing, perhaps a book (usually a Bible) or two, often a musket and possibly a sword, some tools, maybe a cow or a few sheep, possibly an acre of farming land or some salt marsh, but rarely a house or barn. The inventories of the men "slaine in the late Indian war" almost always include some money owed the slain soldier, most often by the men for whom the soldier worked. The listings often include the soldier's military pay "from the county service." The last item that most of the probate records include is a list of debts that the man had acquired, the normal operating debt of colonial life that usually remained invisible. The premature deaths of these young men, however, forced an early reckoning. Quite often, the debts owed exceeded the meager assets, and the creditors were paid shillings on the pound. The probate records of the men who fell in battle confirm their impressment records—these soldiers were relatively young, mostly unmarried men just starting out in life. While their loss was a great sorrow for their families and their towns, it was not (in most cases) a great burden on either the family or the town. It was just as the militia committees had planned.

This relatively benign situation, however, was not always the case. What the committees had wanted to avoid was exactly what happened to the widows of the seven married men from the county who were killed. Very little information is available about these women. When Samuel Stevens of Ipswich died at the Bloody Brook, he left Rebecca, his wife, and their daughter, Sara, a total, in goods and money, of thirty-eight pounds, including one ten-acre lot in Ipswich's Northfield.[88] Rebecca was given control of the minuscule estate and ordered to pay Sara "10 li. at eighteen years of age or marriage with the mother's consent."[89] Nothing else about the two women is known; it is most likely that Sara had to remarry in order to survive. There is certainly no documentation of the family receiving any assistance from the colony. The same was probably true of most widows of the war. The only recorded exception is Sara Pickworth. The Essex County Quarterly Court granted Samuel Pickworth's wife Sara the administration of her husband's estate, including the house and barn, valued at around seventy-three pounds.[90] She had three children and by 1678, still unmarried, was given two shares of town land as a type of poor relief.[91] This was exactly the kind of situation that the committees had hoped to avoid by primarily recruiting single men.

The wounded and the other veterans also had to cope with rebuilding their lives once they returned home. There is very little information available about the men who were wounded. Some did not live long; Daniel Somerby died of his wounds soon after arriving home.[92] Jonathan Emery of Newbury was wounded in the neck by an arrow at the Fort Fight in December 1675. He recovered from his wound and for the rest of his life used a special seal he made: it depicted a lion (representing "the bold Briton inspiring terror") seizing a downward-pointing arrow (for "Indian warfare, which from its position indicates the loin's [*sic*] victory").[93] John Toppan, also of Newbury, fought at Bloody Brook and survived; he "was wounded in the shoulder, [and] concealed himself in a water course that at that time was almost dry, and hauled grass and weeds over his head so that though the Indians sometimes stepped over him he was not discovered."[94] He made it home and lived until 1723.

Sometimes, the colony or the towns tried to help wounded veterans. In Lathrop's company, John Bullock was crippled by his battle wounds and given a sizeable service credit of fifteen pounds and eight shillings. because of it. From Salem, Bullock "was afterwards favored by the General Court and granted a license to keep a 'victualling shop' on January 9, 1680."[95] While help eventually came to Bullock, the four-years wait must have seemed very long. Historian Douglas Edward Leech claimed that there was great support from the towns for the former fighting men: "Wounded veterans, obviously, needed immediate and continuing financial help, for many of them were unable to make an adequate living in the ordinary occupations of the day. Cases were handled on an individual basis, either by special committees or by the regular organs of government. Relief usually took the form of a lump sum payment, occasionally supplemented by certain special privileges such as exemption from taxation or the right to operate a tavern."[96] Despite Leech's contention, there are very few instances, in the records of the towns of Essex County at least, of such assistance being given. If this type of widespread assistance did occur in the county, it has disappeared from the historic record.

Not all the men who fought were wounded physically. In the modern era, it is an accepted fact that combat takes a terrible toll on the psyche of those involved. While the postwar mental repercussions of service were not recognized as an illness in the colonial period, there is no doubt that such effects occurred in early conflicts.[97] Historian Jill Lepore has documented the utter horror of combat in King Philip's War. During the war, New England was "a landscape of ashes, of farms laid waste, of corpses without heads. A place where three-legged cattle wander aimlessly, dragging their guts after them, and Indians strut through the woods wearing belts of human skin and necklaces of rotting fingers. It is difficult to imagine a scene that could do more to assault English notions of order. Towns have been razed and blood spills everywhere. Nearly all that was English had been destroyed—English houses, English farms, English crops, English livestock, English bodies. The tamed wilderness had become wild once again."[98] Most soldiers surely relived these scenes in their nightmares; for some the memories almost certainly haunted them while they were awake.

Edward Ordway and the Richardson brothers from Newbury were all members of Major Appleton's company during the war. An examination of the pay lists suggests that Caleb and Joshua Richardson served from the unit's founding in August 1675 until it was disbanded the following January; Ordway probably joined the company just in time for the Narragansett campaign and its aftermath.[99] All three men saw unimaginable sights in their months on campaign. When they arrived home, the memories apparently got the better of them; they lashed out at the society

Figure 16. Reconstruction of a seventeenth-century Puritan meetinghouse in present-day Danvers, Massachusetts. This structure is likely similar to the meetinghouse in Newbury, the scene of a profound disturbance by three returned veterans of King Philip's War on the night of February 21, 1676. Many members of the community came forward to plead for leniency from the quarterly court on behalf of the veterans, who had "endured hardshipps, & adventured their lives & limbs for the Country." The Meetinghouse at the Rebecca Nurse Homestead, Danvers, Massachusetts. Photo by Kyle F. Zelner.

that had sent them to war. On the night of February 21, 1676, just over a month after the men got back to Newbury, they shattered the windows on the town's meetinghouse and entered the building (see figure 16). Once inside, they broke a pew and a few chairs. According to Anthony Morse, a witness to the destruction, "the windows had been broken several times and the meetinghouse made common by reason of such disorders. The door was daubed with a sarrowans [possibly tree sap] and the key hole stopped up with it so he had difficulty opening the door."[100] There also was "sarrowans put in the corn which was put up in the meetinghouse for security, which was in a cask in the chamber."[101] The pew that the men broke had recently been specially designated for the selectmen of the town, without the town's approval, an action that was very controversial in the community.[102] Yet, the level of destruction in the church went far beyond one pew. It appears that for these three veterans, there was no better symbol against which to strike back than the town's meetinghouse. The building was the center not only of religious affairs in the community, but also of the town's government. Most likely, it was also the meeting place of the militia committee, the very body that had sent them off to such a horrific and horrifying war.

The case against the men did not appear in court while the war still raged, but in March 1677 they were arraigned before the Essex County Quarterly Court in Ipswich. Mr. Samuel Symond (the deputy governor of the colony), Major General Daniel Denison, and Major William Hathorne sat in judgment. The jury found the three men guilty of the destruction at Newbury's meetinghouse and ordered the men "to be whipped or pay a fine, in addition to paying a bond to ensure their good behavior."[103] The incident, however, did not end there. In the court record is a petition, signed by "seventy-six principal inhabitants" of the town.[104] The good citizens wrote the court on April 22, 1677:

> that though they [the townspeople] are far from justifying the outrageous practices of the young men sentenced by the court and they do not question the justice of the court's decision. We do not know any of the young men have bin detected of open crimes but have bin diligent & laborious to promote & support their parents who stand in need of their help. *they have bin imployed in publike service, haue endured hardshipps, & adventured their lives & limbs for the Country*: & they have openly, ingeniously, & solemnly made acknowledgement of their offense, before many assembled to that end.[105]

Unfortunately, no record exists of the court's reaction to the petition of the townspeople. There was a real concern for the men and a hope that they would not be punished too severely for their deeds. Many in the community had sons of their own home from the war and knew that fighting in the horrific conflict had undoubtedly affected the young men. There is also an acknowledgement that their families had suffered from the absence of their sons. It is heartening to think that at least some of the soldiers, upon returning to their communities, were offered a little help, a bit of understanding, and recognition of their sacrifice.

Eventually, some towns offered other forms of assistance to the veterans. Douglas Edward Leech cites a few instances of towns bestowing land grants on veterans; one of his examples comes from Gloucester in Essex

County.[106] The largest land grant came from the government of Massachusetts Bay itself, although it took some time for it to become more than an empty promise. During the 1675 Narragansett campaign, the Massachusetts troops assembled on Dedham plain were told that if they performed well in the upcoming fight they would be rewarded with land.[107] It seems that the promise was forgotten after the war, as the colony recovered from the destruction wrought by the conflict. The men who had served, however, did not forget. In 1685, ten years after the war had begun, a number of veterans from Essex County (from Lynn, Beverly, and Salem) petitioned the colony to fulfill its promise. The colony responded that the men had a just claim. It required them to form a community, find clear title to a tract of land eight miles square, and persuade a minister to join the community for four years. If they could do this, the colony would grant them their land.[108] The men had wanted a simple land grant, not the burden of establishing a new community from scratch. The issue languished another forty-six years.

In 1731, more than fifty-five years after the war ended, the colony finally laid out a series of townships for the veterans (or, in most cases, their descendants) of the Great Swamp Fight. Finding the soldiers and verifying their claim was a slow, difficult, and laborious process: "The grantees were divided into companies or societies, according to their residences, if alive, or according to the residences of their legal representatives, if dead."[109] The government eventually expanded the terms of the grant to include "every Officer and soldier, who served in the said war or the lawful Representatives of such as served and since deceased."[110] In 1733, 840 grantees (either former soldiers or their descendants) were finally recognized by the government and a total of seven townships were established in order to accommodate them.[111] The land to be divided was located either along the Saco River in Maine or in New Hampshire, just north of the Massachusetts border (see figure 17). The townships or districts were named the Narragansett Grants. In some cases it took decades more to establish these townships. It had taken more than fifty-eight years, but the veterans of King Philip's War (in reality their descendants) were finally given some reward for their long suffering and hard service.

While most of the men had to wait for their reward for service during the war, many of these young men reaped one "reward" quickly upon their return. As has been established, most of the men pressed for service were unmarried; of the 357 men, 280 (78 percent) were single. Of the single men, 45 died in the war, leaving 235 men eligible to marry once they

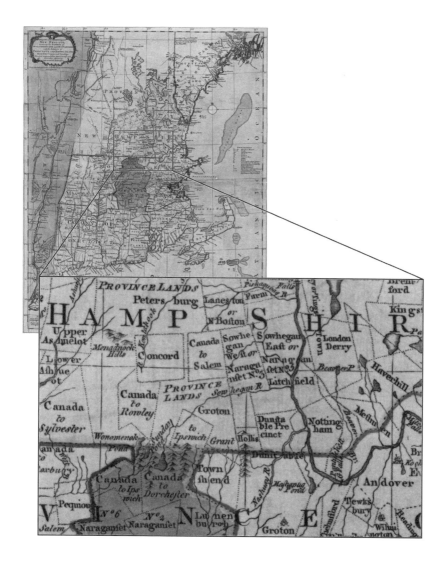

Figure 17. Map detail showing the land set aside for Essex County veterans of the Great Swamp Fight. The township in the middle of the map labeled "Souhegan West or Narraganset No. 3" was granted predominantly to the descendants of soldiers by the government of Massachusetts in 1731. The area later became the town of Amherst, New Hampshire. In the right hand corner of the map, the town of Andover, Massachusetts is visible. Detail from "A map of the most inhabited part of New England, containing the provinces of Massachusets Bay and New Hampshire, with the colonies of Conecticut and Rhode Island" by Carington Bowles (1724-1793). Published in London in January 1771. Photo courtesy of the Library of Congress Geography and Map Division, Washington, D.C.

TABLE 21
Veterans Marrying in the Postwar Period

Year(s)	Number of Men Wed	Percentage Wed of Eligible Men	Cumulative Percentage
WAR YEARS			
1675	5	2%	2%
1676	11	5%	7%
POSTWAR YEARS			
1677	22	9%	16%
1678	16	7%	23%
1679	14	6%	29%
1680	17	7%	36%
1681	16	7%	43%
1682	10	4%	47%
1683–1690	35	15%	62%

were home from the war. Of those single men, there are records showing that 111 (47 percent) married within six years of the war's end (see table 21). It is probable, in fact, that a much higher number of men married in the immediate postwar period than is recorded here.[112] The marriage records of the colony in the first few years after the war are frustratingly incomplete, as many towns were destroyed, town governments were reeling from the shock of the conflict, and people everywhere were on the move as refugees moved back home or to new areas to live. While it is possible that it was simply time for these men to marry (which is plausible because of their average age), it seems likely that the war offered them a new measure of independence or possibly additional leverage when speaking with their parents about the timing of marriage. The men had fought to save their society and proved themselves independent adults. Most families had survived their absence, proving that the sons' labor was not as crucial as had been thought. Most importantly, they had, through their service, simply earned the right to marry. Those who did soon started families of their own and got on with their lives and the rebuilding of the colony.

Afterword
The Military of Massachusetts Bay Transformed

In the midst of King Philip's War, although few in the colony perceived it at the time, a major shift occurred in the way that Massachusetts Bay conducted war. The change in the nature of offensive warfare was subtle, but significant. Amazingly, the exact day that the change transpired can be identified, a rare occurrence for such an important but almost imperceptible shift. The date was May 5, 1676. On that day, the Massachusetts General Court issued a series of orders to its commanders and militia committees. The first set of commands instructed military leaders to "arme & dispatch the Indian soldjers."[1] The second monumental instruction told the militia committees "to take subscriptions from persons willing and able to beare the charge of wages and provisions for the supply of . . . volunteers."[2] With the stroke of a pen, Massachusetts Bay changed the very nature of war making in New England—a change that lasted for over one hundred years.

King Philip's War was the most deadly and important military conflict in the history of colonial New England. Unlike the Pequot War, the conflict that began in 1675 was crucial to the survival of the colonies. The government of the Bay Colony responded to the crisis in the best way that it knew how—it fell back on its legally mandated, persistently local system of militia committees to impress men to fight the war. While a few men volunteered (and a minuscule number hired substitutes) to fight in the early days of the conflict, the war was predominantly fought by pressed men. The trouble was that these pressed men made bad soldiers. And it was not necessarily their fault. The fault should be laid at the feet of the colony's thoughtful, long-established, perfectly logical institution: the committee of militia. The committees employed both civilian and military leaders to make decisions in a way that avoided any grand seizure of power by the central government, a fear that New Englanders carried from the days of

Charles I in Stuart England. At the same time, the Massachusetts militia committees were local. This fit perfectly with New England society, as the colonists had come to cherish and demand local control of almost every aspect of their lives, from politics to religion and even to the military.[3]

The trouble was that militia committees, like Elizabethan lords lieutenant before them, had two masters. The committees were responsible to the governor, the General Court, and society in general to select good soldiers who would fight well. Yet, the committees of militia also had local masters—the towns that demanded that their best sons be spared the press. Why not send the "undesirables" in society instead? When it came time to choose which men to send into combat, the militia committees, manned by local elites, sided almost completely with their communities. They chose, as has been seen, men who had been in trouble with the law, had no connection to the town, were landless and searching for a place to fit in, or had defied authority. These traits were hardly the makings of first-rate soldiers.

Not only were such men poor prospects to be good soldiers, but they often did not show up for service at all, especially those with a predisposition toward contempt of authority. Historian Jenny Hale Pulsipher has detailed high levels of evasion and resistance to the press during King Philip's War.[4] Men who hid or ran from the press just sent the committees scrambling to find more recruits, using the same criteria as before and often finding men just as bad or worse. In his account, Captain Benjamin Church often stressed the inferior martial abilities of pressed soldiers in the early days of King Philip's War.[5] His sentiments mirror those of Barnaby Rich and other English commanders, who complained loudly about the quality and fighting skills of recruits pressed out of taverns and jails for Elizabeth's military adventures in the sixteenth century.[6] The sheer number of ambushes and bungled operations during King Philip's War, such as the surprise raid on the column at Bloody Brook, the unorganized, undisciplined rush to the Great Narragansett Fort, or the disastrous Sudbury rout, are evidence of the poor quality of the locally pressed troops. While bad soldiering was only one element in the inability of the colonists to best their enemy early in the war, it was a crucial one.[7] In theory, the locally controlled impressment system appeared to be the perfect system for the colony; it took New England's political culture into account and preserved the society's military and legal values. The only problem was that as an impressment system with a goal of recruiting able fighting men, it did not work.

What did work by the middle of the war were the special volunteer companies put into the field by the colonies of Connecticut and Plymouth. Benjamin Church established the most famous of these outfits in the days after the Great Swamp Fight. Yet, Massachusetts had its own prototype of a special volunteer company early in the war: Captain Stephen Mosley's company of apprentices, servants, boys, Frenchmen, and privateers.[8] It was Mosley and his men who attempted to rescue Lathrop's impressed company at Bloody Brook and succeeded in driving off the trophy-hunting victors. Mosley's men were also in the vanguard during the Great Swamp Fight and were extremely successful leading the assault. Compared to the armies of impressed men who had stumbled into ambush after ambush and nearly frozen to death during their pursuit of the "conquered" Narragansetts during the Hungry March, the volunteers under Mosley had done remarkably well. The proof of their combat effectiveness can be seen in the General Court's acceptance of Mosley's outrageous demands when he offered to raise a second group of volunteers in May 1676.[9] The General Court not only acquiesced to Mosley's every stipulation (even the highly controversial act of enlisting friendly Indians), it also ordered the militia committees to assist the good captain. On that May day, a notable shift quickly and quietly occurred in the nature of waging war in New England.[10]

By the latter part of the war, fewer and fewer men were being impressed as the colony stopped putting so many of the old-type, mass-impressed militia companies in the field. This was definitely the case in Essex County, where the large impressment drives happened relatively early in the war; in 1675, the towns pressed 292 men for duty in infantry companies, which decreased to a mere 40 men in 1676.[11] By mid-1676, there were simply no more mass levies like the ones that filled Major Appleton's command or Thomas Lathrop's company in 1675. Of the men pressed later in the war, most were levied for defensive garrisons in the backcountry, not for frontline fighting units. The offensive power of New England's military came to reside in the special companies like Mosley's unit or Benjamin Church's Plymouth-based hybrid company. Mosley, Church, and other commanders had come to appreciate the Indians' "skulking way of war" and adapted it to English sensibilities.[12] Many historians credit Church with the creation of the "ranger" concept, specialized units specifically trained to fight Indians in an irregular style.[13] These companies of volunteers, spurred to join by promises of wages, pillage, and bounties, struck the Indians hard in 1676, after Philip and his warriors had already been desperately weakened by a combination of disease, starvation, and attacks by the Mohawk Indians of New York that winter.[14] It was the volunteer force under Church that found and killed King Philip (and scores of other Indian leaders) to end the war in southern New England.

The grand shift in war making had worked and the days of mass *impressed* colonial armies were over. Several historians have argued that the social makeup of soldiers changed in the eighteenth century only as European imperial wars made it necessary to change the militia's original structure.[15] In this conceptualization, as colonial society matured, American fighting men became more like European full-time soldiers, men culled from the lower orders of society.[16] As we now know, this was not the case. A majority of the impressed militiamen of King Philip's War were also of the "lower orders" of society—and not just in an economic sense. Thus, the change in the New England way of war from the seventeenth century to the eighteenth was not due to a change in the type of warfare (from colonial/settlement wars to imperial wars), but to the colonial leaders' realization that impressment did not supply the necessary motivation for soldiers to risk their lives and fight well enough to win on the American frontier. The future of fighting in the colonial Northeast now resided with *volunteer* soldiers because the impressed soldiers had so often failed.

In his definitive study of New England's provincial soldiers, historian Stephen Eames writes that men volunteered to fight for the lure of wages and "special incentives tied to the type of service involved, such as scalp money for scouting and plunder for expeditions."[17] While the men were often of the same social type pressed for service during King Philip's War, their motivation and response to service was now quite different. Regular, adequate wages; land bounties; substantial scalp bounties; government-provided weapons, uniforms, and provisions; exemptions from the military press for defensive garrisons; and the prospect of extensive plunder encouraged many men not only to sign up for military service, but also to excel at their trade.[18] The more land they conquered and the more scalps they took, the more money they made. Military historian John Grenier argues that "the colonial governments had discovered the means to motivate untold numbers of men to take to the field and range against the Indians. In the process, they established the large-scale privatization of war within American frontier communities."[19] This commercialization of military service in the late seventeenth and early eighteenth century perfectly mirrored the rising economic focus of society in general, thus making the new way of war as much a part of the new New England as the committees of militia had been of the old.

Militia committees did not disappear in the Bay Colony, but their focus changed. Instead of impressing men for active service, they supervised the general militia and, in times of war, assisted recruiting officers in enticing men to volunteer.[20] Occasionally, the committees did press men for service. While the press did not disappear entirely, the forced levy was normally reserved as a tool to fill lonely, isolated garrisons in the back-country, not to raise men for fighting companies. On the few occasions when there were not enough volunteers to fill the recruitment quotas of the active-duty companies, men were pressed; they were considered far inferior, however, to the volunteers—who wanted to fight.[21] But this occurred rarely. Provincial companies of volunteers made up the preponderance of colonial forces fighting King William's War (1689–1697), Queen Anne's War (1702–1713), King George's War (1744–1748), and even the French and Indian War (1754–1763).[22] In the backcountry of the colonies, these volunteers created what Grenier calls America's "First Way of War."[23] It is crucial to remember, however, that these pivotal units, the very units that created this new style of war, were themselves conceived amid King Philip's War.

Despite the importance of this new American way of war and the volunteers who invented it, one must not forget those men who came first: the pressed soldiers of 1675 and 1676. While the colonial leaders responsible for the war ultimately rejected impressment by militia committees as flawed, we should not merely dismiss the war service of these pressed men. Despite the problems with the system and the soldiers' lack of motivation, companies of pressed men, under the command of leaders such as Thomas Lathrop, Joseph Gardner, and Samuel Appleton, saved Massachusetts in the early days of the war. Without impressed "undesirables" on the front lines, the colonies would never have had the time to adapt and institute the new military structure necessary for victory. In effect, the "rabble" that made up the early impressed armies of New England made winning the war possible. They saved their society from utter destruction and, in their own way, helped establish the colony's new way of war, which kept Massachusetts secure, if not entirely safe, for the next hundred years.

Appendix 1
The Soldiers of Essex County
in King Philip's War, 1675–1676

Last Name	First Name	Unit
ANDOVER		
Abbot	Joseph	Gardner's company
Ayers	Zechariah	Brocklebank's company
Ballard	John	Gardner's company
Barker	Ebenezer	Gardner's company
Fry	James	Gardner's company
Lovejoy	John Jr.	Gardner's company
Markes	Roger	Appleton's company
Marston	John Jr.	Gardner's company
Parker	John	Gardner's company
Parker	Joseph Jr.	Brocklebank's company
Philips	Samuel	Gardner's company
Preston	John	Gardner's company
Stevens	Nathan	Gardner's company
		Brocklebank's company
Whittington	Edward	Gardner's company
BEVERLY		
Balch	Joseph	Lathrop's company
Bath	William	Gardner's company
Blashfield	Thomas	Gardner's company
Clark	John	Gardner's company
Conant	Lott Jr.	Gardner's company
Dodge	John	Corwin's troop
		Whipple's troop
Dodge	Josiah	Lathrop's company
Dodge	William Jr.	Corwin's troop
Eaton	Joseph	Whipple's troop
Ferrymann	William	Gardner's company
Hascall	Marke	Whipple's troop
Hull	John	Savage's company
Hussband	Richard	Gardner's company
Morgan	Moses	Gardner's company
Mosse	Jonathan	Poole's company
Rayment	John Jr.	Appleton's company
		Whipple's troop

219

Last Name	First Name	Unit
BEVERLY (continued)		
Read	Christopher	Gardner's company
Thorndike	Paul	Lathrop's company
Trask	Edward	Lathrop's company
Woodbury	Peter	Lathrop's company
GLOUCESTER		
Bray	Nathaniel	Poole's company
Clark	Joseph	Syll's company
Davis	Vinesont	Gardner's company
Day	John	Mosely's company
		Poole's company
Duday	Moses	Gardner's company
		Hadley Garrison
Ellery	Issac	Appleton's company
Fitch	John	Poole's company
Haraden	Edward Jr.	Gardner's company
Hascall	John	Poole's company
Jones	Benjamin	Brocklebank's company
Prince	John	Gardner's company
Sargeant	Andrew	Gardner's company
Somes	Joseph	Gardner's company
Stainwood	John	Brocklebank's company
		Lancaster Garrison
Stainwood	Philip Jr.	Brocklebank's company
Stainwood	Samuel	Poole's company
IPSWICH		
Adams	Simon	Appleton's company
		Brocklebank's company
Alhort	Alexander	Chelmsford Garrison
		Quabaug Garrison
Andrews	John Jr.	Lathrop's company
		Appleton's company
Bidford	Richard	Appleton's company
Bishop	Samuel	Willard's troop
Bray	Thomas Jr.	Lathrop's company
Briar	Richard	Appleton's company
Browne	John	Whipple's troop
Browne	John	Brocklebank's company
Burley	Andrew	Appleton's company
Burnam	James	Appleton's company
Chapman	Samuel	Lathrop's company
		Whipple's troop
Chub	John	Hadley Garrison
Clark	Josiah	Brocklebank's company
		Marlboro Garrison
Cross	George	Poole's company
Crumpton	Samuel	Lathrop's company
Cummings	Issac Jr.	Appleton's company
Day	James	Brocklebank's company
Deane	Philemon	Appleton's company

Last Name	First Name	Unit
IPSWICH (*continued*)		
Dennis	Thomas	Marlboro Garrison
Dennison	Jonathan	Appleton's company
Dow	Thomas Jr.	Appleton's company
		Gardner's company
Dutch	Robert Jr.	Appleton's company
Emerson	Nathaniel Jr.	Appleton's company
Emons	Joseph	Lathrop's company
Emons	Philip	Appleton's company
		Gardner's company
Faussee	Thomas	Appleton's company
Fellows	Ephraim	Paige's troop
		Whipple's troop
Fellows	Issac	Willard's troop
Fellows	Joseph	Brocklebank's company
Fitz	Abraham Jr.	Appleton's company
Ford	James	Appleton's company
		Brocklebank's company
		Paige's troop
French	Thomas Jr.	Appleton's company
Gidings	Samuel	Paige's troop
		Whipple's troop
Gilbert	John	Mosley's company
Gourdine	Amos	Gardner's company
Groe	Simon	Henchman's company
		Brocklebank's company
Hodgskin	William	Appleton's company
Hunt	Samuel	Appleton's company
		Turner's company
Ingois	Samuel	Appleton's company
		Williard's company
Jacob	Joseph	Poole's company
Jewett	Joseph Jr.	Appleton's company
		Gardner's company
Knowlton	Abraham	Appleton's company
Knowlton	John	Appleton's company
Line	John	Willard's troop
Lovel	John	Appleton's company
Lurvey	Peter	Appleton's company
Manning	Thomas Jr.	Lathrop's company
Marshall	Joseph	Prentice's company
Mentor	Thomas	Lathrop's company
Neland	Edward	Appleton's company
		Whipple's troop
Newman	Benjamin	Appleton's company
Newman	Thomas Jr.	Paige's troop
		Henchman's company
Newmarsh	Zaccheus	Appleton's company
Pasmore	Richard	Appleton's company
		Wheeler's company
		Groton Garrison

	Last Name	First Name	Unit
IPSWICH *(continued)*			
	Peirce	Samuel	Appleton's company
			Brocklebank's company
	Pengry	John	Appleton's company
			Poole's company
	Pengry	Moses Jr.	Lathrop's company
	Perkins	Issac	Quabaug Garrison
	Perkins	John	Appleton's company
	Perkins	Samuel	Appleton's company
			Brocklebank's company
			Syll's company
	Philips	Thomas	Quabaug Garrison
	Pipin	Samuel	Appleton's company
	Potter	Edmond	Appleton's company
	Potter	John	Wheeler's company
			Groton Garrison
	Prior	Richard	Appleton's company
	Proctor	Joseph	Paige's troop
			Henchman's company
	Ringe	Daniel	Lathrop's company
			Appleton's company
	Ross	Israh	Appleton's company
	Saddler	Abiel	Lathrop's company
			Appleton's company
	Safford	Joseph	Paige's troop
	Sparks	Thomas	Appleton's company
			Poole's company
	Stevens	Samuel	Lathrop's company
	Stimson	George	Appleton's company
	Story	Seth	Appleton's company
	Taylor	Samuel	Appleton's company
	Thomas	John	Appleton's company
	Timson	George	Appleton's company
	Wainwright	Francis Jr.	Billerica Garrison
	Wainwright	Jacob	Lathrop's company
	Wardall	Elihu or Uzall	Paige's troop
			Manning's company
	Wayte	Thomas Jr.	Appleton's company
	Webster	Benjamin	Gardner's company
	Whitteridge	Samuel	Lathrop's company
	Wood	Nathaniel	Appleton's company
	Young	Francis	Lathrop's company
			Appleton's company
	Zachaerias	Lewis	Appleton's company
LYNN			
	Ally	Solomon	Lathrop's company
	Baker	Thomas	Gardner's company
			Brocklebank's company
	Bassett	William	Gardner's company
	Berry	Thadeus	Whipple's troop

	Last Name	First Name	Unit
LYNN (*continued*)			
	Bread	Timothy	Whipple's troop
	Brown	Thomas Jr.	Brocklebank's company
	Burrell	John	Brocklebank's company
	Burrell	Joseph	Poole's company
	Chadwell	Moses	Poole's company
	Coates	Robert Jr.	Turner's company
			Poole's company
			Hadley Garrison
	Cole	George	Lathrop's company
	Collins	Benjamin	Corwin's troop
	Collins	Joseph	Manning's company
	Davis	John	Gardner's company
	Dellow	William	Whipple's troop
	Driver	Robert Jr.	Gardner's company
	Edmonds	John	Prentice's troop
	Farington	John	Gardner's company
	Farrar	Ephraim	Lathrop's company
	Fisk	Samuel	Poole's company
	Fuller	Elisha	Poole's company
	Furnell	Benjamin	Lathrop's company
	Graves	Samuel Jr.	Gardner's company
			Poole's company
	Hartt	Isaack	Gardner's company
	Huchin	Daniel	Gardner's company
	Huchin	Nicholas	Gardner's company
	Hunkens	John	Gardner's company
	Ireson	Samuel	Henchman's company
			Brocklebank's company
	Johnson	Samuel	Manning's company
	Kirtland	Nathaniel Jr.	Manning's company
	Lindsey	John	Gardner's company
	Linsey	Eliazer	Gardner's company
	Looke	Jonthan	Gardner's company
	Mann	John	Gardner's company
	Moore	Jonathan	Manning's company
	Rods	Samuel	Gardner's company
	Tarbox	Samuel	Gardner's company
	Townsend	Andrew	Gardner's company
	Vinton	Blaze	Lathrop's company
	Welman	Iseck	Gardner's company
	Witt	John Jr.	Whipple's troop
	Wyman/Wellman	Stephen	Lathrop's company
MANCHESTER			
	Allen	John	Lathrop's company
	Bennett	John	Lathrop's company
	Carter	Joshua	Lathrop's company
	Knight	John	Poole's company
	Pikworth	Samuel	Gardner's company

Last Name	First Name	Unit

Belinger	Leonerd	Gardner's company
Brock	Philip	Gardner's company
Cary	Peter	Gardner's company
Codner	Henry	Gardner's company
Cole	Peter	Gardner's company
Cooks	Robert	Gardner's company
Dew	William	Lathrop's company
Fferker	Auguster	Gardner's company
Hind	William Jr.	Gardner's company
Hudson	Samuel	Lathrop's company
Jones	Ephraim	Gardner's company
Lawrence	Enoch	Paige's troop
Merrett	John	Lathrop's company
Pittman	Mark	Lathrop's company
Ravensbee	Rowland	Brocklebank's company
Rose	Thomas	Lathrop's company
Russell	Thomas	Gardner's company
Severy	Edward	Gardner's company
Shapligh	David	Gardner's company
Stanford	Thomas	Brocklebank's company
Weymouth	Thomas	Gardner's company

Bartlett	Christopher	Appleton's company
Bodwell	Henry	Lathrop's company Appleton's company
Brabrooke	Samuel	Appleton's company
Breyer	Richard	Appleton's company
Browne	Edmond	Appleton's company
Browne	Richard Jr.	Henchman's company
Chase	Thomas	Appleton's company
Clark	Jonathan	Appleton's company
Cole	Christopher	Appleton's company Brookfield Garrison
Davis	Cornelius	Appleton's company
Davis	Zekeriah	Lathrop's company
Emery	Jonathan	Appleton's company Brocklebank's company
Greenleaf	Steven Jr.	Lathrop's company Appleton's company
Harvey	Jonathan	Appleton's company
Hobbs	John	Lathrop's company
Ilsiey	Issac	Appleton's company
Jones	Morgan	Appleton's company Marlboro Garrison
Kennison	Christopher	Appleton's company
Little	Moses	Turner's company
Lowell	Samuel	Appleton's company
Moore	Edmond	Lathrop's company
Moyer	George	Appleton's company

Last Name	First Name	Unit
NEWBURY (*continued*)		
Noyce	Timothy	Paige's troop
Ordway	Edward	Appleton's company
Plummer	John	Lathrop's company
Poore	Henry	Appleton's company
Poore	Samuel	Appleton's company
Rawlins	Nicholas	Appleton's company
Richardson	Caleb	Lathrop's company
		Appleton's company
Richardson	Joseph	Appleton's company
Rogers	Thomas	Appleton's company
Rolf	Daniel Jr.	Lathrop's company
		Appleton's company
Sawyer	William Jr.	Appleton's company
Sheepard	William	Appleton's company
Smith	Thomas Jr.	Lathrop's company
Somersby	Daniel	Appleton's company
Sparkes	Henry	Lancaster Garrison
Standley	William	Appleton's company
Toppan	John	Lathrop's company
		Appleton's company
Wheeler	John	Lathrop's company
		Appleton's company
Wilcott	John	Prentice's company
ROWLEY		
Bayly	Thomas	Lathrop's company
Boynton	Joshua	Appleton's company
		Brocklebank's company
Brown	William	Appleton's company
Burkby	Joseph	Appleton's company
Cooper	Samuel	Whipple's troop
Gowen	Symon	Appleton's company
Harriman	John	Lathrop's company
Hobson	John	Brocklebank's company
Holmes	Richard Jr.	Lathrop's company
Jackson	Caleb	Appleton's company
Jackson	John	Brocklebank's company
Kilborn	Jacob	Lathrop's company
Lever	Thomas Jr.	Whipple's troop
Leyton	John	Appleton's company
Palmer	John Jr.	Lathrop's company
Palmer	Thomas	Appleton's company
Pearson	Joseph	Lathrop's company
Sawyer	Ezekiel	Lathrop's company
Scales	Matthew	Lathrop's company
Smith	Samuel	Manning's company
Stickney	Andrew	Lathrop's company
Stickney	John	Appleton's company
Tyler	Samuel	Appleton's company
Wicomb	Daniel	Paige's troop
Wood	John	Brocklebank's company

Last Name	First Name	Unit
SALEM		
Alexander	Thomas	Lathrop's company
Allen	William	Gardner's company
Beckett	John	Manning's company
Bell	Thomas	Gardner's company
Boden	John	Gardner's company
Bond	Francis	Billerica Garrison
Bradell	Samuel	Gardner's company
Bridges	Edmond Jr.	Lathrop's company
Brown	Christopher	Gardner's company
Brown	Josiah	Hasey's company
Buffingtog	Thomas	Gardner's company
Bullock	John	Lathrop's company
Burton	Jacob	Turner's company
Butteler	Philip	Gardner's company
Cheever	Peter	Brocklebank's company
Clarke	Adam	Lathrop's company
Cooke	Henry Jr.	Brocklebank's company
Counter	Edward	Gardner's company
Deares	Joseph	Mosley's company
Dees	Joseph	Gardner's company
Flint	Thomas	Gardner's company
Frail	Samuel	Gardner's company
Fuller	Thomas Jr.	Manning's company
Gold	Adam	Gardner's company
Gray	Samuel	Gardner's company
Greene	Thomas	Gardner's company
Hollis	William	Gardner's company
Hooper	Benjamin	Gardner's company
Houlton	Joseph Jr.	Gardner's company
Howard	Thomas	Corwin's troop
Jefford	Frances	Gardner's company
Jennings	Peter	Savage's company
		Brocklebank's company
		Lancaster Garrison
Kenny	Henry	Whipple's troop
Kenny	Thomas	Gardner's company
Keyser	Eleazer	Lathrop's company
King	Joseph	Lathrop's company
Knight	Charles	Gardner's company
Lambard	Richard Jr.	Lathrop's company
Lemon	Benjamin	Gardner's company
Magery	Larance	Gardner's company
Nichols	Francis	Lancaster Garrison
Norman	Richard	Manning's company
Ozzier	Abel	Lathrop's company
Pease	Nathaniel	Brocklebank's company
Pease	Robert	Brocklebank's company
Pilsbury	William Jr.	Springfield Garrison
Polott	John	Gardner's company

	Last Name	First Name	Unit
SALEM (*continued*)			
	Prescote	Peter	Gardner's company
	Price	John	Gardner's company
	Prince	Joseph	Lathrop's company
			Gardner's company
	Pudenter	Jacob	Poole's company
	Read	Isack	Gardner's company
	Rice	Joseph	Gardner's company
	Rich	Henry	Gardner's company
	Ropes	George Jr.	Lathrop's company
	Rumeall	Clement	Gardner's company
	Sibly	Samuel	Turner's company
	Stacey	Marck	Gardner's company
	Stacie	William	Poole's company
	Stacy	John	Gardner's company
	Switchell	Abraham	Gardner's company
	Tossier	Lenard	Gardner's company
	Trask	John	Gardner's company
	Wainwright	William	Mosley's company
	Wall	James	Gardner's company
	Webster	Benjamin	Appleton's company
	Williams	Issac	Corwin's troop
	Wilson	Robert	Lathrop's company
	Wyat	George	Lancaster Garrison
TOPSFIELD			
	Andrews	Robert Jr.	Gardner's company
	Burton	Issac	Gardner's company
	Curtis	Zacheus Jr.	Gardner's company
	Hobbs	Thomas	Lathrop's company
	Peabody	William	Gardner's company
	Perkins	Zachers	Gardner's company
	Wild	John Jr.	Poole's company
			Turner's company
			Sweet's company
WENHAM			
	Abey	Thomas	Appleton's company
	Batchelder	Mark	Gardner's company
	Hutten	Richard Jr.	Gardner's company
	Kemball	Henry Jr.	Sweet's company
	Kemball	Caleb	Lathrop's company
	Kemball	Thomas	Lathrop's company
			Gardner's company
			Brocklebank's company
	Killom	Thomas	Appleton's company
	Moulton	Samuel	Gardner's company
	Welch	Philip	Gardner's company

Appendix 2
Rowley's 1662 Tax List: Ranked by
Family with Soldiers' Families Highlighted

Rank	Company of Soldier in Family	Last Name	First Name	Tax £-s-d	Notes
1ST QUARTILE					
5 Enlisted Soldiers, 1 Officer, 1 Unknown					
1		Gage	Corp.	1-9-8	
2		Rogers	Mrs.	1-6-4	
3	Lathrop	Pearson	John	1-5-7	
4		Jewett	Deacon	1-5-0	
5		Dreser	John	1-2-3	
6		Pichard	John	1-1-4	
7		Tenny	Thomas	1-0-3	
8 (tie)		Dickinson	Uxor	1-0-0	Wife
8 (tie)	Brocklebank	Hobson	Uxor	1-0-0	Wife
10	Appleton, Lathrop	Stickney	William	0-19-4	
11		Swan	Rih	0-18-10	
12	Unknown	Lambart	John	0-16-0	
13		Northen	Ezekiel	0-15-10	
14		Langhorne	Richard	0-15-8	
15		Nelson	Mr.	0-15-7	
16		Elsworth	Jeremiah	0-15-6	
17 (tie)	Brocklebank	Brocklebank	Samuel	0-15-5	
17 (tie)	Lathrop	Palmer	John	0-15-5	
19		Heseltine	Robert	0-15-2	
20		Nelson	Thomas	0-15-0	
21 (tie)		Barker	James	0-14-10	
21 (tie)		Spofford	John	0-14-10	

Rank	Company of Soldier in Family	Last Name	First Name	Tax £-s-d	Notes
2ND QUARTILE *8 Enlisted Soldiers (7 Men—1 Served Twice)*					
23	Lathrop	Bayley	James	0-14-7	
24 (tie)	Appleton	Palmer	Thomas	0-14-3	
24 (tie)		Redington	Abraham	0-14-3	
26	Whipple	Cooper	Peter	0-14-0	
27		Ace	William	0-13-8	
28		Hardy	Good.	0-13-7	
29	Appleton, Brocklebank* (same son)	Jackson	William	0-13-6	
30		Harris	John	0-12-3	
31		Mighill	Uxor	0-12-0	Wife
32	Appleton, Brocklebank* (same son)	Boynton	William	0-11-9	
33		Burbanks	John	0-11-7	
34	Whipple	Leaver	Thomas	0-10-11	
35		Johnson	John	0-10-4	
36 (tie)		Hazen	Edward	0-10-2	
36 (tie)		Prime	Mark	0-10-2	
38		Cumins	John	0-10-0	
39	Brocklebank	Jackson	Nicholas	0-9-10	
40		Langley	Abel	0-9-9	
41		Bixsby	Joseph	0-9-5	
42		Law	William	0-9-4	
MEDIAN (0-9-3)					
3RD QUARTILE *5 Enlisted Soldiers, 1 Quartermaster*					
43		Andrews	Robert	0-9-3	
44		Kingsbury	Henry	0-9-2	
45 (tie)	Lathrop	Killborne	George	0-9-1	
45 (tie)		Scales	John	0-9-1	
47		Foster	William	0-8-11	
48	Lathrop	Harriman	Leonard	0-8-9	
49 (tie)		Riely	Henry	0-8-8	
49 (tie)	Lathrop	Seales	William	0-8-8	
51 (tie)	Lathrop	Holmes	Richard	0-8-6	
51 (tie)	Paige	Wickem	Daniel	0-8-6	
53		Remington	Thomas	0-8-5	
54		Grant	John	0-8-4	

Rank	Company of Soldier in Family	Last Name	First Name	Tax £-s-d	Notes
3RD QUARTILE (*continued*)					
55		Worster	James	0-8-3	
56		Jewett	Abraham	0-8-2	
57		Scott	Benjamin	0-8-1	
58	Manning	Smith	Uxor	0-7-11	Wife
59 (tie)		Boyes	John	0-7-10	
59 (tie)		Mighill	Samuel	0-7-10	
61		Hadley	George	0-7-8	
4TH QUARTILE 5 Enlisted Soldiers					
62 (tie)		Clarke	Richard	0-7-3	
62 (tie)	Brocklebank	Wood	Thomas	0-7-3	
64	Appleton	Browne	Charles	0-7-0	
65	Lathrop	Sawyer	Edward	0-6-11	
66 (tie)		Smith	Robert	0-6-9	
66 (tie)		Stiles	Robert	0-6-9	
68		Bradley	Daniel	0-6-8	
69		Trumble	John	0-6-7	
70		Plats	Samuel	0-5-11	
71	Appleton	Lighton	Richard	0-5-8	
72		Wickem	Richard	0-5-6	
73 (tie)		Bond	John	0-5-5	
73 (tie)		Rogers	Robert	0-5-5	
75		Rayner	John	0-5-1	
76	Appleton	Burkly	Thomas	0-5-0	
77		Mighill	John	0-4-9	
78		Stickney	Samuel	0-4-6	
79		Plats	John	0-4-5	
80		Hindin	Andrew	0-4-3	
81		Peison	Uxor	0-3-11	Wife
82		Starling	Good:	0-3-10	
83		Lumin	Judith	0-1-7	
84		Jewett	Neh.	0-1-3	
85		Perley	Good:	0-1-1	

Source: Matthew Adams Stickney, "Ancient Tax List of Rowley," *New England Historical Genealogical Register* 15 (1861), 253–254; Patricia O'Malley, "Rowley, Massachusetts, 1639–1730: Dissent, Division, and Delimination in a Colonial Town" (Ph.D. diss., Boston College, 1975). Stickney dates the list from 1661–1664, but O'Malley definitively dates it at 1662.

Appendix 3

Topsfield's 1668 Tax List: Ranked by Family with Soldiers' Families Highlighted

Rank	Company of Soldier in Family	Last Name	First Name	Tax £-s-d	Notes
1ST QUARTILE					
5 Enlisted Soldiers					
1	Gardner	Peabody	Francis	1-4-2	Lieutenant Comm. of Militia 1675–76 Selectman
2		Gould	Jon	1-2-0	Ensign Comm. of Militia
3		Reddington	Jon	1-1-10	Sergeant in Chief Comm. of Militia 1675–76 Selectman
4	Gardner	Perkins	Thomas	1-1-6	1675–76 Selectman
5	.	Borman	Daniell	0-14-4	1675–76 Selectman
6		Towne	Edmond	0-14-3	Corporal
7	Poole, Turner	Wilds	John	0-13-3	
8	Lathrop	Hobes	Thomas	0-13-1	
9		Perkins	Mr. William	0-12-9	
10		How	Jon	0-12-6	
11	Gardner	Nickols	William	0-11-8	"Adopted" Issac Burton
12		Towne	William & Joseph	0-11-6	
2ND QUARTILE					
No Enlisted Soldiers, 2 Unknown					
13		Cummings	Issac Jr.	0-10-0	
14		Morall	Jon	0-9-11	
15	Unknown (2 sons)	Estey	Issac	0-9-8	
16		Dorman	Thomas	0-9-6	
16		Hovey	John	0-9-6	
18		Clarke	Daniel	0-9-5	
19		Cuttler	Samuel	0-8-11	

Appendix 3

Rank	Company of Soldier in Family	Last Name	First Name	Tax £-s-d	Notes
		AVERAGE (103 PENCE [D])			
3RD QUARTILE No Enlisted Soldiers, 1 Unknown					
20		French	John	0-8-6	
21		Browning	Thomas	0-8-4	
22		Dorman	Ephraim	0-8-0	1675–76 Selectman
		MEDIAN (94 PENCE [D])			
23	Unknown	Stanley	Mathu	0-7-10	
24		Towne	Jacob	0-7-6	
25		Cummings	Issac Sr.	0-7-3	
26		Baker	Thomas	0-6-6	1675–76 Selectman
27		Avery	William	0-6-0	
28		Peabody	Joseph	0-5-7	
29		Carell	Antony	0-5-6	
29		Donell	Mickall	0-5-6	
31		Prichat	William	0-5-0	
32		Howlett	Ensign	0-4-10	
4TH QUARTILE No Enlisted Soldiers					
33		Bridges	Edmund	0-4-6	
33		Gilbert	Mr.	0-4-6	
35		Smith	William	0-4-4	"Corporal William"
36		Avery	Thomas	0-4-3	
37		Watters	James	0-4-0	
38		Black	Daniel	0-3-6	
39		Robinson	Jon	0-2-10	
40		Nickols	Jon	0-2-9	
41		Boudon	Mickall	0-2-8	
41		Hucker	Mathu	0-2-8	
43		Morles	Evans	0-2-0	
43		Perkins	Deborah	0-2-0	Woman
44		Waklin	Luke	0-1-0	
NOT ON TAX LIST 2 Enlisted Soldiers, 1 Unknown					
	Gardner	Andrews	Robert		Father died 1668
	Gardner	Curtis	Zacheus		
	Unknown	Curtis	Zachariah		

Appendix 4
An Examination of the Age of Essex County Soldiers and Officers in King Philip's War, 1675–1676

Total Number of Enlisted Men: 357
Number with Known Age: 195 (55% of total men)

Average Age: 26.6 years old
Modal Age: 25 years old
Median Age: 25 years old

Enlisted Soldiers' Ages by Decade

Age Group	Number	Percentage	Cumulative Percentage
16–20	33	16.9%	16.9%
20–29	106	54.3%	71.2%
30–39	43	22.0%	93.2%
40–49	10	5.1%	98.3%
50–52	4	2.0%	100.3%

Note: Deviation in percentage totals from 100.0 is a function of rounding.

Breakdown of Men by Age during King Philip's War, 1675–1676

Age during War	52	51	50		49	48	47	46	45	44	43	42	41	40		39	38	37	36	35	34
Number of Men	1	1	2		0	0	1	2	0	2	0	2	0	3		4	2	4	0	3	4

Age during War	33	32	31	30		29	28	27	26	25	24	23	22	21	20		19	18	17	16
Number of Men	6	7	6	7		11	4	7	5	18	10	17	12	8	14		11	10	8	3

In comparison to the numbers for King Philip's War above, Fred Anderson's study of eighteenth-century soldiers of the French and Indian War reports an average of 26.3 years old for enlisted volunteers during the war, with a median age of 23 and a modal age of 18.[1] These numbers are very close to the soldiers considered in this study. In his section on the soldiers of New England who fought during the American Revolution, Charles Neimeyer reports that 72 percent of the men were in their teens and twenties, an almost identical finding to the men of King Philip's War.[2]

ACTIVE-DUTY OFFICERS, 1675–1676

Total Number of Officers: 12

Number with Known Age: 10 (83% of total officers)

Average Age: 46.2 years old

Modal Age: 30 years old

Median Age: 48 Years old

Breakdown of Officers by Age during King Philip's War, 1675–1676

Age during War	65	50	49	47	45	31	30
Number of Officers	2	2	1	1	1	1	2

In comparison to the study of officer ages for King Philip's War above, Harold Selesky's examination of the officers of Connecticut during the French and Indian War reports that the field officers (those above the rank of captain) averaged forty-two years of age, while captains on average were thirty-nine. While the averages are similar to those for King Philip's War described here, Selesky mentions few officers over fifty years old.[3]

ACTIVE-DUTY NONCOMMISSIONED OFFICERS, 1675–1676

Total Number of Noncommissioned Officers: 12
Number with Known Age: 8 (67% of total)

Average Age: 29.9 years old
Modal Age: None
Median Age: 23 years old

Breakdown of Noncommissioned Officers by Age during King Philip's War, 1675–1676

Age during War	52	32	30	23	22	21	19
Number of Noncommissioned Officers	1	1	1	1	1	1	1

Unfortunately, none of the studies of eighteenth-century soldiers make a separate study of noncommissioned officers' ages, so no comparison data is available.

1. Fred Anderson, *A People's Army: Massachusetts Soldiers and Society in the Seven Years' War* (Chapel Hill: University of North Carolina Press, 1984), 53, 231 table 10.

2. Charles Patrick Neimeyer, *America Goes to War: A Social History of the Continental Army* (New York: New York University Press, 1996), 18.

3. Harold E. Selesky, *War and Society in Colonial Connecticut* (New Haven, Conn.: Yale University Press, 1990), 194–215, esp. 196.

Appendix 5
The Occupations of the Soldiers of Essex County, 1675–1676

Occupation	Category	Number Listed
Blacksmith	Craftsmen/Tradesmen	3
Brewer	Craftsmen/Tradesmen	1
Carpenter	Craftsmen/Tradesmen	14
Cooper	Craftsmen/Tradesmen	2
Cordwainer/Shoemaker	Craftsmen/Tradesmen	5
Farm Laborer	Farming/Agriculture	5
Farmer	Farming/Agriculture	16
Fisherman	Maritime Trades	17
Fuller	Craftsmen/Tradesmen	1
Glazier	Craftsmen/Tradesmen	1
Glover	Craftsmen/Tradesmen	1
Gunsmith	Craftsmen/Tradesmen	1
Husbandman	Farming/Agriculture	26
Innkeeper/Ordinary	Merchant	7
Ironworker	Craftsmen/Tradesmen	2
Mariner	Maritime Trades	8
Merchant	Merchant	3
Miller	Craftsmen/Tradesmen	1
Planter	Farming/Agriculture	1
Plowright	Craftsmen/Tradesmen	1
Servant	Servant	22
Shepard	Farming/Agriculture	1
Shipbuilder/Ship Carpenter	Craftsmen/Tradesmen	6
Shoreman	Maritime Trades	4
Tailor	Craftsmen/Tradesmen	4
Tanner	Craftsmen/Tradesmen	4
Trapper/Trader	Merchant	1
Weaver	Craftsmen/Tradesmen	4
Wheelwright	Craftsmen/Tradesmen	1
Yeoman	Farming/Agriculture	15
Total		178

Abbreviations Used in the Notes

Colonial Laws 1672

William H. Whitmore, ed., *The Colonial Laws of Massachusetts: Reprinted from the Edition of 1672 with the Supplements through 1686* (Boston: Published by the Order of the City Council of Boston, 1887).

E C Q C R

George Francis Dow, ed., *Records and Files of the Quarterly Courts of Essex County, Massachusetts*, 8 vols. (Salem, Mass.: Essex Institute, 1911–1918).

M A C

Massachusetts Archives Collection, 1629–1799. (SC1/45x). Massachusetts State Archives, Columbia Point, Massachusetts. Also known as the "Felt Collection."

P R E C

George Francis Dow, ed., *The Probate Records of Essex County, Massachusetts*, 3 vols. (Salem, Mass.: Essex Institute, 1916).

R G C M B

Nathaniel Bradstreet Shurtleff, ed., *Records of the Governor and Company of the Massachusetts Bay in New England.* 5 in 6 vols. (Boston: W. White, Printer to the Commonwealth, 1853).

Notes

INTRODUCTION

1. This recreation of Marblehead's experience in the early days of the war is based on numerous sources, including: George Madison Bodge, *Soldiers in King Philip's War*, reprint of 1906 3rd ed. (Baltimore: Genealogical Publishing, 1967); Benjamin F. Arrington, "Town of Marblehead," in *Municipal History of Essex County in Massachusetts*, ed. Benjamin F. Arrington (New York: Lewis Historical Publishing, 1922); William Hammond Bowden, "Marblehead Town Records," *Essex Institute Historical Collections* 69, nos. 3–4 (1933): 207–293; Christine Leigh Heyrman, *Commerce and Culture: The Maritime Communities of Colonial Massachusetts, 1690–1750* (New York: Norton, 1984); Samuel Roads, *The History and Traditions of Marblehead*, 3rd ed. (Marblehead, Mass.: N.A. Lindsey, 1897).

2. Virginia DeJohn Anderson, *New England's Generation: The Great Migration and the Formation of Society and Culture in the Seventeenth Century* (Cambridge: Cambridge University Press, 1991), 195–196.

3. For a good overview of the period and the trials New England faced, see Francis J. Bremer, *Puritan Experiment: New England Society from Bradford to Edwards*, rev. ed. (Hanover, N.H.: University Press of New England, 1995).

4. For information on the current state of military history and the place of war and society studies within the larger field, see Jeremy Black, *Rethinking Military History* (London: Routledge, 2004), 49–59; Stephen Morillo and Michael F. Pavkovic, *What Is Military History?* (Malden, Mass.: Polity, 2006), 37–43, 61–66; Robert Citino, "Military Histories Old and New: A Reintroduction," *American Historical Review* 112, no. 4 (2007): 1070–1090; Wayne E. Lee, "Mind and Matter—Cultural Analysis in American Military History: A Look at the State of the Field," *Journal of American History* 93 no. 4 (March 2007): 1116–1142; Michael Neiberg, "War and Society," in *Palgrave Advances in Modern Military History*, ed. Matthew Hughes and William J. Philpott, (Basingstoke, England: Palgrave Macmillan, 2006), 42–60. For the state of the study of war and society (or "new military history") in early American history, see Wayne E. Lee, "Early American Ways of War: A New Reconaissance, 1600–1815," *Historical Journal* 44 (March 2001): 269–289; E. Wayne Carp, "Early American Military History: A Review of Recent Work," *The Virginia Magazine of History and Biography* 94, no. 3 (1986):

259–284; Don Higginbotham, "The Early American Way of War: Reconnaissance and Appraisal," *William and Mary Quarterly*, 44, no. 3 (1987): 230–273.

5. Douglas Edward Leech, *Flintlock and Tomahawk: New England in King Philip's War*, reprint of 1958 Macmillian ed. (East Orleans, Mass.: Parnassus Imprints, 1992), 103–104. Leech's earlier works confirm this view; see Douglas Edward Leech, "The Military System of Plymouth Colony," *New England Quarterly* 24, no. 3 (1951): 342–364.

6. Douglas Edward Leech, *Arms for Empire: A Military History of the British Colonies in North America, 1607–1763* (New York: Macmillan, 1973), 21.

7. For a few of the numerous examples of historians accepting this version of early military recruitment, see Russell Bourne, *Red King's Rebellion: Racial Politics in New England, 1675–1678* (New York: Atheneum, 1990), 152–153; Armstrong Starkey, *European and Native American Warfare, 1675–1815* (Norman: University of Oklahoma Press, 1998), 39–42, 57–82; Guy Chet, *Conquering the American Wilderness: The Triumph of European Warfare in the Colonial Northeast* (Amherst: University of Massachusetts Press, 2003), 61–62; Don Higginbotham, "The Military Institutions of Colonial America: The Rhetoric and the Reality," in *War and Society in Revolutionary America: The Wider Dimensions of Conflict*, ed. Don Higginbotham (Columbia: University of South Carolina Press, 1988), 22–23. A few historians have dug a bit more deeply into the specifics of recruitment and offered a more nuanced view. See Jack S. Radabaugh, "The Militia of Colonial Massachusetts," *Military Affairs* 18, no. 1 (1954): 1–18; Jack Sheldon Radabaugh, "The Military System of Colonial Massachusetts, 1690–1740" (Ph.D. diss., University of Southern California, 1965); Jenny Hale Pulsipher, "'The Overture of This New Albion World': King Philip's War and the Transformation of New England" (Ph.D. diss., Brandeis University, 1999), 243–281; Harold E. Selesky, *War and Society in Colonial Connecticut* (New Haven, Conn.: Yale University Press, 1990), 12, 24–25.

8. John Shy, "A New Look at the Colonial Militia," in *A People Numerous and Armed: Reflections on the Military Struggle for American Independence*, reprint of 1976 Oxford ed. (Ann Arbor: University of Michigan Press, 1990), 32.

9. Shy, "New Look," 37.

10. Even careful social historians, who had dedicated themselves to minutely detailed studies, accepted unquestioningly this idea of a representative militia as the truth. One prominent example (of many) is Robert Gross's extensive study of colonial Concord, *The Minutemen and Their World*. Gross goes into great detail about the pre-Revolution life of the community, examining town-church relations, the town's economic web, and interfamily conflicts. Yet, when it came time to examine the men who fought in the famous battle of Lexington and Concord, Gross forwent a study of the soldiers' identities. Instead, he wrote a single page on what he called "a citizen army of rural neighbors . . . that included nearly everyone between the ages of sixteen and sixty." Robert A. Gross, *The Minutemen and Their World* (New York: Hill and Wang, 1976), 70.

11. Richard H. Kohn, "The Social History of the American Soldier: A Review and Prospectus for Research," *American Historical Review* 86, no. 3 (1981): 563.

12. Kohn, "Social History of the American Soldier," 564–565. For a similar call to arms, see also Peter Karsten, "The 'New' American Military History: A Map of the Territory, Explored and Unexplored," *American Quarterly* 36, no. 3 (1984): 390–396.

13. Fred Anderson, *A People's Army: Massachusetts Soldiers and Society in the Seven Years' War* (Chapel Hill: University of North Carolina Press, 1984). Important studies also include: Selesky, *War and Society in Colonial Connecticut*; Stephen Brumwell, *Redcoats: The British Soldier and the War in the Americas, 1755–1763* (Cambridge: Cambridge University Press, 2002); Myron O. Stachiw, *Massachusetts Officers and Soldiers, 1723–1743: Dummer's War to the War of Jenkins' Ear* (Boston: Society of Colonial Wars in the Commonwealth of Massachusetts and New England Historic Genealogical Society, 1979), esp. the introduction.

14. Anderson, *A People's Army*, 26–62. Anderson did not, however, take the data from the muster lists any further; he did not trace the soldiers back to their communities.

15. Steven Rosswurm, *Arms, Country, and Class: The Philadelphia Militia And "Lower Sort" during the American Revolution, 1775–1783* (New Brunswick, N.J.: Rutgers University Press, 1988); Charles Patrick Neimeyer, *America Goes to War: A Social History of the Continental Army* (New York: New York University Press, 1996). For two recent examples, see Caroline Cox, *A Proper Sense of Honor: Service and Sacrifice in George Washington's Army* (Chapel Hill: University of North Carolina Press, 2004); Gregory T. Knouff, *The Soldiers' Revolution: Pennsylvanians and the Forging of Early American Identity* (University Park: Penn State University Press 2003). The issue of soldiers and mobilization in the Revolution is the subject of an entire collection of war and society essays, for which John Shy has written the introduction. See John Resch and Walter Sargent, eds., *War and Society in the American Revolution: Mobilization and Home Fronts* (DeKalb: Northern Illinois University Press, 2007).

16. T. H. Breen, "Persistent Localism: English Social Change and the Shaping of New England Institutions," in *Puritans and Adventurers: Change and Persistence in Early America,* ed. T. H. Breen (New York: Oxford University Press, 1980), 3–24.

A NOTE ON METHOD

1. The identity of the soldiers was determined by using a number of different sources. The main resource in identifying them was George Madison Bodge, *Soldiers in King Philip's War*, reprint of 1906 3rd ed. (Baltimore: Genealogical Publishing, 1967). Bodge, a meticulous antiquarian and historian of the late nineteenth century, combed the account ledgers of John Hull (the wartime treasurer

of Massachusetts Bay) and reconstructed muster lists (based on pay records) for every company and every soldier from Massachusetts Bay in the war. For information on Hull, see Hermann Frederick Clarke, *John Hull, a Builder of the Bay Colony* (Portland, Maine: Southworth-Anthoensen, 1940). For a more detailed account of the men and how these choices were made, see Kyle F. Zelner, "The Flower and Rabble of Essex County: A Social History of the Massachusetts Bay Militia and Militiamen during King Philip's War, 1675–1676" (Ph.D. diss., College of William and Mary, 2003).

2. For a more detailed account of this question, see Zelner, "Flower and Rabble."

3. For information on the special precautions one must use when employing genealogies as a historic source, see Robert M. Taylor and Ralph J. Crandall, eds., *Generations and Change: Genealogical Perspectives in Social History* (Macon, Ga.: Mercer University Press, 1986); Marcia Wiswall Lindberg, *Genealogist's Handbook for New England Research*, 3rd ed. (Boston: New England Historic Genealogical Society, 1993).

4. In 1675, Essex County did not contain the towns of Salisbury or Haverhill, which belonged to (old) Norfolk County. (Old) Norfolk County disappeared in 1679 when New Hampshire became a royal province; at that time, the two towns were designated a part of Essex County, Massachusetts. In 1793, Massachusetts named a newly formed county (located south of Boston) Norfolk County. Because Salisbury and Haverhill were not technically a part of Essex County during the war, their soldiers are not treated here. See Benjamin F. Arrington, ed., *Municipal History of Essex County in Massachusetts*, tercentenary ed., 4 vols. (New York: Lewis Historical Publishing, 1922), 1:40–41; William Francis Galvin, ed., *Historical Data Relating to Counties, Cities, and Towns in Massachusetts* (Boston: New England Historic Genealogical Society, 1997); Louis S. Cook, ed., *History of Norfolk County, Massachusetts 1622–1918*, 2 vols. (New York: S. J. Clarke, 1918).

5. For the classification systems, see Richard Archer, *Fissures in the Rock: New England in the Seventeenth Century* (Hanover, N.H.: University Press of New England, 2001); Edward M. Cook Jr., "Local Leadership and the Typology of New England Towns, 1700–1785," *Political Science Quarterly* 86, no. 4 (1971): 586–608.

6. While some might argue that a study of Hampshire County is more appropriate, given its placement on the frontier and the fact that a large proportion of the war's combat occurred there, that is not the case. Hampshire County is unsuitable for this type of study because it was so recently established in relation to the period of the war. Its population was so small and unstable that relatively few men from the county actually served in active-duty companies during the conflict. In addition, few records from the period exist for Hampshire County, especially when compared to Essex County.

7. For several perspectives on this debate, see Patrick Collinson, "A Comment: Concerning the Name Puritan," *Journal of Ecclesiastical History* 31, no.

4 (1980): 483–488; Peter Lake, "Defining Puritanism—Again?" in *Puritanism: Transatlantic Perspectives on a Seventeenth-Century Anglo-American Faith*, ed. Francis J. Bremer (Boston: Massachusetts Historical Society, distributed by Northeastern University Press, 1993), 3–29.

8. Virginia DeJohn Anderson, *New England's Generation: The Great Migration and the Formation of Society and Culture in the Seventeenth Century* (Cambridge: Cambridge University Press, 1991), 39–40.

CHAPTER 1

1. RGCMB, 1:17–18.

2. RGCMB, 1:17–18.

3. The literature on the militia tradition in England is extensive. See Ian F. W. Beckett, *Amateur Military Tradition, 1558–1945* (Manchester: Manchester University Press, 1991); Lindsay Boynton, *The Elizabethan Militia, 1558–1638* (London: Routledge and Kegan Paul, 1967); C. G. Cruickshank, *Elizabeth's Army*, 2nd ed. (Oxford: Clarendon Press, 1966); John W. Fortescue, *History of the British Army*, 13 vols., vols. 1–2 (London: Macmillan, 1899).

4. Boynton, *Elizabethan Militia*, 9; Darrett Bruce Rutman, "A Militant New World, 1607–1640: America's First Generation: Its Martial Spirit, Its Tradition of Arms, Its Militia Organization, Its Wars" (Ph.D. diss., University of Virginia, 1959), 21.

5. Boynton, *Elizabethan Militia*, 90–125; Richard Winship Stewart, "Arms and Politics: The Supply of Arms in England, 1585–1625" (Ph.D. diss., Yale University, 1986), 207–216, esp. 211–214.

6. Quoted in Rutman, "Militant New World," 25.

7. Boynton, *Elizabethan Militia*, 112.

8. Barnaby Rich, *A Pathway to Military Practise: Containinge Offices, Lawes, Disciplines and Orders to Be Observed in an Army . . .* (London: J. Charlewood for R. Walley, 1587), 23–24, Early English Books Online, 1475–1640, http://eebo.chadwyck.com. See also Cruickshank, *Elizabeth's Army*, 26–30.

9. Cruickshank, *Elizabeth's Army*, 26–30; Frank Tallett, *War and Society in Early Modern Europe, 1495–1715* (London: Routledge, 1992), 86–87.

10. Beckett, *Amateur Military Tradition*, 31–44; D. P. Carter, "The 'Exact Militia' in Lancashire, 1625–1640," *Northern History: A Review of the History of the North of England (Great Britain)* 11 (1976): 87–106.

11. T. H. Breen, "The Covenanted Militia of Massachusetts Bay: English Background and New World Development," in *Puritans and Adventurers: Change and Persistence in Early America* (New York: Oxford University Press, 1980), 29.

12. Breen, "Covenanted Militia," 30–32.

13. Ronan Bennett, "War and Disorder: Policing the Soldiery in Civil War Yorkshire," in *War and Government in Britain, 1598–1650*, ed. Mark Charles Fissel (Manchester: Manchester University Press, 1991), 248.

14. Breen, "Covenanted Militia," 31–32.

15. For the history of the lieutenancy, see Boynton, *Elizabethan Militia*; Cruickshank, *Elizabeth's Army*; Mark Charles Fissel, *English Warfare, 1511–1642* (London: Routledge, 2001); John S. Noland, "The Militarization of the Elizabethan State," *Journal of Military History* 58, no. 3 (1994): 391–420; Victor L. Stater, *Nobel Government: The Stuart Lord Lieutenancy and the Transformation of English Politics* (Athens: University of Georgia Press, 1994); Victor Louis Stater, "The Lord Lieutenancy in England, 1625–1688: The Crown, Nobility, and Local Government" (Ph.D. diss., University of Chicago, 1988); Victor L. Stater, "The Lord Lieutenancy on the Eve of the Civil Wars: The Impressment of George Plowright," *Historical Journal (Great Britain)* 29, no. 2 (1986): 279–296; Gladys Scott Thomson, *Lords Lieutenants in the Sixteenth Century: A Study in Tudor Local Administration* (London: Longmans, Green, 1923); Thomas Garden Barnes, "Deputies Not Principals, Lieutenants Not Captains: The Institutional Failure of Lieutenancy in the 1620s," in *War and Government in Britain, 1598–1650*, ed. Mark Charles Fissel (Manchester: Manchester University Press, 1991), 58–86.

16. Cruickshank, *Elizabeth's Army*, 20–24; Noland, "Militarization," 411.

17. Thomson, *Lord's Lieutenants*, 38–40.

18. Cruickshank, *Elizabeth's Army*, 20–24.

19. Stater, "Lord Lieutenancy in England," 165–167.

20. Fissel, *English Warfare*, 53; Stater, "Lord Lieutenancy in England," 18.

21. Walter Weston Colby Jr., "Adaptations of English Military Institutions in Seventeenth-Century New England" (master's thesis, University of Detroit, 1952), 4; Fissel, *English Warfare*, 53–54.

22. Stewart, "Arms and Politics," 209–210.

23. Breen, "Covenanted Militia," 29; Stater, "Lord Lieutenancy in England," 26–36.

24. Stater, "Lord Lieutenancy in England," 161–167.

25. Stater, "Lord Lieutenancy on the Eve of the Civil Wars," 282–283.

26. On the state of the English militia and how it was mobilized, see Beckett, *Amateur Military Tradition*, 1–59; Boynton, *Elizabethan Militia*, 46–48, 90–126; Cruickshank, *Elizabeth's Army*, 24–26; C. H. Firth, *Cromwell's Army: A History of the English Soldier during the Civil Wars, the Commonwealth, and the Protectorate*, reprint of 1902 ed. (Novato, Calif.: Presido, 1992), 1–14; Noland, "Militarization," 398–401; Stewart, "Arms and Politics," 211–216.

27. Boynton, *Elizabethan Militia*, 108.

28. Boynton, *Elizabethan Militia*, 109; Stewart, "Arms and Politics," 212.

29. Cruickshank, *Elizabeth's Army*, 28.

30. Quoted in Stewart, "Arms and Politics," 212. While many of the trainbands had been "corrupted," those in London still consisted of the rising middle class. See Stewart, "Arms and Politics," 211; Boynton, *Elizabethan Militia*, 122–125, 192–215.

31. Stater, "Lord Lieutenancy in England," 163.
32. Stater, "Lord Lieutenancy in England," 163.
33. Stater, "Lord Lieutenancy on the Eve of the Civil Wars," 284.
34. Cruickshank, *Elizabeth's Army*, 27; Fissel, *English Warfare*, 86.
35. Fissel, *English Warfare*, 86–87.
36. Stater, *Noble Government*, 41.
37. Cruickshank, *Elizabeth's Army*, 28.
38. Stater, "Lord Lieutenancy in England," 165.
39. Stater, "Lord Lieutenancy in England," 165.
40. Stater, "Lord Lieutenancy in England," 165.
41. Breen, "Covenanted Militia," 29.
42. Francis J. Bremer, "The County of Massachusetts: The Governance of John Winthrop's Suffolk and the Shaping of Massachusetts Bay," in *The World of John Winthrop: Essays on England and New England, 1588–1649*, ed. Francis J. Bremer and Lynn A. Botelho (Boston: Massachusetts Historical Society, 2005), 216.
43. RGCMB, 1:85, 1:116.
44. Breen, "Covenanted Militia," 27, 32–45. See also Archibald Hannah Jr., "New England's Military Institutions, 1693–1750" (Ph.D. diss., Yale University, 1950), 1–18; Morrison Sharp, "Leadership and Democracy in the Early New England System of Defense," *American Historical Review* 50, no. 2 (1945): 244–245.
45. In the first year of settlement, the militia of Massachusetts trained as often as once a week. The frequency of training was dramatically reduced over time. There is an extensive literature on the development of training in the Massachusetts militia. See Marie L. Ahearn, *The Rhetoric of War: Training Day, the Militia, and the Military Sermon* (New York: Greenwood, 1989); Allen French, "Arms and Military Training of Our Colonizing Ancestors," *Proceeding of the Massachusetts Historical Society* 67 (1945): 3–21; Richard P. Gildrie, "Defiance, Diversion, and the Exercise of Arms: The Several Meanings of Colonial Training Days in Colonial Massachusetts," *Military Affairs* 52, no. 2 (1988): 53–55; Jack S. Radabaugh, "The Militia of Colonial Massachusetts," *Military Affairs* 18, no. 1 (1954): 1–18.
46. Breen, "Covenanted Militia." For the vast literature on the election of officers in New England militias, see Hannah, "Military Institutions"; Richard Henry Marcus, "The Militia of Colonial Connecticut 1639–1775" (Ph.D. diss., University of Colorado, 1965); Harold E. Selesky, *War and Society in Colonial Connecticut* (New Haven, Conn.: Yale University Press, 1990); John Shy, "A New Look at the Colonial Militia," in *A People Numerous and Armed: Reflections on the Military Struggle for American Independence*, reprint of 1976 Oxford ed. (Ann Arbor: University of Michigan Press, 1990), 29–41; Felix John Zarlengo, "Politics of Defense in the New England Colonies, 1620–1746" (master's thesis, Brown University, 1965).
47. Breen, "Covenanted Militia," 39–43.
48. Breen, "Covenanted Militia," 34–39.
49. RGCMB, 2:42–43.

50. *The Book of the General Lavves and Libertyes Concerning the Inhabitants of the Massachusets . . .* (Cambridge, Mass.: Printed according to order of the General Court, 1660); John D. Cushing, ed., *The Laws and Liberties of Massachusetts, 1641–1691: A Facsimile Edition, Containing Also Council Orders and Executive Proclimations,* 3 vols. (Wilmington, Del.: Scholarly Resources, 1976); Massachusetts General Court, *The Book of the General Lauues and Libertyes Concerning the Inhabitants of the Massachusets . . . Anno 1647* (Cambridge, Mass.: Printed According to Order of the General Court and are to be solde at the shop of Hezekiah Usher in Boston, 1648); and *Colonial Laws 1672.*

51. *Colonial Laws 1672,* 107–116.

52. The continuing concern over an abusive military is best seen in the resistance in 1638 to the establishment of the professional "Artillery Company of Massachusetts Bay." Governor John Winthrop and others were concerned that the group would become an instrument of independent military power and a possible threat to the government in the colony. See Oliver Ayer Roberts, *History of the Military Company of the Massachusetts Now Called the Ancient and Honorable Artillery Company of Massachusetts, 1637–1888* (Boston: Alfred Mudge, 1895); Louise Breen, *Transgressing the Bounds: Subversive Enterprises among the Puritan Elite in Massachusetts, 1630–1692* (Oxford: Oxford University Press, 2001).

53. In 1636, Massachusetts became the first English government to institute its military into permanent regiments, drawn on county lines. In doing so, the colony even preceded England, which did not adopt regular regiments until 1642 during the English Civil War. See Rutman, "Militant New World," 672.

54. *Colonial Laws 1672,* 107.

55. *Colonial Laws 1672,* 111.

56. *Colonial Laws 1672,* 107, 116.

57. *Colonial Laws 1672,* 116.

58. *Colonial Laws 1672,* 108.

59. *Colonial Laws 1672,* 108.

60. Boynton, *Elizabethan Militia,* 111–112.

61. Radabaugh, "Militia of Colonial Massachusetts," 14.

62. *Colonial Laws 1672,* 109. In 1645, boys between ten and sixteen years old were to be instructed in small arms and bows unless their parents objected. See RGCMB, 3:12.

63. *Colonial Laws 1672,* 109.

64. RGCMB, 3:268 and 4:pt. 1, 257.

65. *Colonial Laws 1672,* 109.

66. The post of clerk of the band was extremely unpopular with the soldiers, so much so that the General Court instituted a forty-shilling fine for anyone refusing to serve as clerk if so assigned. *Colonial Laws 1672,* 109.

67. *Colonial Laws 1672,* 108.

68. *Colonial Laws 1672*, 204. Riding the wooden horse was a military punishment that saw the subject forced to sit in intense discomfort on a wooden, triangular "horse" with muskets tied to each foot for weight, often until blood was drawn. Bilboes were an iron bar with sliding fetters to shackle the feet of the offender. "Lying Neck and Heels" meant that the perpetrator was tied with a short length of rope by the neck and ankles so the body was drawn into a ball for a period, which ultimately benumbs the entire body.

69. *Colonial Laws 1672*, 114.

70. Breen, "Covenanted Militia," 39–43.

71. Douglas Edward Leech, "The Military System of Plymouth Colony," *New England Quarterly* 24, no. 3 (1951): 354.

72. *Colonial Laws 1672*, 112.

73. *Colonial Laws 1672*, 111–112.

74. RGCMB, 3:265.

75. *Colonial Laws 1672*, 113.

76. *Colonial Laws 1672*, 113.

77. *Colonial Laws 1672*, 113.

78. RGCMB, 3:268–269.

79. RGCMB, 3:268–269. Magistrates were also known as assistants, as they sat on the Court of Assistants.

80. There was an active Militia Committee of London in England during the English Civil War; because it was associated with Parliament and Parliament's Committee of Safety, however, it was not a local committee and nothing like the Massachusetts committees. See Ian Gentiles, *The New Model Army in England, Ireland, and Scotland, 1645–1653* (Oxford: Blackwell, 1992), 185–187. In 1643, a Massachusetts law was passed in an attempt to establish an official called "shire lieutenant" in each Massachusetts county who could deal with some of the administrative functions of the militia system, which had been reorganized on the county level. See RGCMB, 2:42–43. The shire lieutenant would have been a counterpart to the county sergeants major. No shire lieutenants, however, were ever appointed in Massachusetts Bay. It is likely that the office too closely resembled the much-feared lord lieutenant of England. See Colby, "Adaptations," 35–37; Robert K. Wright, *Massachusetts Militia Roots: A Bibliographic Study* (Washington, D.C.: Departments of the Army and the Air Force, Historical Branch, Office of Public Affairs, National Guard Bureau, 1986), 5–6.

81. Breen, "Covenanted Militia," 40; Francis J. Bremer, *Puritan Experiment: New England Society from Bradford to Edwards*, rev. ed. (Hanover, N.H.: University Press of New England, 1995), 132–133.

82. Breen, "Covenanted Militia," 41.

83. Breen, "Covenanted Militia," 39–43.

84. RGCMB, 3:269.

85. RGCMB, 3:269.
86. RGCMB, 3:344; my emphasis.
87. RGCMB, 3:321.
88. RGCMB, 3:359.
89. RGCMB, 4:pt. 2, 120.
90. RGCMB, 4:pt. 2, 120.
91. RGCMB, 4:pt. 2, 332.
92. *Colonial Laws 1672*, 110.
93. *Colonial Laws 1672*, 110.
94. *Colonial Laws 1672*, 111.
95. *Colonial Laws 1672*, 203; my emphasis.
96. RGCMB, 4:pt. 2, 573. For the Dutch threat, see Harry M. Ward, *The United Colonies of New England, 1643-90* (New York: Vintage, 1961), 270–275.
97. RGCMB, 4:pt. 2, 575.
98. RGCMB, 5:30.
99. This did not apply to the officers put in charge of expeditionary companies during the war. The General Court appointed those officers when the company was established. See George Madison Bodge, *Soldiers in King Philip's War*, reprint of 1906 3rd ed. (Baltimore: Genealogical Publishing, 1967).

CHAPTER 2

1. RGCMB, 5:45.
2. RGCMB, 5:47.
3. RGCMB, 5:47.
4. RGCMB, 5:47–48.
5. For details on weaponry during the war, see Allen French, "Arms and Military Training of Our Colonizing Ancestors," *Proceeding of the Massachusetts Historical Society* 67 (1945): 3–21; Patrick M. Malone, *The Skulking Way of War: Technology and Tactics among the New England Indians* (Baltimore: Johns Hopkins University Press, 1993); Harold L. Peterson, *Arms and Armor in Colonial America, 1526–1783*, unabridged reproduction of the 1956 Stackpole ed. (Mineola, N.Y.: Dover, 2000).
6. RGCMB, 5:49–50.
7. There is a vast literature on the cause of the war and the suggestion that it was brought about by the decline (or declension) of Puritan ideals held by the first generation of settlers. For a few of the more notable examples, see William Hubbard, *The History of the Indian Wars in New England, from the First Settlement to the Termination of the War with King Philip in 1677*, facsimile reprint of the 1864 Samuel Drake ed., 2 vols. in 1 (Bowie, Md.: Heritage, 1990); Increase Mather and Cotton Mather, *The History of King Philip's War by Rev. Increase Mather Also a History of the Same War by the Rev. Cotton Mather*, reprint of the

1862 Samuel G. Drake and J. Munsell ed. (Bowie, Md.: Heritage, 1990); RGCMB, esp. 5:59–63.

8. RGCMB, 5:49–50.

9. RGCMB, 5:49.

10. RGCMB, 5:49.

11. RGCMB, 5:49.

12. RGCMB, 5:50.

13. Ronan Bennett, "War and Disorder: Policing the Soldiery in Civil War Yorkshire," in *War and Government in Britain, 1598–1650*, ed. Mark Charles Fissel (Manchester: Manchester University Press, 1991), 248.

14. RGCMB, 5:50.

15. RGCMB, 5:50.

16. RGCMB, 5:50. Strappado[e] is a form of torture and military punishment in which the subject is lifted off the ground by a rope tied to his wrists (behind the back). In some cases, the victim is then dropped partway to the ground with a jerk, which causes a dislocation of the shoulders; it is highly unlikely that this part of the technique was carried out in Massachusetts Bay. Thanks go to Phyllis Jestice for her clarification of this point.

17. There was quite a debate between various commanders, and the colonies of Massachusetts Bay and Connecticut, over the best strategy to secure the frontier. This debate continued for the first year of the war. For details, see George Madison Bodge, *Soldiers in King Philip's War*, reprint of 1906 3rd ed. (Baltimore: Genealogical Publishing, 1967), 142–154; Douglas Edward Leech, *Flintlock and Tomahawk: New England in King Philip's War*, reprint of 1958 Macmillian ed. (East Orleans, Mass.: Parnassus Imprints, 1992), 73–102.

18. The garrisoned towns included Billerica, Brookfield, Chelmsford, Dunstable, Groton, Hadley, Hatfield, Lancaster, Marlborough, Medfield, Mendon, Northampton, Springfield, Westfield, and Wrentham, among others. For information on the soldiers of these garrisons, see Bodge, *Soldiers*, 355–367.

19. RGCMB, 5:50.

20. RGCMB, 5:48.

21. RGCMB, 5:51.

22. RGCMB, 5:48.

23. RGCMB, 5:51.

24. RGCMB, 5:70.

25. RGCMB, 5:70–71.

26. Leech, *Flintlock and Tomahawk*, 73–102.

27. RGCMB, 5:71–72.

28. RGCMB, 5:71–72.

29. RGCMB, 5:72. No records exist from any militia committee on this subject, so it is not known how many, if any, of these bounties were paid by militia committees.

30. RGCMB, 5:73.

31. RGCMB, 5:76.

32. RGCMB, 5:78.

33. For a few of many examples, see Benjamin P. Mighill and George Brainard Blodgette, eds., *The Early Records of the Town of Rowley, Massachusetts, 1639–1672: Being Vol. 1 of the Printed Records of the Town*, reprint of 1894 Rowley ed. (Bowie, Md.: Heritage, 1984); William Hammond Bowden, "Marblehead Town Records," *Essex Institute Historical Collections* 69, nos. 3–4 (1933): 207–293; *Town Records of Manchester, from the Earliest Grants of Land, 1636 . . .* (Salem, Mass.: Salem Press, 1889); George Francis Dow, *Town Records of Topsfield, Massachusetts, 1659–1778*, 2 vols. (Topsfield, Mass.: Topsfield Historical Society, 1917).

34. James Rusell Trumball, *History of Northampton, Massachusetts from Its Settlement in 1654* (Northampton, Mass: Gazette Printing, 1898), 279.

35. No actual record of the meeting of any militia committee survives. It is not known if any of the small meetings (five men at most) were held publicly (it is doubtful) or if any record, other than the muster lists or reports, was made of the decisions or discussions at the meetings. Other than muster records, there are no published records of such meetings and no originals exist in the Massachusetts State Archives.

36. RGCMB, 5:78.

37. Leech, *Flintlock and Tomahawk*, 91–92.

38. RGCMB, 5:89.

39. RGCMB, 4:pt. 2, 332.

40. RGCMB, 5:89.

41. For the refugee crisis, see William Grant Black, "The Military Origins of Federal Social Welfare Programs: Early British and Colonial American Precedents" (Ph.D. diss., University of Minnesota, 1989), 137–149; Leech, *Flintlock and Tomahawk*, 187–189, 246–249; Michael J. Puglisi, *Puritans Besieged: The Legacies of King Philip's War in the Massachusetts Bay Colony* (Lanham, Md.: University Press of America, 1991), 61–64. For the Irish donation, see Charles Deane, "The Irish Donation in 1676," *New England Historical and Genealogical Register* 2 (1848): 245–250. For the donations from England, see Puglisi, *Puritans Besieged*, 65.

42. RGCMB, 5:79.

43. RGCMB, 5:80.

44. For information on draft evading, see Black, "Social Welfare," 141–147; Leech, *Flintlock and Tomahawk*, 137–138, 184–187; Jenny Hale Pulsipher, "'The Overture of This New Albion World': King Philip's War and the Transformation of New England" (Ph.D. diss., Brandeis University, 1999); Jenny Hale Pulsipher, *Subjects Unto the Same King: Indians, English, and the Contest for Authority in Colonial New England* (Philadelphia: University of Pennsylvania Press, 2005), 160–169. For a different view, see Harold E. Selesky, *War and Society in Colonial Connecticut* (New Haven, Conn.: Yale University Press, 1990), 25.

45. RGCMB, 5:85–87.

46. RGCMB, 5:81. This was not the first time that people had been ordered to stay in the frontier town, but it was the first time that it was enacted as a law. See Puglisi, *Puritans Besieged*, 84–88.

47. Puglisi, *Puritans Besieged*, 85.

48. RGCMB, 5:81.

49. Bodge, *Soldiers*, 151; Leech, *Flintlock and Tomahawk*, 187.

50. RGCMB, 5:81. For a discussion of the backcountry, see Puglisi, *Puritans Besieged*, 84–132; Pulsipher, "Overture," 261–281.

51. Bodge, *Soldiers*, 8.

52. Bodge, *Soldiers*, 11. For the particulars of the Massachusetts militiamen, most notably those under captains John Underhill and Lyon Gardiner, see Bodge, *Soldiers*, 9–19; Darrett Bruce Rutman, "A Militant New World, 1607–1640: America's First Generation: Its Martial Spirit, Its Tradition of Arms, Its Militia Organization, Its Wars" (Ph.D. diss., University of Virginia, 1959), 634–739.

53. Bodge, *Soldiers*, 9–19.

54. RGCMB, 1:192. The qualifications for freeman status changed over time, but generally it meant that the person was male, over twenty-one years of age, owned some land, and was a church member. See B. Katherine Brown, "Freemanship in Puritan New England," *American Historical Review* 59, no. 4 (1954): 865–883.

55. David Richard Millar, "The Militia, the Army, and Independency in Colonial Massachusetts" (Ph.D. diss., Cornell University, 1967), 72–72.

56. Millar, "Militia, the Army, and Independency," 63–65. For a different view, see Rutman, "Militant New World," 744.

57. RGCMB, 4:pt. 2, 120; my emphasis.

58. RGCMB, 4:pt. 2, 121.

59. RGCMB, 4:pt. 2, 121–122.

60. RGCMB, 4:pt. 2, 122–123. If the mission was accomplished earlier, the men would have served for considerably less than six weeks.

61. RGCMB, 4:pt. 2, 123.

62. RGCMB, 4:pt. 2, 572–573. The impressment never occurred. See RGCMB, 4:pt. 2, 575.

63. RGCMB, 5:53.

64. T. H. Breen, "Persistent Localism: English Social Change and the Shaping of New England Institutions," in *Puritans and Adventurers: Change and Persistence in Early America* (New York: Oxford University Press, 1980), 3–24.

65. Quoted in Edwin Martin Stone, *History of Beverly, Civil and Ecclesiastical: From Its Settlement in 1630 to 1842* (Boston: J. Munroe, 1843), 168–169.

66. See for example Douglas Edward Leech, "The Military System of Plymouth Colony," *New England Quarterly* 24, no. 3 (1951): 342–364; James B. Whisker, *The American Colonial Militia*, 5 vols., vol. 1: *Introduction to American Colonial*

Militia (Lewiston, N.Y.: Edwin Mellen, 1997); Louis Morton, "The Origins of American Military Policy," *Military Affairs* 22, no. 2 (1958): 75–82. These are just a few of numerous examples of this myth.

67. Quoted in Bodge, *Soldiers*, 47; my emphasis.

68. See Bodge, *Soldiers*, 47, 53, 55, 105, 161, 171, passim. See also RGCMB, 5:53–54, 65, 72–73, 78, 85, 91. For the exception, see the extensive arrangements that the General Court made for Captain Samuel Mosley, RGCMB, 5:94–95.

69. RGCMB, 5:85, 91, 122.

70. For the workings of the United Colonies during the war, see Harry M. Ward, *The United Colonies of New England, 1643–90* (New York: Vintage, 1961).

71. RGCMB, 5:91.

72. See chapters 3, 4, and esp. 5. The General Court enacted these preferences into law during the continuation of the conflict in Maine in 1677; see RGCMB, 5:144–145.

73. For information on the official policy of the use of transients in the post–King Philip's War era, see RGCMB, 5:123.

74. One possible reason for this is the switch in armaments made by the General Court in the early days of the war, from a force of one-third pike men and two-thirds musketeers to an all-musketeer force.

75. "To the honored major generall [Daniel Dennison] from richard norman, 2 november 1675," vol. 68, document 38, MAC. Often, in order to get a fair accounting, these reports were written after the constables had actually pressed the men and they had mustered. This delay in reporting was more important later in the war, once resistance to and evasion of the draft became commonplace.

76. For information on the duties of a constable, see Samuel Freeman, *Town Officer; or, The Power and Duty of Selectmen, Town Clerks . . .* , 8th ed. (Boston: Printed by Joseph T. Buckingham for Thomas and Andrews, 1815); John Fairfield Sly, *Town Government in Massachusetts 1620–1930* (Hamden, Conn.: Archon, 1967), 39–40.

77. Leech, *Flintlock and Tomahawk*, 104–105.

78. Sarah Loring Bailey, *Historical Sketches of Andover: Comprising the Present Towns of North Andover and Andover* (Boston: Houghton Mifflin, 1880), 170.

79. Bailey, *Historical Sketches of Andover*, 170.

80. Quoted in Bodge, *Soldiers*, 143.

81. Leech, *Flintlock and Tomahawk*, 185. This incident is almost identical to a story from Elizabethan England. See Victor L. Stater, "The Lord Lieutenancy on the Eve of the Civil Wars: The Impressment of George Plowright," *Historical Journal (Great Britain)* 29, no. 2 (1986): 284.

82. For details of Andover's impressment during the war, see chapter 4.

83. See Bodge, *Soldiers*.

84. Quoted in Pulsipher, *Subjects*, 162.

85. Pulsipher, "Overture," 246–247.

86. "Massachusetts Council to Committee of Militia at Woburn, 5 March 1676," vol. 68, document 159a, MAC. Also quoted in Pulsipher, "Overture," 247.

87. Leech, *Flintlock and Tomahawk*, 185–186.

88. Quoted in Daniel Dennison Slade, "Major-General Daniel Dennison," *New England Historical Genealogical Register* 23 (1869): 327.

89. RGCMB, 5:79–80.

90. Pulsipher, "Overture," 255–256.

91. Quoted in Leech, *Flintlock and Tomahawk*, 185.

92. "Orders from the General Court," vol. 68, documents 106 and 117, MAC.

93. RGCMB, 5:78–79.

94. RGCMB, 5:79.

95. RGCMB, 5:79.

96. Black, "Social Welfare," 144; Pulsipher, "Overture," 250–261.

97. ECQCR, 6:132–134.

98. ECQCR, 6:132–133.

99. RGCMB, 5:78–79. Obviously, the General Court had been informed of the details of the Samuel Leech case.

100. *Colonial Laws 1672*, 73.

101. For representative examples, see ECQCR, 2:2, 2:7, 2:32, 2:42, 3:220, 3:241, 3:275, 3:280, 4:163, 4:197, 4:237, 5:293, 5:122, 5:138.

102. RGCMB, 5:48–49.

103. "Massachusetts Council to the Committee of Militia in Woburn, 14 March 1676," vol. 68, document 159a, MAC.

104. See John D. Cushing, ed., *The Laws and Liberties of Massachusetts, 1641–1691: A Facsimile Edition, Containing also Council Orders and Executive Proclamations*, 3 vols. (Wilmington, Del.: Scholarly Resources, 1976). The colony did address the issue of substitution in its laws after 1693. See Abner Cheney Goodell and Melville Madison Bigelow, eds., *The Acts and Resolves, Public and Private, of the Province of the Massachusetts Bay; to Which Are Prefixed the Charters of the Province*, vol. 1, 1692–1714 (Boston: Wright and Potter, 1869), 134.

105. Pulsipher, "Overture," 245–246.

106. "Records of the Suffolk County Court, 1671–1680: Phillips Agt. Smith, 16 May 1676," *Publications of the Colonial Society of Massachusetts* 30 (1933): 683.

107. ECQCR, 6:89.

108. "John How to Major General Dennison, 30 November 1675," vol. 68, document 70, MAC.

109. Pulsipher, *Subjects*, 162–164.

110. Pulsipher, *Subjects*, 162–164. Pulsipher only accounts for nine known substitutions (including Zachary Curtis). Those nine, combined with John Laighton of Rowley, makes the number of known substitutions ten. In an impressment pool from Massachusetts Bay of over one thousand men, ten substitutes means that only around 1 percent of men pressed during the war hired someone to fight

for them. While these numbers are not exact, even if the number of substitutes were doubled, tripled, or quadrupled, substitutes would account for an insignificant number of soldiers during the war.

111. RGCMB, 5:76.

112. Bodge, *Soldiers*, 63. At least four men from Essex County served with Mosley, one each from Ipswich and Gloucester and two from Salem.

113. RGCMB, 5:71.

114. RGCMB, 5:94–95.

115. RGCMB, 5:95–96.

116. RGCMB, 5:95.

117. Black, "Social Welfare," 143.

118. George William Ellis and John Emery Morris, eds., *King Philip's War; Based on the Archives and Records of Massachusetts, Plymouth, Rhode Island and Connecticut, and Contemporary Letters and Accounts* (New York: Grafton, 1906); Russell Bourne, *Red King's Rebellion: Racial Politics in New England, 1675–1678* (New York: Atheneum, 1990).

119. Felix John Zarlengo, "Politics of Defense in the New England Colonies, 1620–1746" (master's thesis, Brown University, 1965), 20.

120. Leech, "Military System of Plymouth," 350.

121. See chapters 3 and 4 on the details of impressment in the towns of Essex County.

122. Richard Henry Marcus, "The Militia of Colonial Connecticut 1639–1775" (Ph.D. diss., University of Colorado, 1965), 60–61.

123. RGCMB; Rutman, "Militant New World." Only once in the war was a land grant made to regular soldiers (not in a special volunteer company). During the Narragansett campaign in December 1675, the colony offered the men (those already impressed and assembled in their units) land if they fought well. This was a reward for good service and not an incentive to volunteer, as the men did not know of the bonus beforehand. See Leech, *Flintlock and Tomahawk*, 124.

124. For the colony's attempt to keep costs down by limiting service, see RGCMB, 4:pt. 2, 121–122.

125. For pay amounts, see Selesky, *War and Society in Colonial Connecticut*, 23; Bodge, *Soldiers*.

126. For wealth and prices in Essex County, see William I. Davisson, "Essex County Wealth Trends: Wealth and Economic Growth in 17th Century Massachusetts," *Essex Institute Historical Collections* 103, no. 4 (1967): 291–342; William I. Davisson, "Essex County Price Trends: Money and Markets in 17th Century Massachusetts," *Essex Institute Historical Collections* 103, no. 2 (1967): 144–185.

127. Fred Anderson, *A People's Army: Massachusetts Soldiers and Society in the Seven Years' War* (Chapel Hill: University of North Carolina Press, 1984), 26–62, esp. 39.

128. Leech, *Flintlock and Tomahawk*, 104. For another example of this view,

based on Leech's work, see Eugene Francis Madigan, "Development of the New England Colonial Militia, 1620–1675" (master's thesis, Kansas State University, 1975), 21.

129. Leech, *Flintlock and Tomahawk*, 103–104.

130. Leech does briefly mention the role of the committees in his later work, although he does not recognize their magnitude in the system of recruitment. See Douglas Edward Leech, *Arms for Empire: A Military History of the British Colonies in North America, 1607–1763* (New York: Macmillan, 1973), 20–21.

131. George H. Martin, "Glimpses of Colonial Life in Lynn in the Indian War Days," *The Register of the Lynn Historical Society* 17 (1913): 106.

CHAPTER 3

1. Historians and genealogists have studied Salem extensively; see Sidney Perley, *The History of Salem, Massachusetts*, 3 vols. (Salem, Mass.: S. Perley, 1924); James Duncan Phillips, *Salem in the Seventeenth Century* (Boston: Houghton Mifflin, 1933); Richard P. Gildrie, *Salem, Massachusetts, 1626–1683: A Covenant Community* (Charlottesville: University Press of Virginia, 1975).

2. For information on Newbury, see John J. Currier, *History of Newbury, Mass., 1635–1902* (Boston: Damrell and Upham, 1902); Robert Lord Goodman, "Newbury, Massachusetts, 1635–1685: The Social Foundations of Harmony and Conflict" (Ph.D. diss., Michigan State University, 1974); Joshua Coffin and Joseph Bartlett, *A Sketch of the History of Newbury, Newburyport, and West Newbury, from 1635 to 1845* (Boston: S. G. Drake, 1845). For Lynn, see George H. Martin, "Glimpses of Colonial Life in Lynn in the Indian War Days," *The Register of the Lynn Historical Society* 17 (1913): 98–122; Alonzo Lewis and James Newhall, *History of Lynn*, 2nd ed. (Lynn, Mass.: George C. Herbert, 1897).

3. David Grayson Allen, *In English Ways: The Movement of Societies and the Transferal of English Local Laws and Custom to Massachusetts Bay in the Seventeenth Century* (New York: Norton, 1982), 118–119.

4. Allen, *In English Ways*, 119.

5. Allen, *In English Ways*, 136–139.

6. Allen, *In English Ways*, 134.

7. Allen, *In English Ways*, 119–120. Allen also points out how this mind-set affected land distribution, with the town granting huge tracts of land to those in leadership. See Allen, *In English Ways*, 121–131.

8. Alison Isabel Vannah, "'Crotchets of Division': Ipswich in New England, 1633–1679" (Ph.D. diss., Brandeis University, 1999), 696.

9. Vannah, "'Crotchets of Division,'" 693.

10. In New England, which practiced partible inheritance, younger sons could expect to inherit some land (usually, in the first few generations, a livable estate). However, towns in Essex County might not give younger sons extra

land allotments, since they were not householders, as first sons were because of the expectation that they would inherit the family's main property and dwelling house. See John J. Waters, "Family, Inheritance, and Migration in Colonial New England: The Evidence from Guilford, Connecticut," *William and Mary Quarterly* (1982): 64–86.

11. Vannah, "'Crotchets of Division,'" 723–782.

12. See Allen, *In English Ways*, 143–144; Vannah, "'Crotchets of Division,'" 696–701.

13. Vannah, "'Crotchets of Division,'" 702–704.

14. Vannah, "'Crotchets of Division,'" 708–722.

15. Vannah, "'Crotchets of Division,'" 810.

16. Thomas Franklin Waters, Sarah Whipple Goodhue, and John Wise, *Ipswich in the Massachusetts Bay Colony* (Ipswich, Mass.: Ipswich Historical Society, 1905), 160–162; ECQCR, 1:117; George Madison Bodge, *Soldiers in King Philip's War*, reprint of 1906 3rd ed. (Baltimore: Genealogical Publishing, 1967), 142, 282; Vannah, "'Crotchets of Division,'" 243–244, 1037–1045.

17. Daniel Dennison Slade, "Major-General Daniel Dennison," *New England Historical Genealogical Register* 23 (1869): 312–335.

18. For sociopolitical rankings of the citizens of Ipswich, see Vannah, "'Crotchets of Division,'" 1021–1139.

19. Vannah, "'Crotchets of Division,'" 834.

20. Vannah, "'Crotchets of Division,'" 834.

21. In her dissertation, Vannah claims that about a third of townsmen served (around 180 men) from 1675 to 1677. There are a number of reasons why the number in this study is different. Vannah included on her list those soldiers from Ipswich who served in Maine during 1676–1677, a sizeable group not included in this study. In addition, she used the muster lists in Bodge, *Soldiers*, without culling those men who were paid for some service but cannot be placed in an actual fighting or garrison company. She also uses, with caution, a listing of soldiers from Ipswich in Waters, Goodhue, and Wise, *Ipswich in the Massachusetts Bay Colony*, 218–224, which includes, as she states, some men not from Ipswich. Because of this discrepancy in the number of men who served, Vannah's conclusions are used with caution here. See Vannah, "'Crotchets of Division,'" 836–842, 847–855, esp. note 817.

22. Vannah estimates the 1675 number of adult males (16–60) in Ipswich at 470; she further argues that 30 men in town had been exempted from militia service because of their age or some other condition. See Vannah, "'Crotchets of Division,'" 847–848, note 817.

23. For the value of first sons, see Daniel Scott Smith, "Parental Power and Marriage Patterns: An Analysis of Historical Trends in Hingham, Massachusetts," *Journal of Marriage and the Family* 35, no. 3 (1973): 422–423; John J. Waters, "The Traditional World of the New England Peasants: A View from Seventeenth-

Century Barnstable," *New England Historical Genealogical Register* 130, no. 1 (1976): 8–9.

24. Occupational data comes from a number of sources, most often court and probate records. See PREC; ECQCR. See also Vannah, "'Crotchets of Division,'" 1022–1139.

25. These listings take into account the fact that some men had multiple occupations listed; thus, the number of occupations (fifty-seven) is higher than the number of men (fifty). For the occupation data for the entire county, see appendix 5.

26. Vannah, "'Crotchets of Division,'" 841. Vannah's distributions are slightly different, because her population is different.

27. Vannah, "'Crotchets of Division,'" 841.

28. See Christine Leigh Heyrman, *Commerce and Culture: The Maritime Communities of Colonial Massachusetts, 1690–1750* (New York: Norton, 1984).

29. Throughout most of this study, a different scale for discerning the families' position in a given town's economy is used. Allison Vannah's systematic and exhaustive study of Ipswich's economy and every family's place in it is substituted in this section, however, because of its scope and authoritative nature. For her methods and listings, see Vannah, "'Crotchets of Division,'" 117–204, 567–688, 1022–1139.

30. Donald Warner Koch, "Income Distribution and Political Structure in Seventeenth-Century Salem, Massachusetts," *Essex Institute Historical Collections* 105, no. 1 (1969): 52. See also Manfred Jonas, "The Wills of Early Settlers of Essex County, Massachusetts," *Essex Institute Historical Collections* 96, no. 3 (1960): 230; Gloria L. Main and Jackson Turner Main, "Economic Growth and the Standard of Living in Southern New England, 1640–1774," *Journal of Economic History* 48, no. 1 (1988): 27–46; Charles R. Lee, "'This Poor People': Seventeenth-Century Massachusetts and the Poor," *Historical Journal of Massachusetts* 9, no. 1 (1981): 41–50.

31. Vannah, "'Crotchets of Division,'" 810.

32. For the county criminal records, see ECQCR.

33. Edwin Powers, *Crime and Punishment in Early Massachusetts, 1620–1692: A Documentary History* (Boston: Beacon, 1966), 405.

34. Based on Ipswich's impressment quota, which was based on population. Ipswich sent 25 percent of the county's soldiers; if its population was 25 percent of the county, it would be responsible for, on average, around twenty-one of the county's eighty-five crimes per year.

35. Increase Mather, *An Earnest Exhortation to the Inhabitants of New-England* (Boston: Printed by John Foster, and are to be sold over against the Dove, 1676), microform; Increase Mather, *A Brief History of the War with the Indians in New-England: From June 24, 1675* (London: R. Chiswell, 1676), microform.

36. RGCMB, 5:59–63.

37. For her assessment of crime in 1660–1670s Ipswich, see Vannah, "'Crotchets of Division,'" 805–836.

38. ECQCR, 5:283, 5:292, 5:318–321, 5:413–414, 5:416.

39. Quoted in Vannah, "'Crotchets of Division,'" 814.

40. Vannah, "'Crotchets of Division,'" 814.

41. ECQCR, 4:46–47.

42. ECQCR, 5:311.

43. ECQCR, 3:338, 4:416, 5:337, 5:368.

44. ECQCR, 3:27, 5:31–32.

45. ECQCR, 6:72.

46. ECQCR, 4:124–126, 5:141, 5:303, 6:127.

47. Vannah, "'Crotchets of Division,'" 805–816.

48. ECQCR, 5:304–306.

49. ECQCR, 5:35, 5:38, 5:315–316, 6:329, 6:372.

50. ECQCR, 5:143, 5:231–232.

51. ECQCR, 5:140.

52. ECQCR, 4:143–145.

53. The men were Freegrace Norton, John Knowlton, John Browne, and Thomas Dennis.

54. Andrew Burley, Samuel Crumpton, George Timson, and Simon Groe.

55. For the refugee situation in Ipswich, see Vannah, "'Crotchets of Division,'" 842–846.

56. ECQCR, 5:306, 5:315, 5:318, 5:411–414.

57. Vannah, "'Crotchets of Division,'" 700–701.

58. This does not include men who had numerous problems within each category, just those men with a negative factor in more than one of the main areas: socioeconomic status, crime, debt, or no town connection.

59. For servants lashing out at society, see Lawrence W. Towner, "'A Fondness for Freedom': Servant Protest in Puritan Society," *William and Mary Quarterly* 19, no. 2 (1962): 201–219.

60. Bodge, *Soldiers*, 142–158.

61. For younger sons and their place in the family hierarchy, see Smith, "Parental Power," 422–423; Waters, "Traditional World," 8–9; Philip J. Greven, *Four Generations: Population, Land, and Family in Colonial Andover, Massachusetts* (Ithaca, N.Y.: Cornell University Press, 1970), 72–99; Daniel Vickers, *Farmers and Fishermen: Two Centuries of Work in Essex County, Massachusetts, 1630–1850* (Chapel Hill: University of North Carolina Press, 1994), 19, 67–68.

62. Thomas Gage, *The History of Rowley Anciently Including Bradford, Boxford, and Georgetown from the Year 1639 to the Present Time* (Boston: F. Andrews, 1840); Amos Everett Jewett, Emily Mabel Adams Jewett, and Jewett Family of America, *Rowley, Massachusetts, "Mr. Ezechi Rogers Plantation," 1639–1850* (Rowley, Mass.: Jewett Family of America, 1946).

63. Jewett, *Mr. Ezechi Rogers Plantation*, 11.

64. Patricia O'Malley, "Rowley, Massachusetts, 1639–1730: Dissent, Division, and Delimination in a Colonial Town" (Ph.D. diss., Boston College, 1975), 22.

65. O'Malley, "Rowley," 22–35.

66. Of the fifty-four men in town with Rogers in 1639, forty-one were full members of Rogers's church, while twenty-six out of the forty-three latecomers arriving by 1660 also joined. Jewett, *Mr. Ezechi Rogers Plantation*, 23. See also O'Malley, "Rowley," 23–27.

67. For the controversy at Newbury, see Coffin and Bartlett, *History of Newbury*, 72–112. For the religious conflict in Salem, see Richard P. Gildrie, "Contention in Salem: The Higginson-Nicholet Controversy, 1672–1676," *Essex Institute Historical Collections* 113, no. 2 (1977): 117–139.

68. O'Malley, "Rowley," 49–83; David Thomas Konig, *Law and Society in Puritan Massachusetts: Essex County, 1629–1692* (Chapel Hill: University of North Carolina Press, 1979), 101–105.

69. O'Malley, "Rowley," 77–78.

70. Allen, *In English Ways*, 24–25.

71. Allen, *In English Ways*, 31.

72. Allen, *In English Ways*, 37; Gage, *History of Rowley*, 138–141; O'Malley, "Rowley," 36–40.

73. Allen, *In English Ways*, 31–32; O'Malley, "Rowley," 35–40.

74. Allen, *In English Ways*, 31–32; O'Malley, "Rowley," 35–40.

75. Allen, *In English Ways*, 40–41.

76. Allen, *In English Ways*, 38.

77. Allen, *In English Ways*, 42–43. On town governments, see Kenneth A. Lockridge, *A New England Town: The First Hundred Years, Dedham, Massachusetts, 1636–1736* (New York: Norton, 1970).

78. Allen, *In English Ways*, 38–54.

79. O'Malley, "Rowley," 38.

80. Quoted in O'Malley, "Rowley," 32.

81. O'Malley, "Rowley," 33.

82. Gage, *History of Rowley*, 179.

83. George B. Blodgette, "Early Records of the Town of Rowley, Mass," *Essex Institute Historical Collections* 8 (1877): 253–262; Jewett, *Mr. Ezechi Rogers Plantation*; Benjamin P. Mighill and George Brainard Blodgette, eds., *The Early Records of the Town of Rowley, Massachusetts, 1639–1672: Being Vol. 1 of the Printed Records of the Town*, reprint of 1894 Rowley ed. (Bowie, Md.: Heritage, 1984).

84. Gage, *History of Rowley*, 383; RGCMB, 5:2.

85. RGCMB, 5:77.

86. Only Corporal John Palmer and Andrew Stickney survived. See Bodge, *Soldiers*, 136–138.

87. For the Rowley men with Brocklebank, see table 3. For a full list of the company, see Bodge, *Soldiers*, 206–207.

88. Bodge, *Soldiers*, 282–283.

89. The men were John Harriman and Thomas Lever.

90. For information on wealth, see William I. Davisson, "Essex County Wealth Trends: Wealth and Economic Growth in 17th Century Massachusetts," *Essex Institute Historical Collections* 103, no. 4 (1967): 291–342; Jonas, "Wills of Early Settlers"; Koch, "Income Distribution"; Main and Main, "Economic Growth."

91. Several of the soldiers had fathers who died before the war began: William Hobkinson (Hobson), William Stickney, Francis Lambert, Thomas Palmer Sr., Peter Cooper, Hugh Smith, and Edward Sawyer all died before the start of the war. In addition, the fathers of the two men compensated by the colony with no known active service, Joseph Jewett and Thomas Lambert, died before the war. See PREC, passim.

92. The size of house lots was remarkably uniform in Rowley. When the land was originally laid out around 1643, there were fifty-nine original house lots, ranging from six acres to one and a half acres in size. The eight largest lots were assigned to major founders and were situated in the center of town between the meetinghouse and training field. Twenty-two families who were minor contributors each got two-acre lots, while the majority of inhabitants, twenty-eight families who did not contribute to the founding of the town, received one-and-a-half-acre lots. These smaller lots were situated on the outer edges of town. See Gage, *History of Rowley*, 123–134.

93. See O'Malley, "Rowley," 36.

94. See Matthew Adams Stickney, "Ancient Tax List of Rowley," *New England Historical Genealogical Register* 15 (1861): 253–254. Stickney dates the list from 1661–1664, but O'Malley definitively dates it at 1662. See O'Malley, "Rowley," 10. The tax rate was based on total property. As David Grayson Allen points out, Rowley's unique situation of being a textile center meant that total property, not just land holdings, was crucial to status in town. Unlike traditional farming towns, Rowley families had more of their wealth tied up in moveable property (rather than land), making the tax list the most important measure of economic status. Allen, *In English Ways*, 25–26.

95. Rowley's stability and isolation over the years makes the tax list of 1662, while not a perfect mirror of the 1675 town, an invaluable resource for understanding Rowley at the time of the war. For information on Rowley's quiet in-migration, see O'Malley, "Rowley," 44–45.

96. The gate system was a direct import from Yorkshire, which had been home to most of the inhabitants. Allen, *In English Ways*, 33.

97. A survey by Patricia O'Malley lists the number of gates that many families held in 1678, three years after the war. The families at the top of the tax hierarchy

are generally high on the gates hierarchy list sixteen years later in 1678, while those lower on the tax list remained near the bottom of the gates list. O'Malley, "Rowley," 243–252.

98. For Rowley's wealth distribution, see Allen, *In English Ways*, 23–25.

99. Allen, *In English Ways*, 38–54, esp. 49.

100. For details on Pearson, see Jewett, *Mr. Ezechi Rogers Plantation*, 105.

101. Jeremiah Jewett, son of the prominent Joseph Jewett, received compensation during the war, but no active service can be traced to him. Joseph Jewett, Jeremiah's brother, was impressed for service in Ipswich, where he lived. See Bodge, *Soldiers*, 164–165.

102. The families were the Mighills, Reyners, Careltons, Barkers, Bellinghams, Bringhams, Rogers, and Nelsons. See O'Malley, "Rowley," 36.

103. Allen, *In English Ways*, 31–32.

104. William Hobson, John's father, bought the land in 1652 from Sebastian Bringham, who went back to England. Gage, *History of Rowley*, 129. Thomas Lambert, one of the two men with unknown service in Rowley, was adopted by his uncle Thomas Barker and possibly raised in this elite section of town in Barker's house.

105. The history of family settlement, when each family came to town and was given land, is set out in Gage, *History of Rowley*, 122–135. See also O'Malley, "Rowley," 187–193, for an analysis of this data.

106. O'Malley, "Rowley," passim.

107. This figure does not include Captain Brocklebank, who was an original founder, because as an officer he was appointed to his post, not recruited.

108. O'Malley, "Rowley," 187–193.

109. A militiaman was counted in one camp or the other based on either his or a prominent member of his family's (usually his father's) signature on a petition or mention in a court case. These names fluctuated over time, but a general sense of each family's standing can be found by looking at the records. For the petitions, see Gage, *History of Rowley*, 74–77; Jewett, *Mr. Ezechi Rogers Plantation*; O'Malley, "Rowley," 243–252. For the court documents, see ECQCR, 6:325–328. In her dissertation, Patricia O'Malley focuses on the controversy and its effects on the town; see O'Malley, "Rowley," 61–111.

110. O'Malley, "Rowley," 74.

111. Allen, *In English Ways*, 18–20.

112. John Wood of Brocklebank's company and Richard Holmes of Lathrop's command.

113. In Appleton's company: Joseph Burkby, Caleb Jackson, and John Leyton. John Jackson and Joshua Boynton were from anti-Shepard families and served with both Appleton and Brocklebank. In Lathrop's company: Thomas Bayly, Jacob Kilborn, Joseph Pearson, Ezekiel Sawyer, and Matthew Scales. Thomas Lever in Whipple's troop was also in the anti-Shepard camp.

114. Patricia O'Malley implies that the town was split two-thirds against Shepard and one-third for him. These percentages in fact fluctuated over time. See O'Malley, "Rowley," 61–78.

115. The documentary record of the minority of families who were pro-Shepard is actually better than the records of the majority who were against him, many of whom were part of a silent majority. The members of the pro-Shepard faction were very vocal in their support and signed petitions and brought court suits frequently. See O'Malley, "Rowley," 61–78.

116. There are few histories of Topsfield. The most important is George Francis Dow, Alice Goldsmith Waters Dow, and Ruth H. Allen, *History of Topsfield, Massachusetts* (Topsfield, Mass.: Topsfield Historical Society, 1940).

117. Topsfield Historical Society, *Town Records of Topsfield Massachusetts, 1659–1778*, 2 vols. (Topsfield, Mass.: Topsfield Historical Society, 1917), 1:vii; Benjamin F. Arrington, "Town of Topsfield," in *Municipal History of Essex County in Massachusetts*, ed. Benjamin F. Arrington (New York: Lewis Historical Publishing, 1922), 161.

118. These figures are taken from Topsfield Historical Society, "County Rate Made the 18th of November 1668 for Topsfield," *Historical Collections of Topsfield Historical Society* 3 (1895): 51. See appendix 3. The list has forty-four names, but a number of them belong to the same families.

119. Walter Goodwin Davis, "The Ancestry of Dudley Wildes of Topsfield," in *Massachusetts and Maine Families in the Ancestry of Walter Goodwin Davis (1885–1966)*, ed. Walter Goodwin Davis (Baltimore: Genealogical Publishing, 1996), 620.

120. For information on the state of the records, see Topsfield Historical Society, *Town Records of Topsfield*, vii.

121. George Francis Dow, *Town Records of Topsfield, Massachusetts, 1659–1778*, 2 vols. (Topsfield, Mass.: Topsfield Historical Society, 1917); ECQCR; RGCMB.

122. RGCMB, 3:336.

123. The General Court passed this in May 1652 (RGCMB, 4:pt. 1, 86) and codified it in the 1672 edition of the *General Laws and Liberties of the Massachusetts Colony*. See William Henry Whitmore, *Colonial Laws of Massachusetts, Reprinted from the Edition of 1660, with the Supplements to 1672: Containing Also, the Body of Liberties of 1641* (Boston: Published by order of the City Council of Boston, 1889).

124. RGCMB, 3:336.

125. For Gould, see RGCMB, 3:427. For Peabody, see Dow, *History of Topsfield*, 125; John H. Towne, "Francis Peabody's Grist Mill," *Historical Collections of the Topsfield Historical Society* 1 (1895): 39–45.

126. Gage, *History of Rowley*, 360–361.

127. Gage, *History of Rowley*, 360–363.

128. ECQCR, 4:397.

129. ECQCR, 4:451–452.

130. ECQCR, 5:21.

131. ECQCR, 5:37.

132. RGCMB, 5:16.

133. The Curtis family, which had two sons fight during the war, served from Topsfield.

134. Most notably, the Tiler family resided in Rowley Village by the late 1670s (possibly earlier) and a Samuel Tiler or Tyler was impressed for Appleton's company from Rowley. See Gage, *History of Rowley*, 182.

135. William Francis. Galvin, ed., *Historical Data Relating to Counties, Cities, and Towns in Massachusetts* (Boston: New England Historic Genealogical Society, 1997), 23.

136. RGCMB, 5:2, 5:77–78, 5:131–132.

137. Dow, *History of Topsfield*, 125–126.

138. Dow incorrectly identifies this soldier as Thomas Towne; see Dow, *History of Topsfield*, 141. The official records name a Thomas Hobbs as serving with Lathrop; see Bodge, *Soldiers*, 133–141, esp. 136, 138.

139. Isaac Cummings Jr., a sometime resident of Topsfield, served in Appleton's company during this campaign; he did so as a recruit of Ipswich, however, and is considered in that section of this study. See Bodge, *Soldiers*, 164–167. See also Albert Oren Cummins, *Cummings Genealogy: Isaac Cummings, 1601-1677 of Ipswich in 1638 and Some of His Descendants* (Montpelier, Vt.: Albert Oren Cummins, 1904); George Mooar, *The Cummings Memorial: A Genealogical History of the Descendants of Issac Cummings, an Early Settler of Topsfield, Massachusetts*, reprint of 1903 B. F. Cummings ed. (New York: New England Historic Genealogical Society, 1993).

140. "John How to Major General Dennison, 30 November 1675," vol. 68 document 70, MAC.

141. Bodge, *Soldiers*, 164–167.

142. Bodge, *Soldiers*, 258–261. There is an extensive literature on the Wild/Wilds/Wildes family; see Davis, "Ancestry of Dudley Wildes"; Walter Davis Jr., "The Wildes Family of Essex County, Massachusetts," *Historical Collection of the Essex Institute* 42, no. 2 (1906): 129–147; Walter Davis Jr., "The Wildes Family of Essex County, Massachusetts," *Historical Collections of Topsfield Historical Society* 11 (1906): 17–35; Ipswich Historical Society, "Probate Records Relating to Topsfield: Estate of John Wild, Jr.," *Ipswich Historical Society Collections* 25 (1920): 115–117. Some claim that John's brother Jonathan also served during the war, but no official record of his service can be found. See Bodge, *Soldiers*.

143. Davis, "Ancestry of Dudley Wildes," 625.

144. Davis, "Ancestry of Dudley Wildes," 625. This was an excessive amount; most soldiers were paid between two and three pounds for their service.

145. Bodge, *Soldiers*, 451.

146. This number assumes that John Wild was impressed. The discrepancy comes about from the unknown status of the Esteys and James Stanley and the fact that Zachariah Curtis hired himself out as a substitute before he could be impressed.

147. Topsfield Historical Society, *Town Records of Topsfield*, 56–57; Topsfield Historical Society, "County Rate 1668."

148. Davis, "Ancestry of Dudley Wildes," 619; Dow, *History of Topsfield*, 35; Walter Goodwin Davis, "Curtis Family of Boxford and Topsfield," in *Massachusetts and Maine Families in the Ancestry of Walter Goodwin Davis (1885–1966)*, ed. Walter Goodwin Davis (Baltimore: Genealogical Publishing, 1996), 333–335.

149. Dow, *History of Topsfield*, 43.

150. Richard Archer, *Fissures in the Rock: New England in the Seventeenth Century* (Hanover, N.H.: University Press of New England, 2001), 165–167.

151. For the links between fathers and sons, see Greven, *Four Generations*, 72–99; Vickers, *Farmers and Fishermen*, 31–83, esp. 64–77.

152. Towne, "Francis Peabody's Grist Mill," 40.

153. Walter Goodwin Davis, "Perkins Family of Topsfield," in *Massachusetts and Maine Families in the Ancestry of Walter Goodwin Davis (1885–1966)*, ed. Walter Goodwin Davis (Baltimore: Genealogical Publishing, 1996): 171–180; Alfred Poor, "Perkins Family," Essex County Manuscript Genealogies, Philips Library, Peabody Essex Museum, Salem, Massachusetts.

154. Davis, "Ancestry of Dudley Wildes," 620–624.

155. Davis, "Ancestry of Dudley Wildes," 620–624.

156. Davis, "Ancestry of Dudley Wildes"; Davis, "The Wildes Family of Essex County, Massachusetts," 17–35.

157. Davis, "Ancestry of Dudley Wildes," 625.

158. One exception to this, among the three men with unknown service, is James Stanley, whose father, Mathu Stanly, was forced to mortgage his house and farm in 1675, placing the family into the subordinate category. See Dow, *History of Topsfield*, 44. However, since his type of service is unknown (and probably was not combat service), as is also the case with the Estey brothers (who fit into the middling category based on the 1668 tax list), the three men are not included in this analysis.

159. He was listed as "Jack Burton" in the initial recruitment report. See "John How to Major General Dennison, 30 November 1675," vol. 68 document 70, MAC.

160. Dow, *History of Topsfield*, 49.

161. Topsfield Historical Society, "County Rate 1668."

162. Dow, *History of Topsfield*, 48–49.

163. Dow, *History of Topsfield*, 48–49.

164. Dow, *History of Topsfield*, 48–49.

165. H. Franklin Andrews, *History of the Andrews Family: A Genealogy of Robert Andrews and His Descendants 1635–1890* (Audubon, Iowa: William E. Brinkerhoff, 1890); Davis, "Curtis Family of Boxford and Topsfield," 333–340.
166. The eight men include Zachariah Curtis (the substitute) and the seven men from known units.
167. Crime was relatively rare in colonial New England, especially when compared to the same period in England. See Archer, *Fissures in the Rock*, 109; Edgar J. McManus, *Law and Liberty in Early New England: Criminal Justice and Due Process, 1620–1692* (Amherst: University of Massachusetts Press, 1993), 149–150; Powers, *Crime and Punishment*; Kermit L. Hall, *The Magic Mirror: Law in American History* (New York: Oxford University Press, 1989); Konig, *Law and Society*.
168. ECQCR, 4:55, 4:99, 4:250.
169. ECQCR, 5:31.
170. ECQCR, 5:63–64.
171. McManus, *Law and Liberty in Early New England*, 51–53; Powers, *Crime and Punishment*.
172. Powers, *Crime and Punishment*, 170–172.
173. ECQCR, 5:63–64.
174. ECQCR, 3:65.
175. ECQCR, 3:65.
176. ECQCR, 3:138.
177. ECQCR, 3:138.
178. ECQCR, 6:5. See also E. N. Hartley, *Ironworks on the Saugus* (Norman: University of Oklahoma Press, 1957).
179. Some might say that this combination of volunteers and impressed undesirables fits many of the long-held beliefs about early military recruitment. This pattern is well established for the imperial wars of the eighteenth century but is disputed here for the seventeenth century. For recruitment in the eighteenth century, see Fred Anderson, *A People's Army: Massachusetts Soldiers and Society in the Seven Years' War* (Chapel Hill: University of North Carolina Press, 1984), 26–62; Stephen C. Eames, "Rustic Warriors: Warfare and the Provincial Soldier on the Northern Frontier, 1689–1748" (Ph.D. diss., University of New Hampshire, 1989), 271–322, esp. 320–322.
180. Heyrman, *Commerce and Culture*, 209.
181. Samuel Roads, *The History and Traditions of Marblehead*, 3rd ed. (Marblehead, Mass.: N. A. Lindsey, 1897), 9–10.
182. Roads, *History of Marblehead*, 12. See also Vickers, *Farmers and Fishermen*, 95–97.
183. Heyrman, *Commerce and Culture*, 207–273.
184. Heyrman, *Commerce and Culture*, 211.
185. Vickers, *Farmers and Fishermen*, 139.
186. Heyrman, *Commerce and Culture*, 223.

187. Heyrman, *Commerce and Culture*, 221; Vickers, *Farmers and Fishermen*, 92–93.

188. Heyrman, *Commerce and Culture*, 224.

189. Roads, *History of Marblehead*, 16.

190. Quoted in Roads, *History of Marblehead*, 16.

191. Heyrman contends that Salem's militia leaders continued to train and oversee Marblehead's militia for a number of years. This seems unlikely. Heyrman, *Commerce and Culture*, 224.

192. There were a few men titled "captain"; they were mariners, however, not militia leaders. See William Hammond Bowden, "Marblehead Town Records," *Essex Institute Historical Collections* 69, nos. 3–4 (1933): 266.

193. Roads, *History of Marblehead*, 23.

194. Roads, *History of Marblehead*, 21.

195. ECQCR, 3:435.

196. ECQCR, 4:275–276, 6:101, 6:234, 7:41–42, 7:67, 7:331, 7:407–408. See also Heyrman, *Commerce and Culture*, 224.

197. Heyrman, *Commerce and Culture*, 224.

198. "Ensign Richard Norman to the General Court, 2 November 1675," vol. 68, document 38, MAC.

199. For his listing as an ensign, see Bowden, "Marblehead Town Records," 266. Ward and Norman, along with John Legg, were listed on an impressment order as members of Marblehead's militia committee after the war. The document is "Committee of Militia from Marblehead to the General Court, 1677." vol. 69, document 50, MAC.

200. Marblehead did not send a deputy to the General Court until 1684. See Heyrman, *Commerce and Culture*, 224.

201. For the prestige of local leaders, see Heyrman, *Commerce and Culture*, 220–222.

202. For information on Marblehead's elite and lawlessness, see Heyrman, *Commerce and Culture*, 220–221.

203. Bowden, "Marblehead Town Records."

204. Bowden, "Marblehead Town Records," 19, 25–26.

205. Bowden, "Marblehead Town Records," 234.

206. Bowden, "Marblehead Town Records," 237–238.

207. The men were William Dew, Samuel Hudson, John Merrett, Mark Pittman, and Thomas Rose. See Bodge, *Soldiers*, 133–141.

208. The men were Leonard Belinger, Philip Brock, Peter Cary, Henry Codner, Peter Cole, Robert Cooks, Auguster Fferker, Ephraim Jones, Thomas Russell, Edward Severy, Davis Shapligh, and Thomas Weymouth. See "Ensign Richard Norman to the General Court, 2 November 1675," vol. 68 document 38, MAC. There is a question whether all twelve men served—Thomas Russell and Thomas Weymouth were listed on the master sheet of the impressment as "these men

wanting their Company." See "Master Impressment List, November 1675," vol. 68 document 98, MAC; Bodge, *Soldiers*, 166–167. Because no record, other than this small notation, exists of the men evading service, including no records of fines or court proceedings, it is assumed here that they did in fact serve.

209. Bodge, *Soldiers*, 85–86, 206–217.

210. Roads, *History of Marblehead*, 13–19.

211. ECQCR, 5:421, 5:437; Bowden, "Marblehead Town Records," 276.

212. Bowden, "Marblehead Town Records," 282.

213. Roads, *History of Marblehead*, 18–19.

214. James Savage, O. P. Dexter, and John Farmer, *A Genealogical Dictionary of the First Settlers of New England . . .* , reprint of the 1860–1862 Boston ed., 4 vols. (Baltimore: Genealogical Publishing, 1990), 3:441.

215. ECQCR, 2:442.

216. Bowden, "Marblehead Town Records," 279.

217. ECQCR, 7:154. Vickers argues that men who worked in the fishing trades on shore or owned land in town were generally the more "settled and sober householders." See Vickers, *Farmers and Fishermen*, 95.

218. Age data comes from a variety of sources, including town histories and vital, town, church, and court records. For Marblehead these include Roads, *History of Marblehead*; Bowden, "Marblehead Town Records"; Joseph Warren Chapman, ed., *Vital Records of Marblehead, Massachusetts, to the End of the Year 1849*, 3 vols. (Salem, Mass.: Essex institute, 1903); PREC; ECQCR. See appendix 4 for overall age data.

219. ECQCR, 4:267. The crime was considered serious enough that the men were to "lie in prison" until they paid their fines, which was unusual for the period.

220. For a discussion of the case, see Heyrman, *Commerce and Culture*, 218–221; Vickers, *Farmers and Fishermen*, 96–97.

221. ECQCR, 3:117. For information on Edward Bishop, see Perley, *History of Salem*, 2:179–182.

222. PREC, 3:35.

223. The names Josiah Codner and Henry and Roger Russell appear on either the 1648 or 1674 householder lists. There is no guarantee that these men were related. See Roads, *History of Marblehead*, 18–19, 26–27.

224. ECQCR, 4:161.

225. ECQCR, 4:161–162, 5:278–279, 5:282, 6:370–371.

226. Quoted in Vickers, *Farmers and Fishermen*, 132.

227. Vickers, *Farmers and Fishermen*, 132.

228. William Hubbard and Samuel Gardner Drake, *The History of the Indian Wars in New England, from the First Settlement to the Termination of the War with King Philip in 1677*, 2 vols. in 1, facsimile reprint of the 1864 Drake ed. (Bowie, Md.: Heritage, 1990), 236–237. For a concurring viewpoint, see Robert Roule's statement in James Axtell, "The Vengeful Women of Marblehead:

Robert Roule's Deposition of 1677," *William and Mary Quarterly* 31, no. 4 (1974): 647–652.

229. Only Thomas Rose survived; Dew, Hudson, Merrett, and Pittman perished. Bodge, *Soldiers*, 133–141.

230. Douglas Edward Leech, *Flintlock and Tomahawk: New England in King Philip's War*, reprint of 1958 Macmillian ed. (East Orleans, Mass.: Parnassus Imprints, 1992), 119.

231. Brian Joe Lobley Berry, *The Shapleigh, Shapley, and Shappley Families: A Comprehensive Genealogy, 1635–1993* (Baltimore: Gateway, 1993).

232. PREC, 3:35.

233. Like professional military leaders in Elizabethan England in the 1500s, some New England officers complained of the quality of impressed soldiers early in the war, especially in comparison to volunteers later in the war who fought for bounties and profit. See Benjamin Church, Thomas Church, and Samuel Gardner Drake, *The History of Philip's War, Commonly Called the Great Indian War, of 1675 and 1676*, reprint of 1716 Boston 2nd ed. (Exeter, N.H.: J. & B. Williams, 1829), esp. 41–45.

234. ECQCR, 4:160–162. Beale was also fined for "breaking Henry Codner's head" while the two scuffled.

235. ECQCR, 4:40, 4:282, 4:403.

236. ECQCR, 5:197, 5:218.

237. ECQCR, 5:278–279.

238. Bodge, *Soldiers*, passim.

CHAPTER 4

1. For the best explanation of the stereotype, see Kenneth A. Lockridge, *A New England Town: The First Hundred Years*, enlarged ed. (New York: Norton, 1985).

2. John Frederick Martin, *Profits in the Wilderness: Entrepreneurship and the Founding of New England Towns in the Seventeenth Century* (Chapel Hill: University of North Carolina Press, 1991).

3. Richard Archer, *Fissures in the Rock: New England in the Seventeenth Century* (Hanover, N.H.: University Press of New England, 2001), 147.

4. Archer, *Fissures in the Rock*, 147.

5. John Josselyn, "Two Voyages to New England 1674," in *John Josselyn, Colonial Traveler: A Critical Edition of Two Voyages to New England*, ed. Paul J. Lindholdt (Hanover, N.H.: University Press of New England, 1988), 190.

6. Dudley and Dennison were appointed to their posts in the 1644 militia organization that established the four counties of Massachusetts Bay Colony and their respective county militias. Thus, Major General Dudley was in charge of all the militia of Massachusetts Bay in 1644 and Sergeant Major Dennison was the commander in chief of the Essex County militia. See Sarah Loring Bailey,

Historical Sketches of Andover: Comprising the Present Towns of North Andover and Andover (Boston: Houghton Mifflin, 1880), 167.

7. ECQCR, 2:101.

8. This was quite common; see Jack Sheldon Radabaugh, "The Military System of Colonial Massachusetts, 1690–1740" (Ph.D. diss., University of Southern California, 1965), 10.

9. ECQCR, 3:375.

10. Abiel Abbot, *History of Andover from Its Settlement to 1829* (Andover, Mass.: Flagg and Gould, 1829); Bailey, *Historical Sketches of Andover.*

11. See George Madison Bodge, *Soldiers in King Philip's War,* reprint of 1906 3rd ed. (Baltimore: Genealogical Publishing, 1967); Bailey, *Historical Sketches of Andover,* 163–177.

12. Philip J. Greven, *Four Generations: Population, Land, and Family in Colonial Andover, Massachusetts* (Ithaca, N.Y.: Cornell University Press, 1970), 34–35.

13. Greven, *Four Generations,* 72–99. While land was plentiful in New England, especially compared to England, most towns limited the amount available for distribution in order to protect some for future generations.

14. Daniel Vickers, *Farmers and Fishermen: Two Centuries of Work in Essex County, Massachusetts, 1630–1850* (Chapel Hill: University of North Carolina Press, 1994), 31–83, esp. 64–77.

15. Bailey, *Historical Sketches of Andover,* 119.

16. Greven, *Four Generations,* 87.

17. The 1679 tax lists include forty-six different family names, while various family histories discuss a few families of the same name (Parker for instance) that had two distinct branches in town. Given this information, an estimate of forty to fifty distinct families (or households) existing in 1675 Andover is assumed here. See Abbot, *History of Andover;* Elinor Abbot, "Transformations: The Reconstruction of Social Hierarchy in Early Colonial Andover, Massachusetts" (Ph.D. diss., Brandeis University, 1989); Bailey, *Historical Sketches of Andover;* Greven, *Four Generations.*

18. For Osgood's sons, see Abbot, *History of Andover,* 19.

19. Abbot, "Transformations," 125.

20. For genealogical information on the families, see Abbot, *History of Andover.*

21. Laurel Thatcher Ulrich, *Good Wives: Image and Reality in the Lives of Women in Northern New England, 1650–1750* (New York: Vintage, 1991), 119; my emphasis.

22. For information on the formation of the Osgood group and its members, see Abbot, "Transformations," 122–125.

23. Abbot, "Transformations," 75–84.

24. For the formation of the southern group and its members, see Abbot, "Transformations," 126–128.

25. See Greven, *Four Generations,* 72–99.

26. With the possible exception of John Marston's family, whose birth order is unknown.

27. Vickers, *Farmers and Fishermen,* 19.

28. Daniel Scott Smith, "Parental Power and Marriage Patterns: An Analysis of Historical Trends in Hingham, Massachusetts," *Journal of Marriage and the Family* 35, no. 3 (1973): 422–423; John J. Waters, "The Traditional World of the New England Peasants: A View from Seventeenth-Century Barnstable," *New England Historical Genealogical Register* 130, no. 1 (1976): 8–9.

29. Vickers, *Farmers and Fishermen,* 67–68.

30. For a discussion of the place of unattached farm laborers in Essex County and comparisons to the situation in England, see Vickers, *Farmers and Fishermen,* 52–64.

31. Bailey, *Historical Sketches of Andover,* 85.

32. The fact that she was still listed as the family's leader as "Widow Stevens" in the 1679 tax list suggests that she had not remarried and still had minor children at home. Otherwise, her other sons, if they were of age, would have taken their portions and Nathan would be listed as the family head. See Abbot, "Transformations," 242–248.

33. Bodge, *Soldiers,* 206–207.

34. Sidney Perley, "Ayer Genealogy," *Essex Antiquarian* 4, no. 10 (1900): 145.

35. Zechariah Ayers's 1679 rate was £0–3–10; see Abbot, "Transformations," 242–248.

36. James Savage, O. P. Dexter, and John Farmer, *A Genealogical Dictionary of the First Settlers of New England: Showing Three Generations of Those Who Came before May, 1692, on the Basis of Farmer's Register,* reprint of the 1860–1862 Boston ed., 4 vols. (Baltimore: Genealogical Publishing, 1990).

37. Bailey, *Historical Sketches of Andover,* 102–103.

38. Greven, *Four Generations,* 46.

39. Bailey, *Historical Sketches of Andover,* 102.

40. Bailey, *Historical Sketches of Andover,* 102–103.

41. PREC, 3:278–281.

42. PREC, 3:278–281.

43. *Vital Records of Andover, Massachusetts, to the End of the Year 1849,* 2 vols. (Topsfield, Mass.: Topsfield Historical Society, 1912).

44. Bailey, *Historical Sketches of Andover,* 103.

45. Even though Captain Brocklebank's company was sent out again in a few weeks to garrison the town of Marlboro, the Andover men did not accompany him as they had been released from service. Bodge, *Soldiers,* 206–217.

46. See Mary Rowlandson, *The Sovereignty and Goodness of God . . . Being a Narrative of the Captivity of Mrs. Mary Rowlandson and Related Documents,* ed. Neal Salisbury (Boston: Bedford, 1997).

47. Quoted in Bailey, *Historical Sketches of Andover*, 171.

48. By April 1676, a number of frontier towns, including Andover, were exempted by law from further impressments, and the men from those towns serving in the army at the time were sent home to help defend the town. See RGCMB, 5:358; Douglas Edward Leech, *Flintlock and Tomahawk: New England in King Philip's War*, reprint of 1958 Macmillian ed. (East Orleans, Mass.: Parnassus Imprints, 1992), 186.

49. ECQCR, 2:288, 3:285.

50. Bailey, *Historical Sketches of Andover*, 138.

51. Bailey, *Historical Sketches of Andover*, 574.

52. Eben. Putnam, *Genealogy of the Descendants of John, Christopher, and William Osgood* (Salem, Mass.: Salem Press, 1894), 1–2.

53. It was usual for a New England father to divide his land and estate among his sons, but John Osgood Sr. must have felt the need to keep his sizeable holdings, and the family's prominent role in Andover, secure. The other sons and daughters were given twenty-five pounds each in cash at their eighteenth birthdays. For the will and an inventory, see Bailey, *Historical Sketches of Andover*, 17–22.

54. For land, see Greven, *Four Generations*, 46, 59–60. For information on Bradstreet, see William H. Whitmore, *The Massachusetts Civil List for the Colonial and Provincial Periods, 1630-1774* (Baltimore: Genealogical Publishing, 1969); Abbot, *History of Andover*, 13–19; Bailey, *Historical Sketches of Andover*, 46–47, 136–139, passim.

55. For Mary, see Bailey, *Historical Sketches of Andover*, 76. For the children, see ECQCR, 2:121, 2:180, 2:345.

56. Abbot, "Transformations," 242–248.

57. ECQCR, 2:153.

58. ECQCR, 5:121.

59. ECQCR, 2:111.

60. For grand jury, see ECQCR, 2:168. For militia, see Bailey, *Historical Sketches of Andover*, 168.

61. Bailey, *Historical Sketches of Andover*, 138.

62. ECQCR, 5:289.

63. Bodge, *Soldiers*, passim.

64. There is ample precedence for this type of payment. See the example of a payment to the constable of Hatfield in the case of Captain Lathrop's company in August 1675 in Bodge, *Soldiers*, 139.

65. Historians of colonial Massachusetts have virtually ignored Manchester. The only dedicated history of the town is D. F. Lamson, *History of the Town of Manchester, Essex County, Massachusetts, 1645-1895* (Manchester, Mass.: Published by the Town, 1895).

66. Lamson, *History of Manchester*, 22–23.

67. *Town Records of Manchester, from the Earliest Grants of Land, 1636* (Salem, Mass: Salem Press, 1889), passim.

68. D. F. Lamson, "Town of Manchester," in *Municipal History of Essex County in Massachusetts*, ed. Benjamin F. Arrington (New York: Lewis Historical Publishing, 1922), 137.

69. *Town Records of Manchester*, 8–17.

70. *Town Records of Manchester*, passim.

71. Robert K. Wright, "Massachusetts Militia Roots: A Bibliographic Study" (Washington, D.C.: Historical Branch, National Guard Bureau, 1986), 11.

72. Bodge, *Soldiers*, 133–141.

73. Bodge, *Soldiers*, 164–167. Lamson had this wrong; he credits Pickworth under Lathrop and even asserts that Pickworth died at the Bloody Brook. See Lamson, *History of Manchester*, 55.

74. ECQCR, 6:132–134. Lamson also had this wrong; he does not credit Knight with service. See Lamson, *History of Manchester*, 55.

75. ECQCR, 6:132.

76. ECQCR, 6:133.

77. ECQCR, 6:132.

78. While this appears to have happened in the fall of 1675 when Elithrop endeavored to impress Leech, it did not come to light until much later (January 21, 1676), in testimony given about an associated case. See ECQCR, 6:132.

79. ECQCR, 6:132.

80. ECQCR, 6:133.

81. ECQCR, 6:133.

82. ECQCR, 6:133.

83. Bodge, *Soldiers*, 258–259.

84. ECQCR, 6:133.

85. ECQCR, 6:133.

86. ECQCR, 6:133.

87. ECQCR, 6:132–133.

88. ECQCR, 6:132.

89. RGCMB, 5:78–79.

90. ECQCR, 6:173.

91. ECQCR, 6:132–134.

92. For Lathrop's role in the Beverly militia, see Edwin Martin Stone, *History of Beverly, Civil and Ecclesiastical: From Its Settlement in 1630 to 1842* (Boston: J. Munroe, 1843), 25–29, 168–169. For the number of men from each town, see Bodge, *Soldiers*, 133–141.

93. Bodge, *Soldiers*, 136–137.

94. Lamson, *History of Manchester*, 20.

95. *Town Records of Manchester*, 3–17.

96. PREC, 3:325–326.

97. John M. Bradbury, *The Bennet Family of Ipswich, Massachusetts* (Boston: D. Clapp and Son, 1875), 5–6.

98. Bradbury, *Bennet Family*, 5–6.

99. Bradbury, *Bennet Family*, 5.

100. Bradbury, *Bennet Family*, 7.

101. Bradbury, *Bennet Family*, 7.

102. Bradbury, *Bennet Family*, 7.

103. ECQCR, 6:60.

104. Bodge lists him as a resident of Salem. Bodge, *Soldiers*, 167.

105. *Town Records of Manchester*, 17.

106. This would explain why his marriage and his children's birth records are recorded in Salem. See *Vital Records of Salem, Massachusetts, to the End of the Year 1849*, 6 vols. (Salem, Mass.: Essex Institute, 1916), 2:176, 4:197.

107. Bodge, *Soldiers*, 164–167.

108. For examples of sergeants being appointed or confirmed in Essex County, see ECQCR, 2:101, 2:332, 3:290, 3:336, 3:337, 3:375.

109. No militia records for Manchester exist. Pickworth may have been a noncommissioned officer in Beverly, but there are no records of this. See *Early Records of the Town of Beverly* (Beverly, Mass.: Allen Print, 1905); *Beverly Town Records, 1665–1709* (Beverly, Mass.: Published by the Town, 1895).

110. Based on his brother's and sisters' baptism dates and the family genealogy. See Sidney Perley, *The History of Salem, Massachusetts*, 3 vols. (Salem, Mass.: S. Perley, 1924), 1:402.

111. *Town Records of Manchester*, 5.

112. *Town Records of Manchester*, 9–13.

113. For numerous land grants, see *Town Records of Manchester*.

114. PREC, 1:428–429.

115. PREC, 1:428–429.

116. PREC, 1:428–429.

117. *Town Records of Manchester*, 10. It is hard to know Samuel Pickworth's status in the town and his family because the records do not mention his age. He did have married sisters, but it is not known if his elder brother John Jr. was married or not. See PREC, 1:428–429.

118. ECQCR, 3:298.

119. *Vital Records of Salem*, 4:197.

120. *Vital Records of Salem*, 2:176.

121. Richard D. Pierce, ed., *The Records of the First Church in Salem Massachusetts, 1629–1736* (Salem, Mass.: Essex Institute, 1974), 30.

122. For an account of this incident, see William Hubbard and Samuel Gardner Drake, *The History of the Indian Wars in New England, from the First Settlement to the Termination of the War with King Philip in 1677*, 2 vols. in 1, facsimile reprint of the 1864 Drake ed. (Bowie, Md.: Heritage, 1990), 141. See also Bodge, *Soldiers*, 167.

123. The youth was probably an apprentice carpenter in the middle of his contract period. PREC, 3:67–68.

124. While it seems unlikely that a married man with three young children would have been impressed, Manchester's small size could have made it difficult to find other candidates; the impressment, however, still appears unlikely.

125. Beverly issued its first warrant in the controversy in September 1675 but did not receive its recruit until January 1676 with the impressment of John Knight. It seems highly unlikely that another warrant for impressment would have been executed (in December 1675, for Gardner's command) amid the controversy over the earlier warrant. See ECQCR, 6:132–134.

126. *Vital Records of Manchester, Massachusetts, to the End of the Year 1849* (Salem, Mass.: Essex Institute, 1903); *Town Records of Manchester*; Lamson, *History of Manchester*.

127. ECQCR, 6:133.

128. *Records of the Court of Assistants of the Colony of the Massachusetts Bay, 1630–1692*, reprint of the Boston and County of Suffolk 1901–1928 ed., 3 vols. (New York: AMS, 1973), passim; ECQCR, passim.

129. ECQCR, 133.

130. There are few historical treatments of Wenham. The classic history of the town is Myron O. Allen, *History of Wenham Civil and Ecclesiastical from Its Settlement in 1639 to 1860*, reprint of the 1860 ed. (Ann Arbor: Edwards Brothers, 1975). It is sparse in its coverage but does have some interesting observations. The more complete is Adeline Cole, ed., *Notes on Wenham History, 1643–1943* (Salem, Mass.: Wenham Historical Association, 1943). There is also a published volume of the town's records, *Wenham Town Records*, 4 vols. (Wenham, Mass.: Wenham Historical Society, 1927), in addition to the standard collection of vital records for the town, *Vital Records of Wenham, Massachusetts, to the End of the Year 1849* (Salem, Mass.: Essex Institute, 1904).

131. Cole, *Wenham History*, 21.

132. Cole, *Wenham History*, 23.

133. Cole, *Wenham History*, 33.

134. *Wenham Town Records*, 33.

135. ECQCR, 5:309–310.

136. A May 1672 law established that the clerks were to collect fines, and if they did not, they could be fined themselves. See William Henry Whitmore, *Colonial Laws of Massachusetts, Reprinted from the Edition of 1660, with the Supplements to 1672: Containing Also, the Body of Liberties of 1641* (Boston: Published by order of the City Council of Boston, 1889), 203. If the men could not afford to pay the fines, they would be subject to "military punishment" such as "riding the Wooden Horse, or By Bilboes, or lying Neck and Heels, or acknowledgement at the head of the company." See Whitmore, *Colonial Laws of Massachusetts*, 204.

137. ECQCR, 5:308–310.

138. ECQCR, 5:308–310.

139. ECQCR, 5:310.

140. ECQCR, 5:373.

141. ECQCR, 5:309.

142. A fine of forty shillings was assessed, as codified in the 1672 edition of the General Laws and Liberties of the Massachusetts Colony. See *Colonial Laws 1672*, 109.

143. For information on firearms in King Philip's War, see Allen French, "Arms and Military Training of Our Colonizing Ancestors," *Proceeding of the Massachusetts Historical Society* 67 (1945): 3–21; Harold L. Peterson, *Arms and Armor in Colonial America, 1526–1783*, unabridged reproduction of the 1956 Stackpole Company ed. (Mineola, N.Y.: Dover, 2000); George Sheldon, *Flintlock or Matchlock in King Philip's War* (Worcester, Mass.: Worcester Society of Antiquity, 1899).

144. See the testimony of William Fiske, John Abbe, and John Waldren in ECQCR, 5:310.

145. ECQCR, 5:309.

146. See the testimony of John Fiske, John Gilbert, John Waldren, Nathaniell Browne, and Tameson Waldren in ECQCR, 5:310.

147. Codified in the 1672 edition of the *General Laws and Liberties of the Massachusetts Colony*. See *Colonial Laws 1672*, 110.

148. *Wenham Town Records*.

149. "Serg. Thomas Fiske to the General Court, 30 November 1675," vol. 68, document 69b, MAC.

150. See Bodge, *Soldiers*, 136–137, 142–158, 166–167, 207, 346–347. In the town histories, several soldiers from Wenham who served in the war are listed; see Allen, *History of Wenham*, 38; and Cole, *Wenham History*, 33. Allen undercounts Wenham soldiers, listing only the five impressed into Gardner's company (Mark Batchelder, Richard Hutton, Thomas Kimball, Samuel Moulton, and Philip Welch). Cole lists the same five and adds three men who "volunteered" (Thomas Abbe, Caleb Kimball, and John Dodge). There is no source for Cole's assertion that these men volunteered. One man, John Dodge, was not a resident of Wenham in 1675 but had moved to Beverly and is not treated in this section. See Dodge, "Dodge Genealogy," Essex County Manuscript Genealogy Collection, Philips Library, Peabody Essex Museum, Salem, Massachusetts; Joseph Thompson Dodge, *Genealogy of the Dodge Family of Essex County, Mass, 1629–1894* (Madison, Wis.: Democrat Printing, 1894).

151. For information on the highly convoluted layers of the Kimball family in Wenham, see Leonard Allison Morrison and Stephen Paschall Sharples, *History of the Kimball Family in America, from 1634 to 1897, and of Its Ancestors the Kemballs or Kemboldes of England, with an Account of the Kembles of Boston, Massachusetts* (Boston: Damrell and Upham, 1897); Marilyn Fitzpatrick, "Correction to Kimball Genealogy," *Essex Genealogist* 20 (2000): 16.

152. "Serg. Thomas Fiske to the General Court, 30 November 1675," vol. 68, document 69b, MAC.

153. For Sweet, see Bodge, *Soldiers*, 342–347. For Brocklebank, see Bodge, *Soldiers*, 206–217.

154. Alexander McMillan Welch, *Philip Welch of Ipswich, Massachusetts 1654 and His Descendants* (Richmond, Va.: William Byrd, 1947).

155. William Grant Black, "The Military Origins of Federal Social Welfare Programs: Early British and Colonial American Precedents" (Ph.D. diss., University of Minnesota, 1989).

156. Only his inclusion on the impressment report of Sergeant Fiske places him in the Wenham impressment group, rather than among the Topsfield or Ipswich men.

157. Leech, *Flintlock and Tomahawk*, 184–185.

158. The following account comes from Welch, *Philip Welch of Ipswich*, 3–11; George Francis Dow, Alice Goldsmith Waters Dow, and Ruth H. Allen, *History of Topsfield, Massachusetts* (Topsfield, Mass.: Topsfield Historical Society, 1940), 90–92.

159. ECQCR, 2:295–296.

160. ECQCR, 2:169, 2:197–198, 2:295–296. Obviously, the ages of the two men in the original documents do not exactly match. It is much more likely that the 1661 document stating their ages is correct.

161. There was some disagreement over the length of his contract. See Welch, *Philip Welch of Ipswich*, 10–11.

162. Welch, *Philip Welch of Ipswich*, 11.

163. Welch, *Philip Welch of Ipswich*, 11.

164. Welch, *Philip Welch of Ipswich*, 16.

165. Bodge, *Soldiers*, 167; Welch, *Philip Welch of Ipswich*, 11.

166. ECQCR, 6:192.

167. Welch, *Philip Welch of Ipswich*, 12–13.

168. The list is printed in Allen, *History of Wenham*, 33.

169. Allen, *History of Wenham*, 39.

170. The position on the tax list and the later relative wealth of certain individuals, based on their probate inventories, even twenty or thirty years later, shows little movement. Richard Kimball, the highest-placed individual on the tax list, retained his high position, and his 1676 probate inventory showed assets of 986 pounds, the highest recorded in town. His brother Henry Kimball, who was near the bottom of the 1659 list, had a 1676 probate inventory of 100 pounds. There are additional examples that confirm this stability. See PREC, 3:72–75.

171. These percentages do not include the nonresident Philip Welch.

172. *Wenham Town Records*, passim; Morrison and Sharples, *Kimball Family*.

173. ECQCR, 4:286. For information about the company, see Louise Breen, *Transgressing the Bounds: Subversive Enterprises among the Puritan Elite in*

Massachusetts, 1630–1692 (Oxford: Oxford University Press, 2001); Oliver Ayer Roberts, *History of the Military Company of the Massachusetts Now Called the Ancient and Honorable Artillery Company of Massachusetts, 1637–1888* (Boston: Alfred Mudge and Son, 1895).

174. The fact that his prominent father died before the war and had his property split among several heirs is the reason for Mark Batchelder's lower-than-expected showing on the tax list. See *Wenham Town Records*; Sidney Perley, "Batchelder Genealogy," *Essex Antiquarian* 7, no. 3 (1903): 105–109; Frederick Clifton Pierce, *Batchelder, Batcheller Genealogy: Descendants of Rev. Stephen Bachiler of England . . . Who Settled the Town of New Hampton, N.H. And Joseph, Henry, Joshua, and John Batcheller, of Essex Co., Mass* (Chicago: W. B. Conkey, 1898).

175. *Wenham Town Records*; Perley, "Batchelder Genealogy"; Pierce, *Batchelder, Batcheller Genealogy*.

176. Perley, "Batchelder Genealogy," 105–109.

177. This was confirmed by examining all court records pertaining to Wenham for the years 1665–1676 in ECQCR.

178. ECQCR, 4:86–87.

179. The crime in Wenham between 1665 and 1675 consisted of: in November 1667 Abner Ordway was declared *"not"* guilty of breech of the peace (ECQCR, 3:462); November 1668 saw "two strangers" in town who committed trivial offenses (ECQCR, 4:86–87); in June 1671 John Whittridge was convicted of drunkenness (ECQCR, 4:416); two servants got in trouble and "fled town" in June 1673 (ECQCR, 5:220); and Walter Fairfield and John Morel of Wenham were convicted of drunkenness in June 1673 (ECQCR, 5:221).

180. ECQCR, 4:73.

181. ECQCR, 4:97.

CHAPTER 5

1. Various lists and accounts from the period, when combined, show that over 434 Essex County men were in some way compensated by the colony during the war years, 1675–1676. Yet, a careful accounting of the actual fighting companies, cross-checked with muster lists and other enlistment records, uncovered only 357 who fought in an active-duty capacity. This figure does not include those men who served as unit commanders or other officers in the expeditionary companies. For a more detailed accounting of this, see Kyle F. Zelner, "The Flower and Rabble of Essex County: A Social History of the Massachusetts Bay Militia and Militiamen During King Philip's War, 1675–1676" (Ph.D. diss., College of William and Mary, 2003).

2. John Shy, "A New Look at the Colonial Militia," in *A People Numerous and Armed: Reflections on the Military Struggle for American Independence*, reprint of 1976 Oxford ed. (Ann Arbor: University of Michigan Press, 1990), 32.

3. Data on the men's ages came from a variety of primary and secondary sources, including birth, church, probate, and court records; town histories; and published and unpublished genealogies. For a detailed breakdown of the men by age, see appendix 4. On the topic of age in New England, see Lisa Wilson, *Ye Heart of a Man: The Domestic Life of Men in Colonial New England* (New Haven, Conn.: Yale University Press, 1999), 143–189.

4. John Demos, *A Little Commonwealth; Family Life in Plymouth Colony* (New York: Oxford University Press, 1970), 148.

5. Daniel Vickers, *Farmers and Fishermen: Two Centuries of Work in Essex County, Massachusetts, 1630–1850* (Chapel Hill: University of North Carolina Press, 1994), 68.

6. Philip J. Greven, *Four Generations: Population, Land, and Family in Colonial Andover, Massachusetts* (Ithaca, N.Y.: Cornell University Press, 1970), 72–99.

7. Vickers, *Farmers and Fishermen*, 69.

8. John J. Waters, "Family, Inheritance, and Migration in Colonial New England: The Evidence from Guilford, Connecticut," *William and Mary Quarterly* 39, no. 1 (1982): 77.

9. Maris A. Vinovskis, "Mortality Rates and Trends in Massachusetts before 1860," *Journal of Economic History* 32, no. 1 (1972): 195–196.

10. Greven, *Four Generations*, 30.

11. Greven, *Four Generations*, 30.

12. Greven, *Four Generations*, 11–13; John J. Waters, "The Traditional World of the New England Peasants: A View from Seventeenth-Century Barnstable," *New England Historical Genealogical Register* 130, no. 1 (1976): 5–7; Waters, "Family, Inheritance, and Migration," 64–86; Daniel Scott Smith, "Parental Power and Marriage Patterns: An Analysis of Historical Trends in Hingham, Massachusetts," *Journal of Marriage and the Family* 35, no. 3 (1973): 423.

13. Birth-order data comes from a variety of sources, including published and unpublished genealogies, vital record collections of the towns (birth volumes), court records, and especially probate records.

14. While Topsfield had a percentage even higher than Lynn, at 100 percent, that finding is skewed by incomplete data and is not treated here.

15. Marriage data comes from a variety of sources, most often vital, probate, and church records and genealogies, but also court and town records.

16. Demos, *Little Commonwealth*, 190.

17. Laurel Thatcher Ulrich, *Good Wives: Image and Reality in the Lives of Women in Northern New England, 1650–1750* (New York: Vintage, 1991), 108.

18. Edmund Sears Morgan, *The Puritan Family: Religion and Domestic Relations in Seventeenth-Century New England*, rev. ed. (New York: Harper and Row, 1966), 29.

19. Morgan, *Puritan Family*, 45.

20. Ulrich, *Good Wives*, 35–50.

21. Ulrich, *Good Wives*, 37.

22. Wilson, *Heart of a Man*, 99.

23. Wilson, *Heart of a Man*, 99–103.

24. Quoted in George Madison Bodge, *Soldiers in King Philip's War*, reprint of 1906 3rd ed. (Baltimore: Genealogical Publishing, 1967), 143.

25. Wilson, *Heart of a Man*, 115.

26. Anne S. Lombard, *Making Manhood: Growing up Male in Colonial New England* (Cambridge, Mass.: Harvard University Press, 2003), 22.

27. Wilson, *Heart of a Man*, 126.

28. Lombard, *Making Manhood*, 30.

29. Lombard, *Making Manhood*, 31.

30. Vickers, *Farmers and Fishermen*, 67.

31. Unlike the distribution of married soldiers, an analysis of fathers sent to the assorted companies at different stages of the war reveals no discernable pattern. Somewhat larger numbers of fathers did serve in Gardner's company and as troopers.

32. Francis J. Bremer, *Puritan Experiment: New England Society from Bradford to Edwards*, rev. ed. (Hanover, N.H.: University Press of New England, 1995), 114.

33. John Winthrop, "A Model of Christian Charity (1630)," in *Settlements to Society 1607–1763: A Documentary History of Colonial America*, ed. Jack P. Greene (New York: Norton, 1975), 67.

34. For one economic view, see John Frederick Martin, *Profits in the Wilderness: Entrepreneurship and the Founding of New England Towns in the Seventeenth Century* (Chapel Hill: University of North Carolina Press, 1991).

35. Virginia DeJohn Anderson, *New England's Generation: The Great Migration and the Formation of Society and Culture in the Seventeenth Century* (Cambridge: Cambridge University Press, 1991), 39–40.

36. Two excellent overviews of this process are Anderson, *New England's Generation*; and Bremer, *Puritan Experiment*.

37. Edmund Sears Morgan, *Visible Saints: The History of a Puritan Idea* (New York: New York University Press, 1963), 88–90.

38. Harry S. Stout, *The New England Soul: Preaching and Religious Culture in Colonial New England* (New York: Oxford University Press, 1986), 18.

39. B. Katherine Brown, "Freemanship in Puritan New England," *American Historical Review* 59, no. 4 (1954): 865–883.

40. Gerald F. Moran, "Religious Renewal, Puritan Tribalism, and the Family in Seventeenth-Century Milford, Connecticut," *William and Mary Quarterly* 36, no. 2 (1979): 245–246.

41. Stout, *New England Soul*, 58.

42. Moran, "Religious Renewal," 245–246.

43. Brown, "Freemanship," passim.

44. Increase Mather, "An Earnest Exhortation To the Inhabitants of New England," in *So Dreadful a Judgment: Puritan Responses to King Philip's War 1676–1677*, ed. Richard Slotkin and James K. Folsom (Middletown, Conn.: Wesleyan University Press, 1978), 172.

45. Mather, "Earnest Exhortation," 179.

46. Moran, "Religious Renewal," 247.

47. T. H. Breen, "Persistent Localism: English Social Change and the Shaping of New England Institutions," in *Puritans and Adventurers: Change and Persistence in Early America*, ed. T. H. Breen (New York: Oxford University Press, 1980), 3–24.

48. Breen, "Persistent Localism," 16.

49. The records for this measure are varied, but include town, court, and even probate records.

50. John Fairfield Sly, *Town Government in Massachusetts, 1620–1930* (Hamden, Conn.: Archon, 1967), 33.

51. Magistrates did have considerable power in the judicial realm and enjoyed considerable influence over town selectmen, but they did not have legally binding authority in town government.

52. Ann Smith Lainhart, *Digging for Genealogical Treasure in New England Town Records* (Boston: New England Historical and Genealogical Society, 1996), 22–23.

53. Sly, *Town Government*, 36.

54. They generally would have been older than the average soldier as well.

55. Sly, *Town Government*, 39. For the listing of duties, see RGCMB, 4:pt. 1, 324–327.

56. Sly, *Town Government*.

57. Anderson, *New England's Generation*, 123.

58. Anderson, *New England's Generation*, 124.

59. Vickers, *Farmers and Fishermen*, 10.

60. Anderson, *New England's Generation*, 31.

61. Vickers, *Farmers and Fishermen*, 51.

62. Occupation data comes from a variety of sources, including court records, town records, tax lists, and probate records. Probate records often list men as having specific types of tools (such as "carpenter's tools"); only if a man was actually labeled with a certain occupation, however, was the man listed as having that occupation. If a man was listed as owning tools and a separate record was available of his employment of that trade (for example, a man who had carpentry tools and was "paid to repair the floor of the meetinghouse"), the occupation *was* listed for that individual.

63. Seventeen men were listed as having more than one occupation. Some of the more interesting combinations include: fisherman/shepherd/ironworker and innkeeper/tanner.

64. Men classified as such were primarily listed as farmers.

65. For a listing of all the tradesmen, see appendix 5.

66. This listing does not include shipwrights, shipbuilders, or ship carpenters. They were listed as craftsmen/tradesmen for the purposes of this study.

67. Vickers, *Farmers and Fishermen*, 53–54.

68. Alison Isabel Vannah, "'Crotchets of Division': Ipswich in New England, 1633–1679" (Ph.D. diss., Brandeis University, 1999), 841.

69. Jill Lepore, *The Name of War: King Philip's War and the Origins of American Identity* (New York: Knopf, 1998), 96.

70. Bodge, *Soldiers*, 135; Douglas Edward Leech, *Flintlock and Tomahawk: New England in King Philip's War*, reprint of 1958 Macmillian ed. (East Orleans, Mass.: Parnassus Imprints, 1992), 108.

71. RGCMB, 5:52.

72. Leech, *Flintlock and Tomahawk*, 109.

73. RGCMB, 5:66.

74. RGCMB, 5:78.

75. James E. McWilliams, *Building the Bay Colony: Local Economy and Culture in Early Massachusetts* (Charlottesville: University of Virginia Press, 2007), 145–157; Vickers, *Farmers and Fishermen*, 98–100.

76. Vickers, *Farmers and Fishermen*, 53–54.

77. Vannah, "'Crotchets of Division,'" 842–843.

78. Sidney Perley, *The History of Salem, Massachusetts*, 3 vols. (Salem, Mass.: S. Perley, 1924), 3:93.

79. Mather, "Earnest Exhortation," 173, 170.

80. Donald Warner Koch, "Income Distribution and Political Structure in Seventeenth-Century Salem, Massachusetts," *Essex Institute Historical Collections* 105, no. 1 (1969): 52.

81. Manfred Jonas, "The Wills of Early Settlers of Essex County, Massachusetts," *Essex Institute Historical Collections* 96, no. 3 (1960): 230–231.

82. William I. Davisson, "Essex County Wealth Trends: Wealth and Economic Growth in 17th Century Massachusetts," *Essex Institute Historical Collections* 103, no. 4 (1967): 291–342; Jonas, "Wills of Early Settlers," 228–235; Koch, "Income Distribution," 50–69; Gloria L. Main and Jackson Turner Main, "Economic Growth and the Standard of Living in Southern New England, 1640–1774," *Journal of Economic History* 48, no. 1 (1988): 27–46.

83. Mather, "Earnest Exhortation," 181, 177.

84. Edwin Powers, *Crime and Punishment in Early Massachusetts, 1620–1692: A Documentary History* (Boston: Beacon, 1966), 149.

85. David Thomas Konig, *Law and Society in Puritan Massachusetts: Essex County, 1629–1692* (Chapel Hill: University of North Carolina Press, 1979), 129.

86. Edgar J. McManus, *Law and Liberty in Early New England: Criminal Justice and Due Process, 1620–1692* (Amherst: University of Massachusetts Press, 1993), 150.

87. McManus, *Law and Liberty*, 151.
88. Mather, "Earnest Exhortation," 176.
89. McManus, *Law and Liberty*, 151.
90. For the court cases, see Powers, *Crime and Punishment*, 405.
91. "This Account of New England (1675): An Account of All the Trading Towns and Ports . . . ," *New England Historical and Genealogical Register* 38 (1884): 379–381. The number of households at Ipswich, 400, is very close to the estimate of 470 adult males made by Vannah, "'Crotchets of Division,'" 847–848, note 817. See also Susan L. Norton, "Population Growth in Colonial America: A Study of Ipswich, Massachusetts," *Population Studies* 25, no. 3 (1971): 433–452; Daniel Scott Smith, "The Demographic History of Colonial New England," *Journal of Economic History* 32, no. 1 (1972): 165–183.
92. Estimating only 1,300 households (which is extremely low because it does not include the seven smaller towns) and a calculation of 5.5 people to a household, the population of the large towns of the county alone would be 7,150. This calculation is based on a formula in Evarts B. Greene and Virginia D. Harrington, *American Population before the Federal Census of 1790* (Baltimore: Genealogical Publishing, 1981), 9, note f. If the figure of 8 people to a household is used, that formula would yield a population of 10,400, based on the work of Greven, *Four Generations*, 30.
93. John Noble and John Francis Cronin, eds., *Records of the Court of Assistants of the Colony of the Massachusetts Bay, 1630–1692*, 3 vols. (Boston: Published by the County of Suffolk, 1901).
94. ECQCR, 4:124–126, 5:141.
95. ECQCR, 5:303, 6:327.
96. RGCMB, 5:59; Mather, "Earnest Exhortation," 176–177.
97. RGCMB, 5:59; Mather, "Earnest Exhortation," 180–181.
98. ECQCR, 5:311.
99. ECQCR, 5:231–232.
100. Mather, "Earnest Exhortation," 177–178, 180–181.
101. ECQCR, 4:441–442.
102. Quoted in Amos Everett Jewett, Emily Mabel Adams Jewett, and Jewett Family of America, *Rowley, Massachusetts, "Mr. Ezechi Rogers Plantation," 1639–1850* (Rowley, Mass.: Jewett Family of America, 1946), 127.
103. Quoted in Jewett, *Mr. Ezechi Rogers Plantation*, 127.
104. Quoted in Jewett, *Mr. Ezechi Rogers Plantation*, 127.
105. Quoted in Jewett, *Mr. Ezechi Rogers Plantation*, 127.
106. Powers, *Crime and Punishment*, 367–399.
107. RGCMB, 6:61.
108. ECQCR, 4:214, 4:270, 5:222, 5:258, 5:266, and 5:363.
109. RGCMB, 6:63.
110. Powers, *Crime and Punishment*, 404–405.

111. ECQCR, 5:250. Marshman's first name in the actual record was recorded as "Xtian."

112. ECQCR, 5:291–292, 5:359.

113. Victor L. Stater, *Noble Government: The Stuart Lord Lieutenancy and the Transformation of English Politics* (Athens: University of Georgia Press, 1994), 40.

114. "Orders from the General Court," vol. 68, documents 106 and 117,
MAC.

115. Victor L. Stater, "The Lord Lieutenancy on the Eve of the Civil Wars:
The Impressment of George Plowright," *Historical Journal (Great Britain)* 29, no.
2 (1986): 84.

116. Charles Patrick Neimeyer, *America Goes to War: A Social History of the Continental Army* (New York: New York University Press, 1996), 17.

117. RGCMB, 5:62.

118. For Salem's controversy, see Richard P. Gildrie, "Contention in Salem:
The Higginson-Nicholet Controversy, 1672–1676," *Essex Institute Historical Collections* 113, no. 2 (1977): 117–139.

119. ECQCR, 5:60–63.

120. ECQCR, 5:222.

121. ECQCR, 4:225, 4:258–259.

122. ECQCR, 5:373.

123. Sly, *Town Government*, 39.

124. ECQCR, 6:60.

125. Konig, *Law and Society*, 82.

126. Konig, *Law and Society*, 82.

127. PREC; Melinde Lutz Sanborn and William P. Upham, *Essex County, Massachusetts Probate Index, 1638–1840*, 2 vols. (Boston: M. L. Sanborn, 1987).

128. Konig, *Law and Society*, 84.

129. The one company that did not, Manning's company, had a relatively small
number of Essex County men compared to the other units, skewing its result.

130. There is a possible pattern. Of the four major Essex companies, Lathrop's,
recruited early in the war, had one of the lowest negative rates (66 percent). While
half of Appleton's troops were recruited at the same time as Lathrop's command,
the other half were recruited in November 1675 for the Narragansett campaign
along with Gardner's company (it is impossible, based on the data available, to
separate Appleton's men by date of recruitment). It may not be a coincidence that
Appleton's (78 percent) and Gardner's companies (75 percent), both (in part for
Appleton) recruited for the dangerous Fort Fight, had the highest percentages of
the "rabble." The difference in the percentages (66, 78, and 75) is quite small, however, and probably not statistically significant. The idea of differing recruitment
patterns based on mission was posited in Kyle F. Zelner, "Massachusetts' Two Militias: A Social History of the 1st Essex Expeditionary Company in King Philip's War,
1675–1676" (master's thesis, Wayne State University, 1993); Kyle F. Zelner, "Essex

County's Two Militias: The Social Composition of Offensive and Defensive Units during King Philip's War, 1675–1676," *New England Quarterly* 72, no. 4 (1999): 577–593. While the premise is not totally without merit, the evidence of town-based recruitment, based on town needs overshadowing military concerns presented here, makes the "mission theory of recruitment" weak.

131. William Hubbard and Samuel Gardner Drake, *The History of the Indian Wars in New England, from the First Settlement to the Termination of the War with King Philip in 1677*, 2 vols. in 1, facsimile reprint of the 1864 Drake ed. (Bowie, Md.: Heritage, 1990), 113. It is quite probable that Hubbard's statement was more a tribute to fallen soldiers than a serious sociological analysis, although many subsequent historians and genealogists have taken the statement as proof of the quality of Lathrop's men.

CHAPTER 6

1. This analysis does not include any companies, even if composed mostly of Essex men, who were sent to fight in Maine from 1676 to 1678, well after the fighting stopped in the south. That conflict and those men are beyond the scope of this study.

2. For information on the causes of the war, see Philip Ranlet, "Another Look at the Causes of King Philip's War," *New England Quarterly* 61, no. 1 (1988): 79–100; Yasuhide Kawashima, *Igniting King Philip's War: The John Sassamon Murder Trial* (Lawrence: University Press of Kansas, 2001); James David Drake, *King Philip's War: Civil War in New England, 1675–1676* (Amherst: University of Massachusetts Press, 1999).

3. George Madison Bodge, *Soldiers in King Philip's War*, reprint of 1906 3rd ed. (Baltimore: Genealogical Publishing, 1967), 27. The cavalry of Massachusetts had been organized into a large unit called the Three County Troop well before the war; see RGCMB, 5:6.

4. Bodge, *Soldiers*, 90.

5. Bodge, *Soldiers*, 85.

6. Darrett Bruce Rutman, "A Militant New World, 1607–1640: America's First Generation: Its Martial Spirit, Its Tradition of Arms, Its Militia Organization, Its Wars" (Ph.D. diss., University of Virginia, 1959), 741–763.

7. Bodge, *Soldiers*, 143. Surprisingly, Appleton's commission as a captain of one hundred men was not dated until September 24, 1675, many weeks after he and his company left for the west.

8. Bodge, *Soldiers*, 63.

9. See John Pynchon, *The Pynchon Papers, 1654–1697*, ed. Carl Bridenbaugh, Juliette Tomlinson, and Colonial Society of Massachusetts, 2 vols., vol. 1: *Letters of John Pynchon, 1654–1700* (Boston: Colonial Society of Massachusetts; distributed by the University Press of Virginia, 1982); Stephen Innes, *Labor in a New*

Land: Economy and Society in Seventeenth-Century Springfield, rev. paperback ed. (Princeton, N.J.: Princeton University Press, 1983).

10. Oliver Ayer Roberts, *History of the Military Company of the Massachusetts Now Called the Ancient and Honorable Artillery Company of Massachusetts, 1637–1888* (Boston: Alfred Mudge and Son, 1895).

11. Bodge, *Soldiers*, 133–134.

12. Increase Mather, "A Brief History of the War with the Indians in New-England," in *So Dreadful a Judgment: Puritan Responses to King Philip's War 1676–1677*, ed. Richard Slotkin and James K. Folsom (Middletown, Conn.: Wesleyan University Press, 1978), 98.

13. William Hubbard, *The History of the Indian Wars in New England, from the First Settlement to the Termination of the War with King Philip in 1677*, ed. Samuel Gardner Drake, 2 vols. in 1, facsimile reprint of the 1864 Drake ed. (Bowie, Md.: Heritage, 1990), 116.

14. Hubbard, *History of the Indian Wars*, 113.

15. Bodge, *Soldiers*, 145.

16. Pynchon, *The Pynchon Papers*, 1:162.

17. This controversy over command, which was at times quite heated, displays the differences between the colonies of Massachusetts Bay and Connecticut under United Colonies' command. It is examined in detail in Bodge, *Soldiers*, 145–152. See also Thomas Franklin Waters, Sarah Whipple Goodhue, and John Wise, *Ipswich in the Massachusetts Bay Colony* (Ipswich, Mass.: Ipswich Historical Society, 1905), 159–224.

18. Douglas Edward Leech, *Flintlock and Tomahawk: New England in King Philip's War*, reprint of 1958 Macmillian ed. (East Orleans, Mass.: Parnassus Imprints, 1992), 98–99.

19. The colonial decision to strike the neutral Narragansett Indians is hotly debated in the historical community. Possible reasons for the attack range from questions of land acquisition to ethnicity and race. See Francis Jennings, *The Invasion of America: Indians, Colonialism, and the Cant of Conquest* (Chapel Hill: University of North Carolina Press, 1976), 298–312; Drake, *King Philip's War*, 114–120; Harry M. Ward, *The United Colonies of New England, 1643–90* (New York: Vintage, 1961), 289–299.

20. For details, see Bodge, *Soldiers*, 179–184.

21. For the final list of the men from Essex in Gardner's company by town, see "A List of ye names of Captain Gardiner's Souldiers named as Impressed for the service of the County, December 1675," vol. 68, document 98, MAC. The same list appears in Bodge, *Soldiers*, 166–167.

22. On Gardner, see Bodge, *Soldiers*, 164–165.

23. David Pulsifer, *Records of the Colony of New Plymouth in New England*, vol. 2: *Acts of the Commissioners of the United Colonies of New England, 1653–1679* (Boston: William White, Printer to the Commonwealth, 1859), 358.

24. For Appleton's men, see Waters, *Ipswich in the Massachusetts Bay Colony*, 200–201.

25. Quoted in Bodge, *Soldiers*, 180.

26. The promise was kept, although not until 1728, when the colony established the Narragansett Grants in the New England backcountry. See Bodge, *Soldiers*, 406–441.

27. Benjamin Church and Thomas Church, *The History of Philip's War, Commonly Called the Great Indian War, of 1675 and 1676*, ed. Samuel Gardner Drake, reprint of 1716 Boston 2nd ed. (Exeter, N.H.: J. & B. Williams, 1829), 58. Obviously, friendly-fire incidents are as old as war itself. For information on Church, see Richard Slotkin and James K. Folsom, eds., *So Dreadfull a Judgment: Puritan Responses to King Philip's War, 1676–1677* (Middletown, Conn.: Wesleyan University Press, 1978), 370–391.

28. Estimates of Indian dead vary widely. One of the best estimates is at least ninety-seven warriors and anywhere from three hundred to one thousand women, children, and the elderly. See Drake, *King Philip's War*, 119–120.

29. Leech, *Flintlock and Tomahawk*, 131.

30. Bodge, *Soldiers*, 167.

31. Bodge, *Soldiers*, 158. By this time, not all of Appleton's men were from Essex County.

32. Leech, *Flintlock and Tomahawk*, 141.

33. For information about Brocklebank and his company, see Bodge, *Soldiers*, 206–217.

34. Bodge, *Soldiers*, 201.

35. For information on Manning and his men, see Bodge, *Soldiers*, 277–278.

36. Leech, *Flintlock and Tomahawk*, 141.

37. Quoted in Leech, *Flintlock and Tomahawk*, 141.

38. For information on the situation in Marlboro, see Bodge, *Soldiers*, 207–217.

39. Bodge, *Soldiers*, 277–278.

40. For details on Captain Poole and his men, see Bodge, *Soldiers*, 258–261.

41. The General Court did not approve of Major Appleton's action, as he did not have the authority to issue field promotions. However, when members of the General Court met Poole, whom Appleton had sent to Boston with dispatches, they were so impressed by him that they restored the commission. See Bodge, *Soldiers*, 258–259.

42. "Reverend John Russell to the General Court, March 16, 1676," vol. 68, document 163, MAC.

43. The Rowlandson 1682 narrative is perhaps the best known and surely one of the most studied events of the war. For the narrative itself, see Mary Rowlandson, *The Sovereignty and Goodness of God Together with the Faithfullness of His Promise Displayed: Being a Narrative of the Captivity of Mrs. Mary Rowlandson and Related Documents*, ed. Neal Salisbury (Boston: Bedford, 1997).

44. "John Osgood to the Council in Boston," vol. 68 document 138, MAC.

45. By April 1676, a number of frontier towns, including Andover, were exempted by law from further impressments and the men from those towns serving in the army at the time were sent home to help with home defense. See RGCMB, 5:358; Leech, *Flintlock and Tomahawk*, 186.

46. "Military Committee's Report, March 29, 1676 with Particulars of Garrisons in Essex County Towns," *Historical Collection of the Essex Institute* 41, no. 4 (1905): 355.

47. Quoted in Joshua Coffin and Joseph Bartlett, *A Sketch of the History of Newbury, Newburyport, and West Newbury, from 1635 to 1845* (Boston: S. G. Drake, 1845), 118.

48. Quoted in Coffin, *History of Newbury*, 118.

49. "Military Committee's Report, March 29, 1676," 355–356.

50. "Military Committee's Report, March 29, 1676," 355–356.

51. "Military Committee's Report, March 29, 1676," 355–356. Marblehead's position on a peninsula jutting out into Massachusetts Bay from the town of Salem bears out the citizens' assessment of their defensive position.

52. For information on Whipple, see Bodge, *Soldiers*, 282–283.

53. See Leech, *Flintlock and Tomahawk*, 161–163; Bodge, *Soldiers*, 212–225; Jill Lepore, *The Name of War: King Philip's War and the Origins of American Identity* (New York: Knopf, 1998), 71–96.

54. Quoted in Bodge, *Soldiers*, 283. Bodge, the most distinguished historian of the men and officers involved in the war, states in defense of his assertion that "Nixon" was in fact Whipple that "I know nothing of a Capt. 'Nixon.'" No commander with that name appears in any colonial records of the war.

55. Quoted in Bodge, *Soldiers*, 282.

56. "Captain Samuel Brocklebank to Massachusetts Council, Marlborough, 28 of 1 [March] 1676," vol. 68, document 180, MAC. See also Bodge, *Soldiers*, 213.

57. "Captain Daniel Dennison to the Massachusetts Council, March 27, 1676," vol. 68 document 179, MAC. See also Bodge, *Soldiers*, 214.

58. Sarah Loring Bailey, *Historical Sketches of Andover: Comprising the Present Towns of North Andover and Andover* (Boston: Houghton Mifflin, 1880), 174.

59. Bailey, *Historical Sketches of Andover*, 175–176.

60. Bailey, *Historical Sketches of Andover*, 174.

61. "John Osgood to the Council in Boston, April 1676," vol. 68 document 202, MAC. See also Bailey, *Historical Sketches of Andover*, 175.

62. Leech, *Flintlock and Tomahawk*, 188.

63. Claude Moore Fuess, *Andover: Symbol of New England* (Andover, Mass.: Andover Historical Society, 1959), 72.

64. Eric B. Schultz and Michael J. Tougias, *King Philip's War: The History and Legacy of America's Forgotten Conflict* (Woodstock, Vt.: Countryman, 1999), 216.

65. See Church, *History of Philip's War*, passim.

66. Leech, *Flintlock and Tomahawk*, 197.

67. For the practice of selling captives into slavery, see Lepore, *Name of War*, 150–170; Drake, *King Philip's War*, 135–136.

68. Some Essex men would soon find themselves pressed for service in Maine, but that is beyond the scope of this study.

69. For the aftermath of the war, see Stephen Saunders Webb, *1676, the End of American Independence* (New York: Knopf, 1984); Colin G. Calloway, *After King Philip's War: Presence and Persistence in Indian New England*, (Hanover, N.H.: University Press of New England, 1997); Drake, *King Philip's War*; Lepore, *Name of War*; Michael J. Puglisi, *Puritans Besieged: The Legacies of King Philip's War in the Massachusetts Bay Colony* (Lanham, Md.: University Press of America, 1991); T. H. Breen, "War, Taxes, and Political Brokers: The Ordeal of Massachusetts Bay, 1675–1692," in *Puritans and Adventurers: Change and Persistence in Early America* (New York: Oxford University Press, 1980), 81–105.

70. Leech, *Flintlock and Tomahawk*, 242; Schultz and Tougias, *King Philip's War*, 4–5.

71. Edward Randolph, "Extracts from Edward Randolph's Report to the Council of Trade, October 12, 1676," in *Documents Relating to the Colonial History of the State of New York*, 15 vols., ed. John Brodhead, Berthold Fernow, and E. B. O'Callaghan (Albany: Weed, Parsons, 1853–1857), 3:242–243.

72. N[athaniel] S[altonstall], "A New and Further Narrative of the State of New England (1676)," in *Narratives of the Indian Wars, 1675–1699*, ed. Charles H. Lincoln (New York: Scribner's, 1913), 98.

73. Schultz and Tougias, *King Philip's War*, 5.

74. James Axtell, *Beyond 1492: Encounters in Colonial North America* (New York: Oxford, 1992), 239.

75. The figures for killed in action come from many sources, including town histories, vital records, probate records, and Bodge, *Soldiers*. Most battle deaths were recorded in at least two places.

76. Ian K. Steele, *Warpaths: Invasions of North America* (New York: Oxford University Press, 1994), 108.

77. Charles Henry Peabody and Selim Hobart Peabody, eds., *Peabody Genealogy* (Boston: Charles H. Pope, 1909); James Savage, O. P. Dexter, and John Farmer, *A Genealogical Dictionary of the First Settlers of New England: Showing Three Generations of Those Who Came before May 1692, on the Basis of Farmer's Register*, reprint of the 1860–1862 Boston ed., 4 vols. (Baltimore: Genealogical Publishing, 1990), 1:297.

78. Hubbard, *History of the Indian Wars*, 113.

79. The men were Samuel Stevens, John Harriman, Robert Wilson, Peter Woodbury, John Merrett, and Mark Pittman.

80. PREC, 3:67–68.

81. Bodge, *Soldiers*, 247. For the Falls Fight, see Bodge, *Soldiers*, 241–257; Schultz and Tougias, *King Philip's War*, 220–225.

82. For a discussion of war and noncombatants, or even the usefulness of that term in colonial warfare, see John Grenier, *The First Way of War: American War Making on the Frontier, 1607–1814* (New York: Cambridge University Press, 2005).

83. PREC, 3:57.

84. PREC, 3:57.

85. PREC, 3:35.

86. PREC, 3:35–36.

87. PREC, 3:36–37.

88. PREC, 3:19–20.

89. PREC, 3:19–20.

90. PREC, 3:67–68.

91. *Town Records of Manchester, from the Earliest Grants of Land, 1636 . . .* (Salem, Mass.: Salem Press, 1889), 17.

92. Coffin, *History of Newbury*, 117.

93. Judith Elaine Burns, *Revised Genealogical Records of the Descendants of John Emery of Newbury, Massachusetts*, rev. ed. (Baltimore: Gateway, 1982), 20.

94. Daniel Langdon Tappan, *Tappan-Toppan Genealogy: Ancestors and Descendants of Abraham Toppan of Newbury, Massachusetts, 1606–1672* (Arlington, Mass.: Privately printed, 1915), 95.

95. Bodge, *Soldiers*, 138.

96. Leech, *Flintlock and Tomahawk*, 247.

97. Herbert Hendlin and Ann Pollinger Haas, "Posttraumatic Stress Disorder in Veterans of Early American Wars," *The Psychohistory Review* 12, no. 4 (1984): 25–30.

98. Lepore, *Name of War*, 72.

99. Bodge, *Soldiers*, 154–158, 371.

100. For the quote, ECQCR, 6:259–260. An investigation of the term "sarrowans" in English language sources (colonial period and modern) did not produce any results. Several staff members of the Plimoth Plantation museum, particularly Kate LaPrad and Richard Pickering, suggested the term might be of Indian origin. Jesse Little Doe Baird of the *Wopanaak* (Wampanoag) Language Reclamation Project conducted a linguistic analysis of the term. The closest match to the term in *Wopanaak* is "sus8wunum" (the 8 represents the dropped "r" sound in Algonquian languages), which translates as plaster. The source for this translation is the 1636 *Wopanaak Bible*, from (Leviticus 14:42): "Kah nak peesh neemunumwak ôkutakeesh qusuqanash, kah peesh nee wunôpatawunâw, y8sh qusuqanash; kah peesh neemunum ôkutak pupusây, kah peesh *wusus-8wunumun* weetyuwômut" (English gloss: "And they shall take other stones, and put them in the place of those stones; and he shall take other mortar, and shall

plaster the house"). Little Doe Baird believes that the most likely substance used by the local Native Americans for plaster was interior tree sap (not tree pitch, which has its own *Wopanaak* word). It is quite possible the colonists used this Indian phrase. Tapping a tree for sap was something that the local Indians did on a regular basis (for maple sugar), which quite possibly was a new technique to the English colonists. Jesse Little Doe Baird, private e-mail correspondence and telephone interview, June 20 and 27, 2008.

101. ECQCR, 6:259–260. Note that corn was being stored in the meeting-house for safekeeping, proving that New Englanders were going to great lengths to preserve their food supply during the war.

102. ECQCR, 6:260.

103. ECQCR, 6:259.

104. Coffin and Bartlett, *History of Newbury*, 119.

105. ECQCR, 6:259–260; my emphasis.

106. Leech, *Flintlock and Tomahawk*, 248.

107. Bodge, *Soldiers*, 180.

108. Bodge, *Soldiers*, 407.

109. John J. Currier, *History of Newbury, Mass., 1635–1902* (Boston: Damrell and Upham, 1902), 513.

110. Bodge, *Soldiers*, 408.

111. Bodge, *Soldiers*, 412.

112. This is especially true as the highest percentage of those recorded as married was only 62 percent, even fourteen years after the war, when most of the men would have been almost forty years old. It was extremely unusual for men of this age to be unmarried, certainly much less that 38 percent of the population. Thus, the missing marriages in the immediate postwar years are much more likely missing marriage records.

AFTERWORD

1. RGCMB, 5:86–87.

2. RGCMB, 5:95.

3. T. H. Breen, "Persistent Localism: English Social Change and the Shaping of New England Institutions," in *Puritans and Adventurers: Change and Persistence in Early America* (New York: Oxford University Press, 1980), 3–24.

4. Jenny Hale Pulsipher, *Subjects Unto the Same King: Indians, English, and the Contest for Authority in Colonial New England* (Philadelphia: University of Pennsylvania Press, 2005), 160–178; Jenny Hale Pulsipher, "'The Overture of This New Albion World': King Philip's War and the Transformation of New England" (Ph.D. diss., Brandeis University, 1999), 243–281. While Pulsipher may overemphasize *the amount* of resistance to the draft to prove her point about the breakdown of authority in colonial Massachusetts, her evidence on the level of resistance is compelling.

5. Church describes several incidents in which the pressed men's poor discipline and lack of respect for authority caused serious military difficulties. He relates stories of men shouting to each other despite being under orders of silence, thus giving away their position, and another of men refusing to stop smoking tobacco, which then led the enemy to their hiding place. See Benjamin Church and Thomas Church, *The History of Philip's War, Commonly Called the Great Indian War, of 1675 and 1676*, ed. Samuel Gardner Drake, reprint of 1716 Boston 2nd ed. (Exeter, N.H.: J. & B. Williams, 1829), 38, 41–45.

6. Barnaby Rich, *A Pathway to Military Practise* (London: J. Charlewood for R. Walley, 1587), Early English Books Online, 1476–1640, http://eebo.chadwyck.com; C. G. Cruickshank, *Elizabeth's Army*, 2nd ed. (Oxford: Clarendon, 1966), 26–28.

7. For another view on what made second-generation New Englanders so bad at fighting wars, see Guy Chet, *Conquering the American Wilderness: The Triumph of European Warfare in the Colonial Northeast* (Amherst: University of Massachusetts Press, 2003).

8. George Madison Bodge, *Soldiers in King Philip's War*, reprint of 1906 3rd ed. (Baltimore: Genealogical Publishing, 1967), 63.

9. RGCMB, 5:94–95.

10. King Philip's War was a turning point in the history of New England in many ways. Not only was it a pivotal moment in the way that war was waged in the region, but it was also a turning point politically and in Indian/English relations. For the war as a political turning point, see Pulsipher, *Subjects*; T. H. Breen, "War, Taxes, and Political Brokers: The Ordeal of Massachusetts Bay, 1675–1692," in *Puritans and Adventurers: Change and Persistence in Early America* (New York: Oxford University Press, 1980), 81–105; Michael J. Puglisi, *Puritans Besieged: The Legacies of King Philip's War in the Massachusetts Bay Colony* (Lanham, Md.: University Press of America, 1991). On the subject of Indian/English relations, see James David Drake, *King Philip's War: Civil War in New England, 1675–1676* (Amherst: University of Massachusetts Press, 1999); Colin G. Calloway, *After King Philip's War: Presence and Persistence in Indian New England* (Hanover, N.H.: University Press of New England, 1997).

11. The reason for the discrepancy between the total here (332) and the total of men in the study (357) is that the number of men listed here are from active-duty companies, which does not, in this case, include garrison soldiers.

12. For an important and fascinating study of cultural adaptation in the warfare of New England, see Patrick M. Malone, *The Skulking Way of War: Technology and Tactics among the New England Indians* (Baltimore: Johns Hopkins University Press, 1993).

13. John Grenier, *The First Way of War: American War Making on the Frontier, 1607–1814* (New York: Cambridge University Press, 2005), 34. For an alternative view of Church and the American way of war idea, see Chet, *Conquering the American Wilderness*.

14. Richard I. Melvoin, *New England Outpost: War and Society in Colonial Deerfield* (New York: Norton, 1989), 107–123; Grenier, *First Way of War*, 33–34.

15. John Shy, "A New Look at the Colonial Militia," in *A People Numerous and Armed: Reflections on the Military Struggle for American Independence,* reprint of 1976 Oxford ed. (Ann Arbor: University of Michigan Press, 1990), 37.

16. Shy, "New Look."

17. Stephen C. Eames, "Rustic Warriors: Warfare and the Provincial Soldier on the Northern Frontier, 1689–1748" (Ph.D. diss., University of New Hampshire, 1989), 271.

18. Eames, "Rustic Warriors," 270–292.

19. Grenier, *First Way of War*, 41.

20. Eames, "Rustic Warriors," 299–305.

21. Eames, "Rustic Warriors," 295.

22. On the early imperial wars, see Carole Doreski, ed., *Massachusetts Officers and Soldiers in the Seventeenth-Century Conflicts* (Boston: Society of Colonial Wars in the Commonwealth of Massachusetts: New England Historic Genealogical Society, 1982); Eames, "Rustic Warriors"; Myron O. Stachiw and Massachusetts Archives, *Massachusetts Officers and Soldiers, 1723–1743: Dummer's War to the War of Jenkins' Ear* (Boston: Society of Colonial Wars in the Commonwealth of Massachusetts and New England Historic Genealogical Society, 1979); Robert E. MacKay, ed., *Massachusetts Soldiers in the French and Indian Wars, 1744–1755* (Boston: By the New England Historic and Genealogical Society for the Society of Colonial Wars in the Commonwealth of Massachusetts, 1978). On the French and Indian War, see Fred Anderson, *A People's Army: Massachusetts Soldiers and Society in the Seven Years' War* (Chapel Hill: University of North Carolina Press, 1984); K. David Goss and David Zarowin, eds., *Massachusetts Officers and Soldiers in the French and Indian Wars, 1755–1756* (Boston: By the New England Historic and Genealogical Society for the Society of Colonial Wars in the Commonwealth of Massachusetts, 1985).

23. Grenier, *First Way of War*.

Selected Bibliography

PUBLISHED PRIMARY SOURCES

Bailey, Frederic William. *Early Massachusetts Marriages Prior to 1800.* Reprint of the 1897–1914 ed. Baltimore: Genealogical Publishing, 1968.

Barrow, Thomas C. "The Town Records of Ipswich." *Essex Institute Historical Collections* 97, no. 4 (1961): 294–302.

Beverly Town Records, 1665–1709. Beverly, Mass.: Published by the Town, 1895.

Blodgette, George B., ed. *Church Records of Rowley, Mass. Admissions and Baptisms, 1665–1783.* Salem, Mass.: Salem Press, 1898.

———. "Early Records of the Town of Rowley, Mass." *Essex Institute Historical Collections* 8 (1877): 253–262.

Bodge, George Madison. *Soldiers in King Philip's War.* Reprint of 1906 3rd ed. Baltimore: Genealogical Publishing, 1967.

Bowden, William Hammond. "Marblehead Town Records." *Essex Institute Historical Collections* 69, nos. 3–4 (1933): 207–293.

Church, Benjamin, and Thomas Church. *The History of Philip's War.* Edited by Samuel Gardner Drake. Facsimile reprint ed. Bowie, Md.: Heritage, 1989.

Coldham, Peter Wilson, ed. *The Complete Book of Emigrants.* 4 vols. Baltimore: Genealogical Publishing, 1987.

———, ed. *Supplement to the Complete Book of Emigrants.* Baltimore: Genealogical Publishing, 1992.

Cushing, John D., ed. *The Laws and Liberties of Massachusetts, 1641–1691: A Facsimile Edition.* 3 vols. Wilmington, Del.: Scholarly Resources, 1976.

Doreski, Carole, ed. *Massachusetts Officers and Soldiers in the Seventeenth-Century Conflicts.* Boston: The Society of Colonial Wars in Massachusetts and the New England Historic Genealogical Society, 1982.

Dow, George Francis, ed. *The Probate Records of Essex County, Massachusetts.* 3 vols. Salem, Mass.: Essex Institute, 1916.

———, ed. *Records and Files of the Quarterly Courts of Essex County, Massachusetts.* 8 vols. Salem: Essex Institute, 1911–1918.

———, ed. *Town Records of Topsfield, Massachusetts, 1659–1778.* 2 vols. Topsfield, Mass.: Topsfield Historical Society, 1917.

Early Records of the Town of Beverly. Beverly, Mass.: Allen Print, 1905.

Hammatt, Abraham, ed. *Hammatt Papers: Early Inhabitants of Ipswich, Massachusetts, 1633–1700.* Baltimore: Genealogical Publishing, 1980.

Hubbard, William. *The History of the Indian Wars in New England.* Edited by Samuel Gardner Drake. Facsimile reprint of the 1864 ed. Bowie, Md.: Heritage, 1990.

Lincoln, Charles Henry, ed. *Narratives of the Indian Wars, 1675–1699.* New York: Scribner's, 1913.

Lynn Historical Society. *Records of Ye Towne Meetings of Lyn.* Lynn, Mass.: Lynn Historical Society, 1949.

Mather, Increase. "A Brief History of the War with the Indians in New-England." In *So Dreadfull a Judgment: Puritan Responses to King Philip's War 1676–1677,* edited by Richard Slotkin and James K. Folsom, 79–163. Middletown, Conn.: Wesleyan University Press, 1978.

———. "An Earnest Exhortation: To the Inhabitants of New England." In *So Dreadfull a Judgment: Puritan Responses to King Philip's War 1676–1677,* edited by Richard Slotkin and James K. Folsom, 165–206. Middletown, Conn.: Wesleyan University Press, 1978.

Mather, Increase, and Cotton Mather. *The History of King Philip's War by Rev. Increase Mather Also a History of the Same War by the Rev. Cotton Mather.* Reprint of the 1862 Samuel G. Drake and J. Munsell ed. Bowie, Md.: Heritage, 1990.

Mighill, Benjamin P., and George Brainard Blodgette, eds. *The Early Records of the Town of Rowley, Massachusetts, 1639–1672.* Reprint of 1894 Rowley ed. Bowie, Md.: Heritage, 1984.

"Military Committee's Report, March 29, 1676 with Particulars of Garrisons in Essex County Towns." *Historical Collection of the Essex Institute* 41, no. 4 (1905): 355–356.

Noble, John, and John Francis Cronin, eds. *Records of the Court of Assistants of the Colony of the Massachusetts Bay, 1630–1692.* 3 vols. Boston: The County of Suffolk, 1901.

Pierce, Richard D., ed. *The Records of the First Church in Salem Massachusetts 1629–1736.* Salem, Mass.: Essex Institute, 1974.

Pulsifer, David. *Records of the Colony of New Plymouth in New England.* Vol. 2: *Acts of the Commissioners of the United Colonies of New England, 1653–1679.* 12 vols. Boston: William White, Printer to the Commonwealth, 1859.

Pynchon, John. *The Pynchon Papers, 1654–1697.* Edited by Carl Bridenbaugh and Juliette Tomlinson. 2 vols. Boston: The University Press of Virginia for the Colonial Society of Massachusetts, 1982.

Rich, Barnaby. *A Pathway to Military Practise.* London: J. Charlewood for R. Walley, 1587. Early English Books Online, 1476–1640. http://eebo.chadwyck.com.

Rowlandson, Mary. *The Sovereignty and Goodness of God . . . Being a Narrative of the Captivity of Mrs. Mary Rowlandson and Related Documents.* Edited by Neal Salisbury. Boston: Bedford, 1997.

Sanborn, Melinde Lutz. *Supplement to Torrey's "New England Marriages Prior to 1700."* Baltimore: Genealogical Publishing, 1991.

Sanborn, Melinde Lutz, and William P. Upham. *Essex County, Massachusetts Probate Index, 1638–1840.* 2 vols. Boston: M. L. Sanborn, 1987.

Savage, James, O. P. Dexter, and John Farmer. *A Genealogical Dictionary of the First Settlers of New England.* 4 vols. Reprint of the 1860–1862 Boston ed. Baltimore: Genealogical Publishing, 1990.

Shurtleff, Nathaniel Bradstreet, ed. *Records of the Governor and Company of the Massachusetts Bay in New England.* 5 in 6 vols. Boston: W. White, Printer to the Commonwealth, 1853.

Stickney, Matthew Adams. "Ancient Tax List of Rowley." *New England Historical Genealogical Register* 15 (1861): 253–254.

Topsfield Historical Society. "County Rate Made the 18th of November 1668 for Topsfield." *Historical Collections of Topsfield Historical Society* 3 (1895): 51.

———. *Town Records of Topsfield Massachusetts, 1659–1739.* Topsfield, Mass.: Topsfield Historical Society, 1917.

Torrey, Clarence Almon. *New England Marriages Prior to 1700.* Rev. ed. Baltimore: Genealogical Publishing, 1985.

Town Records of Manchester, from the Earliest Grants of Land, 1636 . . . Salem, Mass.: Salem Press, 1889.

Town Records of Salem, 1634–1680. 2 vols. Salem, Mass.: Essex Institute, 1913.

Trumball, J. Hammond, ed. *The Public Records of the Colony of Connecticut from 1665 to 1678; with the Journal of the Council of War, 1675 to 1678.* 2 vols. Facsimile reprint ed. Baltimore: Heritage, 1993.

Upham, William P., ed. *Records of the First Church in Beverly, Massachusetts, 1667–1772.* Salem, Mass.: Essex Institute, 1905.

Wenham Town Records. 4 vols. Wenham, Mass.: Wenham Historical Society, 1927.

Whitmore, William H., ed. *The Colonial Laws of Massachusetts: Reprinted from the Edition of 1672 with the Supplements through 1686.* Boston: Published by Order of the City Council of Boston, 1887.

———. *The Massachusetts Civil List for the Colonial and Provincial Periods, 1630–1774.* Baltimore: Genealogical Publishing, 1969.

Winthrop, John. "The Journal of John Winthrop 1630–1649." Edited by Richard S. Dunn and Laetitia Yeandle. Cambridge, Mass.: Belknap, 1996.

———. "A Model of Christian Charity (1630)." In *Settlements to Society, 1607–1763: A Documentary History of Colonial America,* edited by Jack P. Greene, 66–69. New York: Norton, 1975.

SECONDARY SOURCES

Abbot, Abiel. *History of Andover from Its Settlement to 1829.* Andover, Mass.: Flagg and Gould, 1829.

Ahearn, Marie L. *The Rhetoric of War: Training Day, the Militia, and the Military Sermon.* New York: Greenwood, 1989.

Allen, David Grayson. *In English Ways: The Movement of Societies and the Transferal of English Local Laws and Custom to Massachusetts Bay in the Seventeenth Century.* New York: Norton, 1982.

Allen, Myron O. *History of Wenham Civil and Ecclesiastical from Its Settlement in 1639 to 1860.* Reprint ed. Ann Arbor: Edwards Brothers, 1975.

Anderson, Fred. *A People's Army: Massachusetts Soldiers and Society in the Seven Years' War.* Chapel Hill: University of North Carolina Press, 1984.

Anderson, Terry L. "Economic Growth in Colonial New England: 'Statistical Renaissance.'" *Journal of Economic History* 39 (1979): 243–257.

———. "The Economic Growth of Seventeenth-Century New England: A Measurement of Regional Income." *Journal of Economic History* 33, no. 1 (1973): 299–301.

Anderson, Terry L., and Robert Paul Thomas. "White Population, Labor Force, and Extensive Growth of the New England Economy in the Seventeenth Century." *Journal of Economic History* 33, no. 1 (1973): 634–667.

Anderson, Virginia DeJohn. *New England's Generation: The Great Migration and the Formation of Society and Culture in the Seventeenth Century.* Cambridge: Cambridge University Press, 1991.

Archer, Richard. *Fissures in the Rock: New England in the Seventeenth Century.* Hanover, N.H.: University Press of New England, 2001.

Axtell, James. *Beyond 1492: Encounters in Colonial North America.* New York: Oxford, 1992.

———. "The Vengeful Women of Marblehead: Robert Roule's Deposition of 1677." *William and Mary Quarterly* 31, no. 4 (1974): 647–652.

Babson, John James. *History of the Town of Gloucester and Cape Ann.* Reprint ed. Salem, Mass.: Higginson, 1995.

Bailey, Sarah Loring. *Historical Sketches of Andover: Comprising the Present Towns of North Andover and Andover.* Boston: Houghton Mifflin, 1880.

Beckett, Ian F. W. *Amateur Military Tradition, 1558–1945.* Manchester: Manchester University Press, 1991.

Belknap, Henry Wyckoff. *Artists and Craftsmen of Essex County, Massachusetts.* Salem, Mass.: Essex Institute, 1927.

———. *Trades and Tradesmen of Essex County, Massachusetts.* Salem, Mass.: Essex Institute, 1929.

Bennett, Ronan. "War and Disorder: Policing the Soldiery in Civil War Yorkshire." In *War and Government in Britain, 1598–1650*, edited by Mark Charles Fissel, 248–273. Manchester: Manchester University Press, 1991.

Benton, Josiah H. *Warning Out in New England.* Boston: W. B. Clarke, 1911.

Bissell, Linda Auwers. "From One Generation to Another: Mobility in Seventeenth-Century Windsor, Connecticut." *William and Mary Quarterly* 31, no. 1 (1974): 79–110.

Boyett, Gene W. "Aging in Seventeenth-Century New England." *New England Historical Genealogical Register* 134 (1980): 181–193.

Boynton, Lindsay. *The Elizabethan Militia, 1558–1638.* London: Routledge and Kegan Paul, 1967.

Breen, Louise. *Transgressing the Bounds: Subversive Enterprises among the Puritan Elite in Massachusetts, 1630–1692.* Oxford: Oxford University Press, 2001.

Breen, T. H. "The Covenanted Militia of Massachusetts Bay: English Background and New World Development." In *Puritans and Adventurers: Change and Persistence in Early America,* 25–45. New York: Oxford University Press, 1980.

———. "Persistent Localism: English Social Change and the Shaping of New England Institutions." In *Puritans and Adventurers: Change and Persistence in Early America,* 3–24. New York: Oxford University Press, 1980.

———. *Puritans and Adventurers: Change and Persistence in Early America.* New York: Oxford University Press, 1980.

———. "Who Governs: The Town Franchise in Seventeenth-Century Massachusetts." *William and Mary Quarterly* 27, no. 3 (1970): 460–474.

Breen, T. H., and Stephen Foster. "The Puritans' Greatest Achievement: A Study of Social Cohesion in Seventeenth-Century Massachusetts." *Journal of American History* 60, no. 1 (1973): 5–22.

Bremer, Francis J. *Puritan Experiment: New England Society from Bradford to Edwards.* Rev. ed. Hanover, N.H.: University Press of New England, 1995.

———. *Puritanism: Transatlantic Perspectives on a Seventeenth-Century Anglo-American Faith.* Boston: Massachusetts Historical Society, distributed by Northeastern University Press, 1993.

Brown, B. Katherine. "Freemanship in Puritan New England." *American Historical Review* 59, no. 4 (1954): 865–883.

Calloway, Colin G. *After King Philip's War: Presence and Persistence in Indian New England.* Hanover, N.H.: University Press of New England, 1997.

Cave, Alfred A. *The Pequot War.* Amherst: University of Massachusetts Press, 1996.

Chet, Guy. *Conquering the American Wilderness: The Triumph of European Warfare in the Colonial Northeast.* Amherst: University of Massachusetts Press, 2003.

Coffin, Joshua, and Joseph Bartlett. *A Sketch of the History of Newbury, Newburyport, and West Newbury, from 1635 to 1845.* Boston: S. G. Drake, 1845.

Cole, Adeline, ed. *Notes on Wenham History 1643–1943.* Salem, Mass.: Wenham Historical Association, 1943.

Cole, Thomas R. "Family, Settlement, and Migration in Southeastern Massachusetts, 1650–1805: The Case for Regional Analysis." *New England Historical Genealogical Register* 132 (1978): 171–185.

Cook, Edward M., Jr. "Local Leadership and the Typology of New England Towns, 1700–1785." *Political Science Quarterly* 86, no. 4 (1971): 586–608.

Coquillette, Daniel R., ed. *Law in Colonial Massachusetts, 1630–1800.* Boston: The Colonial Society of Massachusetts and the University Press of Virginia, 1984.

Crandall, Ralph J. "New England's Second Great Migration: The First Three Generations of Settlement, 1630–1700." *New England Historical Genealogical Register* 129, no. 3 (1975): 347–360.

Crane, Ellery. "The Early Militia System of Massachusetts." In *Proceedings of the Worcester Society of America for the Year 1888,* 105–126. Worcester, Mass.: Worcester Society of America, 1889.

Cress, Lawrence Delbert. *Citizens in Arms: The Army and the Militia in American Society to the War of 1812.* Chapel Hill: University of North Carolina Press, 1982.

Currier, John J. *History of Newbury, Mass., 1635–1902.* Boston: Damrell and Upham, 1902.

Cruickshank, C. G. *Elizabeth's Army.* 2nd ed. Oxford: Clarendon, 1966.

Davis, Harrison Merrill. "Local Government under the First Charter." *Historical Collection of the Essex Institute* 66, no. 2 (1930): 161–181.

Davisson, William I. "Essex County Price Trends: Money and Markets in 17th Century Massachusetts." *Essex Institute Historical Collections* 103, no. 2 (1967): 144–185.

———. "Essex County Wealth Trends: Wealth and Economic Growth in 17th Century Massachusetts." *Essex Institute Historical Collections* 103, no. 4 (1967): 291–342.

Davisson, William I., and Dennis J. Dugan. "Commerce in Seventeenth Century Essex County, Mass." *Essex Institute Historical Collections* 107, no. 2 (1971): 113–142.

Dederer, John Morgan. *War in America to 1775: Before Yankee Doodle.* New York: New York University Press, 1990.

Demos, John. *A Little Commonwealth: Family Life in Plymouth Colony.* New York: Oxford University Press, 1970.

Dow, George Francis, Alice Goldsmith Waters Dow, and Ruth H. Allen. *History of Topsfield, Massachusetts.* Topsfield, Mass.: Topsfield Historical Society, 1940.

Drake, James David. *King Philip's War: Civil War in New England, 1675–1676.* Amherst: University of Massachusetts Press, 1999.

Dummer, Jos. N. *Rowley, 1640–1936: A History of the Town of Rowley, Massachusetts.* Rowley, Mass.: Jewel Mill, 1989.

Ellis, George William, and John Emery Morris, eds. *King Philip's War.* New York: Grafton, 1906.

Felt, Joseph Barlow. *Annals of Salem.* 2 vols. Salem, Mass.: W. & S. B. Ives, 1849.

———. *History of Ipswich, Essex, and Hamilton.* Reprint ed. Bowie, Md.: Heritage, 1991.

Ferling, John. "The New England Soldier: A Study in Changing Perceptions." *American Quarterly* 33, no. 1 (1981): 26–45.

———. *A Wilderness of Miseries: War and Warriors in Early America.* Westport, Conn.: Greenwood, 1980.

Fissel, Mark Charles. *English Warfare, 1511–1642.* London: Routledge, 2001.

———, ed. *War and Government in Britain, 1598–1650.* Manchester: Manchester University Press, 1991.

Foster, Stephen. "The Massachusetts Franchise in the Seventeenth Century." *William and Mary Quarterly* 24, no. 4 (1967): 613–623.

Freeman, Samuel. *Town Officer.* 8th ed. Boston: Printed by Joseph T. Buckingham for Thomas and Andrews, 1815.

French, Allen. "Arms and Military Training of Our Colonizing Ancestors." *Proceeding of the Massachusetts Historical Society* 67 (1945): 3–21.

Frye, John. "Class, Generation, and Social Change: A Case in Salem, Massachusetts, 1636–1656." *Journal of Popular Culture* 11, no. 3 (1977): 743–751.

Fuess, Claude Moore. *Andover: Symbol of New England.* Andover, Mass.: Andover Historical Society, 1959.

Fuess, Claude Moore, and Scott Hurtt Paradise. *Story of Essex County.* 4 vols. New York: American Historical Society, 1935.

Gage, Thomas. *The History of Rowley.* Boston: F. Andrews, 1840.

Gentiles, Ian. *The New Model Army in England, Ireland, and Scotland, 1645–1653.* Oxford: Blackwell, 1992.

Gildrie, Richard P. "Contention in Salem: The Higginson-Nicholet Controversy, 1672–1676." *Essex Institute Historical Collections* 113, no. 2 (1977): 117–139.

———. "Defiance, Diversion, and the Exercise of Arms: The Several Meanings of Colonial Training Days in Colonial Massachusetts." *Military Affairs* 52, no. 2 (1988): 53–55.

———. "'The Gallant Life': Theft on the Salem-Marblehead, Massachusetts Waterfront in the 1680s." *Essex Institute Historical Collections* 122, no. 4 (1986): 284–298.

———. *Salem, Massachusetts, 1626–1683: A Covenant Community.* Charlottesville: University Press of Virginia, 1975.

Ginsburg, Arlin I. "The Franchise in Seventeenth-Century Massachusetts: Ipswich." *William and Mary Quarterly* 34, no. 3 (1977): 446–452.

Greene, Evarts B., and Virginia D. Harrington. *American Population before the Federal Census of 1790.* Baltimore: Genealogical Publishing, 1981.

Grenier, John. *The First Way of War: American War Making on the Frontier, 1607–1814.* New York: Cambridge University Press, 2005.

Greven, Philip J. *Four Generations: Population, Land, and Family in Colonial An-dover, Massachusetts*. Ithaca, N.Y.: Cornell University Press, 1970.

Gross, Robert A. *The Minutemen and Their World*. New York: Hill and Wang, 1976.

Hall, David D. *Worlds of Wonder, Days of Judgment: Popular Religious Belief in Early New England*. New York: Knopf, 1989.

Haller, William, Jr. *The Puritan Frontier: Town Planting in New England Colonial Development, 1630–1660*. New York: Columbia University Press, 1951.

Hambrick-Stowe, Charles E. *The Practice of Piety: Puritan Devotional Disciplines in Seventeenth-Century New England*. Chapel Hill: University of North Carolina Press, 1982.

Haskins, George Lee. *Law and Authority in Early Massachusetts: A Study in Tradition and Design*. New York: Macmillan, 1960.

Hendlin, Herbert, and Ann Pollinger Haas. "Posttraumatic Stress Disorder in Veterans of Early American Wars." *The Psychohistory Review* 12, no. 4 (1984): 25–30.

Heyrman, Christine Leigh. *Commerce and Culture: The Maritime Communities of Colonial Massachusetts, 1690–1750*. New York: Norton, 1984.

Higginbotham, Don. *War and Society in Revolutionary America: The Wider Dimensions of Conflict*. Columbia: University of South Carolina Press, 1988.

Innes, Stephen. *Creating the Commonwealth: The Economic Culture of Puritan New England*. New York: Norton, 1995.

——. *Labor in a New Land: Economy and Society in Seventeenth-Century Springfield*. Rev., shortened paperback ed. Princeton, N.J.: Princeton University Press, 1983.

Jennings, Francis. *The Invasion of America: Indians, Colonialism, and the Cant of Conquest*. Chapel Hill: University of North Carolina Press, 1976.

Jewett, Amos Everett, Emily Mabel Adams Jewett, and Jewett Family of America. *Rowley, Massachusetts, "Mr. Ezechi Rogers Plantation," 1639–1850*. Rowley, Mass.: Jewett Family of America, 1946.

Johnson, Richard R. "Search for a Usable Indian: An Aspect of the Defense of Colonial New England." *Journal of American History* 64, no. 3 (1977): 623–651.

Jonas, Manfred. "The Wills of Early Settlers of Essex County, Massachusetts." *Essex Institute Historical Collections* 96, no. 3 (1960): 228–235.

Karsten, Peter, ed. *Recruiting, Drafting, and Enlisting: Two Sides of the Raising of Military Forces*. New York: Garland, 1998.

Kawashima, Yasuhide. *Igniting King Philip's War: The John Sassamon Murder Trial*. Lawrence: University Press of Kansas, 2001.

Kenny, Robert W. "The Beginnings of the Rhode Island Train Bands." *Rhode Island Historical Society Collections* 33, no. 2 (1940): 25–38.

Koch, Donald Warner. "Income Distribution and Political Structure in Seventeenth-Century Salem, Massachusetts." *Essex Institute Historical Collections* 105, no. 1 (1969): 50–69.

Kohn, Richard H. "The Social History of the American Soldier: A Review and Prospectus for Research." *American Historical Review* 86, no. 3 (1981): 553–567.
Konig, David T. *Law and Society in Puritan Massachusetts: Essex County, 1629–1692.* Chapel Hill: University of North Carolina Press, 1979.
———. "A New Look at the Essex County 'French': Ethnic Frictions and Community Tensions in Seventeenth-Century Essex County, Massachusetts." *Essex Institute Historical Collections* 110, no. 3 (1974): 167–180.
Lake, Peter. "Defining Puritanism—Again?" In *Puritanism: Transatlantic Perspectives on a Seventeenth-Century Anglo-American Faith*, edited by Francis J. Bremer, 3–29. Boston: Massachusetts Historical Society, 1993.
Lamson, D. F. *History of the Town of Manchester, Essex County, Massachusetts, 1645–1895.* Manchester, Mass.: Published by the Town, 1895.
Lapham, Alice Gertrude. *Old Planters of Beverly in Massachusetts and the Thousand Acre Grant.* Cambridge, Mass.: Riverside Press for the Beverly Historical Society and the Conant Family Association, 1930.
Leech, Douglas Edward. *Arms for Empire: A Military History of the British Colonies in North America, 1607–1763.* New York: Macmillan, 1973.
———. *Flintlock and Tomahawk: New England in King Philip's War.* Reprint of 1958 Macmillian ed. East Orleans, Mass.: Parnassus Imprints, 1992.
———. "The Military System of Plymouth Colony." *New England Quarterly* 24, no. 3 (1951): 342–364.
Lee, Charles R. "'This Poor People': Seventeenth-Century Massachusetts and the Poor." *Historical Journal of Massachusetts* 9, no. 1 (1981): 41–50.
Lepore, Jill. *The Name of War: King Philip's War and the Origins of American Identity.* New York: Knopf, 1998.
Lewis, Alonzo, and James Newhall. *History of Lynn.* 2nd ed. Lynn, Mass.: George C. Herbert, 1897.
Little, Ann M. *Abraham in Arms: War and Gender in Colonial New England.* Philadelphia: University of Pennsylvania Press, 2006.
Little, Eliza Adams, and Lucretia Little Ilsley. *The First Parish, Newbury, Massachusetts, 1635–1935.* Newburyport, Mass.: News Publishing, 1935.
Lockridge, Kenneth A. *A New England Town: The First Hundred Years.* Enlarged ed. New York: Norton, 1985.
Lockridge, Kenneth A., and Alan Kreider. "The Evolution of Massachusetts Town Government, 1640–1740." *William and Mary Quarterly* 23, no. 4 (1966): 549–573.
Lombard, Anne S. *Making Manhood: Growing up Male in Colonial New England.* Cambridge, Mass.: Harvard University Press, 2003.
Mahon, John K. "Anglo-American Methods of Indian Warfare, 1676–1794." *Mississippi Valley Historical Review* 45, no. 2 (1958): 254–275.
———. *History of the Militia and the National Guard.* New York: Macmillan, 1983.

Main, Gloria L. *Peoples of a Spacious Land: Families and Cultures in Colonial New England*. Cambridge, Mass.: Harvard University Press, 2001.

Main, Gloria L., and Jackson Turner Main. "Economic Growth and the Standard of Living in Southern New England, 1640–1774." *Journal of Economic History* 48, no. 1 (1988): 27–46.

Malone, Patrick M. *The Skulking Way of War: Technology and Tactics among the New England Indians*. Baltimore: Johns Hopkins University Press, 1993.

Martin, George H. "Glimpses of Colonial Life in Lynn in the Indian War Days." *The Register of the Lynn Historical Society* 17 (1913): 98–122.

Martin, John Frederick. *Profits in the Wilderness: Entrepreneurship and the Founding of New England Towns in the Seventeenth Century*. Chapel Hill: University of North Carolina Press, 1991.

McManus, Edgar J. *Law and Liberty in Early New England: Criminal Justice and Due Process, 1620–1692*. Amherst: University of Massachusetts Press, 1993.

McWilliams, James E. *Building the Bay Colony: Local Economy and Culture in Early Massachusetts*. Charlottesville: University of Virginia Press, 2007.

Mead, Spencer P. "The First American Soldiers." *Journal of American History* 1, no. 1 (1907): 120–128.

Melvoin, Richard I. *New England Outpost: War and Society in Colonial Deerfield*. New York: Norton, 1989.

Moore, Susan Hardman. *Pilgrims: New World Settlers and the Call of Home*. New Haven, Conn.: Yale University Press, 2007.

Moran, Gerald F. "Religious Renewal, Puritan Tribalism, and the Family in Seventeenth-Century Milford, Connecticut." *William and Mary Quarterly* 36, no. 2 (1979): 236–254.

Moran, Gerald F., and Maris A. Vinovskis, eds. *Religion, Family, and the Life Course: Explorations in the Social History of Early America*. Ann Arbor: University of Michigan Press, 1992.

Morgan, Edmund Sears. *The Puritan Family: Religion and Domestic Relations in Seventeenth-Century New England*. Rev. and enlarged ed. New York: Harper and Row, 1966.

———. *Visible Saints: The History of a Puritan Idea*. New York: New York University Press, 1963.

Morton, Louis. "The Origins of American Military Policy." *Military Affairs* 22, no. 2 (1958): 75–82.

Neimeyer, Charles Patrick. *America Goes to War: A Social History of the Continental Army*. New York: New York University Press, 1996.

Norton, Susan L. "Marital Migration in Essex County, Massachusetts, in the Colonial and Early Federal Periods." *Journal of Marriage and the Family* 35, no. 3 (1973): 406–418.

———. "Population Growth in Colonial America: A Study of Ipswich, Massachusetts." *Population Studies* 25, no. 3 (1971): 433–452.

Osgood, Herbert L. *The American Colonies in the Seventeenth Century.* Rev. ed. 4 vols. New York: Columbia University Press, 1930.

Perley, Sidney. *The History of Salem, Massachusetts.* 3 vols. Salem, Mass.: S. Perley, 1924.

Peterson, Harold L. *Arms and Armor in Colonial America, 1526–1783.* Unabridged reproduction of the 1956 Stackpole ed. Mineola, N.Y.: Dover, 2000.

Phillips, James Duncan. *Salem in the Seventeenth Century.* Boston: Houghton Mifflin, 1933.

Powell, Sumner Chilton. *Puritan Village: The Formation of a New England Town.* Middletown, Conn.: Wesleyan University Press, 1963.

Powers, Edwin. *Crime and Punishment in Early Massachusetts, 1620–1692: A Documentary History.* Boston: Beacon, 1966.

Pringle, James Robert. *History of the Town and City of Gloucester, Cape Ann, Massachusetts.* Gloucester, Mass.: Published by the Author, 1892.

Puglisi, Michael J. *Puritans Besieged: The Legacies of King Philip's War in the Massachusetts Bay Colony.* Lanham, Md.: University Press of America, 1991.

Pulsipher, Jenny Hale. *Subjects unto the Same King: Indians, English, and the Contest for Authority in Colonial New England.* Philadelphia: University of Pennsylvania Press, 2005.

Radabaugh, Jack S. "The Militia of Colonial Massachusetts." *Military Affairs* 18, no. 1 (1954): 1–18.

Ranlet, Philip. "Another Look at the Causes of King Philip's War." *New England Quarterly* 61, no. 1 (1988): 79–100.

Roads, Samuel. *The History and Traditions of Marblehead.* 3rd ed. Marblehead, Mass.: N. A. Lindsey, 1897.

Roberts, Oliver Ayer. *History of the Military Company of the Massachusetts Now Called the Ancient and Honorable Artillery Company of Massachusetts, 1637–1888.* Boston: Alfred Mudge and Son, 1895.

Rutman, Darrett Bruce, and Anita H. Rutman. *Small Worlds, Large Questions: Explorations in Early American Social History, 1600–1850.* Charlottesville: University Press of Virginia, 1994.

Schultz, Eric B., and Michael J. Tougias. *King Philip's War: The History and Legacy of America's Forgotten Conflict.* Woodstock, Vt.: Countryman, 1999.

Selesky, Harold E. *War and Society in Colonial Connecticut.* New Haven, Conn.: Yale University Press, 1990.

Sharp, Morrison. "Leadership and Democracy in the Early New England System of Defense." *American Historical Review* 50, no. 2 (1945): 244–260.

Shea, William L. *The Virginia Militia in the Seventeenth Century.* Baton Rouge: Louisiana State University Press, 1983.

Shy, John. "A New Look at the Colonial Militia." In *A People Numerous and Armed: Reflections on the Military Struggle for American Independence,* 29–41. Rpt. of 1976 Oxford ed. Ann Arbor: University of Michigan Press, 1990.

Slotkin, Richard, and James K. Folsom, eds. *So Dreadfull a Judgment: Puritan Responses to King Philip's War, 1676–1677.* Middletown, Conn.: Wesleyan University Press, 1978.

Sly, John Fairfield. *Town Government in Massachusetts, 1620–1930.* Hamden, Conn.: Archon, 1967.

Smith, Daniel Scott. "'All in Some Degree Related to Each Other': A Demographic and Comparative Resolution of the Anomaly of New England Kinship." *American Historical Review* 94, no. 1 (1989): 44–79.

———. "Child-Naming Practices, Kinship Ties, and Change in Family Attitudes in Hingham, Massachusetts, 1641 to 1880." *Journal of Social History* 18, no. 4 (1985): 541–566.

———. "The Demographic History of Colonial New England." *Journal of Economic History* 32, no. 1 (1972): 165–183.

———. "Parental Power and Marriage Patterns: An Analysis of Historical Trends in Hingham, Massachusetts." *Journal of Marriage and the Family* 35, no. 3 (1973): 419–428.

———. "Underregistration and Bias in Probate Records: An Analysis of Data from Eighteenth-Century Hingham, Massachusetts." *William and Mary Quarterly* 32, no. 1 (1975): 100–110.

Stachiw, Myron O., and Massachusetts Archives. *Massachusetts Officers and Soldiers, 1723–1743: Dummer's War to the War of Jenkins' Ear.* Boston: Society of Colonial Wars and New England Historic Genealogical Society, 1979.

Starkey, Armstrong. *European and Native American Warfare, 1675–1815.* Norman: University of Oklahoma Press, 1998.

Stater, Victor L. "The Lord Lieutenancy on the Eve of the Civil Wars: The Impressment of George Plowright." *Historical Journal* (Great Britain) 29, no. 2 (1986): 279–296.

———. *Nobel Government: The Stuart Lord Lieutenancy and the Transformation of English Politics.* Athens: University of Georgia Press, 1994.

Stone, Edwin Martin. *History of Beverly, Civil and Ecclesiastical: From Its Settlement in 1630 to 1842.* Boston: J. Munroe, 1843.

Stout, Harry S. *The New England Soul: Preaching and Religious Culture in Colonial New England.* New York: Oxford University Press, 1986.

Thomson, Gladys Scott. *Lords Lieutenants in the Sixteenth Century: A Study in Tudor Local Administration.* London: Longmans, Green, 1923.

Towner, Lawrence W. "'A Fondness for Freedom': Servant Protest in Puritan Society." *William and Mary Quarterly* 19, no. 2 (1962): 201–219.

Ulrich, Laurel Thatcher. *Good Wives: Image and Reality in the Lives of Women in Northern New England, 1650–1750.* New York: Vintage, 1991.

———. "It 'Went Away Shee Knew Not How': Food Theft and Domestic Conflict in Seventeenth-Century Essex County." In *Foodways in the Northeast,* edited by Peter Benes, 94–105. Boston: Boston University Press, 1984.

Vickers, Daniel. *Farmers and Fishermen: Two Centuries of Work in Essex County, Massachusetts, 1630–1850.* Chapel Hill: University of North Carolina Press, 1994.

Vinovskis, Maris A. "Mortality Rates and Trends in Massachusetts before 1860." *Journal of Economic History* 32, no. 1 (1972): 184–213.

Wall, Robert Emmet, Jr. "The Decline of the Massachusetts Franchise: 1647–1666." *Journal of American History* 59, no. 2 (1972): 303–310.

Ward, Harry M. *The United Colonies of New England, 1643–90.* New York: Vintage, 1961.

Waters, John J. "Family, Inheritance, and Migration in Colonial New England: The Evidence from Guilford, Connecticut." *William and Mary Quarterly* 39, no. 1 (1982): 64–86.

———. "The Traditional World of the New England Peasants: A View from Seventeenth-Century Barnstable." *New England Historical Genealogical Register* 130, no. 1 (1976): 3–21.

Waters, Thomas Franklin, Sarah Whipple Goodhue, and John Wise. *Ipswich in the Massachusetts Bay Colony.* Ipswich, Mass.: Ipswich Historical Society, 1905.

Webb, Stephen Saunders. *1676, the End of American Independence.* New York: Knopf, 1984.

Wilson, Lisa. *Ye Heart of a Man: The Domestic Life of Men in Colonial New England.* New Haven, Conn.: Yale University Press, 1999.

Wright, Robert K. "Massachusetts Militia Roots: A Bibliographic Study." Washington, D.C.: National Guard Bureau, 1986.

Young, Alexander. *Chronicles of the First Planters of the Colony of Massachusetts Bay, 1623–1636.* Boston: C. C. Little and J. Brown, 1846.

Young, Christine Alice. *From "Good Order" to Glorious Revolution: Salem, Massachusetts, 1628–1689.* Ann Arbor: UMI Research, 1980.

Zelner, Kyle F. "Essex County's Two Militias: The Social Composition of Offensive and Defensive Units during King Philip's War, 1675–1676." *New England Quarterly* 72, no. 4 (1999): 577–593.

DISSERTATIONS AND THESES

Abbot, Elinor. "Transformations: The Reconstruction of Social Hierarchy in Early Colonial Andover, Massachusetts." Ph.D. diss., Brandeis University, 1989.

Andresen, Martin W. "New England Colonial Militia and Its English Heritage: 1620–1675." Master's thesis, United States Army Command and General Staff College, 1979.

Black, William Grant. "The Military Origins of Federal Social Welfare Programs: Early British and Colonial American Precedents." Ph.D. diss., University of Minnesota, 1989.

Colby, Walter Weston, Jr. "Adaptations of English Military Institutions in Seventeenth-Century New England." Master's thesis, University of Detroit, 1952.

Eames, Stephen C. "Rustic Warriors: Warfare and the Provincial Soldier on the Northern Frontier, 1689–1748." Ph.D. diss., University of New Hampshire, 1989.

Gates, Stewart Lewis. "Disorder and Social Organization: The Militia in Connecticut Public Life, 1660–1860." Ph.D. diss., University of Connecticut, 1975.

Goodman, Robert Lord. "Newbury, Massachusetts, 1635–1685: The Social Foundations of Harmony and Conflict." Ph.D. diss., Michigan State University, 1974.

Hannah, Archibald, Jr. "New England's Military Institutions, 1693–1750." Ph.D. diss., Yale University, 1950.

Madigan, Eugene Francis. "Development of the New England Colonial Militia, 1620–1675." Master's thesis, Kansas State University, 1975.

Marcus, Richard Henry. "The Militia of Colonial Connecticut 1639–1775." Ph.D. diss., University of Colorado, 1965.

Michalek, Adolpf Frank. "Social and Economic Problems in Essex County as Revealed in the Records and Files of the Quarterly Courts of Essex County, Massachusetts, 1636–1683." Master's thesis, University of Chicago, 1931.

Millar, David Richard. "The Militia, the Army, and Independency in Colonial Massachusetts." Ph.D. diss., Cornell University, 1967.

Moran, Gerald F. "The Puritan Saint: Religious Experience, Church Membership, and Piety in Connecticut, 1636–1776." Ph.D. diss., Rutgers University, 1974.

Norton, Susan L. "Age at Marriage and Marital Migration in Three Massachusetts Towns, 1600–1850." Ph.D. diss., University of Michigan, 1981.

O'Malley, Patricia. "Rowley, Massachusetts, 1639–1730: Dissent, Division, and Delimination in a Colonial Town." Ph.D. diss., Boston College, 1975.

Perzel, Edward Spaulding. "The First Generation of Settlement in Colonial Ipswich, Massachusetts, 1633–1660." Ph.D. diss., Rutgers University, 1967.

Pinkham, Harold Arthur. "The Transplantation and Transformation of the English Shire in America: Essex County, Massachusetts, 1630–1768." Ph.D. diss., University of New Hampshire, 1980.

Puglisi, Michael J. "Legacies of King Philip's War in the Massachusetts Bay Colony." Ph.D. diss., College of William and Mary, 1987.

Pulsipher, Jenny Hale. "'The Overture of This New Albion World': King Philip's War and the Transformation of New England." Ph.D. diss., Brandeis University, 1999.

Radabaugh, Jack Sheldon. "The Military System of Colonial Massachusetts, 1690–1740." Ph.D. diss., University of Southern California, 1965.

Rutman, Darrett Bruce. "A Militant New World, 1607–1640: America's First Generation: Its Martial Spirit, Its Tradition of Arms, Its Militia Organization, Its Wars." Ph.D. diss., University of Virginia, 1959.

Stater, Victor Louis. "The Lord Lieutenancy in England, 1625–1688: The Crown, Nobility, and Local Government." Ph.D. diss., University of Chicago, 1988.

Stewart, Richard Winship. "Arms and Politics: The Supply of Arms in England, 1585–1625." Ph.D. diss., Yale University, 1986.

Vannah, Alison Isabel. "'Crotchets of Division': Ipswich in New England, 1633–1679." Ph.D. diss., Brandeis University, 1999.

Zarlengo, Felix John. "Politics of Defense in the New England Colonies, 1620–1746." Master's thesis, Brown University, 1965.

Zelner, Kyle F. "The Flower and Rabble of Essex County: A Social History of the Massachusetts Bay Militia and Militiamen during King Philip's War, 1675–1676." Ph.D. diss., College of William and Mary, 2003.

———. "Massachusetts' Two Militias: A Social History of the 1st Essex Expeditionary Company in King Philip's War, 1675–1676." Master's thesis, Wayne State University, 1993.

Permissions

Below is additional information regarding the following figures in the book.

Fig. 1. Woodcut from *The art of Warre; or, Militarie discourses* by Sieur Du Praissac. Courtesy of the Birmingham Central Library, United Kingdom.

Fig. 2. Woodcut detail from *The Military Art of Trayning* by Jacob de Gheyn. © British Library Board. All rights reserved C.27a21.

Fig. 3. Woodcut detail from *The Faithful, yet Imperfect, Character of a Glorious KING, KING CHARLES I.* Written by a Person of Quality. © British Library Board. All rights reserved E.1799.(1.).

Fig. 4. Woodcut detail from *The Exercise of the English* by an anonymous author. © British Library Board. All rights reserved E.136[23].

All four figures are published with permission of ProQuest. Further reproduction is prohibited without permission. Image produced by ProQuest as part of Early English Books Online. Inquiries maybe made to: ProQuest, 789 E. Eisenhower Parkway, Box 1346, Ann Arbor, MI 48106–1346, USA. Telephone: 734-761-4700; E-mail: info@il.proquest.com; Web page: www.il.proquest.com.

Fig. 5. *Captain George Corwin.* Painting attributed to Thomas Smith, Boston, 1675. All but head repainted by Hannah Crownshield about 1819; retouched by Howarth, Boston, 1864. Oil on canvas, 49x39 inches. Photograph courtesy of Peabody Essex Museum. Negative/Catalog #: 4134.1.

Fig. 14. *John Leverett.* Unknown artist, attributed to Sir Peter Lely, c. 1655. Oil on canvas, 43½x35 inches. Photograph courtesy of Peabody Essex Museum. Negative/Catalog #: 106819.

Fig. 15. *Major Thomas Savage.* Attributed to Thomas Smith, 1679. Oil on canvas, 42x37⅛ inches. Museum of Fine Arts, Boston. Bequest of Henry Lee Shattuck in memory of the late M. Gray. Photograph © 2009 Museum of Fine Arts, Boston.

Index

Abbe, John Jr., 139
Abbe, Thomas, 133
Abbot, Joseph, 115
Abbott, George, 198
Abbott, Joseph, 198, 204
Abbott, Timothy, 198
Adams, Nathaniel, 160
age. *See* impressment factors; soldiers
Allen, John, 122, 126
Allen, William, 126
Amherst, New Hampshire, 211f
Anderson, Fred, 7, 68
Anderson, Virginia DeJohn, 17, 153, 158
Andover, Massachusetts, 109–121, 194–195, 198–199; as agricultural town, 110; allied family groups in, 112–115, 119, 121; attack on, 198–199; committee of militia of, 59, 110–121; crime in, 115; families recruited from, 59; family size in, 146; fear of Indian attack, 119; founding of, 110; on frontier, 194–195; garrison houses in, 195–196, 198; geographical division in, 113–115; militia of, 58, 110–121; possibility of volunteer soldiers from, 115–118; socioeconomic status in, 111–115; soldiers of, 48, 110–121, 141, 149, 152–153, 162, 174, 177; town layout of, 110; war casualties in, 204

Andrews, Robert, 93, 97
Anglo-Dutch Wars: First (1652–1654), 35; Second (1664–1667), 50, 102; Third (1672–1674), 51
Appleton, John, 73, 195
Appleton, Samuel, 49, 71, 73, 77–79, 145, 184–185, 187–193, 217
Appleton's company, 73, 79–80, 83, 145, 150, 177, 184–185, 187–193, 202–203, 207
Ayers, Zechariah, 118–119

Baker, Ebenezer, 111–112
Ballard, John, 115
Bassett, William, 175
Batchelder, Mark, 133, 138
Bath, William, 171
Beale, William, 104–106
Beers, Richard, 184
Beers's company, 184–185
Belanger, Leonard, 106
Bennett, Henry, 126–127
Bennett, John, 122, 126–127, 130, 175
Beverly, Massachusetts, 2, 52; families recruited from, 59; involved in Manchester militia, 140; soldiers of, 153, 167, 173, 175, 178; war casualties in, 203
Bigsby, Joseph, 91–92
birth order. *See* impressment factors; *individual town listings*
Bishop, Edward, 105

Shy, John, 6
Smith, William, 91
Smith's Garrison, Rhode Island, 188,
191–192
socioeconomic status. *See* impressment
factors; *individual town listings*
soldiers: age of, 142–146, 235–237ap-
pendix; clothing, 55, 58; common
characteristics, 8–9, 141–180; food
of, 58; in garrisons, 43, 73–74;
identity and character of, 2, 4–9;
payment of, 68; poor performance
of, 214–215; posttraumatic stress
disorder of, 207–209; probate inventories of, 204–206; in troops, 45,
145–146; wills of, 205–206. *See also*
impressment factors; volunteers;
individual town listings
Somerby, Daniel, 206
Spofford, Thomas, 170
Springfield, Massachusetts, attack on,
186
Stainwood, John, 171
Stainwood family, of Gloucester, 59
Stamford, Thomas, 107
Stanley, James, 94
Stater, Victor, 173
Stevens, Nathan, 118–119
Stevens, Rebecca, 206
Stevens, Samuel, 206
Stevens, Sara, 206
Stimson, George, 78
Story, Seth, 77
substitution. *See* militia, Massachusetts
Bay; *individual town listings*
Sudbury, Massachusetts, attack on,
199–202, 214
Swan, Richard, 83
Swansea, Plymouth, attack on,
181–182
Sweet's company, 133
Symonds, Samuel, 134–135, 209

Thomas, John, 78–79
Toppan, John, 206
Topsfield, Massachusetts, 90–100;
crime in, 97; founding of, 90–91;
garrison houses in, 196; militia of,
91–100; militia committee of, 93–
100; militia controversy in, 91–93;
outlying areas of, 96–97; possible
volunteers from, 95; socioeconomic
situation in, 94; soldiers of, 93–100,
108, 141, 149, 153, 162, 167, 173–
174, 177; substitute soldier in, 93;
tax list (1668), 233–234appendix;
town records of, 91; war casualties
of, 203; Welch, Philip, possible resident of, 135–136. *See also* Rowley
Village, Massachusetts
town records, lack of during King
Philip's War, 46–47
Towne, Edmund, 91
troop (cavalry). *See* militia, Massachusetts Bay
Turner, William, 202
Turner's company, 93–94, 96, 202

Ulrich, Laura Thatcher, 112, 148
United Colonies of New England
(New England Confederation), 53,
58, 161 units. *See individual militia
companies listings*

Vannah, Allison, 73
volunteers, 49–51, 66–68, 115–118,
133–134, 200–201; age as a factor in,
143–144, as way to gain temporary
independence, 95; birth order of,
116–117; independent companies,
215. *See also* militia, Massachusetts
Bay; *individual town listings*

Wadsworth, Samuel, 200
Wampanoag tribe, 181–183

About the Author

KYLE F. ZELNER is Assistant Professor of History and a Fellow of the Center for the Study of War and Society at the University of Southern Mississippi in Hattiesburg, Mississippi.